GENERATIONS
Your Family in Modern American History

THIRD EDITION

GENERATIONS
Your Family in Modern American History

THIRD EDITION

J. F. WATTS
The City College of the City University of New York

ALLEN F. DAVIS
Temple University

McGraw-Hill, Inc.
New York   St. Louis   San Francisco   Auckland   Bogotá
Caracas   Lisbon   London   Madrid   Mexico   Milan
Montreal   New Delhi   Paris   San Juan   Singapore
Sydney   Tokyo   Toronto

Third Edition
9876
Copyright © 1988, 1978, 1974 by Alfred A. Knopf, Inc.

Library of Congress Cataloging in Publication Data

Main entry under title:

Generations : your family in modern American history.
  I. United States—Social life and customs—Addresses, essays, lectures.   2. United States—History—Addresses, essays, lectures.   3. United States—Biography—Addresses, essays, lectures: 4. United States—Geneology—Addresses, essays, lectures.   I. Watts, J. F. (Jim), 1935-   .   II. Davis, Allen Freeman, 1931-
E161.G4   1983 ·   973   82-21336

ISBN 0-07-554365-6

Text and Cover Design: Lorraine Hohman

Cover Photograph: From the Collection of the Library of Congress, Washington, D.C.

Picture Editor: R. Lynn Goldberg

Manufactured by R. R. Donnelley & Sons Co. Harrisonburg, Va.

SINCE THIS PAGE CANNOT LEGIBLY ACCOMMODATE ALL THE COPYRIGHT NOTICES, THE PAGES FOLLOWING CONSTITUTE AN EXTENSION OF THE COPYRIGHT PAGE.

Grateful acknowledgment is extended for permission to reprint the following:

Reprinted from *The World We Have Lost,* 2nd edition, by Peter Laslett, with the permission of Charles Scribner's Sons. Copyright © 1965 by Peter Laslett.

"The Estate of Michael D. Davis, 1800–1837—Vermont Sheep Farmer," courtesy, Allen F. Davis.

From "The View from Old Sturbridge Village" by P. E. Beall, W. Leon, P. S. O'Connell, and E. K. Rothman, *Journal of Family History,* Volume 6, Number 1 (Spring 1981), p. 9 (chart). Copyright © 1981 by the National Council on Family Relations. Reprinted by permission.

"Nineteenth-Century Rural Self-Sufficiency" by Jo Ann Carrigan, *Arkansas Historical Quarterly,* Volume XXI (Summer 1962). Reprinted by permission of the Arkansas Historical Association and the author.

A Day in the Life of a Mid-Western Farmer's Wife, *Independent,* Volume LVIII (February 9, 1905), pp. 295–296.

From *Main Street on the Middle Border* by Lewis Atherton. Copyright © 1954 by Indiana University Press. Reprinted by permission of the publisher.

"Tomatoes Were Not Worth Growing—90 Years Ago" by Ruth Tirrell, from *The New York Times,* January 13, 1974. © 1974 by The New York Times Company. Reprinted by permission.

From *Going to America* by Terry Coleman. Copyright © 1972 by Terry Coleman. Reprinted by permission of Pantheon Books, a Division of Random House, Inc., and The Hutchinson Publishing Group, Ltd.

"English Immigrants," *Wisconsin Magazine of History,* Volume 47 (Spring 1964), pp. 225–233. Reprinted by permission of the State Historical Society of Wisconsin.

From "Jens Granbek to Her Brother-in-Law" by Jens Granbek, *Norwegian Studies,* Volume 21, pp. 46–48. Reprinted by permission of the Norwegian–American Historical Association.

From *Rosa: The Life of an Italian Immigrant* by Marie Hall Ets. Copyright © 1970 by the University of Minnesota Press, Minneapolis. Reprinted by permission of the publisher and the author.

From *Jews Without Money* by Michael Gold. Published 1930 by Horace Liveright, Inc. Reprinted by permission of The Evelyn Singer Agency, Inc.

Excerpts from *Blood of My Blood* by Richard Gambino, pp. 1–3. Copyright © 1974 by Richard Gambino. Reprinted by permission of Doubleday & Company, Inc.

From *Stelmark: A Family Recollection* by Harry Mark Petrakis. First published by David McKay. Copyright © 1970 by Harry Mark Petrakis. Used by permission of Toni Strassman, Agent.

From "A Diary of the Front Lines," Anonymous, in *The Cannoneers Have Hairy Ears,* pp. 3–5,' 137–139, 168, 181–182. J. H. Sears & Company, 1927.

"Letters of Negro Migrants of 1916–1918," collected under the direction of Emmett J. Scott, *Journal of Negro History* (July and October 1919). Copyright © by the Association for the Study of Negro Life and History, Inc.

Excerpts from *Today and Tomorrow* by Henry Ford, pp. 1–6. Copyright 1926 by Doubleday & Company, Inc. Reprinted by permission of the publisher.

From "Confessions of a Ford Dealer," as told to Jesse Rainsford Sprague, *Harper's Monthly Magazine,* Volume 155 (June 1927), pp. 26–35.

From "Corncobs for Hair-Cuts: How a Modern Farm Woman Gets on by Swap and Dicker" by Evelyn Harris, *The Survey,* Volume LIX (February 1, 1928), pp. 579–581.

From "Petting and the Campus" by Eleanor Rowland Wembridge, *The Survey* (July 1, 1925).

"The Weary Blues" by Langston Hughes, in *The Selected Poems of Langston Hughes,* pp. 33–34, Alfred A. Knopf, Inc., copyright © 1979. Reprinted by permission.

From "Booze, Here and There" by Ernest W. Mandeville, *The Outlook* (March 18, 1925).

From "Reaffirming the Sacco–Vanzetti Verdict," *The Literary Digest,* Volume XCIV (August 20, 1927), pp. 5–7.

From Bartolomeo Vanzetti to Mrs. Maude Pettyjohn,

December 11, 1926, in *The Letters of Sacco and Vanzetti*, pp. 217–233, edited by Marion Denman Frankfurter and Gardner Jackson. Copyright 1928 by The Viking Press, Inc. Copyright renewed 1956 by The Viking Press, Inc. Used by permission of Viking Penguin Inc.

From " 'Babe' Ruth's Record-Breaking World Series," *The Literary Digest*, Volume XCIX (October 27, 1928).

From *The American Worker in the Twentieth Century: A History through Autobiographies* by Eli Ginzberg and Hyman Berman, pp. 203–206, 210–213. Copyright © by The Free Press, a Division of Macmillan Publishing Co., Inc.

From *Hard Times: An Oral History of the Great Depression* by Studs Terkel. Copyright © 1970 by Studs Terkel. Reprinted by permission of Pantheon Books, a Division of Random House, Inc.

"Choosing a Dream: Italians in Hell's Kitchen" by Mario Puzo. Originally published in *McCall's* magazine. Excerpted from the book *The Immigrant Experience* by Thomas Wheeler. Copyright © 1971 by The Dial Press. Reprinted by permission of The Dial Press.

From "Heroism: 'Commando' Kelly's One Man War" by Sergeant Charles E. Kelly [and Pete Martin]. Reprinted by permission from *The Saturday Evening Post*. Copyright 1944 by The Curtis Publishing Company.

From *State of the Nation* by John Dos Passos. Copyright by Elizabeth H. Dos Passos. Reprinted by permission of Houghton Mifflin Company.

"Of Thee I Sing" by Martha Weinman Lear, *New York Times Magazine* (July 4, 1976). © 1976 by The New York Times Company. Reprinted by permission.

Abridged from *A Choice of Weapons* by Gordon Parks, pp. 252, 256–259, 261–264, 265–267, 269–272. Copyright © 1965, 1966 by Gordon Parks. Reprinted by permission of Harper & Row, Publishers, Inc.

Japanese American Evacuation and Relocation Records, The Bancroft Library, University of California, Berkeley. Published by permission of the Director, The Bancroft Library, University of California, Berkeley.

From *The Names: A Memoir* by N. Scott Momaday, pp. 83–91. Copyright © 1976 by N. Scott Momaday. Reprinted by permission of Harper & Row, Publishers, Inc.

From *The Peace Corps and Pax Americana* by Marshall Windmiller, pp. 38–50, Public Affairs Press, 1970. Copyright © 1970 by Marshall Windmiller. Reprinted by permission.

From *Stinking Creek* by John Fetterman. Copyright © 1967 by John Fetterman. Reprinted by permission of the publishers, E. P. Dutton.

Excerpted from *Coming of Age in Mississippi* by Anne Moody. Copyright © 1968 by Anne Moody. Reprinted by permission of The Dial Press.

"SNCC Statement on Vietnam," *Freedomways Magazine*, Volume 6, Number 1 (Winter 1966), pp. 6–7. Reprinted by permission from *Freedomways Magazine*, published at 799 Broadway, New York City.

From *Born on the Fourth of July* by Ron Kovic, pp. 16–17, 25–26, 46, 54–56, 71–75, 220–222. Copyright © 1976 by McGraw-Hill Book Company. Reprinted by permission.

From "Take a Memo, Mr. Smith" by Robin Morgan, *Going Too Far*, pp. 69–70, Random House, Inc., copyright © 1977. Reprinted by permission.

Excerpts from *America in Our Times* by Godfrey Hodgson, pp. 326–333, 336–340, 349–352. Copyright © 1976 by Godfrey Hodgson. Reprinted by permission of Doubleday & Company, Inc.

"An 18-Year-Old Looks Back on Life" by Joyce Maynard. Copyright © 1972 by Joyce Maynard. First published in the *New York Times Magazine* from the book *Looking Back* by Joyce Maynard. Reprinted by permission of Doubleday & Company, Inc.

From *Global Reach: The Power of the Multi-National Corporation* by Richard J. Barnet and Ronald E. Muller, pp. 13–17. Copyright © 1974 by Richard J. Barnet and Ronald E. Muller. Reprinted by permission of Simon & Schuster, a Division of Gulf & Western Corporation.

From "The Melting Pot: The Latest Pursuers of the American Dream" by Acel Moore and Murray Dubin, *The Philadelphia Inquirer* (March 28, 1978). Reprinted by permission.

From "Hers: Whites Say I Must Be on Easy Street" by Nell Irvin Painter, *The New York Times* (December 10, 1981). Copyright © 1981 by the New York Times Company. Reprinted by permission.

From "Graciela Mendoza Peña Valencia" by June Namias, in *First Generation in the Words of Twentieth Century American Immigrants*, pp. 177–179, Beacon Press, 1978. Copyright © 1978 by June Namias. Reprinted by permission of Beacon Press.

Excerpts from *Listen America!* by Jerry Falwell, pp. 101–103, 232–233. Copyright © 1980 by Jerry Falwell. Reprinted by permission of Doubleday & Company, Inc.

From *Future Shock* by Alvin Toffler. Copyright © 1970 by Alvin Toffler. Reprinted by permission of Random House, Inc.

Illustration Sources

13 New York Public Library/Picture Collection; 17 The Granger Collection; 26 Courtesy, Records of the Veterans Administration; 32 Lin Caufield Photographers, Inc.; 37 Library of Congress; 41 Library of Congress; 42 Culver Pictures; 45 Library of Congress; 60 Library of Congress; 64 Public Health Services/National Archives; 73 Office of the Secretary of Agriculture/National Archives; 81 Library of Congress; 87 With permission of the Boonin Family. Photograph courtesy, Philadelphia Genealogy Society; 89 UPI; 95 Photograph by Jacob A. Riis, The Jacob A. Riis Collection, Museum of the City of New York; 96 Photograph by Lewis Hine, George Eastman House; 100 Photograph by Jacob A. Riis, The Jacob A. Riis Collection, Museum of the City of New York; 109 National Archives; 111 National Archives; 117 Danny Lyon/Magnum; 118 Library of Congress; 122 Library of Congress; 123 National Archives; 127 Library of Congress; 135 National Archives; 141 *top and middle* National Archives; 141 *bottom* Library of Congress; 147 National Archives; 149 Library of Congress; 153 National Archives; 154 Library

of Congress; 161 UPI; 163 Courtesy, Allen F. Davis; 174 *top and bottom* Library of Congress; 175 *top and bottom* Library of Congress; 179 *top and bottom* Library of Congress; 184 Library of Congress; 189 Collection, Museum of the City of New York, Photograph by Charles von Urban; 193 *left* Wide World Photos; 193 *right* UPI; 195 Brown Brothers; 203 U.S. Information Agency/National Archives; 205 National Archives; 206 Library of Congress; 210 Library of Congress; 212 Courtesy, Raymond and Malvina Phillips; 215 *top* UPI; 215 *bottom* National Archives; 218 U.S. Information Agency/National Archives; 220 U.S. Information Agency/National Archives; 221 *top and bottom* U.S. Information Agency/National Archives; 229 Franklynn Peterson/Black Star; 231 *top and bottom* Library of Congress; 232 *top and bottom* Library of Congress; 233 UPI; 236 Library of Congress; 238 *top* U.S. Information Agency/National Archives; 238 *bottom* National Archives; 240 Library of Congress; 247 National Archives; 257 Library of Congress; 259 Courtesy, Soil Conservation Service; 264 *top and bottom* National Archives; 265 National Archives; 273 Neil Benson; 275 Neil Benson; 286 Arthur Greenspon/Nancy Palmer Agency; 290 *left and right* New York Public Library/Picture Collection; 291 *top and bottom* Neil Benson; 297 UPI; 299 Neil Benson; 310 *top and bottom* Harvey Stein; 311 *top* Philip Teuscher; 311 *bottom* Charles Gatewood; 317 Courtesy, McDonalds; 322 *top* Fred R. Conrad/New York Times Pictures; 322 *bottom* Neal Boenzi/New York Times Pictures; 326 UPI; 330 *top and bottom* Howard Petrick/Nancy Palmer Agency; 336 Neil Benson; 345 Department of Housing and Urban Development; 349 *top left and bottom* Allen F. Davis; 349 *top right* Jim Watts; 353 *top left* Courtesy, The Balch Institute, Philadelphia; 353 *top, middle, bottom right* National Archives; 355 *left* Allen F. Davis; 355 *right* Smithsonian Institution Photo; 356 Courtesy, University of Illinois at Chicago Circle; 357 "The Wilkes Family," Collection of Vincent J. Wallace, Courtesy of "A New York Album," Pace University; 359 *left and right* Courtesy, Elizabeth D. Flynn; 360 *left and right* Allen F. Davis; 361 Allen F. Davis; 365 National Archives.

Acknowledgments

The publication of this new edition provides a third opportunity to express my appreciation for places and people. Many of the names do change as time pushes on, but much remains the same. I had the great advantage of growing up in the country, near Oswego, New York, in a responsible and loving family. The legacy of my late father, James F. (Jake) Watts, will last me my lifetime. My mother, Mary Sullivan Hughes Watts, still looks as good as in her wedding picture, prominently featured later in this book. My sister Marianne and my brothers Mike and Pat remain good friends and good influences. My daughter Jennifer Kate is wonderful. My son Nathaniel is super. For nearly two decades I have enjoyed and profited from the challenges and rewards of teaching at The City College and living in New York, a great place to be in all seasons. Among its cast of characters who have recently contributed to my education are Richard Lieberman, Stuart Feder, Andra Crawford, Oscar Cohen, Richard Epstein, Jon Levy, Jack Beckett, and Jimmy Moriarity.

J. F. WATTS

Many students at Temple University have contributed to *Generations* by studying the history of their families and sharing their discoveries with me. This book also owes a great debt to my family. Harold F. Davis, my late father, talked to me about my own family and helped me relate the past to the present. My sons, Gregory and Paul, went on many expeditions with me in search of ancestors. Leone and Roscoe Cobb helped me to rediscover my hometown. Those who attended institutes and short courses at Skidmore College, Emory University, Monroe County Community College, The University of Pennsylvania, The Smithsonian Institution, and New York University all made useful suggestions. Neil Benson, Harry Boonin, Jean Yellin, and Frances A. Keegan provided photographs.

ALLEN F. DAVIS

Preface to
the Third Edition

We are pleased that the continued success of *Generations: Your Family in Modern History* has warranted the publication of this third edition. It was nearly fifteen years ago that we conceived the idea of focusing the study of American history on students' own families as a way of making history more accessible and meaningful. In this edition we have retained many of the features of the other editions, including chapters on the preindustrial age, the great migrations, plus an extensive Appendix. In response to suggestions of many instructors who have used the earlier editions, we have added new chapters on the 1920s, the 1960s, and the 1970s. In this regard, we want to recognize the preceptive suggestions of Professors James Findlay, University of Rhode Island, Paul Preising, Evergreen Valley College, and Susan Porter Benson, Bristol Community College. We have also added new material and new photographs in the other chapters. While the strategy of the earlier editions was circular, the book is now organized more chronologically. This edition, suggested to us by David Follmer, was expertly copy edited by Susan Gilbert. Over the whole process presided our superb editor, Elaine Rosenberg, whose professional expertise and calm demeanor provided a remarkably smooth publication. We hope *Generations,* third edition, will continue to be useful in the classroom, and that even more people will discover the joys of relating their own personal past to the larger forces of history.

Contents

SEVEN

EIGHT

Appendix: Materials for Research and Writing 347

GENERATIONS
Your Family in Modern American History

THIRD EDITION

Introduction: Why Study Family History?

If you have grown up and gone to school in the United States, you have studied American history for almost as long as you can remember. From the first or second grade when you colored pictures of Lincoln and cut out cherry trees and hatchets, to later grades when you memorized the special meaning of dates like 1607 or 1863, American history has been a required subject. You have been buffeted by facts about Puritans, the westward movement, the Age of Jackson, Civil War battles, overseas expansion, the New Deal, and the New Frontier, but the facts have probably had little meaning and surely have been forgotten more quickly than they were memorized. Although there is a certain intellectual excitement in sorting out the conflicting interpretations of past events, that kind of intellectual game often leaves out the human element.

Perhaps a few historical facts have remained with you because of a personal experience—a visit to a local battle site or a historic house, a tour of a restored village, coming across some old news clippings or letters preserved by a relative, or perhaps just seeing some striking old pictures. They gave you a glimpse of a different kind of past, one remote from that in history books and inhabited by real people with problems and hopes and desires. But the glimpse was, no doubt, fleeting and soon disappeared. Perhaps while reading a novel or watching a

3

movie, you got another brief look at the past, as a panorama of human suffering, lust and love, failure and triumph; but that is not supposed to be history—or is it?

All of us, through our parents, grandparents, great-grandparents, and other ancestors, are a part of history, stretching back into a dim and distant past. You will probably search in vain for a really famous person in your family background. Everyone, however, has ancestors whose lives were altered by the forces of history—by wars, depressions, population movements, shifts in national boundaries, changes in farming methods, the process of industrialization. You can begin to understand some of the dimensions of human existence, some of the process of change, by looking at your own family, studying your own particular ethnic group, and examining the community in which you live.

The best way to begin the study of the past is with yourself. Where do you fit in? What makes you similar to your friends? What makes you different? How do you explain your own special situation? Does it have something to do with the generation in which you were born? The accident of birth, for example, caused those born in the 1930s, a time of low birth rate, to have had much greater employment opportunities than you can expect to have if you were born in the early 1960s, a time of high birth rate. Perhaps it is not so much time and generation as sex, race, or religion that you see as crucial in defining your place and identity. Then, being a woman, a black, an Italian, or a Jew will become the most important fact in your life. And social class, too, can be significant in defining your life style, especially if you are either very rich or very poor.

Probably the most crucial influence

on your life was your own family. Whether you grew up in a nuclear family (made up of husband, wife, and children) or an extended family (a group of assorted relatives living together and functioning as a unit), you have, no doubt, been radically affected by your interaction with your parents, brothers and sisters, and other relatives. These interactions constitute a unique story—a history. There are "official" records of this history: deeds, marriage certificates, divorce decrees, various court records, the discharge papers of one released from the army. But behind these recorded events are human stories of pathos and triumph and tragedy. A baby dies, a son leaves home, a daughter marries, children rebel against their parents. There are moments of joy and periods of success, individual accomplishments and family pride. There is bitterness and remorse and failure, or perhaps resignation. All these are universals which touch every family at one point or another.

Both continuity and change characterize these universal human experiences. To put it another way, over the past five generations in your family, sixty-two people participated in your creation. Your thirty-two great-, great-, great-grandparents must seem like characters out of ancient history to you, yet they lived only about a century and a half ago, a short period in historical time. They—and even your more distant ancestors as well—were in some ways just like you. Survival, after all, has always compelled men and women to find the means to acquire food, shelter, and clothing. And being human has always required confronting births and deaths, experiencing pleasure and enduring pain, seeking both solitude and association. With respect to the latter, peoples over the centuries have tended

4

to identify themselves with others, with family or community, by region or nationality, with ethnic groups, or religion. Although your thirty-two great-, great-, great-grandparents may remain beyond your knowledge in most ways, you may be sure that they shared with you many of the experiences of the human condition.

We tend to forget the continuities of existence because of the extraordinary changes the world has undergone in the relatively recent past. Indeed, your ancestors beyond the third and fourth generations past lived in a world amazingly different from what you have known. Their world began to disappear when machines became the primary factor in the production and distribution of goods and services. The age-old patterns of life that were rather quickly destroyed by industrialization offer a striking contrast to the way we live today. We have paid a price for our material progress: the destruction of much that was valuable, as an examination of the days of our preindustrial ancestors will reveal.

Industrialization is just one of the ways the life style of your family has been affected by the events of the past. Another force of major importance was the movement of peoples. Perhaps your family came from Ireland in the great migration after the potato famine in the 1840s; or maybe they were Jews who left Russia in the early 1900s. Possibly you are descended from the slaves who survived the passage from Africa, or perhaps you can trace your ancestry back to the migration from England in the seventeenth and eighteenth centuries. Whatever your own special background, unless you are a pure-blooded Indian, your ancestors went through the process of being uprooted from one culture and establishing themselves in an-

other. Even if your background can be traced to the Native Americans, you too have a heritage of movement and change. The wrenching moves from one land to another that your parents or grandparents made, the hopes and fears, dreams and heartaches they had, constitute a widely shared American experience.

There are, of course, some for whom the effects of immigration are too distant to be felt. But even if your parents or grandparents are not recent immigrants, the chances are that your family has moved from farm to city, from small city to metropolis, from East to West, or from South to North. Americans have always been a mobile people, and they continue to be so even today. It is now an unusual American family that has lived for more than two generations in the same community, let alone in the same house. Every move meant leaving friends and often possessions, although it did not necessarily mean leaving behind the memories of a place. The human dimension of American mobility can be probed by asking questions of your family.

Just as geographic mobility has helped shape the American character, so too has belief in the American Dream—the notion that America is a land of opportunity where poor men and women, if they work hard, can improve their situation or at least create a better life for their children. Almost everyone, except those who came as slaves, believed this dream in the past, but how many really succeeded in creating a better life in a new land?

A person's success, or lack of it, has been affected by many factors, not the least of which, in the twentieth century, have been the Great Depression and the war that followed it. These large historical forces are discussed extensively in history books, mainly from the viewpoint of their effect on political processes and society in the abstract. Both events had very personal sides to them, however, as any member of your family who lived through those decades can attest. For nearly everyone who experienced the depression of the thirties, the hope for a continuously improving life was shattered. True, that hope was revived for some by the prosperity and sense of purpose that World War II gave back to the country. But not everyone shared in this wartime optimism—certainly not those black Americans who fought for a freedom they did not have at home nor those Japanese-Americans interned in concentration camps for the accident of their ethnic heritage—and even for those who did, the memory of bad times was too vivid to ever allow them freedom from naggingly practical concerns. If there is a gap between generations today manifested in what parents and children are concerned with and in what their expectations for the future are, surely it has been conditioned by the differences between the periods of history through which the two generations have lived. Those differences can be laid out and, if not reconciled, at least understood through a comparison of your own family's recollections of living through the past and your remembrances of the time during which you grew up.

The strategy of this book, then, is to help you gather information and to ask questions about yourself and your family and about the movements and events that have influenced history.

Why should I be interested in studying my ancestors? you may ask. My family is not important. My grandfather and great-grandmother cannot be very interesting, because I know they were poor and "ordinary"—common people. Is it not more important and usually more interesting to study famous people, the kings, presidents, and generals who really made a difference in history? Or, if we must study families, why not the famous ones, such as the Adams family, the Roosevelts, or the Rockefellers?

These are natural questions, and there are many answers to them. Perhaps the most basic reason to explore your family's history is that in finding out where you came from, you may learn more about who you are. To discover where your parents were born, to appreciate the struggles that your great-grandparents endured, to re-create what it felt like to live in another time and place, and to imagine what it must have been like for those who came before you is to uncover something important about yourself.

Studying your family's history is much more than a self-serving exercise, however. Until recently, most historical writing has been the story of the famous and the infamous. All too often, it has been the story of famous white men. Even genealogy (that is, the careful investigation of family lineage) has been reserved for those who came from an Anglo-Saxon Protestant background and could trace their family at least to the American Revolution and perhaps even to the arrival of the *Mayflower* in 1620. Most of us are from ordinary families (as were most of those who sailed on the *Mayflower* and fought in the Revolution five generations later). By tracing our past we can learn something about the ways anonymous Americans lived in the past. We can begin to appreciate what travel across the ocean or across the continent really meant to the men, women, and children who made those voyages. We can observe depressions and wars not from the point

6

of view of the leaders but from the vantage point of the people who had to suffer and die. We may come to understand how the passage of time has changed the way we live, altered the landscape, and transformed work and transportation and housing. We can also learn that some things stay the same.

During the 1970s, there was a renewed interest in family and community history, stimulated, partly, by the Bicentennial celebration and a growing sense of ethnic identity. But the basic need to find one's roots was also provoked by the uncertainty of the times. It became important to establish a connection with a personal past, to extend generational memory at a time when the future seemed so uncertain. The phenomenal commercial success of Alex Haley's *Roots*, in book and televised forms, was both a result and a cause of this growing interest in discovering a personal past. The millions who read or watched *Roots* were certainly attracted to the human story of triumph and tragedy, of courage and survival against great odds; but they were also intrigued by the process that Alex Haley, an American black and a twenty-year veteran of the Coast Guard, used to discover his family history all the way back to his "furthest back person," an African.

Many people thrilled by the human side of the *Roots* story set out to find their own family history. Of course, without the time and financial resources needed, and often without Haley's luck, novice researchers were not able to duplicate his success. Yet many family historians did trace their roots back several generations, and many more recovered an oral tradition from living relatives that otherwise would have been lost.

Alex Haley's story of discovery, though familiar, is worth summarizing, because it contains lessons that are relevant to anyone who wishes to discover a personal past. The story begins with a memory from Haley's boyhood: he is sitting on the porch of his grandmother's house in Henning, Tennessee, listening to his grandmother talk to other relatives about family stories and legends. They especially talk of "the African" whose name was "Kin-tay," who said "ko" for banjo, "Kamby Bolong" for river; they tell how the African had been kidnapped while chopping wood to make himself a drum.

One day in 1965, on impulse Haley went into the National Archives building in Washington, D.C., and, after a long search, he found some of the family names on microfilmed census records. "It wasn't that I hadn't believed Grandma," he recalled. "You just didn't not believe my Grandma. It was simply so uncanny actually seeing those names in print and in official U.S. Government records."

Stimulated by his success, Haley enlisted the help of African experts. He learned that "Kamby Bolong" probably meant "Gambia River," that "Kin-tay" was "Kinte," an old African clan. He flew to Africa where an African *griot*, who preserved and recited oral legends of the tribe, told him the same story that he had heard from his grandmother: that a young man many years before had been kidnapped while cutting wood to make a drum. Later he discovered the record of the slave ship that carried his African ancestor from the Gambia River to Annapolis. He then combined historical research with a vivid imagination to produce *Roots*. While some critics expressed reservations about Haley's methodology, nothing dims the fascination of his story. In fact, much of the interest and appeal of *Roots* is Haley's search for a personal past—a search you can take part in.

Your time and resources will be more limited than were Haley's, but the same excitement and thrill of discovery await you as you uncover your own family history, find one of your ancestors listed in an official government document, or visit a place where one of your people lived.

Some families, of course, are easier to trace than are others, but at some point every family disappears into a great unknown. There are some family roots that are impossible to discover. Some people may return to the site of a grandfather's house to find a parking lot or a high-rise apartment building in its place. Some may be blocked from success by a name change or a break in the chain of family memory. Every successful search always includes a certain amount of luck, and a large amount of failure. But even if you fail to trace your family's roots for many generations, you will have experienced some of the thrill of historical research, and you will have learned something about the way people really lived in other times and places. Whatever you find will also have a special meaning because it is your own special history.

ASSIGNMENT 1

Beginning Your Study of Family History

Your first assignment is to begin the process of generating data for your own family's history. The Appendix of this book provides a number of aids for this task. The most logical starting point is the section in the Appendix entitled "Researching and Writing Your Family History" (pp. 347–372), which supplies clues on how to go about finding information.

After reading this section, you should start collecting information. First, fill in the form on "Yourself" (p. 377) and as much of the genealogical chart (either one of the two supplied on pp. 375 and 376) as you can. Next, if you live at home, gather information requested about the other members of your family on the remaining forms (pp. 378–387). If you are living away from home, write a letter explaining what you are doing, and ask that the information be sent to you. At your next opportunity, see what you can discover around your house. (Ask permission when appropriate!) You may turn up photographs, certificates, wills, deeds, diaries, family Bibles, and so on. Try to find out the specific places where your ancestors spent their lives, both in this country and, if possible, in the society of their birth if other than the United States. Where feasible, write letters to officials in those places (to the city or county clerk, probate court, or foreign consulates in the United States) to find out how to obtain pertinent family documents. Let your librarian or instructor help you to locate these places on a map and suggest ways of establishing contacts.

PART TWO

The World We
Have Lost

Think for a moment about your grandparents. Imagine, if you can, the time when they were your age. They were, once, you know. If you begin to count the ways in which their world differed from your world, you will realize how profound many of the changes are, or at least seem to be. No television or radio, probably no automobiles, electricity, or indoor plumbing. Certainly no suburbs, Super Bowls, or supermarkets. And no toothpaste in a tube or *Time* magazine, rock music, or six-packs.

Now imagine your great-grandparents and great-great-grandparents and on to those anonymous ancestors even further back in time. We all have eight great-grandparents and sixteen great-great-grandparents. If you could go back nine generations beyond your parents, you would have 1,024 direct ancestors. How did all those people, especially the ones born before the middle of the nineteenth century, think about their lives? How did they spend their days?

There are, of course, some things that remain constant over the many centuries—birth, death, childhood, old age, marriage, and sexual relationships, as well as work, obtaining food, eating, and sleeping. But even here, differences between you and your distant relatives can be discerned. Attitudes toward childhood, death, and sex, for example, have changed dramatically over 200 years.

The kind of work most people do and the processes of growing and preparing food have also been altered by time. Even family living has changed. Although recent historical investigation reveals that in the Western world, at least from the seventeenth century, most people have lived in nuclear rather than in extended families (that is, they have lived in a household with mother, father, and children, with few people from another generation), still family relationships and the ways families live have certainly changed markedly over three centuries.

Generations vary a great deal in length, but if you could discover your sixty-four great-great-great-great-grandparents they would probably have lived about the time of the American Revolution. Where they lived would have influenced their life style, their hopes and fears and dreams. But whether they were members of an African tribe, peasants in eastern Europe, farmers in Ireland or Italy, or millers and merchants in America, they probably would have much more in common with each other than any of them would have with your generation.

For centuries, most men and women in all parts of the world lived close to the land. They probably died near where they were born, and they knew little of what went on beyond their village. They raised almost all they needed, and their work was closely related to their home and family. Their days and years were bounded and controlled by climate, weather, and the seasons.

We should not be overly nostalgic about this world of small communities where work was closely related to family routines and the rhythm of the seasons, for it was also a world of disease and early death, of constant struggle and frequent disaster. Then, more commonly than now, a strong religious faith provided both explanation and sustenance in the face of inevitable tragedies.

Wealth, position, and class have always made a difference in life style and even in life expectancy. To be a big landowner or a merchant was always to have an advantage over a peasant or an indentured servant. But even the wealthy in the seventeenth century fell victim to yellow fever epidemics and had to use candles for light, a fireplace for heat, and an outdoor privy.

Everyday life has been transformed in the last 150 years by a series of accelerating revolutions that are sometimes lumped together and called "industrialism." These revolutions have influenced every area of life, not just the process of manufacturing and production. Contemplate for a moment the changes that have occurred in transportation. Before the railroad began to connect cities in the mid-nineteenth century, the only way to travel overland was on horseback or in a horse-drawn vehicle (or, in some parts of the world, a vehicle drawn by another animal). People were limited to a distance of twenty-five or thirty miles a day. Travel was difficult and dangerous. The railroad, the automobile, and the airplane have made it possible to travel great distances with ease and comfort. It may now be impossible to find a person who remembers when the first railroad was built, but there are many who can remember when travel by train was still somewhat novel, and many others can recall the first automobile in town or the first airplane they ever saw. You probably have memories of the first man to land on the moon. The rocket has not yet altered our daily lives to any great extent, but the railroad, the automobile, and the airplane make our lives very different from those who lived in the eighteenth century.

A similar revolution has occurred in communication. In the eighteenth century a letter or a newspaper sometimes took three months to go from Boston to London, and those living in the small communities away from the urban centers were even more isolated from news. The nineteenth-century inventions of the telegraph, the cable, and the telephone, and the twentieth-century inventions of radio and television, make any news event today instantly available in almost every part of the world. These inventions have certainly had a visual and audible impact on our lives that those living in the eighteenth century could not have imagined.

Other developments, such as electricity, indoor plumbing, food processing, refrigeration, the growth of large industry and advertising also make our lives very different from those of our ancestors. Artificial heat, light, and air conditioning, together with our great concern with the clock and the division of the day into hours and minutes, have divorced our lives from the natural rhythm of climate, weather, and the seasons.

The revolutions that have transformed daily existence have taken place more rapidly in some parts of the world than in others. There are still pockets even in the United States where life has not changed a great deal since the eighteenth century. Perhaps you can discover such a place, or at least some people born in the 1880s or 1890s who remember life before electricity, indoor plumbing, and the internal-combustion engine. If you try, you can recover something of the world we have lost. Just as important, you may come to appreciate how history has shaped your life and the lives of your ancestors.

The Preindustrial Family

PETER LASLETT

In the following essay Peter Laslett tries to re-create the life of a family of bakers in London in the early seventeenth century. It was a time when work was closely related to family life, when children were also workers, and when a wife was clearly subservient to her husband. It was surely no golden age, but it was a time quite unlike our own. Most of our ancestors were probably not bakers in London, but wherever they lived and whatever their occupations they probably had much more in common with these bakers than with anyone living in the last quarter of the twentieth century.

As you read this essay notice how much the author is able to read into one document. That technique may be useful to you as you attempt to recover the history of your own family. Try to determine how the life style of these men, women, and children differs from your own. Whether you decide that we have made great progress since 1619 or have in some ways declined, you will agree with the author that things have changed dramatically. We are, as the author notes at the end, "very different from our ancestors."

In the year 1619 the bakers of London applied to the authorities for an increase in the price of bread. They sent in support of their claim a complete description of a bakery and an account of its weekly costs. There were thirteen or fourteen people in such an undertaking: the baker and his wife, four paid employees who were called journeymen, two apprentices, two maidservants and the three or four children of the master baker himself. Six pounds ten shillings a week was reckoned to be the outgoings of this establishment of which only eleven shillings and eightpence went for wages: half a crown a week for each of the journeymen and tenpence for each of the maids. Far and away the greatest expense was for food: two pounds nine shillings out of the six pounds ten shillings, at five shillings a head for the baker and his wife, four shillings a head for their helpers and two shillings for their children. It cost much more in food to keep a journeyman than it cost in money; four times as much to keep a maid. Clothing was charged up too, not only for the man, wife and children, but for the apprentices as well. Even school fees were claimed as a justifiable charge on the price of bread for sale, and sixpence a week was paid for the teaching and clothing of a baker's child.

What does this illustration suggest about the nature of family life and its relationship to work? What time of day might this be? How do you explain the scene in terms of Laslett's emphasis on the small scale of urban life?

A London bakery was undoubtedly what we should call a commercial or even an industrial undertaking, turning out loaves by the thousand. Yet the business was carried on in the house of the baker himself. There was probably a *shop* as part of the house, *shop* as in *workshop* and not as meaning a retail establishment. Loaves were not ordinarily sold over the counter: they had to be carried to the open-air market and displayed on stalls. There was a garner behind the house, for which the baker paid two shillings a week in rent, and where he kept his wheat, his *sea-coal* for the fire and his store of salt. The house itself was one of those high, half-timbered overhanging structures on the narrow London street which we always think of when we remember the scene in which Shakespeare, Pepys or even Christopher Wren lived. Most of it was taken up with the living-quarters of the dozen people who worked there.

It is obvious that all these people ate in the house since the cost of their food helped to determine the production cost of the bread. Except for the journeymen they were all obliged to sleep in the house at night and live together as a family.

14 The only word used at that time to describe such a group of people was "family." The man at the head of the group, the entrepreneur, the employer, or the manager, was then known as the master or head of the family. He was father to some of its members and in place of father to the rest. There was no sharp distinction between his domestic and his economic functions. His wife was both his partner and his subordinate, a partner because she ran the family, took charge of the food and managed the women-servants, a subordinate because she was woman and wife, mother and in place of mother to the rest.

The paid servants of both sexes had their specified and familiar position in the family, as much part of it as the children but not quite in the same position. At that time the family was not one society only but three societies fused together; the society of man and wife, of parents and children and of master and servant. But when they were young, and servants were, for the most part, young, unmarried people, they were very close to children in their status and their function. Here is the agreement made between the parents of a boy about to become an apprentice and his future master. The boy covenants to dwell with his master for seven years, to keep his secrets and to obey his commandments.

> Taverns and alehouses he shall not haunt, dice, cards or any other unlawful games he shall not use, fornication with any woman he shall not commit, matrimony with any woman he shall not contract. He shall not absent himself by night or by day without his master's leave but be a true and faithful servant.

On his side, the master undertakes to teach his apprentice his *"art, science or occupation with moderate correction."*

> Finding and allowing unto his said servant meat, drink, apparel, washing, lodging and all other things during the said term of seven years, and to give unto his said apprentice at the end of the said term double apparel, to wit, one suit for holydays and one suit for worken days.

Apprentices, therefore, and many other servants, were workers who were also children, extra sons or extra daughters (for girls could be apprenticed too), clothed and educated as well as fed, obliged to obedience and forbidden to marry, often unpaid and dependent until after the age of twenty-one. If such servants were workers in the position of sons and daughters, the sons and daughters of the house were workers too. John Locke laid it down in 1697 that the children of the poor must work for some part of the day when they reached the age of three. The children of a London baker were not free to go to school for many years of their young lives, or even to play as they wished when they came back home. Soon they would find themselves doing what they could in *bolting*, that is sieving flour, or in helping the maidservant with her panniers of loaves on the way to the market stall, or in playing their small parts in preparing the never-ending succession of meals for the whole household.

We may see at once, therefore, that the world we have lost, as I have chosen to call it, was no paradise or golden age of equality, tolerance or loving kindness. It is so important that I should not be misunderstood on this point that I will say at once that the coming of industry cannot be shown to have brought economic oppression and exploitation along with it. It was there already. The patriarchal arrangements which we have begun to explore were not new in the England of

Shakespeare and Elizabeth. They were as old as the Greeks, as old as European
history, and not confined to Europe. And it may well be that they abused and
enslaved people quite as remorselessly as the economic arrangements which had
replaced them in the England of Blake and Victoria. When people could expect to
live for so short a time, how must a man have felt when he realized that so much of
his adult life must go in working for his keep and very little more in someone else's
family?

But people very seldom recognize facts of this sort, and no one is content to
expect to live as long as the majority in fact will live. Every servant in the old
social world was probably quite confident that he or she would some day get
married and be at the head of a new family, keeping others in subordination. If it is
legitimate to use the words exploitation and oppression in thinking of the economic arrangements of the pre-industrial world, there were nevertheless differences in the manner of oppressing and exploiting. The ancient order of society was
felt to be eternal and unchangeable by those who supported, enjoyed and endured
it. There was no expectation of reform. How could there be when economic organization was domestic organization, and relationships were rigidly regulated
by the social system, by the content of Christianity itself?

Here is a vivid contrast with social expectation in Victorian England, or in
industrial countries everywhere today. Every relationship in our world which can
be seen to affect our economic life is open to change, is expected indeed to change
of itself, or if it does not, to *be* changed, made better, by an omnicompetent
authority. This makes for a less stable social world, though it is only one of the
features of our society which impels us all in that direction. All industrial societies, we may suppose, are far less stable than their predecessors. They lack the
extraordinarily cohesive influence which familial relationships carry with them,
that power of reconciling the frustrated and the discontented by emotional
means. Social revolution, meaning an irreversible changing of the pattern of social relationships, never happened in traditional, patriarchal, pre-industrial
human society. It was almost impossible to contemplate.

■ ■ ■

. . . There are reasons why a baker's household might have been a little out of
the ordinary, for baking was a highly traditional occupation in a society increasingly subject to economic change. [And] . . . a family of thirteen people, which
was also a unit of production of thirteen, less the children still incapable of work,
was quite large for English society at that time. Only the families of the really
important, the nobility and the gentry, the aldermen and the successful merchants, were ordinarily as large as this. In fact, we can take the bakery to
represent the upper limit in size and scale of the group in which ordinary people
lived and worked. Among the great mass of society which cultivated the land, . . .
the family group was smaller than a substantial London craftsman's entourage.
There are other things we should observe about the industrial and commercial
scene.

It is worth noticing to begin with, how prominently the town and the craft
appear in the folk-memory we still retain from the world we have lost. Agriculture and the countryside do not dominate our recollections to anything like the
extent that they dominated that vanished world. We still talk to our children

16   about the apprentices who married their master's daughter: these are the heroes. Or about the outsider who marries the widow left behind by the father/master when he comes to die: these unwelcome strangers to the family are the villains. We refer to bakers as if they really baked in their homes; of spinsters who really sit by the fire and spin. A useful, if a rather arbitrary and romantic guide to the subject in hand, is the famous collection of Fairy Tales compiled by the brothers Grimm in Germany nearly 150 years ago, where the tales we tell to our children mostly have their source. Even in the form given to them by Walt Disney and the other makers of films and picture-books for the youngest members of our rich, leisurely, powerful, puzzled world of successful industrialization, stories like Cinderella are a sharp reminder of what life was once like for the apprentice, the journeyman, the master and all his family in the craftsman's household. Which means, in a sense, that we all know it all already.

■ ■ ■

. . . Let us emphasize again the scale of life in the working family of the London baker. Few persons in the old world ever found themselves in groups larger than family groups, and there were few families of more than a dozen members. The largest household so far known to us, apart from the royal court and the establishments of the nobility, lay and spiritual, is that of Sir Richard Newdigate, Baronet, in his house of Arbury within his parish of Chilvers Coton in Warwickshire, in the year 1684. There were thirty-seven people in Sir Richard's family: himself; Lady Mary Newdigate, his wife; seven daughters, all under the age of sixteen; and twenty-eight servants, seventeen men and boys and eleven women and girls. This was still a family, not an institution, a staff, an office or a firm.

Everything physical was on the human scale, for the commercial worker in London, and the miner who lived and toiled in Newdigate's village of Chilvers Coton. No object in England was larger than London Bridge or St. Paul's Cathedral, no structure in the Western World to stand comparison with the Colosseum in Rome. Everything temporal was tied to the human life-span too. The death of the master baker, head of the family, ordinarily meant the end of the bakery. Of course there might be a son to succeed, but the master's surviving children would be young if he himself had lived only as long as most men. Or an apprentice might fulfil the final function of apprenticehood, substitute sonship, that is to say, and marry his master's daughter, or even his widow. Surprisingly often, the widow, if she could, would herself carry on the trade.

This, therefore, was not simply a world without factories, without firms, and for the most part without economic continuity. Some partnerships between rich masters existed, especially in London, but since nearly every activity was limited to what could be organized within a family, and the lifetime of its head, there was an unending struggle to manufacture continuity and to provide an expectation of the future.

■ ■ ■

When we insist on the tiny scale of life in the pre-industrial world, especially on the small size of the group in which nearly everybody spent his or her

How is the scene in this preindustrial bakery similar to other productive facilities prior to industrialization? What does the picture suggest about the quality and quantity of the work? What does a modern bakery look like?

life, there are certain occasions and institutions which we must not overlook. There were the military practices, an annual muster of the ablebodied men from every county, which took place after harvest in Tudor times. There were regular soldiers too, though not very many of them; variegated bands of the least promising of men straggling behind the banner of some noble adventurer. Much more familiar to Englishmen, at least in the maritime areas, must have been the sailors; twenty, thirty, even fifty men at sea, sometimes for days, or even weeks on end.

Lilliputian, we must feel, when we compare such details with the crowds we meet in our society. The largest crowd recorded for seventeenth-century England, that is the Parliamentary Army which fought at Marston Moor, would have gone three, four or even five times into the sporting stadium of today. Other organizations and purposes which brought groups of people together were the Assizes in the County Towns; the Quarter Sessions of the County Justices; the meetings of the manorial courts in the villages, of the town councils in the towns, of the companies or craftsmen there, each one to a trade or occupation; the assemblies which sometimes took place of clergy or of nonconformist ministers. Most regular of all, and probably largest in scale and most familiar to ordinary men and women were the weekly market days and the annual fairs in each locality. Then there were the 2,000 schools in England, one for every fifth parish but very few large enough to have more than a single teacher, and the two universities, with less than 10,000 men between them. Then there was Parliament itself. All these occasions and institutions assembled men in some numbers for purposes which could not be called familial. Women too assembled, though, save to the markets, they came as spectators rather than as participants.

The fact that it is possible to name most of the large-scale institutions and occasions in a sentence or two makes the contrast with our own world more telling than ever. We have only to think of the hundreds of children sitting every day, all over the country, in their classrooms, the hundreds and thousands together in the factories, the offices, the shops, to recognize the difference. The detailed study of the pre-industrial social world makes this question of scale more critical still. Wherever the facts of economic life and technology required a working group different in size and constitution from the working family, there was discontinuity. Hence the crew of a ship, the team of workers on a building, the fifty or sixty grown men who might be required to work a mine or an armaments manufactory, were all looked upon as exceptional. As indeed they were, so much so that the building trade had had its own society from medieval times, and the miners were a community apart wherever they were found.

Not only did the scale of their work and the size of the group which was engaged make them exceptional, the constitution of the group did too. In the baking household we have chosen as our standard, sex and age were mingled together. Fortunate children might go out to school, but adults did not usually go out to work. There was nothing to correspond to the thousands of young men on the assembly line, the hundreds of young women in the offices, the lonely lives of housekeeping wives, which we now know only too well. We shall see that those who survived to old age in the much less favourable conditions for survival which then were prevalent, were surprisingly often left to live and die alone, in their tiny cottages or sometimes in the almshouses which were being built so widely in the England of the Tudors and the Stuarts. Poor-law establishments, parochial in purpose and in size, had begun their melancholy chapter in the history of the English people. But institutional life was otherwise almost unknown. There were no hotels, hostels, or blocks of flats for single persons, very few hospitals and none of the kind we are familiar with, almost no young men and women living on their own. The family unit where so great a majority lived was what we should undoubtedly call a "balanced" and "healthy" group.

When we turn from the hand-made city of London to the hand-moulded immensity of rural England, we may carry the same sentimental prejudice along with us. To every farm there was a family, which spread itself over its portion of the village lands as the family of the master-craftsman filled out his manufactory. When a holding was small, and most were small as are the tiny holdings of European peasants today, a man tilled it with the help of his wife and his children. No single man, we must remember, would usually take charge of the land, any more than a single man would often be found at the head of a workshop in the city. The master of a family was expected to be a householder, whether he was a butcher, a baker, a candlestick maker or simply a husbandman, which was the universal name for one whose skill was in working the land. Marriage we must insist, and it is one of the rules which gave its character to the society of our ancestors, was the entry to full membership, in the enfolding countryside, as well as in the scattered urban centres.

But there was a difference in scale and organization of work on the land and in

the town. The necessities of rural life did require recurrent groupings of households for common economic purposes, occasionally something like a crowd of men,
women and children working together for days on end. Where the ground was still
being tilled as open fields, and each household had a number of strips scattered all
over the whole open area and not a compact collection of enclosures, ploughing
was co-operative, as were many other operations, above all harvesting, and this
continued even after enclosure. We do not yet know how important this element
of enforced common activity was in the life of the English rural community on the
eve of industrialization, or how much difference enclosure made in this respect.
But whatever the situation was, the economic transformation of the eighteenth
and nineteenth centuries destroyed communality altogether in English rural life.
The group of men from several farmsteads working the heavy plough in spring-
time, the bevy of harvesters from every house in the village wading into the high
standing grass to begin the cutting of the hay, had no successors in large-scale
economic activity. For the arrangement of these groups was entirely different in
principle from the arrangement of a factory, or a firm, or even of a collective farm.

Both before and after enclosure, some peasants did well: their crops were
heavier and they had more land to till. To provide the extra labour needed then,
the farming householder, like the successful craftsman, would extend his working
family by taking on young men and women as servants to live with him and work
the fields. This he would have to do, even if the land which he was farming was not
his own but rented from the great family in the manor house. Sometimes, we have
found, he would prefer to send out his own children as servants and bring in other
children and young men to do the work. This is one of the few glimpses we can get
into the quality of the emotional life of the family at this time, for it shows that
parents may have been unwilling to submit children of their own to the discipline
of work at home. It meant, too, that servants were not simply the perquisites of
wealth and position. A quarter, or a third, of all the families in the country
contained servants in Stuart times, and this meant that very humble people had
them as well as the titled and the wealthy. Most of the servants, moreover, male
or female, in the great house and in the small, were engaged in working the land.

The boys and the men would do the ploughing, hedging, carting and the heavy,
skilled work of the harvest. The women and the girls would keep the house,
prepare the meals, make the butter and the cheese, the bread and the beer, and
would also look after the cattle and take the fruit to market. At harvest-time,
from June to October, every hand was occupied and every back was bent. These
were the decisive months for the whole population in our damp northern climate,
with its single harvest in a season and reliance on one or two standard crops. So
critical was the winning of the grain for bread that the first rule of gentility (a
gentleman never worked with his hands for his living) might be abrogated.

We have hinted that a fundamental characteristic of the world we have lost
was the scene of labour, which was universally supposed to be the home. It has
been implied in the case of industry and in towns, that the hired man who came in
to work during the day and went home to his meals at night was looked on as
exceptional. Apart from the provisions about journeymen, who were, in fact, the
focus of whatever difficulty in "labour relations" was experienced at this time in
the towns, no standard arrangement has been found which contemplated any
permanent division of place of living and place of employment. That such divisions
existed, and may even have been commonplace in town and in country, cannot be

in doubt. There is evidence that a clothmaker in a big way, in the city of Beauvais in France at any rate, would have machinery in his house for more men than could possibly have lived there. It is thought that men walked in from the villages to Beauvais to do their day's work, just as men used to walk from the villages to the towns to work on the building sites in Victorian England. In those areas of England which first became industrial, there are signs that, like those in Beauvais, they too must have contained economic units which had to be supplied by daily wage labour. It came also, maybe, from the surrounding country, but certainly from the grown sons of families living in the town as well, young men, perhaps, even older men and married men, who cannot have been working where they lived. But when all this is said, the division of dwelling place and working place was no recognized feature of the social structure of the towns which our ancestors inhabited. The journey to work, the lonely lodger paying his rent out of a factory wage or office salary, are the distinguishing marks of our society, not of theirs. We are forced to suppose that in industrial and commercial matters the working family was assumed to be self-sufficient in its labour, in spite of the vicissitudes of the market.

But the level of activity in agriculture is fundamentally rhythmic, and its labour demands inevitably vary with the time of the year, the weather in the week, as well as with the prices of its products on the market. To work the land at all, especially as we have already hinted with the climate and geology of England, provision had to be made for a pool of labour, which the farming family could use or not as the farmer himself should decide. The manner in which this economic necessity was provided for shows how well the traditional, patriarchal structure of society could be adapted to meet the needs of a particular economy. It has to be traced in the life stories of the men and the women who lived in the villages and worked the land, or who pursued those occupations which were settled in the countryside, and were as much a part of its life as what went on in the stables and the barns. Let us begin with the life cycle of a poor inhabitant of an English village.

A boy, or a girl, born in a cottage, would leave home for service at any time after the age of ten. A servant-in-husbandry, as he might be called if he were a boy, would usually stay in the position of servant, though very rarely in the same household, until he or she got married. Marriage, when and if it came, would quite often take place with another servant. All this while, and it might be twelve, fifteen or even twenty years, the servant would be kept by the succession of employers in whose houses he dwelt. He was in no danger of poverty or hunger, even if the modest husbandman with whom he lived was worse housed than his landlord's horses, and worse clothed than his landlord's servants. "His landlord's horses," wrote a contemporary of the lowly husbandman, "lie in finer houses, than he, and his meanest servant wears a cloth beyond him." But the husbandman had his own servant, nevertheless, for when he said family prayers after a day's exhausting toil "the wife is sleeping in one corner, the child in another, the servant in a third."

But poverty awaited the husbandman's servant when he got married, and went himself to live in just such a labourer's cottage as the one in which he had been born. Whoever had been his former master, the labourer, late servant in husbandry, would be liable to fall into want directly [after] his wife began to have

children and he lost the earnings of his companion. Once he found himself outside 21
the farming household his living had to come from his wages, and he, with every
member of his family, was subject for his labour to the local vagaries in the
market. Day-labourer was now his full description, for he earned what money
came his way by contracting for work a day at a time with the gentlemen, yeomen,
and husbandmen of his village. This was a source of the variable casual labour
needed to keep agriculture going, and the poor cottager could expect mainly
seasonal employment at a wage fixed, as indeed his wage as a servant had been
fixed, by the justices of the peace. Two forms of wage were laid out in the
published tables, with and without meat and drink. The day-labourer visiting a
farm for his work could claim his place at the table along with the servants
living-in; it might be said that he was made a member of the working family for
that day by breaking bread with the permanent members. It was almost a
sacramental matter.

But his own casual earnings were not the only fund on which the labourer had
to live. There was the produce of the little plot of land lying round his cottage to
begin with. Elizabeth's government had decreed that it should be four acres in
size though this cannot have been anything like a general rule. Then there were
the pennies thrown to his children for bird scaring, or catching vermin, or minding
sheep—the little boy blue who burst into tears in the nursery rhyme might easily
have been of nursery age. But above all, there were the earnings of his wife and
the whole of his little family at "industrial" occupations. A little family because
every grown child would have to leave, and because death came quickly. It was
the cottagers of England who carried on the great woollen industry of England,
spinning the yarn which the capitalist clothiers brought to their doors. Industry,
in fact, kept the poor alive in the England of our ancestors, and the problem of
poverty in their own opinion could only have been solved by the spread of
industrial activity. Though men did not seem to have seen it in quite this way, the
existence of industry also helped to ensure that enough people lived on the land to
meet the seasonal demands of agriculture.

The men and women whose livelihood came from crafts, agricultural and
industrial, lived under the same system of servanthood until marriage. So indeed
did the merchants and the shopkeepers. Not all households took part in this
system all the time. At any moment a quarter or a third of the households of a
community would contain servants, and a similar proportion would have children
absent from home and in service. The households which remained would at that
point in time be unaffected by the system of service, but many of them, perhaps
most, would at other stages of their development either yield up or take in
servants. This is the sense in which it could be said that service was practically a
universal characteristic of pre-industrial English society.

Industry at this time was carried on not only by individual productive units,
like the bakery in London, but by the *putting-out* system, in which several
households were set on work by one middleman, the clothier-capitalist we have
referred to. Much of it was done in the spare time of the farming population, not
simply by the labourers, but by the farmers and their families as well, the simpler
operations, that is to say, the sorting and carding and spinning of the wool. But
the weaving, the dyeing and dressing of the cloth was usually the work of families
of weavers, shearmen or dyers who did nothing else for nine months of the year. If

22   they worked on the land of the villages where they lived it was only in harvest-time, from late June, when the haymaking began, till late September when the last of the wheat or the barley would be brought home.

Hence it came about that the English village contained not simply the husbandmen, the labourers and their families, with the smith, the ploughwright, the miller and the men who plied the agricultural trades, but textile workers too. In the Midlands there were nailers and miners, and everywhere everyone might also work on the land, during the crisis of harvest-time. Such are the rough outlines of the system whereby the independent household was preserved, yet made to collaborate with other independent households in the working of the land, and in the production of cloth. Capitalism, we must notice, was a feature of the system, that store of wealth and raw materials in the hands of the clothier which made it possible for him to give work to the villagers and yet not move them from the village. In the world we have lost, then, industry and agriculture lived together in some sort of symmetry, and the unity of the family was in no way in jeopardy.

■ ■ ■

The word alienation is part of the cant of the mid-twentieth century and it began as an attempt to describe the separation of the worker from his world of work. We need not accept all that this expression has come to convey in order to recognize that it does point to something vital to us all in relation to our past. Time was when the whole of life went forward in the family, in a circle of loved, familiar faces, known and fondled objects, all to human size. That time has gone for ever. It makes us very different from our ancestors.

The Estate of Michael D. Davis,

1800-1837

Vermont Sheep Farmer

One technique historians use to reconstruct the everyday life of the past is to examine the estate inventories that are preserved in probate records. Michael D. Davis, a sheep farmer in Vermont, died unexpectedly in 1837, leaving a widow and two small children. Before his estate could be settled, an inventory was conducted listing all his possessions.

His one cash crop was probably wool, although he might, in addition, have sold or traded some grain, potatoes, and hay. If he had died in the spring rather than in the fall, he would not have had such a large supply of these items on hand. His large kettle, which was broken and awaiting repair, had many uses, including the separation from hardwood ashes of potash, a product used in the manufacture of soap and glass that might also be sold.

Davis seemed to have raised most of the food he needed; he even made his own maple sugar. His meat was salted and stored in one of the barrels, the most common means for storing and transporting all products in his day. His wife used the two spinning wheels to make most of the clothes the family wore. Notice that the only book he owned was a Bible, and that one of his most valuable possessions was a bay mare that, among other things, provided him transportation to the Congregational Meeting House on Sunday. When his horse and wagon took him to town, he could visit the miller, the blacksmith, the harness maker, or the cooper. He might purchase salt at the store, for that was one of the few items he could not grow. His best shoes may have been made by the shoemaker, his best pantaloons by a tailor. But he probably made the boots himself, and his wife made the rest of the clothes—even coats, vests, and hats. For a man his age, in that part of the country, he was reasonably well off. Notice, however, that most of his wealth was in land.

How would a list of your possessions compare with his?

55 acres of land off from Lot no 74 first division of the original Right of John Pyanger in the township of Wolcott together with the buildings attached thereto at $700.00

The whole of Lot no 69 first Division of the Right of Derrick L. Goes supposed to contain one hundred acres being in said Wolcott at 400.00

3 Pews in the Congregational Meeting House in said Wolcott at 10 Dollars each 30.00

1 Brindle Cow	16.00
1 Red Cow	14.00
1 2 year old Bull	10.00
3 calves @ 4.00	12.00
27 sheep	40.50
23 sheep	33.75
28 sheep	28.00
20 lbs sugar	1.80
1 saddle	5.00
200 old sap buckets	8.00
70 new " "	5.60
1 gun and equipment	4.00
4 pelts	2.00
1 new axe	1.50
1 1/2 B salt	1.67
1 Linnen Wheel	1.00
1 Woollen "	1.00
2 meat Barrells	1.00
1 bushel Basket	.34
1 Large Bible	3.00
1 Over Coat	5.00
1 Light "	5.00
1 pr blue Pantaloons	1.00
1 pr grey "	2.00
1 pr blue "	2.75
1 thick vest	2.00
1 thin vest	2.00
1 pr thin boots	1.50
1 " " shoes	1.50
1 " horse hyde shoes	.50
1 neck stock	1.00
3 soft hats	6.00
Lot Pine Lumber	25.00
1 wood saw	1.00
a hay knife	.75
1 iron square	.38
1 set of bench planes	1.25
a auger	.34
1 pr Large Steel yards	1.00
1 pr Small " "	.50
1 Cook Stove, pipe etc	20.00

1 Bay Mare	57.50
20 Tons Hay	120.00
18 B. Wheat	25.50
25 B. Oats	8.75
200 B. Potatoes	40.00
500 lb pork in the hog	37.50
1 Single Sleigh	18.00
1 old "	4.00
1 harness	3.25
1 no. 1 caldron kettle (broken)	3.50
1 cart	6.00
1 gig wagon	12.00
3 shoats	15.00
1 chain	1.67
1 single harness & bells	8.00
244 lbs wool	85.40
1 wood clock	8.00
a pail pot	1.00
1 tea kettle	.75
1 Spider	.50
1 broken kettle	.20
1 tin Baker	.50
1 4 foot table fall leaf	2.00
1 pine leaf table	.50
1 light stand	1.00
7 dining chairs	3.50
6 kitchen "	1.50
1 old desk	2.00
1 bureau	6.00
1 looking glass	.50
1 trunk	1.75
1 dozen printed plates	1.25
1 " edged "	.42
1 Tea set	1.00
1 Nappy	.17
1 pitcher	.20
1 stone cream pot	.50
1 stone preserve pot, tin pans	1.45
2 earthen pans, 1 shaker pail	.62
1 case knives and forks	.50
1 Bed and Bedding	15.00
1 Bed and Bedding	12.00
1 small Bed and Bedding	3.00
Debts due the estate Book note, some doubtful	150.00

ISAAC PENNOCK JR., EPHRAM LADD appraisers __$2067.96__

Whole Amount of Real Estate	1130.00
Whole Amount of Personal Estate	937.96

The Freeman Family of

Sturbridge, Massachusetts

Social historians also use another technique to understand what life was like in another era: it is called family reconstruction. Using the census, vital records, cemeteries, tax records, and genealogies the historian reconstructs the history of a family over two or more generations.

Study this table. What can you learn about the history of the Freeman family from these impersonal statistics? At what age did Pliny and his wife, Delia, marry? How soon after that did they have their first child? How do you explain the spacing between the children? How old were the parents when the youngest child left home? How do you suppose life was different for Silas, the oldest child, from Dwight, the youngest child? Does that perhaps have something to do with the age that Silas married and where he lived? Notice the age and place where each child died. What does that tell you about longevity and mobility? How soon after his first wife died did Pliny remarry? Who took care of him in his old age? What else can you learn from this information? Perhaps you can reconstruct the history of your family in this way.

A. Freeman Household in 1820
Husband: Pliny Freeman   Age 40   Occupation: Farmer
Wife: Delia M.   Age 39
Son: Silas Marsh   Age 17
Son: Pliny   Age 14
Daughter: Beulah   Age 13
Daughter: Delia   Age 10
Daughter: Florella   Age 8
Daughter: Augusta   Age 5
Son: Dwight   Age 1

B. Freeman, Pliny
Occupation: Farmer
Real Estate: in 1824
     1 House and Barn, 70 Acres Improved Land $500.
     59 Acres Unimproved Land $300.
Personal Estate:
     1 Horse, 2 Oxen, 6 Cows, 1 Young Cow, 2 Calves, 2 Swine $164.
     Total Taxable Estate: $964.
Rank on Tax List: 117/320, Second Fifth

BOUNTY LAND CLAIM.

Form of Declaration for Widow of a deceased Officer or Soldier.

State of *Ohio*
County of *Wyandot* { ss.

On this *Ninth* day of *January* A.
D. one thousand eight hundred and *Fifty two* personally appeared before me,
a *Justice of the Peace* within and for the County and State aforesaid,
Elizabeth Bowsher aged *Seventy one (71)* years,
a resident of *Wyandot County* in the State of *Ohio* who
being duly sworn according to law, declares, that she is the widow of *Peter Bowsher*
deceased, who was a *Lieutenant* in the Company
commanded by Captain *David List* in the
Regiment of *James Denny* in the *Ohio Militia*, in the war with
Great Britain, declared by the United States on the 18 day of June 181
That her said husband *Peter Bowsher* at *Circleville Ohio*
on or about the *fifteenth* day of *July* an indefinite term
A. D. *1813* was drafted for an indefinite term
and continued in actual service in said war for the term of *more than forty days* and
was *honorably discharged* at *Frankliston, Ohio* in the the
the month of *August*
A. D. *1813* *or therabout* *had a discharge given him, which*
has been lost *NB Please consult the Muster Rolls*

She further states that she was married to the said *Peter Bowsher, in the county of*
Northumberland, Pennsylvania on the *twenty fifth* day of
December A. D. *1800* that there is no justice or priest
record of the marriage and that her name before her said marriage was *Elizabeth*
Harpster that her said husband died *near Auburn*
Indiana on the *First* day of *April*
A. D. *1846* and that she is still a widow.

She makes this declaration for the purpose of obtaining the bounty land to which she may be entitled under the
act passed September 28th, 1850.

Sworn to and subscribed before me the day and year above written.

Elizabeth her *Bowsher* [SEAL]
mark

Abraham Myers J.P.

AFFIDAVIT OF WITNESSES.

State of
County of { ss.

On this day of A. D. one thousand
eight hundred and personally appeared before me, a
within and for the State and County aforesaid and
and County of residents of the State of
and being duly sworn according to law, declare that

N.B. Widow Bowsher is unable to state the Number
of the Regiment, or the exact time of her husband's
entering the service or his discharge. *R.P. Smith atty*

The government awarded land to veterans of the Revolution and the War of 1812 and to their widows. These Bounty Land Claims are among the many federal records housed in the National Archives in Washington, D.C., which contain family information.

C. Freeman Family

Husband:	Pliny	b. 9/24/1780	d.	10/10/1855 in Webster, Mass.
Wife:	Delia	b. 4/21/1781	d.	3/20/1839
Married:	10/5/1802			
Children:	*Silas Marsh*	b. 8/7/1803	m.	3/27/1831 to Maria R. Upham of Sutton, Mass.
			d.	11/4/1880 in Millbury, Mass.
	Pliny	b. 4/14/1806	m.	9/8/1835 in Cleveland, Ohio
			d.	11/2/1894 in Genesco, Illinois
	Beulah	b. 12/6/1807	m.	4/1/1832 to Walter S. Rosenbrooks
			d.	7/5/1835 in Oxford, Mass.
	Delia	b. 4/4/1810	m.	4/4/1833 to John S. W. May of Leicester, Mass.
			d.	11/2/1864 in Webster, Mass.
	Florella	b. 5/26/1812	m.	12/11/1833 to Bradford Baylis of Southbridge, Mass.
			d.	11/27/1876 in Bristol, Penna.
	Augusta	b. 12/25/1815	m.	3/30/1841 to Holowell A. Perrin
	Dwight	b. 1/15/1819	m.	6/14/1852 in Webster, Mass.
2nd Wife:	Mrs. Mary Pease Widow	b. 8/7/1784 Boston, Mass.	d.	2/3/1850
Married:	7/1/1840			
Children:	None			

Nineteenth-century

Self-sufficiency

A Planter's and Housewife's
"Do-It-Yourself" Encyclopedia

JO ANN CARRIGAN

Most rural women living in the nineteenth century, or for that matter anytime before the nineteenth century, in addition to being wives and mothers often ran a domestic factory and served as nurse, pharmacist, veterinarian, and engineer. The way many women actually lived contrasted sharply with the image of women in their day as weak, submissive, pure, and defenseless.

This essay is based on a family manuscript and illustrates many aspects of everyday life. Perhaps you can find a similar document among your own family's papers or, by talking to your grandparents, you may be able to recover an oral tradition that includes home remedies, recipes, and a family folklore.

The nineteenth-century rural housewife baked her own bread, cakes, and pies; preserved the food products of the farm; made her own soap, candles, furniture polish, and other basic household items, as well as her feminine luxuries such as cologne and curling liquid. In addition to his basic knowledge of farming, the planter needed considerable information at his fingertips regarding the care of his farm animals and the treatment of diseases to which they might fall victim. Furthermore, it was not at all uncommon for farmers to practice medicine among their families, and slaves if they owned any, during the ante bellum period. Since the nearest physician ordinarily was many miles away and licensing requirements were practically nonexistent, manuals of instruction in "Domestic Medicine" as well as the drugs used in regular medical practice were readily available to all who had the price. An intelligent planter who had read and absorbed several medical handbooks and incorporated with that knowledge his own common sense and empirical outlook could be expected to have at least as much success as many self-styled doctors or poorly trained ones. From the baking of one's own bread to the practice of one's own medicine, the rural individual of the nineteenth century supplied his needs and solved his problems in an essentially different fashion from that of the participants in today's interdependent socio-economic framework.

A manuscript discovered in southwest Arkansas several years ago provides a good reflection of this nineteenth-century rural self-sufficiency through hundreds of specific illustrations which it contains. Filed away in an old bookcase in the home of Mrs. Carrie Carrigan in Ozan (Hempstead County), Arkansas, this small hard-backed composition book had been forgotten and unopened for many years. It seems that this two-hundred-page handwritten compilation of medical remedies, cooking recipes and other practical information was brought to Arkansas from North Carolina in the 1850s by Alfred H. Carrigan and his young bride, Mary E. Moore, along with a number of other books from the Moore family library. Containing a wealth of information arranged topically, in alphabetical order, and even partially indexed, the little manual must have been exceedingly helpful to that young couple settling in a place relatively distant from their former homes. In fact, for a time it was probably the most useful reference book in their entire library.

Approximately the first quarter of the manuscript consists of remedies for the diseases and ailments of man—asthma, bilious fever, bruises, burns, chills and fevers, colds, deafness and earache, hydrophobia, hiccups, itch, nettle rash, poisoning, rheumatism, ringworm, sore throat, toothache, warts, whooping cough, and worms—to list only a few. The treatments described in the handbook incorporated some of the valid procedures as well as the fallacious practices of early and mid-nineteenth-century medicine, in addition to a generous selection of folk remedies, some of value and some absurd.

Immediately following the remedies for human ailments is a section dealing with veterinary medicine, classified under these headings: Horses, Cows, Sheep, Hogs, and Chickens. The first entry relating to horses set forth a detailed description of their teeth at various ages—information which any person wishing to become a good horse trader needed to know. Other entries prescribed remedies for such horse ailments as bots or grubs, breaking-out, colic, founder, galls, heaves, strains, and wounds.

Treatments for diseases and disorders among cows included measures for colic, hoven, kicking, lice, milk fever, sprains, and worms. One of the several alternative entries for colic suggested this course of action:

> Make a band of twisted straw and place it in its mouth and make it fast on top of the head just behind the horns, in the act of chewing the band she will open the gullet & let the air out.

A simple but ingenious method designed to solve the problem of a kicking cow was to "ty a rope round her horns and draw it over a beam, then draw it until it raises her head pretty high but do not raise her fore feet of[f] the ground. . . ." According to the handbook, "she will not only be disabled from kicking but also will let dow[n] the milk."

Under the heading "Sheep," the first item stated that "The seed of broom corn is better than indian corn to fatten sheep." Following that entry, appropriate

treatments were listed for apoplexy, blackmuzzle, rot, flies, wounds, and other
sheep disorders. To prevent sheep rot, the manual advised quite sensibly that the
sheep "always have a lump of salt to lick in their troughs." The one general
medicine prescribed "For the common diseases of pigs" consisted of a compound
of sulphur, madder, saltpeter, and black antimony.

To fatten chickens, the little encyclopedia instructed that they be fed on a
mixture of half-cooked rice, milk, and sugar, noting that "The rice will give a
delicate whiteness to the flesh." Furthermore, that entry advised that "charcoal
broken in small peaces increases the appetite & promotes digestion"—among
chickens, that is. For a poultry ailment called the "Gaps," one might either
"smoke them with tobacco untill they quit crying," or "put asefedity in the water
& in the meal," or "strip a feather except 1 1/2 inches at the end, lay the chicken on
its back, stretch out its neck, put the feather in its windpipe, twist it round, pull it
out." One rather quaint, if seemingly meaningless, remedy for "Chip" among
chickens recommended that one "shut them up for 24 hours without food or
raiment."

In the handbook's section on veterinary medicine a total of seventy-four
separate entries dealt with preventive as well as remedial measures for various
animal diseases and proper care of the farm stock. With such information readily
at hand, presumably a farmer could have handled most medical problems which
might have risen among his animals. The remainder of the manual consists of
cooking recipes and assorted information of obvious value to both the head of the
household and his wife.

A highly practical entry entitled "To ascertain the weight of live stock"
described a method by which one might figure the weight of his animals without
the use of a scale:

> Multiply the length from the root of the tail to the front of the shoulder by the girt and
> this by 23 if it is less than 7 feet & more than five in girt. By 31 when it is less than 9 &
> more than 7. By 16 when less than 5 & more than 3, by a leven when less that 3 feet. For
> a half fatted calf, or a cow which has had a calf, deduct 1 stone in 20, allowing 14 lbs to be
> a stone.

In a similar fashion the farmer was also able to "weigh" his corn (both shelled
and unshelled) by measuring the length, breadth, and thickness of the container.

From a scheme for weighing corn and livestock to helpful hints on transplanting cabbage and removing moss from the housetop, the manuscript supplied
an abundance of miscellaneous information to engage the attention and serve the
interests of the young agriculturalist. His encyclopedia even recorded detailed
instructions for hunting wild bees:

> Provide your self with a tin box that will hold about a pt, put into it a piece of dry honey
> comb, carry in your pocket, a phial of 1/2 honey & 1/2 water, go to piece of new ground
> at a distance from any tame bees, open the box, and pour some of the mixture, on the
> comb, & then hunt among the flowers for a bee, if a bee is found catch it by shuting the
> lid over it, wate untill it becomes still, then open the box, it will fly round the box a few
> times & fly away, wate & in a few minutes it will return with 2 or 3 others, & in 1/2 hour
> they will have a line formed between you & the tree, then set the box over as many as
> possible, then go the edge of the next wood and wait untill they are still then open the
> box etc, untill the tree is found, a pocket spy glass is usefull to see a bee from the top of a
> tree, the time for hunting them is in September or October or in the spring, if a bee

cannot be found to commence operations with burn some honey on a stone & maby some wanderer may smell it. . . .

Since the time of agriculture's primitive beginnings, sowers and reapers have had to concern themselves with the question of the weather, a vital factor in the regulation of farm activities. Unable to control it, the farmer could only adapt his planting and harvesting to its normal course, always with the hope that climatic conditions would work with him and not against him. Naturally, an ability to predict the weather would serve as a decided advantage in planning for the day-to-day activity, and long before the time of scientific meteorology a kind of weather lore—part observation, part superstition—was developed. The handbook included a weather chart listing the probabilities for summer and for winter depending on the "time of the Moon's Change." In addition to the chart, several entries set forth other guides for the weather prophet:

> When the sun sets in a cloud, or rises clear & soon pases behind a cloud look out for foul weather, when a storm clears off in the night time look for rain again soon.
> A circle round the moon indicates foul weather.

Not only did the farmer have to contend with the potential weather hazards posed against a successful outcome of his planting, but he also had to face the problem of pest control—household pests as well as those threatening his growing crops and stored grain. Instead of calling in a professional exterminator or choosing one among the possible dozens of brands and varieties of spray guns, bombs, powders, or pastes (as one might do today), the nineteenth-century individual had to fight off his insect, rodent, and other house and garden pests without the aid of professionals or handy commercial insecticides. Reflecting this serious problem, the manual devoted considerable attention to methods for dealing with a variety of undesirables. Pests of particular interest to the farmer considered in the handbook included cabbage worms, "Bugs on vines," caterpillars, crows and blackbirds, and rats. Among the several anti-pest suggestions listed, these three seem especially interesting for their extreme simplicity, if not for their potential efficacy:

> *Bugs on vines*, lay shingles between the hills in the evening, & in the morning raise up a shingle in each hand, & clasp them togather, & you will kill the bugs that have got on the under side during the night for protection.
> *Caterpillers*, place a wollen rag in your bushes at night, and in the morning you will find them adhering to it.
> *Rats*, fry sponge and put in their way.

For eliminating ants the manual proposed two alternative methods: (1) "Crack shag bark walnuts & lay where you wish to collect them, & then wet the cracks whare they come with corrosive sublihate," or (2) "place a small piece of camphine or sprinkle alkihol whare they frequent." In case of a bed bug problem, there were also several methods among which to choose, one being to "rub the bed stids with green tomato vines." Mixtures designed to kill (or at least to ensnare) the cockroach, still a persistent pest in the southern clime, included a compound of meal, red lead, and molasses and one of "strong pink root and molasses." Another prevalent and extremely annoying southern insect pest, the mosquito, could be repelled by one of two ways, depending on the appropriate circumstances:

(1) "burn a little brown sugar on a shovel of coals," or (2) "place a piece of flannel or sponge wet with camphorated spirits to a thread fastened across the top of the bed posts."

Insecticides or repellants, however, represent only one item among the dozens of common household necessities now bought in the supermarket (if not completely obsolete), but then made at home. The handbook provided complete instructions for the home manufacture of an amazing number of items, such as boot blacking, boot varnish, bottle stoppers, brass cleaner, furniture polish, waterproof varnish, waterproof paste, glue, cement for mending "Crockreware," cement for glass, and cement for grafting. The finished product in each case was simply a mixture of several basic ingredients. For example, the boot varnish consisted of linseed oil, "muton suet," and beeswax, melted together and applied while still warm to the boots or shoes; the bottle stoppers were fashioned from a compound of wax, lard, and turpentine.

The mid-twentieth-century housewife who does not yet own an automatic washer-dryer and has to take her clothes down the street to the laundromat is likely to consider herself extremely underprivileged. What if she had to make her own soap, boil the water, and scrub by hand? The manuscript contains several recipes detailing the process of making soap, one describing the procedure for what must have been a kind of liquid soap in this manner:

Dissolve 18 lbs of potash, in 3 pailfills of water, than add about 25 lbs of grease, boil it over a slow fire 2 hours, turn it into a barrel and fill it up with water.

Another soap recipe was followed by a bit of labor-saving advice:

Put your cloth[es] in soak them overnight & to every pail of water in which you boil add 1/2 lb of soap they will need no scrubbing merely wrence them out.

On the general subject of washing and cleaning, the handbook listed several suggestions for dealing with specific materials, such as flannel, black veils, and silk. For cleaning silk the following method was recommended:

1/2 lb soft soap 1 tee spoon of brandy, 1 pt gin, spread it on both sides, wash it in several waters, & iron it on the rong side.

To remove grease from silk, the manual advised that one "apply a little magnesia to the rong side." Undoubtedly, the nineteenth-century housewife found the following entry of particular interest and value: "*Set colors*, alum desolved in water will prevent calico from fading." In the event that clothes faded, however, as certainly would have been the result of many hard scrubbings with strong soap, the manuscript provided detailed information on how to dye materials green, red, and black.

Now almost obsolete except for ornamental purposes and special occasions, candles used to fulfill a more vital utilitarian function. Certainly one would never think of making his own candles today—not even for chianti-bottle-lamps in an espresso shop. Nevertheless, the manuscript told how to make them:

2 lb of Allum for every 10 lbs of Tallow desolve it in water before the Tallow is put in & then melt Tallow in the water with frequent stirings & it will clarify harden the tallow so as to make a most beautiful candle.

In the age before machines and ready-to-wear clothing, women usually ran what amounted to a domestic factory. They would spin the wool or cotton (or, in this case, flax) into yarn, and then weave it into cloth which would be sewn into clothes. Do today's women have anything in common with this woman?

An extremely important area of activity for the farm family involved the preservation of food, and on that subject the home encyclopedia again supplied valuable reference material. In regard to the preservation of fruit, these two suggestions were set forth:

> *Winter fruit.* pack it in dry sand, & it will keep longer than in any other way.
> *Peaches & Plumbs*, preserved ripe through the winter, put them into equal quantities of water and honey.

During the seasons when eggs were plentiful, the housewife did well to preserve the accumulated supply for the times when the chickens were less productive. According to the handbook, eggs could be preserved in this manner:

> *Eggs to preserve;* take 1 qt of salts, & 3 qts of lime, add water untill the whole stirred up & disolved is of the consistency of cream; then put in the eggs.

Several entries gave directions for preserving meat, a necessary process in an age without refrigeration and when one did not simply march to the market for the fresh meat which is now always available. The manual proclaimed the following recipe "an excellent method of preserving hams. &c.":

> Cover the bottom of the cask with fine salt; lay on the hams with the skin side down, sprinkle over fine salt; then another layer of hams & so on untill you have disposed of all

32

your hams. Then make a brine in the following proportions: water 6 gal; salt 9 lbs; brown sugar, 4 lbs; salt peter, 3 oz; saleratas, 1 oz; Boil & skum, & when cold pour the brine into the cask until the hams are covered.

Other entries described additional methods for curing hams and pickling beef.

A household item used frequently as an ingredient in the home medical remedies as well as in cooking and preparing various foods, vinegar was an exceedingly useful and versatile liquid. Hence, this manuscript entry would have been of considerable interest and value:

Vinegar Preserved for domestic use cork it up in glass bottles, set them on the fire with cold water, & as much hay or straw as will prevent them from knocking to gather; when the water nearly boils take of[f] the pan, let the bottles remain in the hey 1/4 hour, it will never lose its strength though kept for years.

■ ■ ■

Obviously, the task of preparing and cooking meals kept the housewife of the nineteenth century in her kitchen a much greater portion of the time than does the same task today. Baking one's own wheat bread is rapidly becoming a lost art, and pies and cakes are more and more commonly put together with the aid of packaged ready-mixed ingredients. In previous times, however, it was necessary to begin with the making of the yeast. Here are two of the several methods described in the manuscript:

(1) *Yeast,* Boil 1 lb flour 1/2 lb brown sugar, a little salt in two gal water for 1 hour, when milkwarm, bottle & cork it close it will be fit for use in 24 hours, 1 lb will make 16 lb of bread.

(2) *Yeast.* 1 qt of hops & 7 gal water is boiled about 3 hours, pass it through a cullendar & mix with 3 qts of meal or so much that it will make batter, add 1/2 tea cup of salt, when cooled to milk warm, add 1/2 pt yeast, stir it well, & let it stand 15 or 20 hours then add meal enouf to make it dough, make cakes 3 inches in diameter & 1/2 inch thick, dry it on a board by the fire if not dried in 2 or 3 days it will spoil. they will keep 3 months. 1 soaked 1/2 hour in warm not hot water is enough for a large loaf.

The handbook supplied instructions for making ginger bread, rice cakes, "New Years Cookies," fruit cakes, tea cakes, doughnuts, apple "Dumblings," muffins, chicken pie, lemon pie, bread pudding, citron pudding, wheat bread, "Light Biscuit," and a host of other cakes and pastries. One rather unusual recipe was set forth in verse:

Variety Pudding

Of flour take one half a pound
Six eggs all very good & sound
Sugar according to your taste
Of butter do not make a waste.
Just as you like you choose your spices
And when its done tis cut in slices.

To cope with such vague instructions obviously one would have to know something about pudding-making in advance.

In addition to the numerous food recipes, the manuscript also supplied directions for making all sorts of beverages. Aromatic beer, for instance, could be made by pouring two quarts of boiling water into a mixture of oil of spruce, wintergreen, and sassafras, and then adding eight quarts of cold water, one and a half pints of molasses, and one-fourth pint of yeast. After about two hours, it could be bottled. For making ginger beer, the manual prescribed several different techniques, some to be used if the beverage was for immediate consumption and others if one planned to bottle it. To make a drink called "Chery Bounce," one was directed to fill a jug with cherries and to "run it over with aple brandy let it stand a few days, & pore it off, it will keep any length of time." A combination of ten gallons of water, one gallon of molasses, one quart of vinegar, and one-half pound of ginger produced something called "Harvest Drink," apparently a beverage which might be served to a large number of people (perhaps the slaves) to celebrate the harvest. A recipe for making plum wine was the last entry recorded in the manual, an entry added to the reference book some thirty years after it was brought to Arkansas:

Plum Wine

Thoroughly wash the plums, squeeze out the juice and strain through a cloth. To one gallon of juice add three lbs brown sugar. Put in vessels, either bottles or jars and cover with a cloth. Let it stand till the first fermentation ceases, which must be carefully noticed. As soon as fermentation ceases, bottle, cork, and seal air tight.

   If bottled before fermentation ceases the bottles will burst. After the 1st fermentation is over a 2nd sets up, which will make vinegar. The wine will be fit for use as soon as sealed, but the older the better. It takes from 4 to 7 weeks for the 1st fermentation to cease. June 20th 1883.

Although busily engaged with cooking, preserving, washing, manufacturing an endless number of necessary articles, and all her other tasks, the housewife was still after all a woman and not just a machine, and it was only natural that she would be interested in certain feminine vanities. One might well wonder when she had time to fit such things as cologne and curling liquid into her tight schedule, especially when even those articles had to be manufactured at home. Nevertheless, the handbook gave directions for making cologne, curling liquid, and "Hare dye" as well:

Cologne, 12 gtts [drops] of bergamot 120 of leavender, 24 of lemon 60 gr musk, 1 pt of purest alkihol.
   Curling liquid, for ladies, 5 oz of borax, 1 drachm gum senegal, 1 qt of hot water when desolved, add 2 oz of spts of wine strongly impregnated with campher.
   Hare dye, 1 pt pkld herin liquor. 1/2 lb lamp black, 2 oz iron rust boil 2 mts stran it.

As a handy source of information on medicine, animal care, food preservation, cooking, the manufacture of soap, candles, and other necessary household articles, and dozens of other miscellaneous topics, this small volume undoubtedly represented a valuable item in the library of the Alfred H. Carrigan family in southwest Arkansas from the 1850s until sometime in the latter part of the nineteenth century. From the entries in the handbook, one gains an insight into the life of a rural Southern family and a close-up view of the self-sufficiency which circumstances imposed upon them.

A Day in the Life of a Mid-western Farmer's Wife, 1905

Those nostalgic for life on the farm in a less complicated age should ponder the amount of work that this rural woman accomplished before 9 A.M. Of course, unlike the factory worker, she could plan her own schedule. How would life be different for a farm woman today?

Any bright morning in the latter part of May I am out of bed at four o'clock; next, after I have dressed and combed my hair, I start a fire in the kitchen stove, and while the stove is getting hot I go to my flower garden and gather a choice, half-blown rose and a spray of bride's wreath, and arrange them in my hair, and sweep the floors and then cook breakfast.

While the other members of the family are eating breakfast I strain away the morning's milk (for my husband milks the cows while I get breakfast), and fill my husband's dinner-pail, for he will go to work on our other farm for the day.

By this time it is half-past five o'clock, my husband is gone to his work, and the stock loudly pleading to be turned into the pastures. The younger cattle, a half-dozen steers, are left in the pasture at night, and I now drive the two cows a half-quarter mile and turn them in with the others, come back, and then there's a horse in the barn that belongs in a field where there is no water, which I take to a spring quite a distance from the barn; bring it back and turn it into a field with the sheep, a dozen in number, which are housed at night.

The young calves are then turned out into the warm sunshine, and the stock hogs, which are kept in a pen, are clamoring for feed, and I carry a pailful of swill to them, and hasten to the house and turn out the chickens and put out feed and water for them, and it is, perhaps, 6.30 a.m.

I have not eaten breakfast yet, but that can wait; I make the beds next and straighten things up in the living room, for I dislike to have the early morning

35

36 caller find my house topsy-turvy. When this is done I go the kitchen, which also serves as a dining-room, and uncover the table, and take a mouthful of food occasionally as I pass to and fro at my work until my appetite is appeased.

By the time the work is done in the kitchen it is about 7.15 a.m., and the cool morning hours have flown, and no hoeing done in the garden yet, and the children's toilet has to be attended to and churning has to be done.

Finally the children are washed and churning done, and it is eight o'clock, and the sun getting hot, but no matter, weeds die quickly when cut down in the heat of the day, and I use the hoe to a good advantage until the dinner hour, which is 11.30 a.m. We come in, and I comb my hair, and put fresh flowers in it, and eat a cold dinner, put out feed and water for the chickens; set a hen, perhaps, sweep the floors again; sit down and rest, and read a few moments, and it is nearly one o'clock, and I sweep the door yard while I am waiting for the clock to strike the hour.

I make and sow a flower bed, dig around some shrubbery, and go back to the garden to hoe until time to do the chores at night, but ere long some hogs come up to the back gate, through the wheat field, and when I go to see what is wrong I find that the cows have torn the fence down, and they, too, are in the wheat field.

With much difficulty I get them back into their own domain and repair the fence. I hoe in the garden till four o'clock; then I go into the house and get supper, and prepare something for the dinner pail to-morrow; when supper is all ready it is set aside, and I pull a hundred plants of tomato, sweet potato or cabbage for transplanting, set them in a cool, moist place where they will not wilt, and I then go after the horse, water him, and put him in the barn; call the sheep and house them, and go after the cows and milk them, feed the hogs, put down hay for three horses, and put oats and corn in their troughs, and see those plants and come in and fasten up the chickens, and it is dark. By this time it is 8 o'clock p.m.; my husband has come home, and we are eating supper; when we are through eating I make the beds ready, and the children and their father go to bed, and I wash the dishes and get things in shape to get breakfast quickly next morning.

It is now about 9 o'clock p.m., and after a short prayer I retire for the night.

As a matter of course, there's hardly two days together which require the same routine, yet every day is as fully occupied in some way or other as this one with varying tasks as the seasons change. In early spring we are planting potatoes, making plant beds, planting garden, early corn patches, setting strawberries, planting corn, melons, cow peas, sugar cane, beans, popcorn, peanuts, etc.

Oats are sown in March and April, but I do not help do that, because the ground is too cold.

Later in June we harvest clover hay in July timothy hay, and in August pea hay.

Winter wheat is ready to harvest the latter part of June, and oats the middle of July.

These are the main crops, supplemented by cabbages, melons, potatoes, tomatoes, etc.

U.S. Census

Work in Oswego, New York, c. 1880

One of the most intriguing changes over the past century is in the kind of work that people do. Most of the tasks at which the men and women of the late nineteenth century spent their days have now disappeared. In traditional land-based cultures, jobs remained the same generation after generation over millennia; today, with the relentless technological innovations in machinery, the old ways of doing things have been destroyed as ever-changing specialized ways of performing industrial and commercial tasks replace them.

Oswego, New York, is a Lake Ontario port city whose population of about 20,000 has remained nearly the same for a century. The 1880 census enumerates the jobs performed by 3,237 of its men, women, and children.

Look closely at the jobs, including those mentioned in the footnote below the table. How many of them are still performed? Also make note of the average annual wage of workers and compare that with the average wage today—about $12,500.

The following is a summary of the statistics of the manufactures of Oswego, New York, for 1880, being taken from tables prepared for the Tenth Census by A. E. Buell, special agent:

Mechanical and Manufacturing Industries	No. of Establish- ments	Capital	AVERAGE NUMBER OF HANDS EMPLOYED			Total Amount Paid in Wages During the Year	Value of Materials	Value of Products
			Males Above 16 Years	Females Above 15 Years	Children and Youths			
All industries	179	$2,611,238	1,754	272	106	$756,435	$3,646,845	$5,619,944
Blacksmithing (see also Wheelwrighting)	11	3,120	10	—	—	2,782	4,275	14,850
Boots and shoes, including custom work and repairing	16	13,750	25	—	—	9,576	21,556	45,983
Bread and other bakery products	7	42,200	23	4	—	10,021	49,651	74,746
Carpentering	11	21,100	61	—	1	21,960	26,323	55,575
Cooperage	12	24,250	47	—	6	12,637	44,595	66,010
Flouring- and grist-mill products	5	465,000	74	—	—	37,102	1,136,974	1,591,759
Foundery and machine-shop products	5	416,818	363	—	2	153,904	258,311	552,780
Furniture	4	19,500	19	1	—	8,902	17,100	37,000
Liquors, malt	3	68,000	12	—	1	6,146	30,970	55,125
Lumber, planed	4	160,500	111	—	—	47,300	163,605	238,932
Marble and stone work	4	11,500	7	—	—	1,875	3,585	11,399
Painting and paperhanging	6	20,300	38	—	2	13,264	20,000	42,350
Photographing	3	10,150	5	1	—	1,732	3,290	7,857
Plumbing and gasfitting	3	12,000	17	—	—	10,100	33,240	55,054
Printing and publishing	3	110,000	70	—	14	27,956	15,401	66,580
Saddlery and harness	4	4,800	8	—	—	2,950	6,600	12,200
Shipbuilding	7	27,500	58	—	—	23,072	22,030	50,563
Tinware, copperware, and sheet-iron ware	15	19,300	34	—	—	15,394	27,700	63,950
Wheelwrighting (see also Blacksmithing)	5	8,600	13	—	—	5,405	5,400	14,900
All other industries (a)	51	1,152,850	759	266	80	344,357	1,756,239	2,562,331

a Embracing baking and yeast powders; baskets, rattan and willow ware; boxes, cigar; boxes, fancy and paper; carriages and wagons; cement; coffins, burial cases, and undertakers' goods; confectionery; cutlery and edge tools; drain and sewer pipe; drugs and chemicals; dyeing and cleaning; gloves and mittens; hats and caps; hosiery and knit goods; instruments, professional and scientific; iron railing, wrought; leather, curried; leather, tanned; lime; lock- and gunsmithing; looking-glass and picture frames; lumber, sawed; malt; mineral and soda waters; mixed textiles; patent medicines and compounds; pumps; sash, doors, and blinds; shirts, soap and candles; sporting goods; starch; tobacco, cigars and cigarettes; upholstering; watch and clock repairing; window blinds and shades; and wood, turned and carved.

From the foregoing table it appears that the average capital of all establishments is $14,587.92; that the average wages of all hands employed is $354.80 per annum; that the average outlay in wages, in materials, and in interest (at 6 per cent.) on capital employed is $25,474.61.

The Horse is King

Lewis Atherton

The automobile dominates our lives in so many ways today that we find it difficult to imagine a time before the internal-combustion engine changed the world forever. One hundred years ago, however, the horse was almost as important as the auto is today. The amount of change that the "horseless carriage" brought with it is obscured today because we take the invention so much for granted. Certainly, the look of towns is no longer the same. Livery stables, black-smiths' shops, watering troughs, and hitching posts have now almost disappeared. Even the smell of towns has been transformed. But perhaps most important, the social life of the American people has changed. Dating habits are noticeably different today as is the pace of life. As you read the following article, try to isolate the most significant changes that have occurred since the auto replaced the horse.

Village life moved at the pace of horse-drawn transportation. Tourist homes, tourist courts, garages, filling stations, and stores selling automobile accessories lay in the future. There were no concrete curbs, and parking meters were nonexistent; and small-town workmen would have been baffled at the idea of painting parking lines in streets consisting of dust or mud.

The presence of horses was evident everywhere. Droppings in the streets and town stables attracted swarms of flies, and narrow-rimmed wheels of wagons and buggies cut gaping ruts during rainy seasons. Hitching posts, connected with iron chains, surrounded the village square. Until business growth necessitated removal of hitching lots to the edge of business districts, farmers tied their teams around the courthouse square, let down check reins to ease the tired necks of their horses, and walked across the street to do their trading. Thirsty farm teams quickened their step when they approached town pumps and watering troughs, which also doubled as fire-fighting equipment.

Horses were sentient beings, capable of affection, and an unwritten code censured their abuse. In cold and rainy weather farmers paid the modest fee necessary to stable their teams in commercially operated feed barns and livery stables. The occasional drunk who forgot his team was roughly criticized by the village paper after some citizen had removed them late at night to a livery barn for food and shelter.

Even within the town itself business and social life depended on horse-drawn transportation. Most citizens had horse-and-carriage barns at the rear of their homes to shelter driving equipment. Commercial drays hauled freight to and from the depot, did heavy moving for local citizens, and made daily deliveries for stores unable to afford their own private wagons. Most stores, however, owned single-horse, spring wagons, with business advertisements painted on the sides, which made morning and afternoon deliveries to residential areas. Younger clerks enjoyed driving these conveyances at speeds beyond the limits of safety demanded by elderly residents of the town. Local hotel hacks, pulled sometimes by as many as four horses, rushed back and forth from depots at speeds supposed to impress travellers with their efficiency. By loading sample trunks of travelling salesmen smartly and with dispatch, sounding their horns sharply, and dashing off before a rival hack could clear the depot platform, drivers scored a point in favor of the establishment which they represented. Peddling carts, ice wagons, and sprinkler carts moved more sedately, much to the pleasure of children who begged fruit and small chunks of ice or played in the streams of water being sprayed on dusty streets.

Livery stables served those who could not afford to own rigs or who had temporary and unusual demands. Young people courted and eloped with livery stable teams, and circus agents drove them leisurely round the countryside to post bills. Drummers employed drivers and rigs to haul their sample trunks on two- and three-day side trips to hamlets lacking railroad connections. Picnics, celebrations and fairs in nearby towns, baseball trips, sleighing in winter, funerals—all these and more called for livery-stable teams.

A good bay trotter and a fine buggy appealed to the young man of the 1870s much as the convertible does to his great-grandson. At the peak of its development, a truly fine buggy was an expensive item. Polished and varnished ash shafts, rubber-tired wheels with shiny brass inner rims, brass lamps decorated with large glass rubies, and patent-leather dashboards pleased the eye. Even the harness had its charms—gleaming tan leather with brass fittings, rainbow-colored celluloid baubles, and ruby rosettes. The current generation will never know the thrill of spending $1.75 on a horse and buggy for an afternoon and evening of dating. The carriage with its fast team, yellow fly nets, linen lap robe, and beribboned whip lifted the spirit of the young blade as he drove up and down Main Street with one foot hanging over the body bed and a cigar at an angle in his mouth. Loafers shouted at him and received the expected quip in reply, commented on his extravagance, and wondered at his destination. A touch of the whip and he was on his way. With one horse pacing and the other trotting, he passed the fragrant slaughterhouse at the edge of town and on to the meeting with his best girl.

■ ■ ■

Horses could be a nuisance in many ways. In 1876 the Monroe, Wisconsin, editor warned his readers that city ordinances prohibited the riding of horses on sidewalks, even though it was a temptation to do so in muddy times. When a citizen of Chillicothe, Illinois, in 1875 spoke of Saturday as a lively day, with

Horses dominated life up to the middle of the nineteenth century. In many respects, life moved no faster than the horse could move. What difference does the speed of transportation make? What are the advantages and disadvantages of the horse over the automobile? Study the photo of the market square carefully. How would the scene be different today?

vacant lots filled with teams, and then added that he thought he was on Broadway in New York City until he saw "George" and his dogs, he expressed in a lighter vein the problem of congestion and the greater danger of accidents on Saturdays. Occasional runaways added zest for spectators if not for the unfortunate individuals involved. A team belonging to a Mr. Bumpus took fright on State Street in Algona, Iowa, in 1877 and dashed around the corner of Thorington Street, breaking the wagon tongue, the whiffletrees, and creating general havoc. Citizens got inside so quickly during the fracas that the town took on a Sunday air of desertion within a matter of seconds.

Constant activity at private and railroad stockyards in country towns also emphasized the importance of horsedrawn transportation. Produce and livestock had to be concentrated at local shipping points because they could not be moved great distances over muddy and unimproved roads in wagons pulled by horses. Small-town elevators and stockyards thus handled an enormous volume of agricultural produce. During 1878, J. J. Wilson's private yards at Algona, Iowa, shipped almost 350 cars of hogs, wheat, and oats, and several more of minor produce. In return, he received 388 carloads of lumber and coal. From the adjoining new depot stockyards 817 cars departed during the same year with wheat, corn, oats, flax, cattle, hogs, butter, and cheese.

Wagons converged on Algona from all directions during weeks when as many as fifty carloads of cattle and hogs left for Milwaukee. Their drivers ate a noon

42

By the late nineteenth century the many and varied native American tribes had been driven from their ancestral lands and penned up on desolate and im-poverished reserva-tions. How do you account for the deter-mination of succes-sive generations of white Americans to punish American Indians?

meal at the local hotel and bought family supplies in Algona stores. Livery stables, blacksmith shops, harness shops, and feed barns benefited from their presence. In commenting on business during 1878 the Algona editor said that State Street occasionally had been filled with teams and loaded wagons four and five abreast. At times the line had stretched from the elevator and cattle yards at the depot to the City Hotel, a distance of nearly a mile. Dust and mud, bawling cattle and squealing hogs, horses and men, the plank platform of the Fairbanks scales, loading chutes, and lines of box- and cattle-cars on sidings—all have been challenged by the trucks which now travel midwestern highways. But in the 1870s horses and country towns were equally necessary to assemble agricultural produce for market and to supply country homes with merchandise.

As a focal point in the age of horse-drawn transportation, the livery stable had a form, a personality, and an odor as distinctive as that of its twentieth-century successor, the garage and automobile showroom. Brick construction, feed chutes connected directly with the hayloft, and running water in stalls and washrooms marked the more pretentious establishments. Most, however, were large, box-like structures of graying unpainted wood, with oversized doors to permit carriages to enter the central ramp. A few had signs in front, perhaps a horse's head with crossed whips carved in wood, but, as a rule, the only decorations were tin advertising strips of patent remedies for horseflesh nailed at random to exterior walls. All stables had the same mingled smell of horse urine and manure, harness oil, feed and cured hay.

A small office near the door contained a battered desk, a pot-bellied stove, a few chairs, a cot, and a lantern hanging on a wooden peg for the use of an attendant who was on duty twenty-four hours a day to wait on customers and to guard against the constant threat of fire. A slate on the wall near the office or just within listed the names of horses out on trips and rental charges. So far as possible, customers were held accountable for abusing horses by furious driving, for turning rubber-tired conveyances so short as to fray the rubber against the buggy bed, for failing to feed horses on long trips, and for other injurious acts. Some stables posted slogans to encourage better care of equipment:

Whip Light,
Drive Slow.
Pay Cash
Before You Go.

and all gave careful instructions to new patrons.

Well-equipped livery stables possessed a surprising variety of vehicles. Fancy buggies and curved sleighs were rented out for single dates; fringed surreys served for double-dating and more prosaic family trips. Carryalls, with seats along the sides and entrance steps in the rear, were used on special occasions—for Sunday School picnics, to carry visiting ball teams to hotel and the playing field, to take elderly ladies to the cemetery on Memorial Day, and in Autumn to taxi passengers to the fair grounds. Light spring wagons hauled drummers and their sample trunks on visits to country stores and hamlets. Of more somber mien were the hearses, with black enclosed sides and oval windows, fringe and plumes, and elaborate box lights. Hearses decorated in white were preferred for children's funerals. Perhaps one or more of the local doctors kept a team and glass-enclosed coupe at the livery stable. Hotel hacks, the town watering cart, and vegetable wagons added to the variety of conveyances parked along the walls.

Stalls were to the rear, from which horses were led up cleated ramps to the main floor for hitching. A second-floor loft over the stables facilitated the forking down of hay used for feed. Harness for each animal hung on wooden pegs at the front of his stall. Somewhere in the building was the washroom where buggies were washed and wheels were greased. Curry combs, hair clippers, sponges, axle grease, harness soap, and pitchforks were scattered through the building at points most convenient for their use.

■　■　■

44   The livery barn was universally condemned by pious mothers who rated it only slightly above the town saloons. Its robust life shocked those refined people who spoke of bulls as "gentleman cows." Unlike twentieth-century automobile dealers, who move in country-club circles, livery stable owners generally ignored high society. Addicted to slouch attire, sometimes noted for profanity, they were numbered among the few local men of property who avoided religious activities and booster movements. Since the usual explanations—stinginess, a choleric disposition, or free-thinking religious principles—did not apply in their case, they puzzled even their own contemporaries. For these mothers, however, it was enough that they were hard to understand and did not practice the finer points of accepted social conduct. The livery stable also served as a loafing place, especially for those most addicted to betting on horse races. Checkers and playing cards were often in evidence, and liquor was tolerated within limits. Most horrible of all, stallions were offered at service as long as public opinion would tolerate it, usually only until mothers of impressionable boys learned of the presence of "gentleman horses" within the city limits.

■ ■ ■

Probably no other loafing place in town provided so fine a setting for tall stories, and there the town liars competed for supremacy. They told of working for the contractor who built Niagara Falls, of ice worms ruining a whole summer's supply of ice, and of the half-believable hoop snake. Stories of Civil War exploits appealed to an audience composed in large part of veterans, who could relish the ludicrous overtones:

> Still another told of coming on the battle field of Gettysburg on a gunboat in a driving snow storm. It was the morning of the third day of the battle. He had been drinking gun powder in his whiskey to make him brave, and he performed such feats of daring and valor that General Meade, with tears in his eyes, shook his hand and said, "Abel, I won't forget this."

Youngsters found additional attractions. Horseshoe nails could be bent into rings; old bottles and junk lying around the premises were collected and sold. And when the "Tom shows" (Uncle Tom's Cabin) came to town the trained dogs which would chill the local audience by baying on Eliza's trail generally were housed at one of the local livery stables.

Nineteenth-century midwestern civilization was obviously geared to the strength and limitations of horse-drawn transportation. The horse accounted for the carriage sheds and barns in residential sections, for livery and feed barns, for stockyards, harness shops, and blacksmith shops, for the many small carriage factories in country towns, for hitch racks, town pumps, and watering troughs. Cemeteries and schools were laid out with horse-drawn transportation in mind. The horse played a major part in determining trade areas, and his potentialities helped determine nineteenth-century recreational patterns.

Other forces began to play an increasingly important part in shaping midwestern life in the years immediately following the Civil War. Technological and managerial revolutions exerted more and more influence. Railroads were already bringing goods from distant points to be exchanged for crops and livestock, and agencies of short-range communication, like the telephone and trolley line, and

The Union Pacific Railroad midway through Nebraska in 1866. How did the railroad alter the daily lives of ordinary Americans? Did the railroad make the horse obsolete?

then the truck and automobile, would soon appear. Tremendous change generated by them would destroy many small-town crafts, and country towns would suffer from wildly fluctuating trade areas. Greater specialization and a higher standard of living would accompany a declining independence from the outside world. But, for the moment, these were the very characteristics—a low standard of living, relative lack of specialization, and freedom from outside control—which set the country town apart from its twentieth-century successor.

People did things for themselves or did without far more than is either possible or necessary today. They lacked hospitals, funeral homes, florist shops, dry-cleaning-and-pressing establishments, beauty shops, country clubs, plumbers, waterworks, telephones, electric lights, ten-cent stores, commercial laundries, radio and television shops.

Small-town business felt little external control. Though manufacturers and wholesalers were beginning to advertise directly to consumers the unique virtues of their own special packaged branded and trade-marked wares, which finally would compel retailers to stock such items, general stores still carried coffee and calico, not a variety of packaged or labelled brands. Storekeepers were relatively free to select their own stock; their customers in turn needed judgment of quality and price in order to spend their money wisely. Officials at the court house were still county and local officials only; and local banks enjoyed a measure of independence unknown in federal reserve and deposit-insurance days.

46   Even the homes of the period were relatively independent. Storms and blizzards might isolate country towns, and even individual families, without seriously affecting their mode of living. Coal oil lamps, a supply of cordwood in the backyard, meat in the smokehouse, fruits and preserves in the cellar, a cow for milk in the barn—here was food, light and warmth which continued to function when neighbors and the outside world were cut off.

Americans thrill to this saga of independence as their own lives daily become more interdependent. They envy their ancestors, those artisans and storekeepers who rose early in the morning to milk their cows and slop their pigs in order to have their individually owned shops and stores open for early customers. But, as in all Edens, there were serpents. Town ordinances show that conditions were not idyllic. Gallatin, Missouri, in 1873, instructed city authorities to order the removal of "every hog-pen, slaughter house, privy, mud hole, stable . . . in a stinking or unhealthy condition." It was easy to order drastic action, but enforcement in specific cases was another matter because no citizen in a closely-knit community wanted to issue a complaint.

Artisans flourished in the relatively isolated and unspecialized economy. Blacksmiths were able and willing to build wagons and plow, harness shops both made and sold harness, shoemakers and tailors turned leather and cloth into finished goods. The revolutions in transportation, manufacturing, and management ruined such business. Gunsmiths, wagon makers, coopers, millers, tanners, and cigarmakers are gone from the country towns where they were well known in the 1870s. Other artisans have survived by changing to new occupations—from tinsmiths to plumbers, for instance, or most commonly by abandoning all manufacturing in favor of service and repair. The shoe repair man on Main Street today is thus a lineal descendant of the craftsman who actually produced shoes in the 1870s.

Tomatoes

RUTH TIRRELL

This brief essay, while it focuses on a family's involvement with fruits and vegetables over several generations, also provides some illuminating insights into the American past. Notice how easily this family's history reaches back over four generations to the era of John Adams, who was President from 1796 to 1801. Contrast this generation span with that of your own family. In addition, consider the implications of gardening on this scale: where did they find time for such work and why wasn't the produce simply purchased at the corner market? How does your family obtain and prepare food today? How does this differ from the customs of your ancestors? Food can tell you a great deal about a family and a culture.

My mother, who is well along in her tenth decade, still starts tomato seedlings on a sunny window sill each spring (but lets me set them in the ground). Tomatoes, to her, are the No. 1 crop. By careful choice of varieties—one is an early, quick-growing hybrid—we get four months of fresh fruit in suburban Boston.

In my mother's childhood, however, tomatoes were hardly worth the bother, often not ripening until September on the Rhode Island farm of her great-grandmother. And in the latter's childhood—she was born before the eighteenth century ended—most people still regarded the "love apple" as poison. Thomas Jefferson was experimenting with the tomato in Virginia. All her life, she was skeptical of the tomato's value. Under her eye, my mother first planted seeds of peas and beans, not tomatoes.

In the continuity of their gardening, however, matriarch and great-granddaughter, between them, have spanned the eras from John Adams to Richard Nixon. Their lives overlapped for thirteen years.

When Grover Cleveland began his Presidency and my mother was a child, many crops grown on the farm were the same as in colonial days. The "three sisters" of the Indians—squash (or pumpkin), beans and corn—flourished in harmony together. Corn was of three kinds: field corn for the stock; sweet yellow corn to eat on the cob; and white flint corn for the johnnycake meal that Rhode Islanders claim tastes far better than the white corn meal of the South. (It does.) The flat johnnycakes, cooked slowly on a griddle, were served three times a day at the farm. Yeast bread, never.

Corn may have been a small cash crop. Otherwise, all food produced was for the family's benefit, including city relatives like my mother who came to the farm on vacation, when 25 or more people often sat down to the table.

Beans were "string" then, not "snap." Speckled shell beans and corn, fresh or dried, made the Indian dish succotash. Salads were cucumbers and a coarse, curly loose-leaf lettuce, dressed with sugar and vinegar homemade from apples. The lettuce thrived in summer heat and didn't have to be planted. Mature plants self-sowed the next spring.

A staple in summer was beet greens, cooked with bacon and served with vinegar. Beet roots were grown as fodder, and sowings made from mid-April on, and had to be thinned.

Turnip thinnings, which make the favorite cooked greens of the South, were thrown to the hens. Turnips were an important winter vegetable and kept well in a special cellar. Likewise potatoes, onions and cabbage.

Squashes were stored in the attic near the chimney. Carrots, like beets, were for cattle, but parsnips for people. They stayed in the ground and were dug during thaws. The first fresh food of spring was wild dandelions, then rhubarb and asparagus.

Fertilizer was manure—horse, cow, sheep, pig and fowl. Litter was spread on the fields, residues ploughed in, nothing wasted. In most respects, this was an "organic" farm (like all farms once), before the term was coined. But poison— probably paris green—was used on potato bugs. Many pests, including the Japanese beetle and the Mexican bean beetle, hadn't arrived.

Many good things, too, were missing. Vegetables of Italian origin, for instance. No broccoli, no arúgola nor zucchini. The only summer squash was the bright yellow, warty crookneck (which my mother still prefers for its "nutty" texture and flavor). It was a sprawling vine then instead of a compact bush like modern summer varieties.

Unknown—perhaps even by name—were the exotic crops, eggplant and pepper, which once took months of growth in hot weather. The hybrids of today, developed to grow fast in short summers, must still be started inside here in the Northeast.

But looking back, my mother thinks that harvests of fruits were richer and more varied then. The farm had a big strawberry bed and a raspberry plantation, red, yellow and black kinds. Dozens of currant bushes—red, black and white— would be a rare sight now. (As host for the blister rust disease that attacks the white or five-needled pine, currants are now banned from many areas.)

Currants and raspberries—which ripen simultaneously—were often combined in pies and preserves for a marvelous sweet-acid taste better than either alone. Currant clusters, sprinkled with powdered sugar, served as dessert.

Apples of many kinds were a mainstay. A child's favorite was the pretty Snow apple (or Fameuse) with purest flesh and striped purplish-red skin. The Rhode Island Greening stayed fresh until spring packed in barrels of leaves in a cool shed. Apple slices were dried on racks in the sun for winter pies. Apple butter was made outside, too, in a huge cauldron on a cairn of stones. In summer, the cauldron held giant geraniums.

White-fleshed peaches with rosy hearts grew in the poultry yards. The hens fertilized the trees and cleaned up the fallen fruit. The superior fruit seemed to cling to the trees until ripe.

Wild fruits were there for the gathering. Highbush blueberries grew in a deep
swamp where snakes lay on hummocks in the sun. A picker wore boots and a pail
on a rope tied round the waist. Children had their daily quota of 10 to 12 quarts.

Wild blackberries were for jam; elderberries for wine. The wild fox grape
hung high on vines tangled on roadside trees. An ailing person might eat nothing
but grapes for a month and sometimes got cured. At this time, the farm had no
cultivated arbor, though the Concord grape, which is related to the wild fox
grape, had been developed in Concord, Mass., by 1849.

Tiny tart cranberries grew in the family's own wild bog. The matriarch made
sauce by a tedious but effective method that had been taught her great-grandmother by an Indian. Slice each berry in half; soak them overnight. "Play with
your hands" in the water, then lift the berries and the seeds all fall out. Cook as
usual with sugar and a little water. My mother still makes sauce this way, perhaps
needlessly, for the big modern cultivated berries have far fewer seeds.

Everybody kept busy without much letup. After the haying, there was a
family picnic at the beach (Charlestown, R.I.) and "sea-bathing." Or more rowdy
good times at a fresh-water pond on the Connecticut line. Children and old people
didn't go. Farmers from miles around gathered to sharpen their scythes in a
special fine sand, though this custom was beginning to die out in my mother's
childhood.

The Yankee high holiday was Thanksgiving when all the descendants came
back to the farm. Except for sugar, salt, tea and white flour for piecrust, nothing
on the table was "bought."

My mother's family in the city gave gifts and celebrated Christmas, but the
people on the farm, according to the custom of their colonial ancestors, did not.

Pages from the Sears,

Roebuck Catalog

Although it is conventional to cite the building of the transcontinental railroad network as an example of the fundamental changes taking place in late-nineteenth-century America, the social effects of those changes are sometimes passed over.

Without an efficient railroad network, Sears, Roebuck, the "cheapest supply house on earth," could not have functioned. From

its central location in Chicago, Sears, by the 1890s, was able to deliver the items listed in its extraordinary catalog, a publication that was eagerly awaited in isolated farmhouses from Maine to Wyoming.

As its pages clearly indicate, the days of homemade wares were coming to a close, as factory-produced and store-bought goods became more common.

OUR $55.00 A GRADE AND $65.00 AA GRADE TOP BUGGY

☞ **$55.00 IS THE PRICE OF OUR A GRADE COLUMBUS TOP BUGGY IN LEATHER QUARTER.**
$65.00 IS THE PRICE OF OUR AA GRADE COLUMBUS TOP BUGGY IN LEATHER QUARTER.

FOR
FULL
LEATHER
TOP
ADD
$5.00.

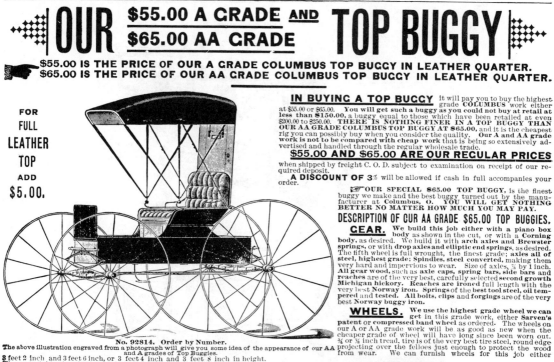

No. 92814. Order by Number.

The above illustration engraved from a photograph will give you some idea of the appearance of our AA and A grades of Top Buggies.

3 feet 2 inch and 3 feet 6 inch, or 3 feet 4 inch and 3 feet 8 inch in height. The material in the wheels is strictly second growth hickory of the very finest quality, and they are put together in the most approved manner possible. Tire is carefully bolted between each spoke. **A set of the wheels used in** this buggy is worth five sets of the common Special B grade.

SHAFTS. Shafts are all made of selected second growth hickory, of the latest design. They are substantially ironed with heavy irons so that the heels will not straighten out in use.

BODY AND SEAT. WE FURNISH THIS JOB IN EITHER PIANO BOX BODY, as illustrated, or **CORNING BODY,** and can furnish the body in either 20, 22 or 25 inch width. **ALL BODIES** are 52 inches long. The **CORNING BODY** is 23 inches wide and 50 inches long. All bodies and seats are made of the **best poplar panels** second growth ash sills, are put together in the best manner, screwed and plugged from inside and outside. **WIDTH OF SEAT,** on 20 inch body, measuring over top of cushion, 26 inches; depth, 16 inches; height of back over cushion, 14 inches. **WIDTH OF SEAT** on 22 inch body, 30 inches; depth, 16 inches; height of back above cushion, 14½ inches. **WIDTH OF SEAT** on 25 inch, or regular sized body, measuring over top of cushion, 31 ins. Depth, 16 inches; height of back over cushion, 14½ inches. On the Corning body, width of seat measuring over top of cushion, 31 ins.; depth 17 inches; height of back above cushion, 15 inches.

TRIMMINGS. We trim the Seat and back in either the very finest imported all wool English green or blue body cloth, or green genuine machine buffed leather. We use the very best spring back and spring seat cushions. The back of the seat is also wood painted same as body. We use a full length velvet carpet, heavy rubber boot over back of body, and dash frame is made of best steel, covered with the very finest enameled leather.

MOUNTINGS. We furnish this Buggy with silver mountings throughout.

PAINTING. Our AA grade buggies are painted in the very highest style of the art, in 13 coats of paint, the first coats rubbed out with pumice stone. Nothing but the very best grade of paints, oils and varnishes are used, and they are given ample time to dry in a dark, dust proof room, which is kept at an even temperature. Bodies are black, gear dark green with suitable gold stripe.

IN OUR AA GRADE BUGGIES we furnish the very best machine buffed leather quarter top, or at **$5.00 extra, full leather top.** All tops have machine buffed solid leather valance, front and rear, sewed on. The head lining is of the very best imported all wool English green dyed body cloth.

IN BUYING A TOP BUGGY it will pay you to buy the highest grade **COLUMBUS** work either at $55.00 or $65.00. You will get such a buggy as you could not buy at retail at less than **$150.00,** a buggy equal to those which have been retailed at even $200.00 to $250.00. **THERE IS NOTHING FINER IN A TOP BUGGY THAN OUR A GRADE COLUMBUS TOP BUGGY at $65.00,** and it is the cheapest rig you can possibly buy when you consider the quality. **Our A and AA grade** work is not to be compared with cheap work that is being so extensively advertised and handled through the regular wholesale trade.

$55.00 AND $65.00 ARE OUR REGULAR PRICES

when shipped by freight C. O. D. subject to examination on receipt of our required deposit. **A DISCOUNT OF 3%** will be allowed if cash in full accompanies your order.

☞ **OUR SPECIAL $65.00 TOP BUGGY,** is the finest buggy we make and the best buggy turned out by the manufacturer at Columbus, O. **YOU WILL GET NOTHING BETTER NO MATTER HOW MUCH YOU MAY PAY.**

DESCRIPTION OF OUR AA GRADE $65.00 TOP BUGGIES.

GEAR. We build this job either with a piano box body as shown in the cut, or with a **Corning** body, as desired. We build it with **arch axles and Brewster springs,** or with **drop axles and elliptic end springs,** as desired. The fifth wheel is full wrought, the finest grade; **axles all of steel, highest grade; Spindles, steel converted,** making them very hard and impervious to wear. Size of axles, ⅞ by 1 inch. All gear wood, such as axle caps, spring bars, side bars and **reaches** are of the very best, carefully selected second growth Michigan hickory. Reaches are ironed full length with the very best **Norway iron.** Springs of the best tool steel, oil tempered and tested. All bolts, clips and forgings are of the very best Norway buggy iron.

WHEELS. We use the highest grade wheel we can get in this grade work. either Sarven's patent or compressed band wheel as ordered. The wheels on our A or AA grade work will be as good as new when the cheaper grade of wheel will have long since been worn out. ¾ or ⅞ inch tread, tire is of the very best tire steel, round edge projecting over the felloes just enough to protect the wood from wear. We can furnish wheels for this job either

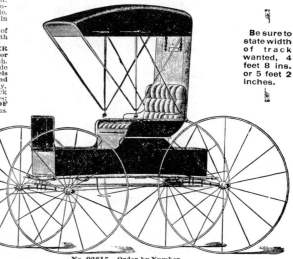

Be sure to state width of track wanted, 4 feet 8 ins. or 5 feet 2 inches.

No. 92815. Order by Number.
The above illustration engraved from a photograph will give you some idea of the appearance of our AA and A grades of Top Buggies.

━ The Bows to the Top are Leather Covered, the Top Prop Nuts are Leather Covered, the Seat Handles are Leather Covered, the Steps have Rubber Covered Step Pads. ━ All these features only to be found on the very finest work. It is not only these little points alone that go to make this Buggy the very best, but the fact that only the most skilled mechanics are allowed to work on the AA grade, none but the very finest material enters into every piece and part of the work, and when completed there is nothing finer in appearance, more durable or better made at any price.

AT $65.00 LEATHER QUARTER TOP, OR $70.00 IN FULL LEATHER TOP, we furnish the AA Grade Columbus Top Buggy with full length Velvet Carpet, Toe Carpet, Panel Carpet, Full Length Side and Back Curtains, Storm Apron, Leather Foot Protectors to both sides of box, Anti-Rattlers and Shafts.

FOR POLE WITH NECKYOKE AND WIFFLETREES complete, in place of Shafts, add $3.50.
FOR BOTH POLE AND SHAFTS add $6.00.

OUR A GRADE AT $55.00 IN FULL LEATHER QUARTER TOP, OR $60.00 IN FULL LEATHER TOP is a buggy exactly like the illustration above, and a buggy that will compare in every way with any buggy you can buy elsewhere at from $75.00 to $100.00. It has the **highest grade wheel, the very best material in every piece and part.** The leather is all genuine machine buffed leather. The difference in price to you is only the difference in cost to us, and that is in trimmings and workmanship. This A Grade Buggy at $55.00 and $60.00 does not have the leather covered bows and leather covered prop nuts, the leather covered seat handles, the rubber covered step pads; it is not painted in 13 coats, nor made and finished by the same class of workmen. It is, however, a STRICTLY HIGH GRADE BUGGY, one that we can recommend in every way, and a buggy we GUARANTEE FOR TWO YEARS, and one that will last a natural life time. We would recommend by all means you buy OUR COLUMBUS, O., A GRADE BUGGY AT $55.00 OR $60.00 if you do not buy our AA GRADE COLUMBUS AT $65.00 OR $70.00.

FOR ADDITIONS TO THE A GRADE COLUMBUS AT $55.00 AND $60.00, add for pole with neckyoke and whiffletrees, in place of shafts, $2.50. For both pole and shafts, $4.50.

THE BUSINESS WE DO IN WATCHES, JEWELRY, ETC., WOULD BE CONSIDERED LARGE FOR THE BIGGEST WHOLESALER IN THE COUNTRY. NO WONDER WHEN YOU SEE OUR PRICES AND LIBERAL TERMS,

MERIT SUNSHINE.

For hard or soft coal or wood, with Reservoir.

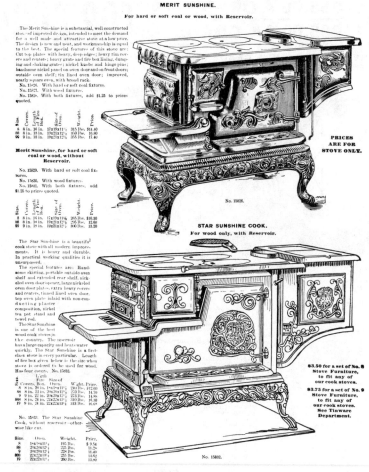

The Merit Sunshine is a substantial, well constructed stove of improved design, intended to meet the demand for a well made and attractive stove at a low price. The design is new and neat, and workmanship is equal to the best. The special features of this stove are: Cut top plates with heavy, deep edges; heavy rim covers and centers; heavy grate and fire box lining, dumping and shaking grate; nickel knobs and hinge pins; handsome nickel panel on oven door and on front doors; outside oven shelf; tin lined oven door; improved, nearly square oven, with broad rack.

No. 15826. With hard or soft coal fixtures.
No. 15827. With wood fixtures.
No. 15828. With both fixtures, add $1.25 to prices quoted.

Size.	Covers.	Length of Fire Box.	Size of Oven.	Weight.	Price.
8	8 in.	16 in.	17x19x11½	315 lbs.	$14.40
88	8 in.	18 in.	19x21x12½	350 lbs.	16.80
99	9 in.	18 in.	19x21x12½	355 lbs.	17.40

Merit Sunshine, for hard or soft coal or wood, without Reservoir.

No. 15829. With hard or soft coal fixtures.
No. 15830. With wood fixtures.
No. 15831. With both fixtures, add $1.25 to prices quoted.

Size.	Covers.	Length of Fire Box.	Size of Oven.	Weight.	Price.
8	8 in.	16 in.	17x19x11½	265 lbs.	$10.80
88	8 in.	18 in.	19x21x12½	295 lbs.	12.60
99	9 in.	18 in.	19x21x12½	300 lbs.	13.20

STAR SUNSHINE COOK.

For wood only, with Reservoir.

The Star Sunshine is a beautiful cook stove with all modern improvements. It is heavy and durable. In practical working qualities it is unsurpassed.

The special features are: Handsome skirting, portable outside oven shelf and extended rear shelf, nickeled oven door opener, large nickeled oven door plates, extra heavy covers and centers, tinned lined oven door, top oven plate inlaid with non-conducting plaster composition, nickel tea pot stand and towel rod. The Star Sunshine is one of the best wood cook stoves in the country. The reservoir has a large capacity and heats water quickly. The Star Sunshine is a first-class stove in every particular. Length of fire box given below is the size when stove is ordered to be used for wood. Has four covers. No. 15832.

Size.	Covers.	Length Fire Box.	Size of Oven.	Weight.	Price.
8	8 in.	20 in.	18x18x11½	230 lbs.	$12.60
88	8 in.	22 in.	20x20x12½	250 lbs.	14.70
9	9 in.	22 in.	20x20x12½	273 lbs.	14.88
888	9 in.	24 in.	22x22x13½	310 lbs.	16.30
19	9 in.	24 in.	22x22x13½	313 lbs.	16.68

No. 15833. The Star Sunshine Cook, without reservoir—otherwise like cut.

Size.	Oven.	Weight.	Price.
8	18x18x11½	195 lbs.	$9.54
88	20x20x12½	225 lbs.	11.28
9	20x20x12½	228 lbs.	11.40
888	22x22x13½	255 lbs.	13.62
19	22x22x12½	260 lbs.	13.80

PRICES ARE FOR STOVE ONLY.

$3.50 for a set of No. 8 Stove Furniture, to fit any of our cook stoves.

$3.75 for a set of No. 9 Stove Furniture, to fit any of our cook stoves. See Tinware Department.

No. 15826.

No. 15832.

Prices named for Stove do not include Pipe or Stove Utensils. Make your own selection from our catalogue.

ASSIGNMENT 2
Discovering Your Community's History

Even your grandparents and your great-grandparents will not be able to recall firsthand the time before industrialism transformed social patterns, but some material artifacts of that preindustrial culture can no doubt still be found in your own community.

Your assignment is to go into the community in search of traces of the world we have lost. You may want to team up with other members of the class. A camera and a notebook will be useful. Start by familiarizing yourself with the community in which you are living. Either by talking to "old settlers" or by consulting materials in a library, museum, or historical society, provide yourself with clues on the probable location of the early buildings, ruins, artifacts, cemeteries, monuments, statues, and so forth. Then, go out and find physical evidences of the culture of the mid-nineteenth century or before. You are expected to return with at least one piece of tangible evidence—a photograph or drawing you have made, an interview with someone who has at least secondhand recollections of the time, or perhaps a tombstone rubbing (see Appendix, pp. 347–372).

PART THREE

Your People

and the

Great Migrations

America has always been a nation on the move. From the earliest settlers who had the courage and the faith to travel across the ocean to an unknown land to the modern family that moves to California in search of a better life, Americans have always been restless. Mobility is a major theme in American history.

Somewhere in the recent past your family has undoubtedly participated in one of the great movements of people that created this country. Someone in your family has been a part of the migration from Europe or Asia or Africa to America, the movement from East to West or from South to North, the transplantation from rural to urban living. Do you know whether your grandparents and/or great-grandparents were born in a foreign country, or whether they made any significant moves within this country?

This section emphasizes the uprooting of people and their resettlement in places where language, customs, and tradition were often quite different. Although the readings are set in the period between the 1850s and World War I, the range of experiences is timeless. They should give you some sense of what your ancestors underwent in this cycle of human drama, punctuated perhaps by the pain of leaving ancestral villages and dear friends, perhaps by a joyful sense of release from poverty and oppression.

Travel has become so easy that we sometimes forget how difficult it was for our ancestors to move from one place to another. Americans remain a mobile people: one out of every five moves every year. Businessmen and vacationers fly to Europe or across the country without a second thought. Americans have become so accustomed to driving hundreds of miles over weekends in their automobiles that the inconvenience of a gasoline shortage a few years ago took on the proportions of a crisis. And, while surely unusual, the example of a man we know who lives in New York and works in Chicago is a sign of our times. Yet the lifetime of this country's "senior citizens" reaches back before the jet plane and automobile, when fifteen to twenty-five miles by horse-drawn wagon was an exhausting day's work. America's railroads in 1880 or 1920 may have offered better service than is available today between most cities, but getting across the ocean or across the continent was often a difficult and dangerous experience, especially for immigrants and other travelers with little money.

Yet the immigrants to the United States arrived in overwhelming numbers from around the globe. In 1910 the census takers discovered that there were 92,228,496 people living in the country. Of that number over 10 percent listed as their native tongue a language other than English. Indeed, over 35 million Europeans came to this country between 1815 and 1915, people of widely varying racial and ethnic stock who carried with them the cultural baggage of dozens of societies. The earliest arrivals were English, French, German, Irish, Scotch, and Scandinavian. Later, central, southern, and eastern European nationals predominated— Greeks, Rumanians, Hungarians, Austri-ans, Italians, Balts, Poles, Russians, and several kinds of Slavs. Indeed, the word "immigrants" almost always brings to mind a picture of people huddled together at Ellis Island in New York harbor shortly after arriving from Italy or eastern Europe. But Europeans were not the only immigrants. The Chinese had come to the West Coast as early as the 1840s, and the Japanese began to arrive in large numbers fifty years later. Mexicans and other Spanish-speaking peoples moved across the Western borderlands. And those Englishmen who came on the *Mayflower*, or the slaves captured and brought against their will from the west coast of Africa, were just as much immigrants as were those who later arrived on ocean liners.

Our ancestors came in search of a better life or merely seeking to survive. While many remained to swell the populations of the coastal cities, millions of newcomers migrated to the frontierlands or to the cities of the interior. Useful generalizations about such a range of experience are difficult to make. One rather constant phenomenon, however, has been discrimination. Long-enduring examples of bias against all nonwhite peoples, including those from Africa, Asia, and Hispanic America, are now fairly well recognized. Intolerance toward Catholics, Jews, Irish, and southern and eastern Europeans has persisted well into the twentieth century. Legislation that discriminated against specific national groups was passed as early as the 1880s; in subsequent decades, an often rabid xenophobia underscored American political life. The culmination of this fear was the passage of a restrictive immigration law in 1924, which limited annual immigration to 2 percent of each national group present in the country in 1890, a clearly discriminatory act against east Europeans and other groups that made up a small proportion of the population in 1890.

The restrictive immigration laws, with a quota system favoring migrants from Northern Europe, remained basically in place until 1965. Even during the period from 1933 to 1944, the restrictive policies limited the number of European refugees accepted into the United States. Only about 250,000 refugees were admitted as immigrants during that time. In fact, during the 1930s, for the first time in its history, more people left the United States than entered.

After World War II, immigration policy relaxed to a limited degree. Certain "displaced persons" were allowed to enter the United States, and those married to United States citizens, including a number of war brides, could legally migrate. The absolute prohibition on Chinese immigration was lifted, but initially only 105 persons could enter the United States each year. The McCarran-Walter Act of 1952 reinforced the restrictive measures, especially against various groups who were considered "undesirable." It was not until the Hart-Celler Act of 1965 lifted the quota system and removed the stigma against Asian immigrants that there finally seemed to be a growing tolerance for ethnic diversity in America. But quotas still remained, and by the 1980s illegal immigrants possibly outnumbered those who entered the country legally. The United States has always had the reputation of being the haven for the oppressed, but in the twentieth century the truth of that reputation was certainly questionable: for many groups were not welcomed, and some were legally prevented from entering the United States.

One effect of racial and ethnic discrimination was the preservation of ma-jor elements of old-country cultural patterns, customs, language, and religious practices. (The image of the United States as a great melting pot where different ethnic and racial groups are melded into Americans never had much basis in fact.) This inclination toward preserving racial and ethnic self-consciousness was also the result of the failure to achieve the American Dream of security and happiness. First- and second-generation immigrants, for the most part, entered the social structure at the bottom. The dream was not at hand but it persisted. However long the hours and low the wages, the memory of the old country's serfdom was worse. The climb up the ladder of success would be long and slow for most members of the ethnic groups, and slower yet for nonwhites. But, sons and daughters would inherit the dream, someday. Their persistent attachment to racial and ethnic self-identification seems to be a reflection of this ambivalent search for the American grail.

Before you read this section, think a bit about your own immigrant roots. Then, as you read, try to associate these selections with the experiences of your own ancestors, their uprooting and resettling, relative assimilation and survival. Perhaps your family came with hope and had their dreams immediately fulfilled in the new land, much like the English house painters you will read about who migrated to Wisconsin. Perhaps your roots go back to the seventeenth or eighteenth centuries, and your ancestors followed the American Dream to the frontier. Possibly your grandmother or great-grandmother came with the same sense of resignation and despair that is described by the immigrant girl Rosa in another selection. Whatever your family's particular experiences and expectations, they probably shared the range of hope and despair shown by the Jews of the Lower East Side of New York City. Whatever your background, whether your family consists of recent immigrants or has been in the country for many years, you will probably find some of the generational conflict and disagreement described in the last two selections.

PRINCIPAL SOURCES OF EUROPEAN EMIGRATION, 1846–1932

Great Britain and Ireland	18,000,000
Russia	14,250,000*
Italy	10,100,000
Austria-Hungary	5,200,000
Germany	4,900,000
Spain	4,700,000
Portugal	1,800,000
Sweden	1,200,000
Norway	850,000
Poland	640,000[†]
France	520,000
Denmark	390,000
Finland	370,000
Switzerland	330,000
Holland	220,000
Belgium	190,000
TOTAL	63,660,000

* Consists of 2,250,000 who went overseas, 7,000,000 who migrated to Asiatic Russia by 1914, 3,000,000 who migrated to the Urals, Siberia, and the Far East from 1927 to 1939 and 2,000,000 who migrated to Central Asia from 1927 to 1939. Since 1939, Russian emigration, free and forced, into the trans-Ural areas, has been the greatest single population movement in the world.
[†] 1920-1932 only.
Source: A. M. Carr-Saunders, *World Population* (Oxford: Clarendon, 1936), pp. 49, 56; and W. S. and E. S. Woytinsky, *World Population and Production* (New York, Twentieth Century Fund, 1953), pp. 69, 93.

Steerage

The Irish Come to America

TERRY COLEMAN

"Steerage" is defined in the Oxford English Dictionary as "the part of a passenger ship allotted to those passengers who travel at the cheapest rate." This benign definition suggests modest but adequate below-deck accommodations for thrifty travelers. Yet millions of our immigrant ancestors would be haunted by this experience the rest of their days.

As diverse as were the immigrant peoples, the horrors of the mid-passage were grimly similar. For up to two weeks on the Atlantic, as many as 900 voyagers were crammed into the steerage, each allotted no more space than their body dimensions.

The fetid underdecks of slowly moving ships reduced individuals—whether Russian Jew or Irishman, Greek or German, man, woman, or child—to an undifferentiated suffering mass.

Here and there, a ship's travelers were fortunate enough to have a tolerable passage. Everywhere, moments of youthful hope helped mask the reality. In the years after 1900, steerage conditions tended to improve, and travel time shrank to a more tolerable six or seven days. Yet relative suffering is suffering nonetheless, as the large literature of steerage recollections makes so wrenchingly clear.

"Before the emigrant has been a week at sea he is an altered man. How can it be otherwise? Hundreds of poor people, men, women, and children, of all ages, from the drivelling idiot of ninety to the babe just born, huddled together without light, without air, wallowing in filth and breathing a fetid atmosphere, sick in body, dispirited in heart, the fevered patients lying between the sound, in sleeping places so narrow as almost to deny them the power of indulging, by a change of position, the natural restlessness of the disease; by their agonised ravings disturbing those around, and predisposing them, through the effects of the imagination, to imbibe the contagion; living without food or medecine, except as administered by the hand of casual charity, dying without the voice of spiritual consolation, and buried in the deep without the rites of the church."

These are the words of Stephen de Vere, a landowner and philanthropist from County Limerick, a distant relative of the former Earls of Oxford, a convert to Rome, and a poet who translated Horace's Odes. He saved Irishmen from the gallows, taught in Irish schools, charged his tenants less than a fair rent for his lands, and for more than twenty years abstained from wine to encourage temperance among the poor. In 1847 he went out to America not in the cabin but as a steerage passenger, to see for himself how poor emigrants were treated.

■ ■ ■

The most detailed account of all is by an Irish gentleman, Vere Foster, who was no relation of Stephen de Vere, and must not be confused with him. Foster sailed in the *Washington* which left Liverpool for New York in October 1850. This was not a year of great disease. The passage was not stormy, although it was winter. The *Washington* was no hulk, but one of the finest American emigrant ships. She was new, strong, and dry. Her two passenger decks were each over seven feet high, and bulwarks more than six feet high protected the deck from sea spray. She had a crew of thirty-one sailors, three boys, four mates, and a captain. She carried a surgeon. She was a great deal better in all ways than the average run of emigrant ships. She left Liverpool on October 25 with 934 passengers and anchored in the Mersey to take on supplies. Next day Foster went on board to sail as one of the cabin passengers. He was the man who had given away 250,000 copies of his *Emigrants' Guide.* He was a philanthropist, and a relative of Lord Hobart, who was with the Board of Trade in London.

One of the first things Foster saw on board was the doling out of the daily water ration. All 900 or so passengers were called forward at once to receive the water, which was pumped into their cans from barrels on deck. The serving out was twice capriciously stopped by the mates, who cursed, abused, kicked, and cuffed the passengers and their tin cans and, having served about thirty people, said there would be no more water that day. Foster gently remonstrated with one of the mates, observing to him that such treatment was highly improper and unmanly, and that the mate would save himself a great deal of trouble and annoyance and win, instead of alienating, the hearts of the passengers, if he would avoid foul language and brutal treatment: the mate replied that if Foster said another word he would knock him down. By October 30, no food at all had been served to the passengers although the contract tickets stated they were to be fed each day. The poorer steerage passengers had brought nothing with them, and for five days had nothing to eat except what they could beg from their better-off companions. Foster began to write a letter of complaint addressed to the captain on behalf of the steerage passengers. He began "Respected Sir," and had got as far as courteously enquiring when they might expect to be fed, when the first mate knocked him flat on the deck with a blow on the face. "When the mate knocked me down," Foster said, "which he did without the smallest previous intimation or explanation, he also made use of the most blasphemous and abusive language." Foster went to his cabin, the mate remarking that if he found him in the 'tween decks again he would not hit him but throttle him. Next day Foster did manage to get to the captain, Page, to present his letter. The captain told him to read it aloud. Foster had read a third of it, when the captain said that was enough; he knew what Foster was—he was a damned pirate, a damned rascal, and he would put him in chains and on bread and water for the rest of the voyage. The first mate added more foul abuse and blasphemy, and was later found heating a thick bar of iron in the kitchen fire and saying he intended to give Foster a singeing with it.

. . . The captain never bothered to visit the steerage, and the first and second mates, the cooks, and the surgeon seldom opened their mouths without prefacing what they had to say with, "God damn your soul to hell," or "By Jesus Christ, I'll rope's end you." Those who gave the cooks money or whisky could get five meals cooked a day. Others who had no money to give, or chose not to give, had one meal a day, or one every other day.

. . . On November 17 the surgeon hurled overboard a great many chamber pots belonging to the women passengers, and told them to come to the privies on deck which were filthy. Foster heard him say: "There are a hundred cases of dysentery on the ship, which will all turn to cholera, and I swear to God that I will not go amongst them; if they want medecines they must come to me." The same morning, the first mate played the hose on the passengers who were in the privies, drenching them. The fourth mate had done the same four days before. One of the passengers who was himself a doctor, went round canvassing for a testimonial to the ship's surgeon, collecting money for a gift to placate him. Nobody wanted to give. The ship's doctor, hearing of this, muttered that the steerage passengers had plenty of money on them, which they would not know what to do with when they got to New York, and that if they would not look after him he would not look after them. Some passengers said they would not mind contributing a shilling each if they thought it might be used to buy a rope to hang him.

The first mate kneed John M'Corcoran, an old man, who afterwards passed blood whenever he went to the privy. The doctor, now he was getting no gift, decided to charge for his services, and extorted half a crown from one passenger and a shilling from another, and charged sixpence for a glass of castor oil. On November 25, a month out, when it had been very cold, another child, making about twelve in all, died of dysentery and from want of proper food. He was thrown into the sea sewn up in a cloth weighted with a stone. No funeral service was conducted: the doctor said the Catholics objected to a layman conducting any such service. The sailors were pulling at a rope, and raising their usual song:

Haul in the bowling, the Black Star bowling
Haul in the bowling, the bowling haul—

and the child was thrown overboard at the sound of the last word of the song, which became a funeral dirge.

On November 30, two days off New York, Foster wrote in his diary: "The doctor came down to the second cabin in company with the first mate, and to display his authority, drew himself up and swelled himself up excessively tremendous, roaring out, 'Now then, clean and wash out your rooms every one of you, God damn and blast your souls to hell.'"

■　■　■

The Atlantic passage in a sailing vessel must by its nature have been an ordeal for most landsmen. Many ships, even the bigger ones, were not dry, particularly when they had a part cargo of iron or railway lines. Captain Schomberg, emigra-

The immigrant ships of the late nineteenth century were much larger than, for example, the slave ships that sailed at the beginning of that century. They carried nearly 10 million people from 1880 to 1900 alone. Were your ancestors part of this wave of migration?

tion officer at Liverpool, tried to superintend the loading, not only to make sure the ship was safe but also to look after the passengers' health. "A deep ship will very probably, under ordinary circumstances, be very wet and uncomfortable, and the people will live up to their knees in water. . . ." Even the cheerful emigrant from Bristol complained that "two holes, cut for air, often admit water upon us, through the ship's heaving."

The crowding itself made decency and comfort impossible. . . .

On board most ships, men and women were indiscriminately berthed together. Sir George Stephen once asked a ship's mate how he managed with marriages at sea; how did he manage to bed the couple on board? To which the mate replied: "There is no difficulty as to that; there is plenty of that work going on every night to keep them all in countenance." George Saul, passenger broker, said that if people wished to be improperly berthed, he shut his eyes to it, thinking he could not make people virtuous if they were disposed to be immoral. . . .

Sylvester Redmond, journalist, was asked if he thought indiscriminate intercourse took place. He said: "I saw on two occasions, in the daytime, persons in very indelicate positions."

"Of different sexes?—Yes."

This is risible; as it was when a captain in the Royal Navy was solemnly questioned about unmarried men on board being able to "view the married women dressing or undressing, and see what is going on." He had to agree that there was "use given to the eyes." But this berthing together must have been intolerable for a modest woman. Sometimes women had to sit up all night on boxes because they could not think of going to bed with strange men, under the same blanket.

60

■ ■ ■

The women got the worst of it in other ways. Those who had no men to look out for them found it difficult to get any food at all. A doctor who had made many voyages from Liverpool to America said that on rough days he had often been obliged to go into the steerage with buckets of water and a bag of biscuits to feed the women to save them from starvation. Women and feeble men went days without a bite. A boarding-house keeper at Liverpool who had made one voyage on a ship with about 400 passengers, said that there was only room for six people to stand and cook at the same time, and there was incessant cooking and fighting from six in the morning till six at night. "The women particularly, who were alone, must have wanted their food."

. . . On many Irish ships the staple diet was a coarse concoction of wheat, barley, rye, and pease, which became saturated with moisture on board ship, where it fermented and became baked into a solid mass "requiring to be broken down with an axe before using."

Many emigrants would not eat unaccustomed food, though it might have been perfectly good. The Irish, although preferring potatoes, which they never got, would eat oatmeal. The English, thinking it food for horses, would not. One passenger said he had seen it thrown into the St. Lawrence. He had seen the river covered with oatmeal. Many emigrants were too poor and ignorant to know what to do with the food they were given. One captain said a third of them did not know what tea was. "It is no uncommon thing to see an Irishman survey his allowance of tea for a while, and then fill his pipe with a portion, and smoke it with evident satisfaction."

■ ■ ■

On September 3, 1853, Delaney Finch, a farmer, sailed from Liverpool to Quebec in the *Fingal*, with 200 other passengers and 1,100 tons of railroad iron. She was lost on the return voyage. Finch said she was a good ship, though the berths broke down. On the voyage of seven weeks, thirty-seven or forty-one passengers died: he could not remember which. Later he was asked what happened. He said: "I should not like to give an opinion, but my impression is, that Epsom salts and castor oil are very improper medecines to administer to persons labouring under the cholera."

"Is that what they gave?—Yes."

"Epsom salts and castor oil?—Yes, and thirty-five drops of laudanum, and then rubbing a man's face with vinegar."

He was asked if any record was of the deaths: "When we got to Quebec, I and Mr. Liefchild, a gentleman who was in the second cabin, had to put down the names of the parties who died on the voyage, but it was more guess-work than certainty."

Then he was asked how the burials were carried out, and he said the bodies were thrown overboard, not covered up or anything.

"Did he [the captain] give directions to have the corpse sewn up in canvas, and thrown over?—No, he did not use his jurisdiction in that matter, because he said in the cabin, 'We are not bound to do it; it is only according to courtesy.'"

From England to Wisconsin

We usually think of nineteenth-century immigrants to the United States as a mass of people speaking one or another foreign language and faced with a difficult adjustment to their new land. Many immigrants, however, came from the British Isles and had no language problems, though in other ways they faced the same trials as did all newcomers. The stream of immigrants from Great Britain continued long after the colonies declared their independence. In fact, the number of British immigrants in the late 1840s increased greatly, possibly even exceeding the number from Ireland, which reached a peak about the same time. Among the migrants from the British Isles were two house painters, Fred Chaney and Frank Johnson. Each left behind a wife and children, who would follow later.

Chaney and Johnson traveled all the way to Fond du Lac, Wisconsin, before they found work. They achieved a measure of success and, following the common immigrant custom, sent for their families. More fortunate probably than most, the Chaneys and Johnsons had been separated for only about eighteen months before the women and children crossed the ocean. The Johnsons were reunited in New York City and remained there. The Chaneys settled in Fond du Lac.

Their letters back and forth during this time provide us with interesting descriptions of the passage across the Atlantic at mid-century as well as the trip to Wisconsin. The route these two immigrants took was similar to the one taken by a great many residents of New England and the Middle Atlantic states as they sought opportunity in the Middle West. The letters even mention "Oregon Fever," the urge to continue the quest for fame and fortune all the way to the West Coast—an urge that these settlers resisted.

For these British immigrants the American Dream seems to have come true. Although they did not make a fortune, they saw America as a land of opportunity, where jobs were plentiful, investment opportunities were everywhere, and the cost of living only half of what it had been in Britain. Yet even for the successful immigrants there were many trials and many difficulties to overcome.

[Autumn], 1849

Dear Ann and Dear Betsey,
We started from London on 24th Augt and sailed from Portsmouth on 1 Sept, and was 5 Weeks on our Passage. We had a Pleasant Voyage, came to New York and had a look around. We had the promises of 3 or 4 Houses in a fortnights time. It would not

do to wait. We went from New York to Albany 150 miles. We had no Luck and went on to Utica 110 Miles further where we now write from. We are rather late for Business here. We are now starting for Buffalow.

Was anxious to let you now our affairs as soon as possible to comfort you a little, and anxious are we to hear how you are in health and circumstances. We feel great concern for you, and believe you do the same for us. I am sorry we could not send better News, but we would not wait any longer writing to you.

America is a fine Country. No man in Existence can truly describe its beauties. We wish we were all settled here together, it would be the greatest happiness we could Experience. God alone knows what he intends to do with us. May we have Grace and Faith to leave all things in his hands.

We wish you to get all the News ready for our Next Letter which we hope to send in a few Days with Directions where to write to us. Remember us to all the Dear Children, give them a kiss apiece for us. Keep up your Spirits and we will do the same. It may be like Old Jacob coming down to Egypt to live.

Give our kind Love to your Mother, John, Henry in particular. Tell him I shall write a long letter to him as soon as we get settled. Richard, Wife and Betsy, Charles, Sarah, not forgetting above all Mr. and Mrs. Farrow, Hugh, William, Wife and Child.

Yours affectionately,

No more at present from Fred and Frank

Dear Betsy, give the babe a kiss for me, Frank. I have been to see a Baptiss Member who is the largest Painter in this town who came here very low and is now a great Man. He Encouraged us very much by saying when we once got into Work we should sure to do well as we can keep a Famely at half the price of beggerly England.

[Autumn], 1849

Dearest Ann, Betsey, Clara and all young ones,

We think by this time you [are] anxiously waiting to hear from us, we are also anxious to hear from you without one moments delay. Our last letter we sent did not hold out much comfort for you or us either, but by the Blessing of a Merciful God we can give you some Good News. We think we have found the Land of Promise at last, and the God of Promises is with us.

I have not room to give any account at present of our travels but suffice it to say we have settled at Fond de Lack, Wisconsin, United States America. We came here heavy hearted after failing all our journey on account for being to late for the season here. God raised us up Good Friends. Arrived here on Saturday Night, went to work on Monday, and earned 6£ in American Money in 5 days at painting, equal to 3£ in English Money. This is a New and Flourishing Town only a few Months started. We have plenty of Work and likely to continue for Years, but the thing is this, in all New Places we are forced to work for Barter so we are now working out 50 Dollars for a Town Lot of Ground that will Build 6 or 8 Houses. We are also working for another Man for Timber to Build your Houses. We are now working for Mr. Edwards who is Building a large House for Shop. Tell Mr. Vinters he knows him well. He kept the Bakhouse that Child [h]as got on the Highway. He was Sectary to the Bakers Society. Desire to be remembered to him, tho 5 Thousand Miles of[f].

We have plenty of London cockneys here and plenty coming every day. This will

An immigrant group probably consisting of several families photographed at Ellis Island. Do they have hope or fear in their faces? Why was so much immigration encouraged by America in the late nineteenth and early twentieth centuries? Will the process of Americanization be easier for the men, the women, or the children? They even look "foreign," do they not? Will that look change in a few years? Perhaps you can imagine one of your ancestors in a group like this, just off the boat.

be a fine place for Business soon, so you see we cannot help you to come out. You must directly think about it as it will take some time to arrange with the Parishes. You must come out about the 1st of March as the lakes are frosen over in Winter.

Ann and Betsey, you must exert yourselves with all your Might, you must throw yourself on the Parish or they will not do anything for you, and that for some time before they will do anything for you. If it is St. Lukes Parish go to Mr. Smith, he knows me well, and see what he can do. If St. Georges go and see Mr. Knight the Rope Maker, he knows me well, he is [a] very kind and liberal Man, he is the first Man in the Parish, and is sure to do what he can. Do not let the parish know that you can work at the Needle, as they would say you could earn your own living. You must push it with all your strength. When you arrive here you will find every thing heart can wish, house of your own, no Rent to pay. We shall be able no doubt to work out a good Cow, and to have a Barrell of Flour by that time.

Everything here is very Cheap, 2 days work will keep a Man for a Week. . . . We have heard a Good deal about America, but never thought it was like this. We can look out from our Window over 50 Miles of Beautiful country, no place in the world to equal America. Plenty work for Dress Makers, first rate pay to.

Tell Betsey Frank wants her to go to Bunyan and ask him to send on a slip of paper the different Colors for Graining. Tell him to send the Names of Colors how to Mix them and for Graining, and Receipts for all Woods. Give Frank['s] kind respects to him.

Now Ann I wish you to be sure to enquire the prices of the Plush, different sorts and colors for making Mens Caps, also the prices of the peaks per Dozen of the same, also prices of Threads, Cottons, pins, Needles, etc., which are very dear here. Our Landlady Makes Caps, and she will send money over by the time you come to bring her some. She and her Husband are the best Creatures in the world. All our prospects, Work and everything is oweing to them, they long to see you all over safe, tho never seen you. Dont forget to send particulars upon any account. If you could get plenty of Beads to bring you would get a capital price for them here. Clara is sure to make Money here.

[Unsigned, but probably also from Fred and Frank]

[Autumn], 1849

Dear Betsey,
You can tell Mr. Powell that there is a good prospect here for a man who has got 2 or 3 Hundred Pounds as he could double it in about 12 Months in Buying Land and Building, as the Houses are let or sold before finished, and will be so for some time to come, as this is a thriving town, as a New Canal is cut from this Town to run into the Main Rivers to convey goods to all parts. We have 2 steamers already running on it. Land very cheap here, but will soon rise high. Last spring there was only 3 Houses in this place, now there is 3 or 4 Hundred, and next year will be Treble that.

Betsey, you can tell Mr. Powell that had I a few Pounds it would be of infinite Value to me at this time. I am sure I could more than double it in a few Months.

Give my kind respects to Mrs. Powell and Mr. Powell, hope they are quite well. Give a kiss to all the young ones for me, and when you come over I will pay you back again.

Your affecly
F[rank] Johnson

Decr. 16, 1849

Dearest Betsey & Dearest Children,
I Received you Letter of 12th Decr., it came from England to New York in 13 days and from New York to me in 11 days more, being only 24 in all, this is quick travelling. I was most happy to hear that you and the dear Children are all well in health. I hope when you receive this you will not lose a day without sending an answer, it is very uncertain that I shall be able to send another Letter, for at this time of Year the Lakes are frose over and the Mail has to travel some Hundred[s] of Miles on Sledges through the snow, and by the time my Letter came to England you, I hope, will have started, so write immediately and send all the News you can.

You wish me to give you a true account [of] how I am getting on. When I came here I found plenty of Work but no Money, it was all done in Barter. I have bought a plot of Ground and Built a cottage on it. I have paid part of the Money in Labour, and have to pay the rest in Labour. I have been very fortunate since I have been here in getting Work, especially as I came just before the Winter set in. Of course I do not care what I do if I dont get work at my own trade. I go to Labouring work, I have now 3 Jobs in hand, and one is to Work out 2 Waggon Loads of Fire Wood, another for a Hundred and Half of Flour, another for Wearing Apparel. There is plenty of Work, but all must be taken out in Goods, so you see I can keep 2 Familys here better than I could keep one in England. Good Flour is only 5s English money, pr Hundred Weight, Prime Beef 2 pence pr pound, and every thing else equally low, and no Rent to pay.

Dear Betsey, I feel very anxious to see you come out and hope the Parish Authority will be kind enough to help you and the Children for to come. I feel very thankful to hear they have acted so kind towards you, and that you have been so comfortable and also that the children are with you. Should be very Glad to hear if your Confinement was over. I feel very anxious about you. Do not fail to send all particulars as to the time of coming out. I would advise you by all means to come out in the Middle of March. The ship will not be so crowded. There will not be any sickness or fever that is some times the case through the Hot Weather.

Dear Betsey save all the Means you are able as it will cost a good bit to bring you from New York to me. You had better bring all the Bed and Bedding you can, as Blankets are very dear here, and any other things that are not to heavy or cumbersome. You wished me to write about the disturbance with the Indians. We have not heard a word about it. We seldom see any of them, but they are very sociable and Quiet People.

We have fine weather here, tho in the Middle of Winter we have always a clear Sky, Warm Sun, no fogs, and from what I have seen not so severe as our winters. Nearly all our Neibours are English People.

> I Remain your Affec. Husband,
> F. Johnson

Apparently Betsey Johnson obtained the coveted parish aid, for some time in 1850 she arrived in New York where Frank joined her and where they remained. In the summer of the same year Ann Chaney and her daughters Clara, Eliza, Emma, and Jane, also with parish assistance, sailed for Canada en route to join Fred Chaney in Wisconsin. In her first letters to her family in England Ann gives a vivid account of life aboard an immigrant ship and records her first ebullient impressions of the strange new world. Clara's first letter to her grandmother is interesting for its contrast of English and American ways and for its evidence of the adaptability of a sixteen-year-old London girl to frontier conditions.

[August, 1850]

My dear Mother, Brother and Sister,
I know you are very anxious to hear from me, as I expect you have not herd of the vessel. We left Hatton Garden at ten o'clock on the 3rd August for the Railway Station, and left there at twelve for Blackwall where [we were met by] some of the

Ladies and Gents, and a widow as sub-Matron. She was not with them. She had aplied for her passage within the last two days of leaving London. All eyes was upon her. She was a respectable looking person, but disguised by licour. All the Girls took a dislike to her.* She was very bussy telling them she would see them done well by, and asking the Gentlemen for instructions. They treated her very cool, and told her I would give them her. Mr. Quickett, after paying for the Children to Toronto, paid me over eight pounds. We joined the Ship at Gravesend, and the Gentry left us there. The Government Oficer ordered the Steward to cook us some beef steaks and Mr. Blackey looked dagers at him. Last fresh meat we had.

We sailed from Gravesend at 4 on Sunday morning. I went on deck and enjoid an hour there, being a delightful morning. At 6 the provisionry was given out for the week for the whole party—biscuits, rice, peas, tea, sugar, pork, beef, plumbs and [?] soup, cheese and butter. Fancy all this stuff in my little Cobard with the addition of this troblesome nuisance. I get Dinner in the best way we could, being very troblesome to get it cooked.

The pilot left us on Sunday evening at the Downs, the weather being rough, cast anchor and sailed earley on Monday morning. We was all getting very sick while the vessel is getting out of the Chanel, it is fact about the sails being shipt very often, the sailors shouting and tossing about the Deck. The Carpenter came to make the boxes fast, the water cans tied.

I appointed two Cooks, but the convenience was very bad. A bad Cook, a littel Black man. We have biscuit eat like baked sawdust, fresh water stinking, pudding boiled in salt water and not half done, peas and rice the same, and hard salt beef. The Girls get disatisfied with their food. Some of them are bold low creatures, and to get order is quite impossible. My cooks very ill. The Doctor divided the party into four meses, each cook for themself. This relieved me very much. I was very sick and low part of the time, but I think if I could have enjoid my food I should have been very well. I am very well now. The Children are all very well. Littel Jean ha[s] been the best Sailour and a general Favourate in particular with the Black Steward.

Now my dear Mother, we are getting very tired of the sea, the wether very rough and contrary winds. I lay in my birth and listen, try to listen, but I cannot distinguish such a confusion of noises. The sea roars, the waves dash against the vesel with such force you would think it had struck against a rock. Then it would heave from one side to the other. Boxes slip, tins and sugar, treacle, rice, cheese, plumbs and everything we had dashed about, the vesel cracking and groaning you would think it must devide or sway under the water.

We had several squals. The men said our ship is the dryest they have sailed in, and she rode through the squals bravely. We had two or three nights and days of this sort, and a day or so quit calm. You can have no idea of the beauty of the sea when the sun sets. I [never?] saw anything so beautifull, the sea deep blue, and sometimes on looking over the side of the vesel can see very curious fish, some like a flat round with a bright cross up them, and other different forms, and when the sea is rough great monsters seem to play in the waves.

Now we are about to enter the Gulf. This night was awful, the rain poured in to torrents, and the wind blew huricans. The water, all thoe the [h]atch was on which all most stifold us, was pouring down. I herd the Cheif Mait tell the people in the sterage that he did not think one of us could see the morning, but thank God mercies came, but

---

*Apparently Ann Chaney was in charge of a party of young women being assisted by the parishes to emigrate to Canada to seek employment, probably as domestics. From the context it would appear that the woman "disguised by licour" was either to serve as Ann's subordinate or was in charge of a similar group of female emigrants.

the hurican continued. The vesel was on its side. The sailors [said?] had that occured in the night we must have been lost. In the afternoon the storm seased to a calm. Now the pilot came on board, this caused much excitement, but he had joined us two hundred miles beyond his station. He had been out some time looking for us.

We enter the river St. Lorance, here we wait for the tide. The senery is delightfull. At last disernible the numerus little hills scatered at the slopes near the water by milk white houses, and the boats come along side. Now we are at dock near the quarintine ground, and if we was not in [h]e[a]lth we should have to stop some time there. Mrs. Sidney Herbert's Brother had been there, we had been expected these three weeks. I would not have sent [this letter?] till we got to Toronto, but I know you are anxious. I shall long to hear from you. We are near Quebec.

I have just been on deck and the sight very impresing. We seam encircled by land and the slopes up from the water, and laid out butifuly, houses with slated roofs, and we see a great water fall.

[Unsigned, but probably from Ann Chaney]

[September, 1850]

My very dear Mother,
I know you are very anxious to hear of me, and I am also very anxious to let you know I am very greived to hear how you was moved.

Well, I will give a sketch from Quebec. We met Mr. a'Court [Harcourt?] there and he accompanyed us, providing cabin fair to Toronto. The weather was very [good?] and the views along very beautiful. In two or three days the Girls was provided with places. I wrote to Fredrick the day I arrived there, and waited three weeks and no answer.

I was treated with great kindness, but still I could not stop any longer, so I packed up and started at a venture at two o'clock in the afternoon, and passed Niagra Fawls that night. We had left the boat and was in horse cars. The night was dark and we could but hear the tremendous roar of the waters and see the white foam to a Great Hight. We stopt [at?] Keep Chipawea [?] 7 miles from there, from there to Buffalo by steam boat, from there to Detroit. Stopt at a Dashing Hotel till morning, then by rail to New Buffalo. Waited till three in the morning, the boat being full, was thought I should not go, but the lugage was at the last minute put on board. I had left the Children with a woman on the warf who had promised to not to leave them, and Clara and me sought the goods. The boat pushed into the lake and I thought all was wright but presently found the Children was left on the warf and ran about like one mad to find the Captain. He was on the second deck. He said they would be sent to me. He tried to get from me, and went down the roaps, I went down the roaps as well as he, and I was left there with the Children, and Clara and the lugage went on to Chicago. I went by the next boat, and found Clara at a respectable hotel, where we all stopt that night, then we left there for Milwacke late at night, and was to go the next morning. We went to the warf, the boat was to full and we could not go that day.

The next morning we went on board and the boat put out into the lake but the weather was to rough to procede. The third morning we left Milwake for Sheboggan. There we stopt one night, then toke a team to go to Fondulake which was forty five miles.

We started this distance, was all through a wood. The trees have been cut down to make a road, and a queer road it was, over stumps of trees and stones, down steaps, up hills, mud, and then you come to a hole partly piled up with sticks, then to a great swamp and bodies of trees put cross to form a road. So you may think this was very rough riding, but thoe the morning was frosty we was not the least cold, the sun out and the weather bright and pleasant, and plenty of Buffalo skins to rap our feet in. These woods are not drery as you would think—hear and there is a open space, been cleared, and a few cottages. A few miles further and another or two. There are several taverns in this wood. We stopt one night at a log tavern, you cannot get through in one day.

I met with a young man in Milwake who knew Fredrick and directed me to the spot. It is in the lower vilage. On a prary ground, there is no trees close, but at a littel distance there is plenty of woods. Well, we was directed over the Bridge, then we was shone his Shanty. We drove to the door of this most splend[id] cottage. It was a wooden house with two windows in it, and one good sized room and one small with two bed steds the old Chap manufactured himself. He was not at home. His nearest neighbour came and insisted on us going to her house to dinner, and sent for him. He was expecting us. He had received and answered my letter but I had not received it. Frederick toke me to see several people all who was very glad to see me, and are very friendly, and we have several visits.

There is very little money here, but traid one with the other. There are stores and they [have] every thing, and you have bills on these stores and take what you want. I have been to one of the largest stores who deal largely in Close, and has promised me work, and we I do think may be comfortable. Fredrick has agreed part material for a better house wich is to be done in the Spring.

My dear Mother, only for the thort that we are so far apart I am very comfortable and my helth is much improved. We are all in good helth.

I have been here five days before I sent this, that I might send you all the news I could. I gave Mr. a'Court your address. He assured me he would call on you. He is Sir Sidney Herbert Wifes Brother. He expected to be in England in three months.

Fredrick had a letter from Frank a few days ago. He has some work at New York and he thinks to come to Fondulack next Spring. They are all well.

Now my dear Mother and Brothers and Sister except our sesear [sincere?] love from your affectionate Daughter and family. Love to John, hope him and his mother is comfortable.

A. F. and C. Chaney

We have a pig near ready to kill and three others not quite ready. I was in Milwakey three days and nights. I received five pounds of Mr. a'Court and spent all I had in travelling. Please to remember me to Mr. and Mrs. Venters and Helen and [H?]inton. I could have called on Mr. [H?]intons famely if I had known there adress.

December, 1850

Dear Grandmother,
Thinking by this time that you and Uncle John will be saying Ah Clara is gone and forgot all about us, but I hope not to deserve this acuseasation, but I thourt it better to defer writing a few weeks after Mother's letter. . . .

. . . A dollar goes much further here than it would in England. Harricot beans a dollar a Bushel. Father brought home for half dollar 2 pounds of sugar, quarter of a pound of tea, a pound and ½ of coffee, this seemed a good deal to us for 2 english shillings. We have to roast and grind our own coffee, bake our own Bread. We mostly have meat for Breakfast. The Yankees generally live well, we have three meals a day, they [call?] the third Supper. They do not have 3 trays like they do in england, they have apple sauce, preserves, meat and several kinds of cakes on the Table at one time. At every meal they have tea or coffee. Dear Grandmother, I think you may see it is much easier to get on here than in england. We are in expectation of a rail road coming near us in the spring, which will make the place very Flourishing and money more plentiful. We are invited to dinner Christmas day by that mans brother that mother took the letter for. Mother and I went with a person from England who are Cabinet makers in the Town to see Mrs. Smiths farm who are also english. These Smiths have not been here two years, they came without a penny but now they are in a Flourishing condition. They rent the farm at 2 hundred dollars a year, but there corn that they grow pays there rent and a hundred dollars over. They have 14 cows, 10 calves, and 2 sheep, 23 pigs, 20 fowls. They have 100 acres of land, 50 in cultivation and the rest in pasture. They made us very welcome. I made a Chrochet cap for which we take out in butter. We have several invitations to different farmers when it is good sleaighing, that will be when the snow gets a little deeper on the ground.

The frost set in about the begining of December, it was very severe for a few days, and frose the lakes and rivers up. The weather is dry and clear and fine sunshiny weather. Teams which are drawn by oxen and mools, sleaighs, cutters, all cross the river and lakes on the ice. The inhabitants look forword with pleasure to deep snow and kalaclate on many pleasant visits. The winter last about six months, snowing and freeseing, snowing and freeseing all the winter.

Dear grandmother, the stoves are very different here to what they are at home, they are in sort of iron box with oven and a pipe going up through the ceiling. They mostly stand in the middle of the room and throw out a great heat. There is no coals burnt here, all wood. The men go up in the woods to get it, and chop or saw it at there own place.

We killed the sow and salted it down, now we have three young ones left which Father means to keep. We give them very little food. They run about the prairies and pick up anything they can eat. Sometimes they will go away for days together.

Dear Grandmother, when you write again please to put James Fredrick instead of Mr. Chaney as the letters stop at the post office until called for, and they make a peice of work if they are not directed so.

Dear Grandmother, I have not room for any more, but hope you will write directly you receive this, and I will write directly I receive your answer. We are all in good health, as we hope you are also. Mother and Father send their love to you and Uncle John, Uncle Charles, Aunt Sarah, Phil, Sally and the baby and all inquiring frends. The children send their love.

I am your ever affectionate [grand] daughter Clara Chaney.

March 1st, 1851

Dear Mother and Charles,
We received your last letter and was very sorry to hear you was so poorly, we hope you are better. We should be glad to have a long letter from you. If you cannot write it, ask Charles to send us a long letter.

We thought you would like to know how we are getting on. We are all in good health, thank the Lord, Ann, Emma and Clara are getting fatter than my Pigs, and no wonder if you could see how they go into it. Plenty to Eat and plenty fine fresh Air. Eliza and Jane are growing very fast and in good health. We have just agreed with a Carpenter to put our House up, we have got the principle of the Materials and expect to have it up very shortly. We are going to have the Ground plowed up and sown with Potatoes, Greens, etc., which will supply us through the Season. We have 3 Pigs and all in thriving condition, expecting every day to be confined. I hope we shall have a Score of Young ones. We have been pretty well off for Work, the Weather is now very fine and we expect to be very Busy this summer. We have had a very fine Winter, not too Cold, we all stood it like trumps.

We have just received a letter from Frank and was very glad to hear he was doing very Comfortable, and expects this summer to do better still. He has written to us to say if we was not doing well where we are to go up to New York, he believes we should do well there. But as a rolling stone gathers no moss we think we can do better hear at least we intend giving it a fair trial. We shall have no Rent to pay here, can grow all our own vegetables, and fatten the principle of our Meat. All this we must pay for at New York. We have several good Ministers here and several Chapels, they are now Building one within a quarter of a Mile of us, Congregationist. Our Neighbours are all very kind and we [get] many invitations. . . .

We have heard and read a good deal about the Worlds Fair, we have just seen a Hansome Engraving of it Gilt in Gold. Suppose it will be a spendid Affair.

Frank says he has written two Letters to England and received no answer. He has lost his last young one 11 months old. I think the California Mania is now at an end. We hear of Numbers that have starved to Death there, and Numbers that have perished in coming home. The Oregon Fever [h]as now started and Numbers are going from this part of America, there. They are giving 320 acres of Land to all that go there. It is 6 Months travelling across the Land about Two Thousand Miles from this part of America. By Sea it is Nineteen Thousand Miles. I do not think I shall ever go there.

We have nearly got rid of the Indians, they will receive their last payment from the Government the latter end of this Year, as the Government Bought them out. They will have to go a Hundred Miles further west, but they are very Quiet peaceable and Good Natured, we never hear any bad accounts of them. They are what are called Civilised, but further West and South they are Savage, Murderous and Cruel. They bring into the Town a good deal of Venison, Sugar, Honey, Fish, etc., etc. We expect we shall have a Railway running through our Town this Summer, if so it will be a busy place. We all like the Country well, we have no wish to return to Old England again, altho some say with all her faults they love her still—Trash— Trash—certainly we should like to see Old Friends and Old Faces, but as that cannot be, God grant we may all Meet together in Heaven.

It is a Beautiful Country, I have travelled about 16 Hundred Miles from East to West, and Ann has travelled about the same distance from North to West. We have seen some fine Citys and Towns, and as to the Views of Scenery it cannot be surpassed, if it can be equalled anywhere.

We all join in our best love and Esteem to you and all Friends and Remain

Yours Affectly
J. F. Chaney

A Norwegian Writes Home About America

Probably most people who immigrated to the United States learned about the new land through letters from a friend or relative who had migrated earlier. Some of these letters spoke of a magic land where streets were paved with gold, others told tales of hardship, but many gave practical advice on how to survive in the new country. The following letter was written, in September 1867, by Jens Gronbek, from Rice County, Minnesota, to his brother-in-law, Christian Heltzen of Hemnes in northern Norway. He advises his brother-in-law that if he can raise $600, then coming to Minnesota would be worthwhile. We do not know whether or not Christian Helzen came to America, but a great many Scandinavians did settle in the upper Midwest. Today, in fact, almost every family in Norway has at least a distant relative in the United States.

Dear Christian,

Thank you for your welcome letter, which was both unexpected and remarkable. I got it from a smith in town who asked if I knew someone named Jans Grønbek. I had not known that Hans Jansen had gone to America, and I have no news of him. I would guess he is somewhere in Minnesota. I was especially glad to learn from your letter that you and dear Laura as well as others of the family live comfortably. But I am very sorry that your Lofoten investment did not turn out well. You ask that I report to you concerning conditions here. This I will do by way of addition to what I have written to you before.

America is a naturally rich land, endowed with virtually everything, except to a dull-witted European who is disappointed not to find money in the streets or who expects to get things without moving his arms. Spring work has been delayed by heavy rains this year. I think we sowed wheat in the middle of May. Now we have harvested and, thanks to God, it is good. The quantity is about average.

There are many thousand acres of available land here—government, school, and railroad land—although it is increasingly in the West. As for government or homestead land, one can take a quarter section or 160 acres free, except for payment of a registration fee of $14 per quarter, and this is almost all arable land. An acre is 4½ Norwegian *maal*. Schools and railroad companies have received large grants of land

Can you imagine what life was like for a family on the "sod house frontier" of the plains? Does the family portrait suggest a close-knit family? Do you feel any great tension with everyone in the small house living so close together? Can you imagine month after month of frozen winter in that house? Why are so many family members dressed in the same cloth? What was the woman's life like? From where do you suppose these people came to the frontier?

for their support, and they sell for 6 shillings American or 75 shillings Norwegian per acre. This land you can use as you wish and can sell when you will, and therefore it is most sought. On homesteads, you are obligated to establish a residence, build a house, and start cultivation. You must live on the claim for six months of each year, and you may not sell it for five years, during which time it is free of taxes or further payments. It is this policy, of course, that makes the American government so generous and good for immigrants.

Now then, if one has land, the most important items are horses or oxen, a wagon, a plow, and other things necessary for a farmer. A pair of good work horses costs $400 to $500, a yoke of oxen, $160 to $200, and a wagon, $140 to $160. A plow, a harrow, and harness for the horses cost $200.

A beginner usually buys a pair of oxen and a wagon and makes out very well. I know farmers, wealthy people, who own many horses, including my employer who still uses oxen for farm work. I am now doing fall plowing with them every day.

This year my employer got about 1,200 to 1,400 bushels of wheat. The price this spring was two specie dollars for No. 1 wheat, 1½ dollars for No. 2, and 1 specie dollar for No. 0. A bushel weighs about 60 pounds.

Do you know what, my dear Christian? If you find farming in Norway unrewarding and your earnings at sea are poor, I advise you, as your friend and brother-in-law, to abandon everything, and—if you can raise $600—to come to Minnesota. Do not believe that all is lies and fables in reports that in one year in America all will be well, for I can testify that it is true, despite the fact that, last fall when I came, I thought for a time I would starve. But an American came to me in friendly fashion and said, "Huad yuh want? Want yuh work? Will yuh have som ting to eat and trink?" That is, did I need anything, did I want work, and was I hungry? I did not understand him and continued hungry even though I had been offered all these good things.

I have now worked for a Norwegian farmer since Christmas and will remain here until October. I have it very good here. Five meals each day of the best food in the world, so that I fear I have become choosy. You can best understand the food here when I say that the cost of board for a week is $5 and for individual meals $1 to $1.80.

Now, dear Christian, if you consider selling and emigrating across the Atlantic Ocean, please write me. Do not be worried about the voyage, either for your wife or for the children. Neither should you be alarmed about Indians or other trolls in America, for the former are now chased away, and the Yankees, that is Americans, are as kind a folk toward a stranger as I can imagine.

I am uncertain whether to make a trip to Norway in the spring or to go farther west and look over the land. If you plan to migrate, I will come to Rana, for one thing is certain: you will need as much money as possible. Andreas and Nils Jørgen bought land this spring, but I have met no acquaintances from Norway since Christmas. Nearly all newcomers want to return to the homeland until they have become American citizens, and then hardly anyone wants to return.

Dear Christian, tell Laura that I will soon see her again. Greet all friends and family.

ROSA

Marie Hall Ets

In many ways the immigrant experience was more difficult for women than for men. Often women traveled to join husbands or lovers who had gone ahead. Sometimes, through arrangements, they came to meet men whom they had never seen before and married in this new and strange land.

Men usually found it easier to learn English and adapt to American ways than women because often women were forced to remain at home, thus missing the same opportunities to become Americanized. But social patterns varied. Many immigrant women were compelled to work long hours in factories or as domestic servants.

Below is a selection from a remarkable autobiography of an Italian woman, told to and written down by a social worker who had befriended her. Rosa is one of those ordinary people who made up the bulk of immigrants from all countries. She grew up in Italian Lombardy, in a silk-making village. There she lived with a foster mother, Mamma Lena, and went to work at an early age. She was attractive and physically mature, and her foster mother feared that she would "get into trouble" with men. Consequently, when she was fifteen a marriage was arranged for her with a man she did not love, a man, as it turns out, who treated her badly. Her new husband left for America, and, after a time, Rosa reluctantly joined him in a Missouri mining village. The year was 1884. Her hopes and dreams and fears, while perhaps not typical, are representative of the experiences of many millions of immigrants who came to America.

So then the time came. I was in church waiting to be married with Santino. The priest was there in front and he was asking me the question. But I couldn't answer. I *couldn't!* I couldn't say yes! I was just there, that was all. I couldn't say anything. But Father Pietro didn't know I didn't answer and he didn't make me. He married me with Santino anyway. But the people all knew. When the people came home to Mamma Lena's for the wedding dinner all the women were saying, "Rosa didn't say yes!"

"Why didn't you say yes, Rosa?"

"You're not married when you don't say yes!"

"Rosa didn't say yes!"

I can't stand it to tell about that marriage and about Santino! I have to leave them out of my story, that's all. I can't tell about them!

75

76   The next day I was back at work in the silk mill of Signor Rossi and bringing my wages to Mamma Lena like before.

One night a few months after the marriage when I came from my work Santino said we were going to the dance hall. I was tired and kind of sick. "Why do you want to go when you don't know to dance?" I asked him. He didn't like it that I asked him why and he didn't answer. Mamma Lena was brushing crumbs from the table to the chickens. She was listening but she said nothing either. So I knew I would have to go. I ate the black bread and cabbage soup that Mamma Lena gave me for my supper, then I washed, put on my sailor dress and leather shoes, and we went.

Santino didn't try dancing himself—he knew he couldn't. But he told me to dance with his friends—a lot of men that were there. He wanted to show them how I could dance. I didn't know those men, but I did like he said—I tried to dance with them. But those men didn't know how at all. It was impossible to dance with them! So I sat down at the side and Santino and his friends sat at the table drinking.

After a little while Pio, the son of the *portinaia* at the mill, came in. I knew Pio when he was a little boy. He was an old friend to me and he was a wonderful dancer. So when Pio asked me to dance with him I was glad. And we danced the whole evening. Then because I was feeling so sick and tired I went home by myself and went to bed. When Santino came home he was drunk and so mad that I had danced with Pio that he said he would kill me. He pulled me out of the bed and threw me on the floor.

Other nights when Santino was drunk and beating me Mamma Lena had sat up in her bed and watched, but she had said nothing. This night—I guess she could see it that he wanted to kill me for sure—she jumped up and came over and stopped him. She pulled him away so he couldn't reach to kick me. When she did that he started fighting with her. He should have known better than to try to fight Mamma Lena! Mamma Lena was so mad she didn't care what she did. She wasn't afraid of hurting him or anything. And in the end she put him out the door and he went rolling down the steps. "And don't ever come back to this house!" she yelled after him. "Don't ever come back! I never want to see you again!"

Before he married me that man was always sweet to Mamma Lena to make her like him. But after the marriage she could see it herself—how bad he was. He was all the time drunk and beating me, and she didn't like him herself.

A few weeks after the fight—Santino was not living in Mamma Lena's— one of those agents from the big bosses in America came to Bugiarno to get men for some iron mines in Missouri. The company paid for the tickets, but the men had to work for about a year to pay them back, and they had to work another year before they could send for their wives and families. So this time when that agent came Santino and some of his friends joined the gang and went off to America. He didn't even come back to the *osteria* [boarding house] to get his clothes.

When I heard that Santino was gone, oh, I was happy! I was thinking that probably I would never see that man again. America was a long way off.

Mamma Lena was better to me now and gave me more to eat. And I kept getting bigger and bigger. And then one day I felt kicking inside of me and I knew it was a baby. How that baby got in there I couldn't understand. But

the thing that worried me most was how it was going to get out! A baby
couldn't make a hole and come out like the moth in a cocoon. Probably the
doctor would have to cut me. I didn't want to ask Mamma Lena, but what
was I going to do? That baby was kicking to get out—I would have to ask
someone. So I told her.

"Well," said Mamma Lena. "You'll have to pray the Madonna. If you
pray the Madonna with all your heart maybe the Madonna will make a
miracle for you and let the baby come out without the doctor cutting you."

And so I started to pray for that miracle. I prayed to the little statue
Madonna over the chicken coop and I prayed to the big Madonna in the
church. And every night I gave myself more Ave Marias to say, so that when
I woke up in the morning I would find the baby there in the bed beside me.
But it never was. It was still inside and kicking.

At last there came a day when I had to leave my work and go home. After
that I didn't know what happened. I was three days without my senses.
Mamma Lena got two doctors—she got the village doctor, then she got the
doctor she had to pay. But both doctors said the same. They said the baby
could not be born—that they would have to take it in pieces. And they were
even scolding her. They said,"How can a girl make new bones when her own
bones are not finished growing? The girl is too young!" Mamma Lena was in
despair. She wanted that baby. So she told the doctors to go and she ran to
the church and prayed to the big Madonna. She told the Madonna that if She
would let the baby be born alive she would give Her that beautiful shawl that
Remo and me won in the dance. (As soon as Mamma Lena had found out
about the prize shawl she had made Zia Teresa bring it to her. And she
would not speak to Zia Teresa for about three weeks because she said Zia
Teresa had helped me deceive her.)

And right then when she was praying, my baby was born—a nice little
boy. She came home and she could hear it crying. Think what a miracle! Two
doctors said that baby couldn't be born! For a long time she didn't know
whether I was going to live or not, but she was so happy to have that baby
that she was thanking the Madonna. She took the shawl to the priest the
next day. And that shawl made so much money in the raffle that the
Madonna got all new paint and a new sky and new stars behind Her.

In the fever that followed the birth of my baby I lost my hair and my
voice. Little by little my hair came back, and my voice to speak came back
too, but I could never sing like before. And as soon as I could walk again I
went back to my work in the mill. They had a special room in the mill just for
nursing the babies. So Mamma Lena would bring the baby to me and I would
stop work and go in there and nurse him. And I nursed him at lunchtime too.

Not long after the baby was born Mamma Lena got five little coral horns
one day from another lady and tied them on a string around his neck. She
said she didn't want anyone to witch that baby with the evil eye and make
him sick. I told her I didn't believe in those things. I said, "Only God and the
Madonna make you sick and make you well. How can people make you sick!"
She didn't scold. She said it was good that I believed only in God and the
Madonna. But she kept those horns around the baby's neck anyway. How
could anyone witch that baby with the evil eye when the Madonna made a
miracle to let him be born? I guess Mamma Lena remembered Braco and she
didn't want to take any chance.

There used to be a lot of men, and women too, in the villages of Lombardy that the people called witches—*maliardi*. The people thought those men and women had the evil eye. In this country too some of the old people believe in the evil eye. When my Visella got the heart trouble and died some of the women were saying it was the evil eye. I said no. I said God wanted her, that was all. But that Braco, I remember him myself. He was all the time singing. But then one day someone witched him and he couldn't talk and he couldn't sing. He was *muto*. Three years he couldn't talk and he couldn't sing. After three years a man appeared and said,"Braco, you're going to sing and you're going to talk again." And when Braco tried, he could! He could sing and he could talk! As quick as he could Braco grabbed a big knife and started after that man to catch him. Braco ran all through the town trying to catch that *maliardo* to kill him. But he never saw him again. That man disappeared entirely. No one knew where he came from or where he went. (Nobody can witch me, though. I'm too strong in believing in God and the Madonna.)

So I was around fifteen years old and I had to be like an old woman. I was not allowed to walk with the young people when they went to the square on Christmas Eve or dance with the masks when they came to the stables in the time of the carnival. I couldn't even sit with the other young girls at lunchtime at the mill. But as I got strong again I began imitating funny people and telling stories again to make the women and girls all laugh. And nighttimes and Sundays I had my baby, my Francesco, to give me joy and make me laugh. And now that I was married Mamma Lena no longer scolded or beat me like before.

"But you did wrong to make that beautiful young girl marry a man like Santino!" Zia Teresa would say.

"Yes, I made a mistake," Mamma Lena would say. "But it was not my fault. I didn't know before how bad he was. And now Rosa is married and has her baby and I don't have to worry anymore."

My Francesco had learned to walk and was learning to talk when here, coming into the *osteria* one Sunday, were some of those men who had gone to America with Santino. I stopped playing with my baby and went and called Mamma Lena from the wine cellar.

"Those men in the iron mines in Missouri need women to do the cooking and washing," said one of the men. "Three men have sent back for their wives, and two for some girls to marry. Santino says for you to send Rosa. He sent the money and the ticket." And the man pulled them from an inside pocket and laid them on the table. Then all four sat down and ordered wine and polenta. Mamma Lena took the ticket and the money and put them in the pocket of her underskirt, and without a word started serving them.

When the men were ready to leave the one who had brought the message spoke again. "In two weeks another gang of men from the villages is leaving for the iron mines in Missouri. Your daughter and the other wives and girls can go with them." But still Mamma Lena didn't tell him if I was going or not going.

After they were gone I helped her clear the table and wash the dishes. Then I took Francesco in my arms and waited for her to speak. She took her rag and started to wipe the table, but instead of wiping it she sat down on the bench beside it.

"Yes, Rosa," she said. "You must go. However bad that man is, he is your husband—he has the right to command you. It would be a sin against God not to obey. You must go. But not Francesco. He didn't ask for Francesco and I would be too lonesome without him."

Me, I was even wanting to sin against God and the Madonna before I would leave my baby and go off to Santino in America! But Mamma Lena said I must go. There was nothing I could do.

Mamma Lena was good to me though. She thought I would be not so lonesome—not so homesick in America—if I had the oil like the poor always had in Bugiarno. So she made me three bottles full and sealed it up so it looked like wine. That oil is made from the seed of the mustard plant— mustard or turnip?—I don't know what it's called in English. You eat the part underground but it's not pinchy like radishes. Only the rich people in the cities in Italy can have the olive oil. We poor people used that oil that the women made themselves.

And so I had to leave Mamma Lena and my baby and go off with that gang of men and one or two women to America.

The day came when we had to go and everyone was in the square saying good-bye. I had my Francesco in my arms. I was kissing his lips and kissing his cheeks and kissing his eyes. Maybe I would never see him again! It wasn't fair! He was *my* baby! Why should Mamma Lena keep him? But then Pep was calling and Mamma Lena took Francesco away and Zia Teresa was helping me onto the bus and handing up the bundles.

"But Rosa, don't be so sad!" It was the other Rosa and Zia Maria in the station in Milan, kissing me good-bye and patting my shoulder. "It is wonderful to go to America even if you don't want to go to Santino. You will get smart in America. And in America you will not be so poor."

Then Paris and we were being crowded into a train for Havre. We were so crowded we couldn't move, but my *paesani* [friends] were just laughing. "Who cares?" they laughed. "On our way to America! On our way to be millionaires!"

Day after day in Havre we were leaving the lodging house and standing down on the docks waiting for a ship to take us. But always the ship was full before it came our turn. "O Madonna!" I prayed. "Don't ever let there be room! Don't ever let there be room!"

But here, on the sixth day we came on. We were almost the last ones. There was just one young French girl after us. She was with her mother and her sister, but when the mother and sister tried to follow, that *marinaro* [sailor] at the gate said, "No more! Come on the next boat!" And that poor family was screaming and crying. But the *marinaro* wouldn't let the girl off and wouldn't let the mother and sister on. He said, "You'll meet in New York. Meet in New York."

All us poor people had to go down through a hole to the bottom of the ship. There was a big dark room down there with rows of wooden shelves all around where we were going to sleep—the Italian, the German, the Polish, the Swede, the French—every kind. And in that time the third class on the boat was not like now. The girls and women and the men had to sleep all together in the same room. The men and girls had to sleep even in the same bed with only those little half-boards up between to keep us from rolling together. But I was lucky. I had two girls sleeping next to me. When the dinner bell rang we were all standing in line holding the tin plates we had to buy in Havre, waiting for soup and bread.

"Oh, I'm so scared!" Emilia kept saying and she kept looking at the little picture she carried in her blouse. "I'm so scared!"

"Don't be scared, Emilia," I told her. "That young man looks nice in his picture."

"But I don't know him," she said. "I was only seven years old when he went away."

"Look at *me*, said the comical Francesca with her crooked teeth. "I'm going to marry a man I've never seen in my life. And he's not *Lombardo*—he's *Toscano*. But I'm not afraid."

Of course Francesca was not afraid. "Crazy Francesca" they called her at the silk mill. She was so happy she was going to America and going to get married that she didn't care who the man was.

On the fourth day a terrible storm came. The sky grew black and the ocean came over the deck. Sailors started running everywhere, fastening this and fastening that and giving orders. Us poor people had to go below and that little door to the deck was fastened down. We had no light and no air and everyone got sick where we were. We were like rats trapped in a hole, holding onto the posts and onto the iron frames to keep from rolling around. Why had I worried about Santino? We were never going to come to America after all! We were going to the bottom of the sea!

But after three days the ship stopped rolling. That door to the deck was opened and some sailors came down and carried out two who had died and others too sick to walk. Me and all my *paesani* climbed out without help and stood in line at the wash-house, breathing fresh air and filling our basins with water. Then we were out on the narrow deck washing ourselves and our clothes—some of us women and girls standing like a wall around the others so the men couldn't see us.

Another time there was fog—so much fog that we couldn't see the masts and we couldn't see the ocean. The engine stopped and the sails were tied down and a horn that shook the whole boat started blowing. All day and all night that horn was blowing. No one could sleep so no one went to bed. One man had a concertina and the ones who knew how to dance were dancing to entertain the others. Me, I was the best one. There was no one there to scold me and tell me what to do so I danced with all my *paesani* who knew how. Then I even danced with some of the Polish and the French. We were like floating on a cloud in the middle of nowhere and when I was dancing I forgot for a little while that I was the wife of Santino going to him in America. But on the third day the fog left, the sails came out, the engine started, and the ship was going again.

Sometimes when I was walking on the steerage deck with Giorgio—the little boy of one woman from Bugiarno who was all-the-way seasick—I would look back and see the rich people sitting on the higher decks with nice awnings to protect them from the cinders and the sun, and I would listen to their strange languages and their laughing. The rich always knew where they were going and what they were going to do. The rich didn't have to be afraid like us poor.

Then one day we could see land! Me and my *paesani* stood and watched the hills and the land come nearer. Other poor people, dressed in their best clothes and loaded down with bundles, crowded around. *America!* The country where everyone could find work! Where wages were so high no one had to go hungry! Where all men were free and equal and where even the poor could own land! But now we were so near it seemed too much to believe. Everyone stood silent—like in prayer. Big sea gulls landed on the deck and screamed and flew away.

This woman is one of "1,000 marriage-able girls" brought over on one ship from eastern Europe in the late nineteenth century. Marriage was thought of as both a religious obligation and a rational decision in eastern European Jewish culture, so that arranged marriages were common. Why has this idea largely been replaced among second- and third-generation Jewish-Americans?

Then we were entering the harbor. The land came so near we could almost reach out and touch it. "Look!" said one of the *paesani*. "Green grass and green trees and white sand—just like in the old country!" The others all laughed—loud, not regular laughs—so that Pep wouldn't know that they too had expected things to be different. When we came through that narrow place and into the real harbor everyone was holding their breath. Me too. There were boats going every-where—all sizes and all kinds. There were smoke chimneys smoking and white sails and flags waving and new paint shining. Some boats had bands playing on their decks and all of them were tooting their horns to us and leaving white trails in the water behind them.

"There!" said Pep, raising his hand in a greeting. "There it is! *New York!*"

The tall buildings crowding down to the water looked like the cardboard scenery we had in our plays at the *istituto* [institute].

"Oh I'm so scared!" said Emilia again. "How can I know that man I am going to marry? And what if he doesn't meet me?"

Us other women and girls were going to meet our husbands, or the men to marry, in the iron mine in Missouri. Only the man to marry Emilia lived in New York and was meeting her here. He didn't work in the mines. He played a trumpet and had his own band.

"Look," said Pep. "Brooklyn Bridge! Just opened this year with fireworks and everything."

"And there's Castle Garden."

"Castle Garden! Which? Which is Castle Garden?"

Castle Garden! Castle Garden was the gate to the new land. Everyone wanted to see. But the ship was being pulled off to one side—away from the strange round building.

"Don't get scared," said Pep. "We go just to the pier up the river. Then a government boat brings us back."

Doctors had come on the ship and ordered us inside to examine our eyes and our vaccinations. One old man who couldn't talk and two girls with sore eyes were being sent back to the old country. "O Madonna, make them send me back too!" I prayed. "Don't make me go to Santino!"

About two hours later me and my *paesani* were back at Castle Garden on a government boat, bumping the dock and following Pep across a boardwalk and leaving our bundles with some officers. I wanted to hold onto my bottles of oil—they might get broken—but the officers made me leave those too. Then one by one we went through a narrow door into Castle Garden. The inside was a big, dark room full of dust, with fingers of light coming down from the ceiling. That room was already crowded with poor people from earlier boats sitting on benches and on railings and on the floor. And to one side were a few old tables where food was being sold. Down the center between two railings high-up men were sitting on stools at high desks. And we had to walk in line between those two railings and pass them.

"What is your name? Where do you come from? Where are you going?"

Those men knew all the languages and could tell just by looking what country we came from.

After Pep, it was my turn.

"Cristoforo, Rosa. From Lombardy. To the iron mine in Missouri."

Emilia was holding me by the skirt, so I stayed a little behind to help her. "Gruffiano, Emilia. From San Paola. What, *signore*? You don't know San Paola?"

"She's from Lombardy too," I said. "But she's going to stay in New York."

"And do you know the man I am going to marry, *signore*?" asked Emilia. "See, here's his picture. He has to meet me in Castle Garden. But how can I know him? He plays the *tromba* and owns his own band."

"Get your baggage and come back. Wait by the visitors' door—there at the left. Your name will be called. All right. Move on!"

There were two other desks—one for railroad tickets and one for American money—but we *Lombardi* had ours already so we went back for our bundles. But I couldn't find my straw-covered bottles. Everybody was trying to help me find them. Then an inspector man came. "What's all the commotion?" he asked. "Oh, so those bottles belonged to her? Well ask her," he said to the interpreter. "Ask her what that stuff was? Was it poison?"

When Pep told him he said, "Well tell her her bottles are in the bottom of the ocean! Tell her that's what she gets for bringing such nasty stuff into America! It made us all sick!"

My *paesani* looked at their feet or at the ground and hurried back into the building. Then they busted out laughing. That was a good one! That was really a good one! And even I had to laugh. I was brokenhearted to lose my good oil but it was funny anyway—how Mamma Lena's nice wine bottles had fooled those men in gold braid.

We *Lombardi* put down our bundles and sat on the floor near the visitors' door. At last after all the new immigrants had been checked, an officer at the door started calling the names. "Gruffiano, Emilia" was the first one.

"*Presente! Presente!*" shouted Pep jumping to his feet and waving his hands. But Emilia was so scared I had to pull her up and drag her along after him.

At the door the officer called the name again and let us pass. Then here came

up a young man. He was dressed—O Madonna!—like the president of the United
States! White gloves and a cane and a diamond pin in his tie. Emilia tried to run
away but Pep pulled her back. *"Non è vero! Non è vero!* It's not true!" she kept
saying.

"But it *is* true!" the young man laughed. "Look at me, Emilia! Don't you
remember Carlo who used to play the *tromba* in San Paola when you were a little
girl?" And he pulled her out from behind us and took her in his arms and kissed
her. (In America a man can kiss the girl he is going to marry!) "But I never
thought you would come like this," he said, holding her off a little and looking at
her headkerchief and full skirt. "I'm afraid to look. Did you come in the wooden
soles too?"

"No," said Emilia, speaking to him for the first time. "My mother bought me
real shoes to come to America!" And she was lifting her feet to show him.

"She looks just the same as when she was seven years old," the young man said
to Pep, and he was happy and laughing. "But I'm going to take her up Broad
Street and buy her some American clothes before I take her home."

I was glad for Emilia that she was going to marry that nice young man, but
why couldn't something like this ever happen to me?

Other visitors were called. Some families separated at Havre found each other
again and were happy. But that nice young French girl, she was there all
alone—nobody could find her mother and her sister. I don't think they ever found
each other again.

When the gate was opened men wearing badges came running in, going to the
different people. One dressed-up man with a cane and waxed mustache came to
us. *"Buon giorno, paesani! Benvenuto!* Welcome to America! Welcome to the new
country!" He was speaking Italian and English too and putting out his hand to
shake hands with Pep. The other *paesani* looked on in wonder. A high man like
that shaking hands with the poor! This was America for sure!

"I heard your talk and knew you were my *paesani*. I came to help you. You
have the railroad tickets and the American money?"

"Si, signore," said Pep and we all showed our tickets and our money.

Then Pep asked about the women's chests that had come on an earlier ship.
"Leave it to me," said our new friend. "Leave it to me, your *paesano*, Bartini. I
will find them and send them to Union. And in three days when your train goes I
will put you on myself so you won't go wrong."

"Three days! But no, *signore!* We want to go today."

"My dear man," laughed Bartini, "you're lucky I found you. There's no train to
Missouri for three days. But don't worry! Bartini will take care of everything.
You can come and eat and sleep in my hotel, comfortable and nice, and in three
days I will take you and put you on the right train."

And in three days he did put us on the train but he took all our money first,
about thirteen dollars each one. He left us not even a crust of bread for our
journey. And we didn't even guess that he was fooling us.

The American people on the train were sorry when they saw we had nothing to
eat and they were trying to give us some of their food. But Pep said no. He was too
proud to take it. Me, I would have taken it quick enough. But I couldn't after Pep
said no—even with that little Giorgio crying with his face in my lap. Those
American people were dressed up nice—the ladies had hats and everything—but
they were riding the same class with us poor—all equal and free together.

"Look, Giorgio," I said, to make him forget his pains. "Horses and cows just like in *Italia*. But here there are no shepherds to watch every blade of grass they eat. Here they can go all around and eat what they want."

At last we were in the station in St. Louis changing trains for Union. We were sick for food but everyone was awake now—everyone excited. Domiano could scarcely wait to see her husband, Masino. And Francesca—"Crazy Francesca" —was trying to find out from Pep what kind of a man was waiting to marry her. All the *paesani* were laughing, but not me. Me, I was hiding my rosary in my hand and kissing the cross and trembling inside. "O Madonna," I prayed, "You've got to help me! That man is my husband—I must do what he wants, to not offend God and offend You! But You've got to help me!"

Then the conductor was calling, "Union! Union!" And everybody was picking up bundles and pushing to the windows. There was a little wooden station ahead and beside it were all our *paesani* from the iron mine with two wagons with horses to meet us.

"Look, Rosa, the one with white teeth and black mustache, he's my cousin, Gionin. I think the young man beside him is the one I'm going to marry!"

"He looks nice, Francesca," I said.

I thought maybe Santino didn't come, or maybe I'd forgotten what he looked like. But then I saw him—a little back from the others—just as I remembered him.

Pep, a bundle on his back, was getting off first—laughing and excited—proud that he had brought us new *paesani* all the way from the old country.

"*Benvenuto*, Pep! *Benvenuto, paesani! Benvenuto!* But *Gesu Maria*! Why those three days doing nothing in New York?"

"Bartini said there were no trains for three days."

"No trains for three days! There come two trains every day to Missouri. Wait till we can get our hands on Bartini! But forget it now. Now we are all together. Just a little ride through the woods and you are in your new home. And in camp there is plenty to eat. Can a girl as beautiful as Rosa help cook it?"

It was like a *festa*. Everybody in their best clothes and everybody talking and laughing.

Francesca's cousin Gionin was introducing Francesca to the man she was going to marry, but they didn't know what to say. They just stood there getting red and red. Masino, the husband of Domiana, was laughing and crying at the same time, hugging Domiana, then taking Giorgio in his arms and kissing him. Without looking I could see Santino still back at one side eying me with his half-closed eyes. He did not come to me and I did not go to him. Instead I stood there talking and laughing with the *paesani* who had come to meet us—mostly young men I had known in Bugiarno. Twelve of them were going to eat in my house. I was to cook for them. "But I don't know how to cook!"

"*Per l'amore di Dio* [For the love of God], don't worry about that. We will teach you!"

"Watch close the way we are going, Rosa." It was Gionin, the cousin of Francesca. He was sitting next to me on the wagon. "You will be walking back here every two or three days to get groceries and ask for mail." He was not *Lombardo* like the others—he and his friend were *Toscani*. I had to listen careful to understand his words. But his talk sounded nice and so respectful. "Here in America they have the courthouse and the jail on the square, in place of a church."

The old *paesani* were all asking questions at once of the new ones. They wanted to know about this one and that one and all that had happened in Bugiarno since they went away. Only Santino said nothing. I could see him out of the corner of my eye sitting up near the driver watching me. But somehow I was not so afraid with Gionin beside me. And Gionin was one of the twelve going to eat in my house.

After two or three miles the wagons came out from the woods and there, below, was the iron mine and the camp. Down there there were no trees and no grass—just some shacks made of boards and some railroad tracks. The sun was going down behind the hills and a few miners with picks and sledgehammers were coming out from a tunnel. Other men down in an open place were wheeling away their tools in wheelbarrows. The new *paesani* grew silent—as if they had expected something else—as if they were no longer sure they were going to be millionaires. And me, looking up to see which shack Gionin was pointing to, met the eyes of Santino.

I had never seen houses like these before—nothing but boards. The one where we stopped was larger than the others and had two doors to go in. Me and Santino were going to live in the side we were going in, and Domiana and Masino in the other. There was one large room with a long table and benches and a big cook stove and some shelves with pans and things. Then behind was a little room with an iron-frame bed and straw mattress. Gionin and some of the other men carried in my two chests. Then they came back and put food on the table.

Bread! White bread! Enough for a whole village! And butter to go on it! I ate until I no longer had any pains in my stomach. Then I went back by the stove to watch Gionin. He had built a fire and was making coffee. Never in my life had I made coffee and I would have to learn if I was going to cook for these men in America.

■ ■ ■

As the weeks went by I grew friendly with other Americans too—with old Mr. Miller and his daughter, Miss Mabel, in the store at Union. They were the boss of the store and of the post office, but they were treating me like I was as good as them. "Here's Rosa!" they would say when they saw me come in. "Hello, Rosa! Come in!" And when they saw how much I wanted to speak English they were helping me. And as it grew cold with the winter they made me come in to dry my feet and get warm. And they gave me coffee.

But those saloons in Union were bad. I didn't even want to walk past. Freddy's saloon was the worst. Some of those bad women who lived upstairs were always standing in the window looking out over the half curtain. And Annie, the friend of Santino, always thumbed her nose at me and made faces. She didn't know that I was more happy when he stayed with her than when he came home. Probably she didn't like it that Santino left most of his pay in the pocket of my underskirt so she and his other friends in Freddy's saloon couldn't get it when he was drunk.

Santino had started getting whiskey from some American men who brought it to the camp. More and more he would come home drunk and start beating me. Probably he would like it better if I was not so meek—if I fought with him. But I didn't want to offend God and the Madonna. Gionin couldn't stand it. He would put his head in his hands. Or he would get up and go out. Gionin really loved me—that I knew. And that made me feel not so lonesome. But Gionin couldn't do anything—Santino was my husband.

Jews Without Money

MICHAEL GOLD

Arriving safely in America was only the first step in an extensive process of adjustment for the immigrant. There was usually a long wait at the port of debarkation, embarrassing questions to answer, forms to fill out, a complicated bureaucracy to get past. Then there was a job to find, housing to locate, a new language to learn. The land was strange, and the customs different. In facing this alien and sometimes hostile environment, most immigrants sought out others from their own country, perhaps from their own village. In the Eastern port cities they formed ghettos that were often isolated from the rest of the city yet dependent on its larger political and economic structures. The new land and the new customs put unusual pressure on the immigrant families and often drove a wedge between husband and wife, parents and children.

In what follows, Michael Gold details a remarkable range of immigrant expectation and reality in New York City at the turn of the century. The tension, pathos, and despair that beset his own family, Jews from eastern Europe, are typical of the reactions of many other immigrants. Did your ancestors come to this country with the same illusions as did Gold's? How did they react to the steady erosion of these dreams? Would you have had the courage to persevere?

SAM KRAVITZ, THAT THIEF

"Why did I choose to come to America?" asked my father of himself gravely, as he twisted and untwisted his mustache in the darkness. "I will tell you why: it was because of envy of my dirty thief of a cousin, that Sam Kravitz, may his nose be eaten by the pox.

"All this time, while I was disgracing my family, Sam had gone to America, and was making his fortune. Letters came from him, and were read throughout our village. Sam, in two short years, already owned his own factory for making suspenders. He sent us his picture. It was marveled at by everyone. Our Sam no longer wore a fur cap, a long Jewish coat and peasant boots. No. He wore a fine gentleman's suit, a white collar like a doctor, store shoes and a beautiful round fun-hat called a derby.

"He suddenly looked so fat and rich, this beggarly cobbler's son! I tell you, my liver burned with envy when I heard my father and mother praise my cousin Sam. I knew I was better than him in every way, and it hurt me. I said to my father, 'Give me money. Let me go at once to America to redeem myself. I will make more money than Sam, I am smarter than he is. You will see!'

"My mother did not want me to go. But my father was weary of my many misfortunes, and he gave me the money for the trip. So I came to America. It was the greatest mistake in my life.

■ ■ ■

"I am not discouraged, children. I will make a great deal of money some day. I am a serious married man now and no greenhorn. But then I was still a foolish boy, and though I left Roumania with great plans in my head, in my heart a foolish voice was saying: 'America is a land of fun.'

"How full I was of all the *Baba* stories that were told in my village about America! In America, we believed, people dug under the streets and found gold

Emigration was often the occasion for a family portrait. This is the Boonin Family of Slutzk, Russia in June 1903 just before Mendell, the twenty-year-old son standing between his parents, sailed for Philadelphia. After arriving in the new country he went on to college and became an engineer. His parents died a few years after this picture was taken, and eventually all the other children came to the United States. Perhaps your family has a similar photograph with its own special story.

88 anywhere. In America, the poorest ragpicker lived better than a Roumanian millionaire. In America, people did little work, but had fun all day.

"I had seen two pictures of America. They were shown in the window of a store that sold Singer Sewing Machines in our village. One picture had in it the tallest building I had ever seen. It was called a skyscraper. At the bottom of it walked the proud Americans. The men wore derby hats and had fine mustaches and gold watch chains. The women wore silks and satins, and had proud faces like queens. Not a single poor man or woman was there; every one was rich.

"The other picture was of Niagara Falls. You have seen the picture on postcards; with Indians and cowboys on horses, who look at a rainbow shining over the water.

"I tell you, I wanted to get to America as fast as I could, so that I might look at the skyscrapers and at the Niagara Falls rainbow, and wear a derby hat.

"In my family were about seventy-five relatives. All came to see me leave Roumania. There was much crying. But I was happy, because I thought I was going to a land of fun.

"The last thing my mother did, was to give me my cousin's address in New York, and say: 'Go to Sam. He will help you in the strange land.'

"But I made up my mind I would die first rather than ask Sam for help.

■ ■ ■

"*Nu*, I will not mention how bad I felt when I saw the cigarmaker uncle's home. It was just a big dirty dark room in the back of the cigar store where he made and sold cigars. He, his wife and four children lived in that one room.

"He was not glad to have me there, but he spread newspapers on the floor, and Yossel and I slept on them.

"What does it matter, I thought, this is not America. To-morrow morning I will go out in the streets, and see the real American fun.

"The next morning [my friend] Yossel and I took a long walk. That we might not be lost, we fixed in our minds the big gold tooth of a dentist that hung near the cigar shop.

"We walked and walked. I will not tell you what we saw, because you see it every day. We saw the East Side. To me it was a strange sight. I could not help wondering, where are all the people running? What is happening? And why are they so serious? When does the fun start?

"We came to Allen Street, under the elevated. To show you what a greenhorn I was, I fell in love with the elevated train. I had never seen anything like it in Roumania.

"I was such a greenhorn I believed the elevated train traveled all over America, to Niagara Falls and other places. We rode up and down on it all day. I paid the fare.

"I had some money left. I also bought two fine derby hats from a pushcart; one for Yossel, and one for me. They were a little big, but how proud we felt in these American fun-hats.

"No one wears such hats in Roumania. Both of us had pictures taken in the American fun-hats to send to our parents.

"This foolishness went on for two weeks. Then all my money was gone. So the cigarmaker told me I should find a job and move out from his home. So I found a

Many immigrants filled the hard manual labor jobs. They sold their strength by the hour to provide for their families. Here a group of men break ground for the first subway in New York City about 1900.

job for seven dollars a month in a grocery store. I lived over the store, I rose at five o'clock, and went to bed at twelve in the night. My feet became large and red with standing all day. The grocerman, may the worms find him, gave me nothing to eat but dry bread, old cheese, pickles and other stale groceries. I soon became sick and left that job.

"For a week I sat in Hester Park without a bite of food. And I looked around me, but was not unhappy. Because I tell you, I was such a greenhorn, that I still thought fun would start and I was waiting for it.

"One night, after sleeping on the bench, I was very hungry in the morning and decided to look up my rich cousin, Sam Kravitz. I hated to do this, but was weak with fasting. So I came into my cousin's shop. To hide my shame I laughed out loud.

"'Look, Sam, I am here,' I laughed. 'I have just come off the boat, and am ready to make my fortune.'

"So my cousin Sam gave me a job in his factory. He paid me twenty-five cents a day.

"He had three other men working for him. He worked himself. He looked sick and sharp and poor and not at all like the picture of him in the fun-hat he had sent to Roumania.

"*Nu*, so your father worked. I got over my greenhorn idea that there was nothing but fun in America. I learned to work like every one else. I grew thin as my cousin.

"Soon I came to understand it was not a land of fun. It was a Land of Hurry-Up. There was no gold to be dug in the streets here. Derbies were not fun-hats for holidays. They were work-hats. *Nu*, so I worked! With my hands, my liver and sides! I worked!

"My cousin Sam had fallen into a good trade. With his machines he manufactured the cotton ends of suspenders. These ends are made of cotton, and are very important to a suspender. It is these ends that fasten to the buttons, and hold up the pants. This is important to the pants, as you know.

"Yes, it was a good trade, and a necessary one. There was much money to be made, I saw that at once.

"But my cousin Sam was not a good business man. He had no head for figures and his face was like vinegar. None of his customers liked him.

"Gradually, he let me go out and find business for him. I was very good for this. Most of the big suspender shops were owned by Roumanians who had known my father. They greeted me like a relative. I drank wine with them, and passed jokes. So they gave me their orders for suspender ends.

"So one day, seeing how I built up the business, Sam said: 'You shall be my partner. We are making a great deal of money. Leave the machine, Herman. I will take care of the inside shop work. You go out every day, and joke with our customers and bring in the orders.'

"So I was partners with my cousin Sam. So I was very happy. I earned as much as thirty dollars a week; I was at last a success.

"So a matchmaker came, and said I ought to marry. So he brought me to your momma and I saw at once that she was a kind and hard-working woman. So I decided to marry her and have children.

"So this was done.

"It was then I made the greatest mistake of my life.

"Always I had wanted to see that big water with the rainbow and Indians called Niagara Falls.

"So I took your momma there when we married. I spent a month's wages on the trip. I showed America to your momma. We enjoyed ourselves.

"In a week we came back. I went to the shop the next morning to work again. I could not find the shop. It had vanished. I could not find Sam. He had stolen the shop.

"I searched and searched for Sam and the shop. My heart was swollen like a sponge with hate. I was ready to kill my cousin Sam.

"So one day I found him and the shop. I shouted at him, 'Thief, what have you done?' He laughed. He showed me a paper from a lawyer proving that the shop was his. All my work had been for nothing. It had only made Sam rich.

"What could I do? So in my hate I hit him with my fist, and made his nose bleed. He ran into the street yelling for a policeman. I ran after him with a stick, and beat him some more. But what good could it do? The shop was really his, and I was left a pauper."

■ ■ ■

My proud father. He raved, cursed, worried, he held long passionate conversations with my mother.

"Must I peddle bananas, Katie? I can't do it; the disgrace would kill me!"

"Don't do it," my mother would say gently. "We can live without it."

"But where will I find work?" he would cry. "The city is locked against me! I am a man in a trap!"

"Something will happen. God has not forgotten us," said my mother.

"I will kill myself! I can't stand it! I will take the gas pipe to my nose! I refuse to be a peddler!"

"Hush, the children will hear you," said my mother.

I could hear them thrashing it out at night in the bedroom. They talked about it at the supper table, or sat by the stove in the gloomy winter afternoons, talking, talking. My father was obsessed with the thought of bananas. They became a symbol to him of defeat, of utter hopelessness. And when my mother assured him he need not become a peddler, he would turn on her and argue that it was the one way out. He was in a curious fever of mixed emotions.

Two weeks [later] . . . he was in the street with a pushcart, peddling the accursed bananas.

He came back the first night, and gave my mother a dollar bill and some silver. His face was gray; he looked older by ten years; a man who had touched bottom. My mother tried to comfort him, but for days he was silent as one who has been crushed by a calamity. Hope died in him; months passed, a year passed, he was still peddling bananas.

I remember meeting him one evening with his pushcart. I had managed to sell all my papers and was coming home in the snow. It was that strange, portentous hour in downtown New York when the workers are pouring homeward in the twilight. I marched among thousands of tired men and women whom the factory whistles had unyoked. They flowed in rivers through the clothing factory districts, then down along the avenues to the East Side.

I met my father near Cooper Union. I recognized him, a hunched, frozen figure in an old overcoat standing by a banana cart. He looked so lonely, the tears came to my eyes. Then he saw me, and his face lit with his sad, beautiful smile—Charlie Chaplin's smile.

"Ach, it's Mikey," he said. "So you have sold your papers! Come and eat a banana."

He offered me one. I refused it. I was eleven years old, but poisoned with a morbid proletarian sense of responsibility. I felt it crucial that my father *sell* his bananas, not give them away. He thought I was shy, and coaxed and joked with me, and made me eat the banana. It smelled of wet straw and snow.

"You haven't sold many bananas to-day, pop," I said anxiously.

He shrugged his shoulders.

"What can I do? No one seems to want them."

It was true. The work crowds pushed home morosely over the pavements. The rusty sky darkened over New York buildings, the tall street lamps were lit, innumerable trucks, street cars and elevated trains clattered by. Nobody and nothing in the great city stopped for my father's bananas.

"I ought to yell," said my father dolefully. "I ought to make a big noise like other peddlers, but it makes my throat sore. Anyway, I'm ashamed of yelling, it makes me feel like a fool."

I had eaten one of his bananas. My sick conscience told me that I ought to pay for it somehow. I must remain here and help my father.

"I'll yell for you, pop," I volunteered.

"Ach, no," he said, "go home; you have worked enough to-day. Just tell momma I'll be late."

But I yelled and yelled. My father, standing by, spoke occasional words of praise, and said I was a wonderful yeller. Nobody else paid attention. The workers drifted past us wearily, endlessly; a defeated army wrapped in dreams of home. Elevated trains crashed; the Cooper Union clock burned above us; the sky grew black, the wind poured, the slush burned through our shoes. There were thousands of strange, silent figures pouring over the sidewalks in snow. None of them stopped to buy bananas. I yelled and yelled, nobody listened.

My father tried to stop me at last. "*Nu,*" he said smiling to console me, "that was wonderful yelling, Mikey. But it's plain we are unlucky to-day! Let's go home."

I was frantic, and almost in tears. I insisted on keeping up my desperate yells. But at last my father persuaded me to leave with him. It was after nightfall. We covered the bananas with an oilcloth and started for the pushcart stable. Down Second Avenue we plodded side by side. For many blocks my father was thoughtful. Then he shook his head and sighed:

"So you see how it is, Mikey. Even at banana peddling I am a failure. What can be wrong? The bananas are good, your yelling was good, the prices are good. Yes, it is plain; I am a man without luck."

■　■　■

"Ach, Gott, what a rich country America is! What an easy place to make one's fortune! Look at all the rich Jews! Why has it been so easy for them, so hard for me? I am just a poor little Jew without money."

"Poppa, lots of Jews have no money," I said to comfort him.

"I know it, my son," he said, "but don't be one of them. It's better to be dead in this country than not to have money. Promise me you'll be rich when you grow up, Mikey!"

"Yes, poppa."

"Ach," he said fondly, "this is my one hope now! This is all that makes me happy! I am a greenhorn, but you are an American! You will have it easier than I; you will have luck in America!"

"Yes, poppa," I said, trying to smile with him. But I felt older than he; I could not share his naïve optimism; my heart sank as I remembered the past and thought of the future. At the age of twelve I carried in my mind a morbid load of responsibility.

I had been a precocious pupil in the public school, winning honors not by study, but by a kind of intuition. I graduated a year sooner than most boys. At the exercises I was valedictory orator.

My parents were proud, of course. They wanted me to go on to high school, like other "smart" boys. They still believed I would be a doctor.

But I was morbid enough to be wiser than my parents. Even then I could sense that education is a luxury reserved for the well-to-do. I refused to go to high school. More than half the boys in my graduating class were going to work; I chose to be one of them.

It was where I belonged. I figured it out on paper for my parents. Four years of high school, then six years of college before one could be a doctor. Ten years of study in all, with thousands of dollars needed for books, tuition, and the rest.

There were four of us in my family. My mother seemed unable to work. Would my father's banana peddling keep us alive during those ten years while I was studying?

Of course not. I was obstinate and bitter; my parents wept, and tried to persuade me, but I refused to go to high school.

Miss Barry, the English teacher, tried to persuade me, too. She was fond of me. She stared at me out of wistful blue eyes, with her old maid's earnestness, and said:

"It would be a pity for you to go into a factory. I have never seen better English compositions than yours, Michael."

"I must work, Miss Barry," I said. I started to leave. She took my hand. I could smell the fresh spring lilacs in the brass bowl on her desk.

"Wait," she said earnestly, "I want you to promise me to study at night. I will give you a list of the required high school reading; you can make up your Regents' counts that way. Will you do it?"

"Yes, Miss Barry," I lied to her sullenly.

I was trying to be hard. For years my ego had been fed by every one's praise of my precocity. I had always loved books; I was mad about books; I wanted passionately to go to high school and college. Since I couldn't, I meant to despise all that nonsense.

"It will be difficult to study at night," said Miss Barry in her trembly voice, "but Abraham Lincoln did it, and other great Americans."

"Yes, Miss Barry," I muttered.

She presented me with a parting gift. It was a volume of Emerson's Essays, with her name and my name and the date written on the flyleaf.

I thanked her for the book, and threw it under the bed when I got home. I never read a page in it, or in any book for the next five years. I hated books; they were lies, they had nothing to do with life and work.

It was not easy to find my first job. I hunted for months, in a New York summer of furnace skies and fogs of humidity. I bought the *World* each morning, and ran through the want ads:

Agents Wanted—Addressers Wanted—Barbers Wanted—Bushelmen Wanted—Butchers Wanted—Boys Wanted—

That fateful ad page bringing news of life and death each morning to hundreds of thousands. How often have I read it with gloomy heart. Even to-day the sight of it brings back the ache and hopelessness of my youth.

There was a swarm of boys pushing and yapping like homeless curs at the door of each job. I competed with them. We scrambled, flunkeyed and stood at servile attention under the boss's eye, little slaves on the block.

No one can go through the shame and humiliation of the job-hunt without being marked for life. I hated my first experience at it, and have hated every other since. There can be no freedom in the world while men must beg for jobs.

I rose at six-thirty each morning, and was out tramping the streets at seven. There were always hundreds of jobs, but thousands of boys clutching after them. The city was swarming with these boys, aimless, bewildered and as hungry for work as I was.

I found a job as errand boy in a silk house. But it was temporary. The very first morning the shipping clerk, a refined Nordic, suddenly realized I was a Jew. He politely fired me. They wanted no Jews. In this city of a million Jews, there was much anti-Semitism among business firms. Many of the ads would read: Gentile Only. Even Jewish business houses discriminated against Jews. How often did I slink out of factory or office where a foreman said Jews were not wanted. How often was I made to remember I belonged to the accursed race, the race whose chief misfortune it is to have produced a Christ.

At last I found a job. It was in a factory where incandescent gas mantles were made, a dark loft under the elevated trains on the Bowery near Chatham Square.

This was a spectral place, a chamber of hell, hot and poisoned by hundreds of gas flames. It was suffocating with the stink of chemicals.

I began to sweat immediately. What was worse, I could not breathe. The place terrified me. The boss came up and told me to take off my coat. He was a grim little man, thick as a cask about the middle, and dressed in a gaudy pink silk shirt. He chewed a cigar. His face was morbid and hard like a Jewish gangster's.

"Monkey Face," he called, "show this new kid what to do."

An overgrown Italian boy approached, in pants and undershirt streaked with sweat. His slit nose, ape muzzle, and tiny malicious eyes had earned him his appropriate nickname.

"Come here, kid," he said. I followed him down the loft. There were thirty unfortunate human beings at work. Men sat at a long table testing mantles. Their faces were death masks, fixed and white. Great blue spectacles shielded their eyes.

Little Jewish and Italian girls dipped racks of mantles in chemical tanks. Boys stood before a series of ovens in which sixty gas jets blazed. They passed in the racks for the chemicals to burn off. Every one dripped with sweat; every one was haggard, as though in pain.

"Where did yuh work last?" growled Monkey Face.

"It's my first job. I'm just out of school."

"Yeh?" he snickered. "Just out of school, huh? Well, yuh struck a good job, kid; it'll put hair on your chest. Here, take dis."

I took the iron rack he gave me, and dropped it at once. It scorched my hand. Monkey Face laughed at the joke.

"You son-of-a-bitch!" I said, "it's hot."

He pushed his apish face close to mine.

"Yuh little kike, I'll bite your nose off if yuh get fresh wit' me! I'm your boss around here."

He went away. I worked. Racks of mantles were brought me, and I burned them off. Hell flamed and stank around me. At noon the boss blew a whistle. We sat on benches for our half-hour lunch. I could not eat for nausea. I wanted air, air, but there was no time for air.

There was no time for anything but work in that evil hell-hole. I sweated there for six months. Monkey Face tortured me. I lost fifteen pounds in weight. I raged

Child labor was common in your grandparents' or great-grandparents' generation. Cigars, requiring unskilled drudgery for their manufacture, were often produced by family groups in their tenement flats. Even outside larger urban areas, children were hired to run dangerous machinery for up to sixteen hours a shift. What effect might child labor have had on the family as a social unit? How is the family affected today when fewer young people need to work?

in nightmares in my sleep. I forgot my college dreams; I forgot everything, but the gas mantles.

My mother saw how thin I was becoming. She forced me to quit that job. I was too stupefied to have done this myself. Then I read the Want Ads for another month. I found a job in a dark Second Avenue rat-hole, a little printing shop. Here I worked for another five months until I injured my hand in a press.

Another spell of job-hunting. Then a brief interval in a matzoth bakery. Job in an express company. Job in a mail order house. Job in a dry goods store.

Jobs, jobs. I drifted from one to the other, without plan, without hope. I was one of the many. I was caught like my father in poverty's trap. I was nothing, bound for nowhere.

A young spinner working in a Carolina cotton mill. Did this child benefit in any way from this kind of work? Why did so many people defend work, even for young children, as character building?

At times I seriously thought of cutting my throat. At other times I dreamed of running away to the far west. Sex began to torture me. I developed a crazy religious streak. I prayed on the tenement roof in moonlight to the Jewish Messiah who would redeem the world. . . . I spent my nights in a tough poolroom. I needed desperate stimulants; I was ready for anything. At the age of fifteen I began drinking and whoring . . .

And I worked. And my father and mother grew sadder and older. It went on for years. I don't want to remember it all; the years of my adolescence. Yet I was only one among a million others.

A man on an East Side soap-box, one night, proclaimed that out of the despair, melancholy and helpless rage of millions, a world movement had been born to abolish poverty.

I listened to him.

O workers' Revolution, you brought hope to me, a lonely, suicidal boy. You are the true Messiah. You will destroy the East Side when you come, and build there a garden for the human spirit.

O Revolution, that forced me to think, to struggle and to live.

O great Beginning!

Blood of My Blood

RICHARD GAMBINO

The process by which immigrants adjusted to American society often led to conflict between generations. The first generation usually held onto the old ways—to the religion, language, and customs of the old country—as a means of surviving in the new land. Their sons and daughters, on the other hand, often rejected those old ways (and sometimes their parents) in their efforts to become Americanized. In this short selection Richard Gambino, a third-generation Italian, recounts a childhood incident that vividly demonstrated to him how his grandmother and his parents differed over the old and new ways.

During the first sixteen years of my life I lived in Red Hook, Brooklyn. Still largely Italian today, the area then was almost exclusively composed of Italian-American families, many of whose men were longshoremen on Brooklyn's large waterfront. It was typical of the many "Little Italies" in America, and, incidentally, is the area where Arthur Miller chose to set his forceful play about an Italian-American longshore family, *A View from the Bridge.* Also typical of many families in the Little Italies, I lived with my parents (my father emigrated from Palermo, Sicily, at age thirteen; my mother was born in Red Hook shortly after her parents came from Palermo), and my maternal grandparents.

One of my early memories is of an event that happened when I was perhaps seven years old. One of my closest friends was an Italian immigrant boy named Tony. One winter day, I forget why, Tony and I fought. We tumbled on the ground and hit at each other. Somehow, Tony's nose began to bleed. The sight of the blood on the dirty snow terrified both of us, and we each ran home. Because both my parents worked during the day, I went to my grandparents' basement flat rather than to my own, immediately above it. Of course I kept silent about the fight and the blood, preferring to shiver in fear next to the hot coal stove. In a few minutes, the inevitable happened. The doorbell rang, and I watched with a sense of doom as my grandmother walked the long corridor to the outside "gate" of the old brownstone. I thought my fate was sealed a minute later when I heard her call to me in the uniquely sharp, decisive Sicilian dialect, *Veni icca!* (come here!) My second-generation mother had taught me that fighting was wrong, that hurting someone was wrong, and sometimes reinforced these and other lessons of American morality by spankings. I was thus totally unprepared for the scene I found at the gate. There was my grandmother, a big woman, standing in the doorway facing Tony's mother, totally blocking the latter's view. My grandmother stood squarely on both feet, hands resting on hips, palms turned *outward* from the body—the reverse of the American manner. In the body language of Southern Italy, the stance's meaning was unmistakable—"Don't tread on me or mine!" The two women were engaged in delivering ritual insults to each other, in hissing voices, almost spitting as they spoke. Southern Italians have a name for a game of ritualized oratory—*passatella*. The gist of my grandmother's part of this serious passatella was that Tony was a worthless son of worthless blood and it was a *vergogna* (outrage) to allow him to walk the streets with her *nipotino* (fine little grandson). This was news to me—my grandmother often saw me play with Tony and previously had spoken to his mother with courtesy, hence as a peer. After the confrontation, back inside the house, my grandmother asked me what had happened. Her only comment upon my explanation was that since I shed Tony's blood, *he* must have committed some *infamia* (infamy)!

I was astonished. My mother, when informed by my teacher of some misbehavior on my part in school, had automatically taken the teacher's side and promised me a beating when I came home—a promise kept. But my grandmother's only punishment to me was a one-sentence lecture on choosing my companions more carefully. She did not even mention the incident to my "American" parents.

My parents were embarked on the *via nuova* (new way), and I suppose my grandmother, in accordance with a Sicilian proverb, considered them too far down the road to recognize what was demanded in such a family confrontation. The proverb is, *Chi lascia la via vecchia per la nuova, sa quel che perde e non sa quel che trova*—"Whoever forsakes the old way for the new knows what he is losing but not what he will find."

Stelmark: A Family Recollection

HARRY MARK PETRAKIS

Sometimes the conflict between generations extended beyond the family into the community and even involved something as ordinary as food. In this selection, Harry

Petrakis recalls how he was taught a lesson about his Greek heritage by a neighborhood grocer.

"You were the one," he said, finally, in a harsh voice.

I nodded mutely.

"Why did you come back?"

I stood there unable to answer.

"What's your name?"

"Haralambos," I said, speaking to him in Greek.

He looked at me in shock. "You are Greek!" he cried. "A Greek boy attacking a Greek grocer!" He stood appalled at the immensity of my crime. "All right," he said coldly. "You are here because you wish to make amends." His great mustache bristled in concentration. "Four plums, two peaches," he said. "That makes a total of 78 cents. Call it 75. Do you have 75 cents, boy?"

I shook my head.

"Then you will work it off," he said. "Fifteen cents an hour into 75 cents makes"—he paused—"five hours of work. Can you come here Saturday morning?"

"Yes," I said.

"Yes, Barba Nikos," he said sternly. "Show respect."

"Yes, Barba Nikos," I said.

"Saturday morning at eight o'clock," he said. "Now go home and say thanks in your prayers that I did not loosen your impudent head with a solid smack on the ear." I needed no further urging and fled.

Saturday morning, still apprehensive, I returned to the store. I began by sweeping, raising clouds of dust in dark and hidden corners. I washed the windows, whipping the squeegee swiftly up and down the glass in a fever of fear

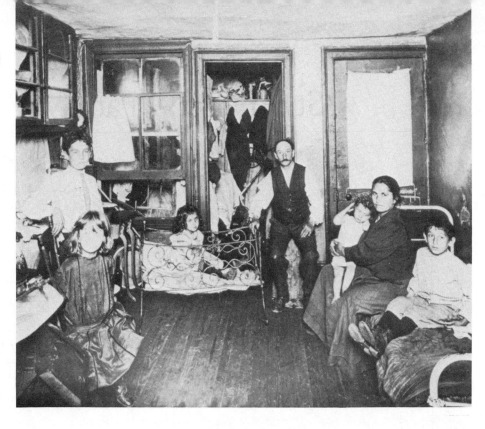

Having survived the sea voyage in crowded, unsanitary ships, immigrants who settled in cities often faced a similar situation in their living quarters. The one-room flats that families generally occupied made privacy impossible and increased family tensions.

that some member of the gang would see me. When I finished I hurried back inside.

For the balance of the morning I stacked cans, washed the counter, and dusted bottles of yellow wine. A few customers entered, and Barba Nikos served them. A little after twelve o'clock he locked the door so he could eat lunch. He cut himself a few slices of sausage, tore a large chunk from a loaf of crisp-crusted bread, and filled a small cup with a dozen black shiny olives floating in brine. He offered me the cup. I could not help myself and grimaced.

"You are a stupid boy," the old man said. "You are not really Greek, are you?"

"Yes, I am."

"You might be," he admitted grudgingly. "But you do not act Greek. Wrinkling your nose at these fine olives. Look around this store for a minute. What do you see?"

"Fruits and vegetables," I said. "Cheese and olives and things like that."

He stared at me with a massive scorn. "That's what I mean," he said. "You are a bonehead. You don't understand that a whole nation and a people are in this store."

I looked uneasily toward the storeroom in the rear, almost expecting someone to emerge.

"What about olives?" he cut the air with a sweep of his arm. "There are olives of many shapes and colors. Pointed black ones from Kalamata, oval ones from Amphissa, pickled green olives and sharp tangy yellow ones. Achilles carried black olives to Troy and after a day of savage battle leading his Myrmidons, he'd rest and eat cheese and ripe black olives such as these right here. You have heard of Achilles, boy, haven't you?"

"Yes," I said.

"Yes, Barba Nikos."

"Yes, Barba Nikos," I said.

He motioned at the row of jars filled with varied spices. "There is origanon there and basilikon and daphne and sesame and miantanos, all the marvelous flavorings that we have used in our food for thousands of years. The men of Marathon carried small packets of these spices into battle, and the scents reminded them of their homes, their families, and their children."

He rose and tugged his napkin free from around his throat. "Cheese, you said. Cheese! Come closer, boy, and I will educate your abysmal ignorance." He motioned toward a wooden container on the counter. "That glistening white delight is feta, made from goat's milk, packed in wooden buckets to retain the flavor. Alexander the Great demanded it on his table with his casks of wine when he planned his campaigns."

He walked limping from the counter to the window where the piles of tomatoes, celery, and green peppers clustered. "I suppose all you see here are some random vegetables?" He did not wait for me to answer. "You are dumb again. These are some of the ingredients that go to make up a Greek salad. Do you know what a Greek salad really is? A meal in itself, an experience, an emotional involvement. It is created deftly and with grace. First, you place large lettuce leaves in a big, deep bowl." He spread his fingers and moved them slowly, carefully, as if he were arranging the leaves. "The remainder of the lettuce is shredded and piled in a small mound," he said. "Then comes celery, cucumbers, tomatoes sliced lengthwise, green peppers, origanon, green olives, feta, avocado, and anchovies. At the end you dress it with lemon, vinegar, and pure olive oil, glinting golden in the light."

He finished with a heartfelt sigh and for a moment closed his eyes. Then he opened one eye to mark me with a baleful intensity. "The story goes that Zeus himself created the recipe and assembled and mixed the ingredients on Mount Olympus one night when he had invited some of the other gods to dinner."

He turned his back on me and walked slowly again across the store, dragging one foot slightly behind him. I looked uneasily at the clock, which showed that it was a few minutes past one. He turned quickly and startled me. "And everything else in here," he said loudly. "White beans, lentils, garlic, crisp bread, kokoretsi, meat balls, mussels and clams." He paused and drew a deep, long breath. "And the wine," he went on, "wine from Samos, Santorini, and Crete, retsina and mavrodaphne, a taste almost as old as water . . . and then the fragrant melons, the pastries, yellow diples and golden loukoumades, the honey custard galatobouriko. Everything a part of our history, as much a part as the exquisite sculpture in marble, the bearded warriors, Pan and the oracles at Delphi, and the nymphs dancing in the shadowed groves under Homer's glittering moon." He paused, out of breath again, and coughed harshly. "Do you understand now, boy?"

He watched my face for some response and then grunted. We stood silent for a moment until he cocked his head and stared at the clock. "It is time for you to leave," he motioned brusquely toward the door. "We are square now. Keep it that way."

I decided the old man was crazy and reached behind the counter for my jacket and cap and started for the door. He called me back. From a box he drew out several soft, yellow figs that he placed in a piece of paper. "A bonus because you worked well," he said. "Take them. When you taste them, maybe you will understand what I have been talking about."

I took the figs and he unlocked the door and I hurried from the store. I looked back once and saw him standing in the doorway, watching me, the swirling tendrils of food curling like mist about his head.

I ate the figs late that night. I forgot about them until I was in bed, and then I rose and took the package from my jacket. I nibbled at one, then ate them all. They broke apart between my teeth with a tangy nectar, a thick sweetness running like honey across my tongue and into the pockets of my cheeks. In the morning when I woke, I could still taste and inhale their fragrance.

I never again entered Barba Nikos's store. My spell of illness, which began some months later, lasted two years. When I returned to the streets I had forgotten the old man and the grocery. Shortly afterwards my family moved from the neighborhood.

Some twelve years later, after the war, I drove through the old neighborhood and passed the grocery. I stopped the car and for a moment stood before the store. The windows were stained with dust and grime, the interior bare and desolate, a store in a decrepit group of stores marked for razing so new structures could be built.

I have been in many Greek groceries since then and have often bought the feta and Kalamata olives. I have eaten countless Greek salads and have indeed found them a meal for the gods. On the holidays in our house, my wife and sons and I sit down to a dinner of steaming, buttered pilaf like my mother used to make and lemon-egg avgolemono and roast lamb richly seasoned with cloves of garlic. I drink the red and yellow wines, and for dessert I have come to relish the delicate pastries coated with honey and powdered sugar. Old Barba Nikos would have been pleased.

But I have never been able to recapture the halcyon flavor of those figs he gave me on that day so long ago, although I have bought figs many times. I have found them pleasant to my tongue, but there is something missing. And to this day I am not sure whether it was the figs or the vision and passion of the old grocer that coated the fruit so sweetly I can still recall their savor and fragrance after almost thirty years.

ASSIGNMENT 3

An Essay on the Migration of Your People

In this assignment you will work with your instructor and librarian to locate your ancestors in the stream of the great migrations. Your emphasis will be on history rather than on biography, however, as you study the uprooting and movement of the group to which your ancestors belonged.

To begin, ask yourself where any one of your ancestors lived one hundred years ago today. Locate that place on a map. Gather some basic information on that country and/or locality from your library. Have your librarian help you to find pertinent information from microfilmed newspapers, government documents, magazines, and photographs. Check pages 368–372 in the Appendix for a list of books on immigration and on specific ethnic groups. Among the topics that you might focus on are the patterns of family life, the religious beliefs, the distribution of land, foods, value systems, educational and social facilities, male-female relationships, songs, legends, celebrations, and the like, in the place your ancestors lived.

You should also look for statistics on the migration patterns of members of your ancestor's ethnic or racial group, where they tended to go, when, and in what numbers. You might construct a line or bar graph that illustrates the movement of that people over time to the United States. In some cases longstanding patterns of settlement would later change dramatically. This is particularly true of the Afro-American experience. After forced migration on slave ships, many generations of blacks resided in the South during the slave period and for two or three generations thereafter. The movement of the majority of black Americans from the rural South to the urban North constitutes a second major migration, a pattern that has also been followed by other American immigrant groups to a lesser extent. On the other hand, you may be a representative of a family that is unusual by American standards of mobility in that it has remained rooted for a century or more. If so, ample family records should be close at hand. Most Americans, however, must look to an "old place" to find their past.

Although the primary objective of this assignment is the gathering of information, you might use your historical studies to construct a theory explaining why so many of your ancestor's people were forced to leave home and find a new life elsewhere. If you do this, try to locate some materials that describe the "mid-passage" of people like your ancestor. How did they travel across seas or on land, and under what conditions?

This assignment is based on the assumption, in Alex Haley's words, that "Any individual's past is the essence of the millions." Although you may not have the factual data at hand to write specifically of your own ancestors, enough primary and secondary sources exist to permit you to reconstruct both the causes and effects of a move like the one your ancestors once made. Be sure you have a sense of conditions in the old place (either here or in another country), including prevailing cultural patterns, social and economic class structure, migration trends, and so on.

America Comes of Age: The Great War and the Twenties

By the end of the 1920s, American life had become more complex than were earlier periods. In fact, the American landscape of the twenties has more similarity to our own times than to the preindustrial "world we have lost." Automobiles, advertising, spectator sports, consumerism, and concern about moral decline emerged as major pleasures and preoccupations during this period.

The dynamics of the decade produced a variety of lasting images, the most appealing of which is the caricature of an endless party. Bathtub gin, jazz, speakeasies, bootleggers, racoon coats, and Stutz Bearcat cars surrounded the era's heroes and villains. Principal players included Babe Ruth, Al Capone, Calvin Coolidge, Jack Dempsey, Gene Tunney, Henry Ford, Charles Lindbergh, Charlie Chaplin, Clara Bow, flappers, and fundamentalists. Even Presidents lent themselves to appropriate stereotyping. Warren Gamaliel Harding personified the backroom poker games, drinks, and cigars of the small-town Main Street businessman. Coolidge, the grim-faced, silent reminder of stern Puritanical manners, somehow proved a popular figure in a hell-raising age. While the image of a decade lost in revelry does suggest some of the period's essential significance, there is much more worth examining.

The twenties immediately followed what was once known as "the Great War," an event of enormous importance both in world affairs and in the lives of countless young Americans. Hundreds of thousands of men and boys were swept up from conventional lives in cities and towns and country crossroads, often transported to exotic places, to experiences of danger and adventure. This generation brought to the twenties its energy and unconventional spirit.

In the new decade, enthusiasms threatened tradition in many, often conflicting, ways. One major drive was the making of money. While President Coolidge solemnly intoned that "The business of America is business," millions of big and small entrepreneurs, stock speculators and company managers, went after production and profit with a frenzy.

None spoke for this class and its ideals better than did Henry Ford. He lifted to a new high the American genius for applying scientific theories to useful products. By the twenties, Ford had developed a functional automobile in the square black Model T, had perfected a cheap and efficient assembly line for its mass production, and paid his workers enough so that they bought Fords as well as made them. Ford not only put America on wheels, itself an unsettling change, he also attempted to provide a philosophical justification for an American value system centered around business, production, and consumption.

For many Americans, materialism, with its windfall of new and exciting products, transformed life in the most fundamental ways. What we now take for granted amazed our ancestors. Imagine experiencing, for the first time, electricity and all it could power; ordinary homes filled up with radios, small appliances, refrigerators, phono-graphs, telephones, indoor plumbing, even fountain pens. Moving pictures talked and became America's favorite form of relaxation. Americans bought up and delighted in these products that quickly changed the ways in which they lived, worked, and enjoyed themselves. And many younger Americans did enjoy themselves in ways that their elders found scandalous.

Divorce rates increased throughout the decade; and there was a general sense of decline in modesty. Preachers delivered endless sermons decrying immorality, particularly among young women, many of whom had begun to clothe themselves without benefit of traditional layers of undergarments. Automobiles provided the young with mobility and privacy. Cigarette smoking became fashionable. Many Americans flouted both propriety and legality by openly violating Prohibition laws, in the process consuming oceans of often-vile homemade alcoholic concoctions.

Perhaps these displays of social adventurism were the normal results of a generation experiencing the first fruits of a newly mature economy that was spewing forth consumer goods. Some Americans undoubtedly found material pleasures a welcome relief from the idealism that took the country into the brutal failure of the Great War. Millions upon millions lay dead or maimed by a war that caused more problems than it solved. Writers and artists rejected the military rhetoric and the narrowness of the Calvin Coolidge–Henry Ford world view, reinforcing the mood of relaxed morality and social adventure. The twenties witnessed an astonishing explosion of superb novels, plays, poetry, music, and painting. In New York City's Harlem, an artistic black renaissance combined high aesthetic form with black rage, a feeling that would remain submerged for another generation.

While these changes began to emerge, tradition was still the way of life across the American landscape. Rural America in the 1920s was little affected by either the social and cultural trends or by the business boom. Indeed, many farmers' incomes declined steadily as the foreign markets created by the war disappeared. In some rural areas, modernity was met head on. In 1925, the dozing country town of Dayton, Tennessee, hosted a criminal trial of the local biology teacher, John Scopes, who stood accused of teaching the evolutionary theories of Charles Darwin. Modern science locked horns with fundamental religion in a struggle that has not yet ended.

Other traditionalist reactions included the roundup of political subversives and a general intolerance of dissent, particularly from "foreigners," a term often applied to the new generation of immigrants. In the winter of 1919–1920, a so-called "Big Red Scare" brought in suspected radicals, many of whom were deported. Affected by this event, and later arrested tor armed robbery and murder on the flimsiest circumstantial evidence, were two Boston-area Italian workers, Nicola Sacco and Bartolomeo Vanzetti. Their subsequent trial and execution became a cause for the entire generation. At the same time, Congress passed exclusionary immigration laws; and racism and segregation continued, sometimes through Ku Klux Klan activity.

The conflicts over social and cultural values were set in a context dominated by dynamic business and technological change. Major corporations developed and expanded. Machines performed miracles and begat better and more complex machines, which produced almost without regard for the individual worker. Skilled craftsmen became machine tenders. The extraordinary reception given Charles Lindbergh in 1927 suggests a celebration of one individual's ability to tame and use a complicated machine for his own purposes. "The Lone Eagle" provided a reminder of American individualism in a new technological age.

The same need produced the "golden era" of American sports heroes: home-run hitter Babe Ruth, boxers Jack Dempsey and Gene Tunney, football hero Harold "Red" Grange, and tennis star. Bill Tilden. Spectator sports emerged from the decade as a permanent preoccupation, presaging the time when more Americans would use technology to watch others play sports than to participate themselves.

The twenties created tendencies and forces that were soon to dominate modern American lite: technological advances, consumerism, and a dominant business culture. America remains delighted with its seemingly endless capacity to produce and consume. Yet even in today's corporate age, Americans emulate their ancestors by insisting on seeing themselves as individualists, questioning even as they accept, searching for personal fulfillment amidst standardized productivity. Eccentricity is probably losing the social and cultural battle, but eccentrics continue to defy the dominance of mass culture.

A Diary of the Front Lines

The effects of World War I can hardly be overestimated. Ancient empires collapsed, revolutionary socialism triumphed in Russia, the United States emerged as the world's leading economic power, and the European states began a period of instability that was to culminate in an even greater cataclysm twenty years later. More than 65 million men had been mobilized for this first modern war. Within five years, 40 million had been killed or wounded.

Over a million Americans played a role in the war, which began in August 1914 and ended in November 1918. Even before the United States finally entered the stalemated struggle, many Americans had volunteered for the Allied cause. The United States' entry in the spring of 1917, with its war production and about 1 million officers and men, began to tip the military balance on the western front. The 115,000 American fatalities and the unsatisfactory aftereffects of this unsuccessful "crusade" convinced most Americans that the spending of money and lives had been a tragic error.

This American army, the first to fight in Europe, returned home having been "educated" by harsh yet revealing experiences. An anonymous junior officer's reflections follow. This generation of young Americans headed into the postwar years with a new angle on what life offered. Most of them were prepared to accept and exploit a society quite different from the America of their parents.

HORSES, MEN AND GUNS

Up and At 'Em

VALDAHON, *August 22, 1918.*—Doc Duffy says I probably will live if I can make it as far as the Front where men are men and hospitals are few. He says I've had influenza—which seems to be the medical equivalent of a disorderly conduct charge. I have it yet, for that matter, but raw eggs and cognac seem to be easing the pain between my knees and furnishing an excuse for a slight mental wooziness.

It is now that witching hour just after taps and the camp is theoretically silent. The war that Duff talked about an hour ago seems to be quite a distance from here. This is the top of the world where it is always twilight. There is a misty glow to the southeast where France steps up into the Alps. White roads blend with it. The groves over there on the rim of the plateau are frosty under it.

World War I recruiting posters appealed to young men's patriotism and masculinity. It was easy to believe that one was making the world safe for democracy. Was there a difference between the ideal pictured here and the reality of war?

One might sit here and become quite romantic over the wistful beauty of this lovely butcher shop, were it not for the yammering of the female warriors in comic opera uniforms who occupy the Y.M.C.A. barracks next door. The girls apparently have their hearts in their work. All day long they rush at breakneck speed in their little flivver trucks from one Y.M.C.A. hut to another Y.M.C.A. hut and back again, much as Joan of Arc might have done had she been a Y.M.C.A. truck driver—each striving to win the war in her own little way. And at night they are too tired to sleep and so discuss tactics and maneuver with one another while a phonograph blats the martial strains of "Allah's Holiday," "There's a Long, Long Trail," "Over There," and "Missouri Waltz."

And to-morrow all this is over for us.

"We pull out at 2 o'clock," Duff said when he came in with his raw eggs. "I told Hackett you'd be O.K. for the trip. You may croak on the road—that's a chance—

but if you stay here you'll have to go to the post hospital and in a week they'll be hanging your boots on a strange horse and dragging you out to a permanent emplacement on a Fifth Division caisson. . . . Take your pick, kid. . . ."

So Duff dressed me and packed my trunk for shipment to the American Express dump in Paris. He'll be back after me in the morning and then, God willing, we shall set out arm in arm or stirrup to stirrup to do deeds of high emprise. As executive I shall be in command of the column as far as Besançon or some such silly place while the battery commander rides forward to take ready for us on the loading platform, and even in my present delirium I can foresee that the battery is likely to find itself in Switzerland unless the raw eggs and alcohol hold out. . . . But, what ho! maybe the Doc will be able to see the road and it is time that he learned something about artillery maneuver. He can have the parade. I shall watch him with interest, providing I am able to stick on the horse.

In the meantime I am sitting here pinned in a blanket, looking out upon the sheer beauty of a moonlit night and starting upon this journal, which one day may enlighten an expectant world and then again may come to an ignominious and useless end in the mud of a ditch.

A woman—one of the Y.M.C.A. ladies—is telling the palpitant night that she "won't come back till it's over, over there." A woman . . . possibly the loneliness wouldn't seem quite so poignant—the old life so far away—if she could contrive somehow to leave music to the nightingales.

To-morrow there will be no women even remotely connected with our lives. You are going to the wars, my lads, to the jolly old wars . . . horses and men and guns and men and horses. The Great Adventure. . . . That's what we came here for . . . what we've been asking for. But it may not be all delirium that suggests the thought that some of us are going forward gayly to a permanent berth in Ragnarok.

Across the parade ground the men's barracks are still. The Cannoneers don't know yet, probably, that to-morrow's reveille will see them on their way to green fields and pastures new. If they have been told in advance it is likely that all of them feel the same as I do about the projected trip. They know also that death has enlisted with us, but of course they feel only an impersonal interest in the matter. Every cannoneer knows that somebody will presently be mustered out. But each one knows that he will not be the one. The psychology of battles is that somebody else's widow is going to collect the insurance.

■ ■ ■

LIMBERS FRONT AND REAR

Mark Time

BOUÇONVILLE, *September 12, Three P.M.*—At three o'clock the prisoners began to come in. The battle had reached its third phase. . . . First the withdrawal of the wounded . . . second the advance of the engineers . . . third the prisoners. . . .

The men arose from their beds in the mud and went forward to give the newcomers greeting. There was no doubting the genuineness of the interest they

Strict rules of segregation were maintained throughout the war, in combat and on the homefront. This photograph shows a black social club in Newark, New Jersey, in 1918.

displayed in the procession of *feld grau*. For the first time they were face to face with the Boche and they were anxious to see how he fitted in with his press notices.

The cannoneers expected to see stalwart Prussians, fierce of mien and proud of bearing. It was not to be expected that our mysterious targets out there in the blue would prove to be anything like the Heinies we used to know in Milwaukee and St. Louis. Thanks to advertising the soldats had unconsciously endowed this warrior— "the Hun"—with a sort of diabolical personality. Hence curiosity mingled with distrust as four complete gun crews lined the road to watch the passing of the enemy.

They were disappointed. In the lead was a young lieutenant . . . A Prussian— his cap button branded him for that—but otherwise an everyday sort of lad. He was chubby and pink. As ferocious as a fat, contented baby. The haughty demeanor, the pride of position, supposedly so essential to the German officer's well-being, were lacking here. The warrior didn't have time to be haughty. He was too busy displaying his pleasure at having been captured.

Doubtless he had expected to be bayoneted promptly—for Americans, according to the Boche propaganda issued for home consumption, were a wild lot with no regards for the rights or hide of a loyal German. After recovering from his disappointment at being allowed to remain alive, the lieutenant decided to act like a good loser. And he did.

Behind him were two boys about fourteen years old, thin, hollow-eyed and frightened. They had in their woe-begone faces that hungry-dog look that a man cannot steel himself against.

The men by the roadside looked on in surprised silence. Could this be a sample of the wonderful German army? Some of these children wore the emblem of the guards. Was it possible that this crack organization was so near dissolution that fourteen-year-old boys were admitted to its rolls?

They pondered these things as the bedraggled procession passed on.

One youth, fifteen years old perhaps, a fat, redheaded lad of the butcher-boy type, was staggering forward under the weight of his own machine gun. He was smiling at everybody who cast a glance his way. Behind him was a taller boy, maybe a year older, seeing nothing, hearing nothing. The tears were streaming down his wan cheeks and the stamp of disgrace was evident in every feature.

Two others, both under seventeen years, carried a stretcher. A third boy was under the gray blanket, unconscious. Lieut. Stier looked down at his impassive face as they passed by.

"Good God!" he exclaimed. "Have we been pumping cyanogen for ten hours on to these kids?"

"Probably not," I told him. "The lads who got the cyanogen won't be here. They're still up on Mont Sec."

But to all who looked at the captured ones there had come suddenly a changed point of view—a new appraisal of the enemy. As a foeman he must still be respected but rather as a spent fighter who summons all his strength for a losing battle than as the legendary paladin of yesterday. If these prisoners are typical of Germany's man power, then Germany is about finished.

The prisoners looked wonderingly at the concentration of artillery—all of their march since their entry into the allied lines had been for miles and miles between rows of active guns. They seemed to realize now something of the resources pitted against them.

"Verdun," murmured one hatchet-faced sergeant gazing over the field where as far as the eye could see rifles and howitzers lay scattered scarcely ten meters apart. And everyone—German and American—understood what he meant.

■ ■ ■

Shell-fire and Ooze

STILL HERE, *September 24.*—Well, somebody has discovered that our range in this lovely bower is so limited that we can only shoot ourselves in the foot. So we are going to move out. We'll probably nest again in some swamp where the ammunition dumps will be marked by buoys. *C'est la guerre!*

Just before we pulled in here we discovered a good excuse for fighting this war.

An American balloon was up—somewhere over near Esnes. As we stood blocked in the road a Boche aëroplane came out of a cloud bank to attack. The air had cleared a bit since morning and the sun was in sight late in the day, but there were still enough remnants of storm to give Heinie cover in his approach and he was on top of the balloon and opening up with his machine gun before the crew below started to haul it in. Then it was too late. There was the usual burst of flame. The observer jumped.

About a thousand feet down the parachute opened and all of us stood by to watch a ghastly drama. The burning sausage was dropping about twice as fast as the parachute and squarely above it. The observer didn't have a Chinaman's chance.

There was something sickening about the whole thing. Thousands of soldiers along the American Front must have been standing as we stood, nauseated and helpless, while the flame came tumbling down.

But horrible as it was, the Boche aviator seemed to think that something was lacking in the tragedy. He swooped past the balloon and straightened out above the parachute and to one side. Once more he let go the machine gun.

A helpless foe hung there as his target and he emptied his clip. It made no difference to the observer of course. His doom was hardly twenty seconds above him when the Boche left. But the cold-blooded murder of it brought a roar from a hundred thousand throats . . . a massed curse that would have silenced a barrage. Nobody who heard will ever forget it.

■ ■ ■

Letters from Black Migrants*

Among the paradoxes that abound in history is the equivocal effect of war. World War I, occasion of hideous carnage on the battlefields of Europe, provided opportunity for black people in America. Brutalized by Jim Crow segregationist rule throughout the South, blacks sought salvation in Northern cities, where a combination of full war production and labor shortages meant steady work at decent pay. One indication of this mass movement is revealed in census records, which show staggering net population losses of blacks in the Deep South between 1910 and 1920: 130,000 from Mississippi, 70,000 from Alabama, 74,000 from South Carolina, 75,000 from Georgia. Where did they go? To New York City and Philadelphia, to Cleveland and the other industrial cities of Ohio, to Chicago, Detroit, and St. Louis. This was the beginning of a major demographic movement that has continued into the 1980s, a movement with profound implications in twentieth-century American history. Although the statistical data are sterile, the letters that follow, written to The Defender, a Chicago black newspaper, indicate the full range of human emotions accompanying this extraordinary uprooting.

Dallas, Tex., April 23, 1917.

Dear Sir: Having been informed through the Chicago Defender paper that I can secure information from you. I am a constant reader of the Defender and am contemplating on leaving here for some point north. Having your city in view I thought to inquire of you about conditions for work, housing, wages and everything necessary. I am now employed as a laborer in a structural shop, having worked for the firm five years. I stored cars for Armour packing co. 3 years, I also claims to know something about candy making, am handy at most anything for an honest living. I am 31 yrs. old, have a very industrious wife, no children. If chances are available for work of any kind let me know. Any information you can give me will be highly appreciated.

Memphis, Tenn., May 22nd, 1917.

Sir: As you will see from the above that I am working in an office somewhat similar to the one I am addressing, but that is not the purpose with which I sat out to write.

---

*Arrangement of letters and headings is supplied by the editors.

What I would like best to know is can you secure me a position there? I will not say that I am capable of doing any kind of labor as I am not. Have had an accidental injury to my right foot; hence I am incapable of running up and down stairs, but can go up and down by taking my time. I can perform janitors duties, tend bar, or grocery store, as clerk. I am also a graduate of the Law Department, Howard University, Washington, D. C. Class of '85 but this fact has not swelled my head. I am willing to do almost anything that I can do that there is a dollar to it.

I am a man of 63 years of age. Lived here all of my life, barring 5 or 6 years spent in Washington and the East. Am a christian, Baptist by affiliation.

Have been a teacher, clerk in the government department, Law and Pension offices, for 5 years, also a watchman in the War Dept., also collector and rental agent for the late R. R. Church, Esq. Member of Canaan Baptist Church, Covington, Tenn. Now this is the indictment I plead to.

Sir, If you can place me I will be willing to pay anything in reason for the service. I have selected a place to stop with a friend of earlier days at——, whenever I can get placed there. An early reply will be appreciated by yours respectfully.

Palestine, Tex., Mar. 11th, 1917.

Sirs: this is somewhat a letter of information I am a colored Boy aged 15 years old and I am talented for an artist and I am in search of some one will Cultivate my talent I have studied Cartooning therefore I am a Cartoonist and I intend to visit Chicago this summer and I want to keep in touch with your association and too from you knowledge can a Colored boy be an artist and make a white man's salary up there I will tell you more and also send a fiew samples of my work when I rec an answer from you.

Alexandria, La., June 6, 1917.

Dear Sirs: I am writeing to you all asking a favor of you all. I am a girl of seventeen. School has just closed I have been going to school for nine months and I now feel like I aught to go to work. And I would like very very well for you all to please forward me to a good job. but there isnt a thing here for me to do, the wages here is from a dollar and a half a week. What could I earn Nothing. I have a mother and father my father do all he can for me but it is so hard. A child with any respect about her self or his self wouldnt like to see there mother and father work so hard and earn nothing I feel it my duty to help. I would like for you all to get me a good job and as I havent any money to come on please send me a pass and I would work and pay every cent of it back and get me a good quite place to stay. My father have been getting the defender for three or four months but for the last two weeks we have failed to get it. I dont know why. I am tired of down hear in this——/ I am afraid to say. Father seem to care and then again dont seem to but Mother and I am tired tired of all of this I wrote to you all because I believe you will help I need your help hopeing to here from you all very soon.

New Orleans, La., June 10, 1917.

Kind Sir: I read and hear daly of the great chance that a colored parson has in Chicago of making a living with all the priveleg that the whites have and it mak me the most ankious to want to go where I may be able to make a liveing for my self. When you read this you will think it bery strange that being only my self to support that it is so hard, but it is so. everything is gone up but the poor colerd peple wages. I have made sevle afford to leave and come to Chicago where I hear that times is good for us but owing to femail wekness has made it a perfect failure. I am a widow for 9 years. I have very pore learning altho it would not make much diffrent if I would be throughly edacated for I could not get any better work to do, such as house work, washing and ironing and all such work that are injering to a woman with femail wekness and they pay so little for so hard work that it is just enough to pay room rent and a little some thing to eat. I have found a very good remady that I really feeling to belive would cure me if I only could make enough money to keep up my madison and I don't think that I will ever be able to do that down hear for the time is getting worse evry day. I am going to ask if you peple hear could aid me in geting over her in Chicago and seeking out a position of some kind. I can also do plain sewing. Please good peple dont refuse to help me out in my trouble for I am in gret need of help God will bless you. I am going to do my very best after I get over here if God spair me to get work I will pay the expance back. Do try to do the best you can for me, with many thanks for so doing I will remain as ever,
Yours truly.

Mobile, Ala., April 25, 1917.

Sir: I was reading in that paper about the Colored race and while reading it I seen in it where cars would be here for the 15 of May which is one month from to day. Will you be so kind as to let me know where they are coming to and I will be glad to know because I am a poor woman and have a husband and five children living and three dead one single and two twin girls six months old today and my husband can hardly make bread for them in Mobile. This is my native home but it is not fit to live in just as the Chicago Defender say it says the truth and my husband only get $1.50 a day and pays $7.50 a month for house rent can hardly feed me and his self and children. I am the mother of 8 children 25 years old and I want to get out of this dog hold because I dont know what I am raising them up for in this place and I want to get to Chicago where I know they will be raised and my husband crazy to get there because he know he can get more to raise his children and will you please let me know where the cars is going to stop to so that he can come where he can take care of me and my children. He get there a while and then he can send for me. . . .

Houston, Texas, April 20, 1917.

Dear Sir: . . . I am 30 years old and have Good Experence in Freight Handler and Can fill Position from Truck to Agt. would like Chicago or Philadelphia But I dont Care where so long as I Go where a man is a man. . . .

Almost 5,000 blacks were the victims of lynchings in the fifty years following Reconstruction, many in the North and West. Most died by hanging, but there were other hideous mob actions. Is the decline in such overt violence a sign of improved race relations? The era of World War I marked a major movement of blacks from the rural South to the urban North. In what ways did this move affect the lives of black Americans?

Troy, Ala., Oct. 17, 1916.

Dear Sirs: I am enclosing a clipping of a lynching again which speaks for itself. I do wish there could be sufficient presure brought about to have federal investigation of such work. I wrote you a few days ago if you could furnish me with the addresses of some firms or co-opporations that needed common labor. So many of our people here

It has been estimated that by the end of 1918 more than 1 million blacks had left the South. Why did Southern whites react with alarm to this mass migration? How were blacks treated when they arrived in Northern cities?

are almost starving. The government is feeding quite a number here would go any where to better their conditions. If you can do any thing for us write me as early as posible.

Brookhaven, Miss., April 24, 1917.

Gents: The cane growers of Louisiana have stopped the exodus from New Orleans, claiming shortage of labor which will result in a sugar famine.

Now these laborers thus employed receive only 85 cents a day and the high cost of living makes it a serious question to live.

. . . Please dont publish this letter but do what you can towards helping them to get away. If the R. R. Co. would run a low rate excursion they could leave that way. Please ans.

Memphis, Tenn., 4-23-17.

Gentlemen: I want to get in tuch with you in regard of a good location & a job I am for race elevation every way. I want a job in a small town some where in the north where I can receive verry good wages and where I can educate my 3 little girls and demand respect of intelegence. I prefer a job as cabinet maker or any kind of furniture mfg. if possible.

Let me hear from you all at once please. State minimum wages and kind of work.

Macon, Ga., May 27, 1917.

Dear Mary: . . . I got a card from Mrs. Addie S—— yesterday she is well and say washington D. C. is a pretty place but wages is not good say it better forther on Cliford B—— an his wife is back an give the North a bad name Old lady C—— is in Cleavon an wonte to come home mighty bad so Cliford say. I got a hering from Vick C—— tell me to come on she living better than she ever did in her life Charlie J—— is in Detroit he got there last weak Hattie J—— lef Friday Oh I can call all has left here Leala J—— is speaking of leaving soon There were more people left last week then ever 2 hundred left at once the whites an colored people had a meeting Thursday an Friday telling the people if they stay here they will treat them better an pay better. Huney they are hurted but the haven stop yet. The colored people say they are too late now George B—— is on his head to go to Detroit Mrs. Anna W—— is just like you left her she is urgin everybody to go on an she not getting ready May you dont no how I mis you I hate to pass your house Everybody is well as far as I no Will J—— is on the gang for that same thing hapen about the eggs on Houston road. His wife tried to get him to leave here but he woulden Isiah j—— is going to send for Hattie. In short Charles S—— wife quit him last week he aint doin no better. . . . I received the paper you sent me an I see there or pleanty of work I can do I will let you no in my next lettr what I am going to do but I cant get my mind settle to save my life. Love to Mr. A——. . . .

Chicago, Illinois.

My dear Sister: I was agreeably surprised to hear from you and to hear from home. I am well and thankful to say I am doing well. . . . Please remember me kindly to any who ask of me. The people are rushing here by the thousands and I know if you come and rent a big house you can get all the roomers you want. You write me exactly when you are coming. I am not keeping house yet I am living with my brother and his wife. My sone is in California but will be home soon. He spends his winter in California. I can get a nice place for you to stop until you can look around and see what you want. I am quite busy. I work in Swifts packing Co., in the sausage department. My daughter and I work for the same company—We get $1.50 a day and we pack so many sausages we dont have much time to play but it is a matter of a dollar with me and I feel that God made the path and I am walking therein.
Tell your husband work is plentiful here and he wont have to loaf if he want to work. . . .

120

Pittsburg, Pa., May 11, 1917.

My dear Pastor and wife: . . . I am in this great city & you no it cool here right now the trees are just peeping out. fruit trees are now in full bloom but its cool yet we set by big fire over night. I like the money O.K. but I like the South betterm for my Pleasure this city is too fast for me they give you big money for what you do but they charge you big things for what you get and the people are coming by cal Loads every day its just pack out the people are Begging for some whears to sta If you have a family of children & come here you can buy a house easier than you cant rent one if you rent one you have to sign up for 6 months or 12 month so you see if you dont like it you have to stay you no they pass that law becaus the People move about so much. . . .

Hattiesburg, Miss. Chicago, Illinois, 11/13/17.

Dear M——: . . . M——, old boy, I was promoted on the first of the month I was made first assistant to the head carpenter when he is out of the place I take everything in charge and was raised to $95. a month. You know I know my stuff.

Whats the news generally around H/burg? I should have been here 20 years ago. I just begin to feel like a man. It's a great deal of pleasure in knowing that you have got some privilege My children are going to the same school with the whites and I dont have to umble to no one. I have registered—Will vote the next election and there isnt any "yes sir" and "no sir"—its all yes and no and Sam and Bill.

Florine says hello and would like very much to see you.

All joins me in sending love to you and family. How is times there now? Answer soon, from your friend and bro.

Today and Tomorrow

HENRY FORD

Henry Ford (1863–1947) lived the American Dream. From modest beginnings, he created industrial and philanthropic empires, making his name synonymous with wealth and power. A tinkerer with machines, Ford built an inexpensive automobile, designed an efficient system of mass production, and put millions of Americans on the road in Model Ts and Model As.

As a success story in the wholly American idiom, Ford confidently preached a homespun philosophy. In this selection,

written during the twenties when the Ford Motor Company was at the peak of its power, Henry Ford proclaimed that American leaders like himself knew the secrets of permanent progress and the elimination of unemployment and poverty. He sharply answered those critics who emphasized the dishonest and dehumanizing characteristics associated with major business enterprises. What aspect of American life in 1926 do you feel confirmed Henry Ford in these beliefs?

WE ARE BEING BORN INTO OPPORTUNITY

For hundreds of years men have been talking about the lack of opportunity and the pressing need of dividing up things already in existence. Yet each year has seen some new idea brought forth and developed, and with it a whole new series of opportunities, until today we already have enough tested ideas which, put into practice, would take the world out of its sloughs and banish poverty by providing livings for all who will work. Only the old, outworn notions stand in the way of these new ideas. The world shackles itself, blinds its eyes, and then wonders why it cannot run!

Take just one idea—a little idea in itself—an idea that any one might have had, but which fell to me to develop—that of making a small, strong simple automobile, to make it cheaply, and pay high wages in its making. On October 1, 1908, we made the first of our present type of small cars. On June 4, 1924, we made the ten millionth. Now, in 1926, we are in our thirteenth million.

That is interesting but perhaps not important. What is important is that, from a mere handful of men employed in a shop, we have grown into a large industry directly employing more than two hundred thousand men, not one of whom receives less than six dollars a day. Our dealers and service stations employ another two hundred thousand men. But by no means do we manufacture all that we use.

Henry Ford put America on wheels. Can you imagine some social and economic consequences as the car replaced the horse as the most common mode of transportation? This photo is of the parking lot outside Soldiers' Field, Chicago, during the Notre Dame—Southern California football game on November 16, 1927. (Notre Dame won 13—12.)

Roughly, we buy twice as much as we manufacture, and it is safe to say that two hundred thousand men are employed on our work in outside factories. This gives a rough total of six hundred thousand employees, direct and indirect, which means that about three million men, women, and children get their livings out of a single idea put into effect only eighteen years ago. And this does not take into account the great number of people who in some way or other assist in the distribution or the maintenance of these cars. And this one idea is only in its infancy!

These figures are given not with any thought of boastfulness. I am not talking about a specific person or business. I am talking about ideas. And these figures do show something of what a single idea can accomplish. These people require food, clothing, shoes, houses, and so on. If they and their families were brought together in one place and those needed to supply their wants gathered around them, we should have a city larger than New York. All this has matured in less time than a child matures. What nonsense it is to think or speak of lack of opportunity! We do not know what opportunity is.

There are always two kinds of people in the world—those who pioneer and those who plod. The plodders always attack the pioneers. They say that the pioneers have gobbled up all the opportunity, when, as a plain matter of fact, the plodders would have nowhere to plod had not the pioneers first cleared the way.

122

Think about your work in the world. Did you make your place or did someone make it for you? Did you start the work you are in or did someone else? Have you ever found or made an opportunity for yourself or are you the beneficiary of opportunity which others have found or made?

We have seen the rise of a temper which does not want opportunities—it wants the full fruits of opportunity handed to it on a platter. This temper is not American. It is imported from lands and by races that have never been able to see or use opportunity—that have existed on what was given them.

Now the fact is that a generation ago there were a thousand men to every opportunity while today there are a thousand opportunities for every man. Affairs in this country have changed just that much.

However, when industry was growing up, opportunities were limited. Men saw along one track and all of them wanted to get on that one track. Naturally, some of them were shoved off; there were more men than opportunities. That is why we had so much fierceness and cruelty of competition in the old days. There were not enough of the big opportunities to go around.

But, with the maturing of industry, a whole new world of opportunity opened up. Think how many doors of creative activity every industrial advance has opened. It has turned out, through all the fierce competitive fights, that no man could succeed in his own opportunity without creating many times more opportunities than he could begin to grasp.

It is almost impossible to understand the rise of industry without recognizing the former scarcity of opportunity. Some forms of business seem to have gone onward, but our accounts of them mostly come from those who were beaten.

But there is enough of fact to indicate that, when industry was being evolved under the pressure of the people's needs (and that is the only force that brought it into being), some men had large vision while others had limited vision. The men of

Charles Lindbergh became an instant hero by flying across the Atlantic alone in 1927. Here he is shown on board ship returning to America together with his plane "The Spirit of St. Louis." How do you explain the fact that he became an enduring American hero for this one feat? Do we have comparable heroes today?

larger vision naturally bested the others. Their methods were sometimes immoral, but it was not their immoral methods that accounted for their success—it was their larger vision of needs, and ways and means to fulfill them. There must be a tremendous amount of right vision in anything if it is to survive dishonest or cruel methods. To attribute success to dishonesty is a common fallacy. We hear of men "too honest to succeed." That may be a comforting reflection to them, but it is never the reason for their failure.

Dishonest men do sometimes succeed. But only when they give a service which exceeds their dishonesty. Honest men sometimes fail because they lack other essential qualities to go with their honesty. It is safe to say that in the success of men who are dishonest, all that is touched by dishonesty sloughs off.

Those who do not believe in opportunity will still find places within the opportunities that others have created; those who cannot direct their work successfully will always find it possible to be directed by others.

But are we moving too fast—not merely in the making of automobiles, but in life generally? One hears a deal about the worker being ground down by hard labour, of what is called progress being made at the expense of something or other, and that efficiency is wrecking all the finer things of life.

It is quite true that life is out of balance—and always has been. Until lately, most people have had no leisure to use and, of course, they do not now know how to use it. One of our large problems is to find some balance between work and play, between sleep and food, and eventually to discover why men grow ill and die. Of this more later.

Certainly we are moving faster than before. Or, more correctly, we are being moved faster. But is twenty minutes in a motor car easier or harder than four hours' solid trudging down a dirt road? Which mode of travel leaves the pilgrim fresher at the end? Which leaves him more time and more mental energy? And soon we shall be making in an hour by air what were day's journeys by motor. Shall we all then be nervous wrecks?

But does this state of nervous wreckage to which we are all said to be coming exist in life—or in books? One hears of the worker's nervous exhaustion in books, but does one hear of it from the workers?

Go to the people who are working with the actual things of the world, from the labourer travelling to his work on the street car to the young man who hops across a continent in a day. You will find quite a different attitude. Instead of cringing away from what has come, they are looking with eager expectancy toward what is coming. Always they are willing to scrap today in favour of tomorrow. That is the blessedness of the active man, the man who is not sitting alone in a library trying to fit the new world into the old moulds. Go to the labourer in the street car. He will tell you that just a few years ago he came home so late and so tired that he had no time to change his clothes—just got his supper and went to bed. Now he changes his clothes at the shop, goes home by daylight, has an early supper, and takes the family out for a drive. He will tell you that the killing pressure has let up. A man may have to be a little more businesslike on the job than formerly, but the old endless, exhausting drive has quit.

The men at the top, the men who are changing all these things, will tell you the same. They are not breaking down. They are marching the way progress is going and find it easier to go along with progress than to try to hold things back.

And just there is the secret: those who get headaches are trying to hold the world back, trying to wrap it up again in their small definitions. It cannot be done.

The very word "efficiency" is hated because so much that is not efficiency has masqueraded as such. Efficiency is merely the doing of work in the best way you know rather than in the worst way. It is the taking of a trunk up a hill on a truck rather than on one's back. It is the training of the worker and the giving to him of power so that he may earn more and have more and live more comfortably. The Chinese coolie working through long hours for a few cents a day is not happier than the American workman with his own home and automobile. The one is a slave, the other is a free man.

In the organization of the Ford work we are continually reaching out for more and more developed power. We go to the coalfields, to the streams, and to the rivers, always seeking some cheap and convenient source of power which we can transform into electricity, take to the machine, increase the output of the workers, raise their wages, and lower the price to the public.

Into this train of events enter a great and ever-increasing number of factors. You must get the most out of the power, out of the material, and out of the time. This has taken us apparently far afield, as, for instance, into railroading, mining, lumbering, and shipping. We have spent many millions of dollars just to save a few hours' time here and there. Actually, however, we do nothing whatsoever which is not directly connected with our business—which is the making of motors.

The power which we use in manufacturing produces another power—the power of the motor that goes into the automobile. About fifty dollars' worth of raw material is transformed into twenty horsepower mounted on wheels. Up to December 1, 1925, we had, through cars and tractors, added to the world nearly three hundred million mobile horsepower, or about ninety-seven times the potential horsepower of Niagara Falls. The whole world uses only twenty-three million stationary horsepower, of which the United States uses more than nine million.

Confessions of a Ford Dealer

One Ford dealer during the 1920s who had read Henry Ford's book took issue with the company's managerial practices, although he proclaimed his agreement with the great man's theories. These "confessions" provide a description of sleezy selling tactics that, according to the anonymous author, salesmen were forced to use because of higher sales quotas imposed by the Ford Motor Company. In contrast to the general prosperity of the decade, business condi-tions were poor in this dealer's rural area because of the farm depression.

A new economic relationship between major national corporations and small Main Street businessmen is clearly illus-trated by this essay. The practices that major national corporations use reflect their own national interests and difficulties, yet small businessmen are compelled to accept these methods despite prevailing local conditions.

The former Ford dealer said:

Things have changed a lot around here since 1912, when I bought out the man who had the Ford agency and paid him inventory price for his stock, plus a bonus of five hundred dollars for good-will. A dealer didn't have to hustle so hard then to make both ends meet. You kept a few cars on your floor and when you needed more you bought them. You were your own boss. There weren't any iron-clad rules laid down for you saying how you had to run your business.

Sometimes I wonder if Mr. Ford knows how things have changed. I have just finished reading his book, and in one place he says: "Business grows big by public demand. But it never gets bigger than the demand. It cannot control or force the demand."

Understand me, I think Mr. Ford is a wonderful man. They say he is worth a billion dollars; and no one can make that much money unless he has plenty of brains. Still and all, when Mr. Ford says business cannot control or force the demand I can't quite think he means it. Or maybe it's his little joke. You *can* force demand if you ride people hard enough. And, believe me, you have only to get on the inside of a Ford agency to learn how.

Take my own case, for instance. Like I say, when I first took the agency I was my own boss like any other business man, selling as many cars as I could and buying more when I needed them. I didn't have to make many sales on install-ments, because people who wanted cars usually saved up in advance and had the cash in hand when they got ready to buy. Occasionally some man that I knew would want a little time, in which case I just charged it the same as if it was a bill of dry goods or groceries, and when the account fell due he paid me. There was no such thing then as putting a mortgage on the car and taking it away from him if he didn't pay up. If I didn't believe a man was honest I simply didn't give him credit.

I did a pretty good business this way and by 1916 was selling an average of about ten cars a month. Then one day a representative of the Company came to see me. I'll call him by the name of Benson, though that was not his real name. In fact wherever I mention a man's name in giving my experiences I shall call him something different because some of them probably would not like to be identified. Well, anyway, this man that I call Benson came into my place at the time I speak of and said ten cars a month was not enough for a dealer like me to sell. It seems the Company had made a survey of my territory and decided that the sales possibilities were much greater. Benson said my quota had been fixed at twenty cars a month, and from then on that number would be shipped to me.

Naturally, I got a little hot under the collar at this kind of a proposition, and I told Benson where he could get off at. I said I was doing all the business that could be done and I intended to buy only the cars that I needed. The Company could ship me as many as they wanted to, but I would pay for what I could sell, and no more.

Benson was pretty hard boiled. He said there was no need of my getting mad at him because he was only doing what he had been ordered to do, and I could take my choice. Either I could buy twenty cars a month or the Company would find another agent. There were plenty of live wires who would jump at the chance.

Of course I knew this last was true. I had got to making a little money during the four years I was Ford agent, and there are always fellows who will go into a thing when someone else has done the hard sledding. My wife had got used to living pretty well and, beside that, my boy was fixing to go away to college. I

The automobile influenced the life of almost all middle-class Americans. It gave them more mobility, changed dating habits, and even inspired trips into the country such as this circa 1915 photo depicts. Almost every family took photos of their autos, which became prized possessions. Can you find similar pictures in your family album?

knew there would be an awful roar at home if I gave up a sure thing and started over again at something else. Still, I couldn't see how I could possibly sell twenty cars a month in my territory. There were only about nine thousand people in the town, and possibly that many more on the farms. Most of them were poor folks. It wasn't, I told Benson, like an Eastern manufacturing community where there are a lot of moneyed people and a big bunch of well-paid mechanics who can afford to have their own cars.

Benson only laughed and said that didn't make any difference. There was a certain population in my territory that called for a certain number of sales, and the Company would show me how to do business. All I had to do was to follow instructions.

Well, I finally decided to take a chance on twenty cars a month rather than lose the agency. I had read a lot of nice things about Mr. Ford in the newspapers and I felt sure he wouldn't ask me to do anything he wouldn't be willing to do himself. Benson said he was glad I looked at things in a businesslike way and promised me plenty of assistance in moving my twenty cars a month. But I sure got it in the neck when the slump of 1920 came on. If anyone wants to know what hard times are he ought to try to do business in a Western farming community during a panic. Almost overnight half of our sheep men went bankrupt when wool dropped from sixty cents a pound to twenty cents, and hardly any buyers at that price. The potato growers couldn't get enough for their stuff to pay freight to the Chicago market, and most of them let their crop rot in the ground. Of our four banks in town two went into the hands of receivers and the other two had to call in every possible loan in order to save their own necks. A lot of our Main Street retailers fell into the hands of their creditors that year, too.

I was in about as bad a fix as anyone else. By then I had agreed to take thirty Fords a month, which was a pretty heavy job to get away with in good times, to say nothing of the sort of a situation we were going through. These cars came in each month, regular as clock work, and I had stretched my credit at the bank about as far as it would go in paying for them as they arrived. The bank kept hounding me all the time to cut down my loan, which I couldn't do with my expenses running on all the time and hardly any business going on. From September to January that year I sold exactly four cars.

Pretty bad? I'll say it was. But the worst was yet to come. Altogether I had more than one hundred and forty new cars on hand, besides a lot of trade-ins, and no immediate prospect of selling any. Then all of a sudden came notice that a shipment of fifteen Fords was on the way to me, and that I would be expected to pay for them on arrival. I thought there must be some mistake, and got the branch manager in the city on the long distance. He was a pretty hard-boiled egg named Blassingham.

"What's the meaning of these fifteen cars that are being shipped me?" I asked. "I've already taken my quota for the month."

"It don't mean anything," Blassignham answered, "except that you're going to buy fifteen extra cars this month."

I tried to explain to him that I was in no position to get hold of the cash for such a purchase, and even if I was I wanted to know the whys and wherefores.

"You know as much about it as I do," he snapped. "Those are the orders, and my advice to you is to pay for those cars when they arrive."

Of course I sensed the reason later on, when it came out in the newspapers

How does this 1925 automobile advertisement differ from modern car ads? Why may the price range of the different Star models be deceivingly inexpensive?

about Mr. Ford's little tilt with the money sharks down in New York, how they tried to get a hold on his business and how he fooled them by getting the cash without their help and then told them to go chase themselves.

If you ask me, I'd say Mr. Ford is an absolute humdinger when it comes to handling a lot of crooks who are bent on feathering their own nests off other people. At the moment, however, I was too busy with personal problems to think much about the battles of Big Business. Like I say, my credit at the bank was used up, and the bank had no money to loan, anyhow. I was taking in enough cash to pay my mechanics in the garage, but I had to stand off the office help Saturday nights with part of their wages and ask them to wait on me for the balance. I couldn't sleep much for worrying, and I guess my wife worried as much as I did because at three and four o'clock in the morning she would ask me if I had been to sleep yet and when I would say no, she would say she hadn't either.

I had fully made up my mind I was going on the rock pile when just a couple of days before the extra shipment of Fords was due to arrive I had an unexpected stroke of luck. There was a sheep man named Flanagan I knew who had made a trip out west to Salt Lake City just before the market broke and closed out his entire holdings for something like a hundred thousand dollars in cash, which he put into Liberty Bonds. He had a Ford that he ran around in sometimes, and one day when he drove up to the garage I happened to think about his money and asked him how he would like to come in with me as a silent partner. To make a long story short, he became interested in the proposition and bought a third interest. Of course I had to sell him his share for a lot less than it was worth, but it saved my scalp.

■ ■ ■

I am willing to confess that we rode the public a little ourselves while we were getting rid of our big surplus of cars. There are always some people that you can sell anything to if you hammer them hard enough. We had a salesman named Nichols who was a humdinger at running down prospects, and one day he told me he had a fellow on the string with a couple of hundred dollars who would buy a car if we would give him a little extra time on the balance. This prospect was a young fellow that had come out West on account of his health and was trying to make a living for his family as an expert accountant. Just at that time the referee in bankruptcy was doing most of the accounting business around town, and I knew the young fellow wasn't getting on at all. He had about as much use for a car as a jack rabbit. I told Nichols this, but you know how plausible these go-getter salesmen are; he told me it wasn't our business whether the young fellow had any use for a Ford or not; the main thing was he had two hundred dollars in cash.

Well, we went ahead and made the sale, but we never got any more payments. The young fellow took to his bed just after that, and the church people had to look out for him and his family until he died. In the final showdown it turned out that the two-hundred dollar equity in the car was everything they had on earth, and by the time we replevined it and sold it as a trade-in there wasn't anything at all. I gave twenty dollars toward his funeral expenses. I know this sounds pretty tough; but when it's a case of your own scalp or some other fellow's you can't afford to be too particular.

■ ■ ■

Half the time I didn't know whether I was in business for myself or whether I was only a hired man. The branch manager up in the city had a corps of inspectors who went around all the time to check up on local agents and keep them on their toes. Of course these inspectors had to make a showing in order to justify their jobs, but sometimes it was pretty irritating. It seemed to be part of their policy to find some fault or other. Sometimes they would tell you that your show windows weren't clean enough, or that your cars weren't properly displayed on the sales floor, or that the papers in your office were disorderly. On one occasion I got wind in advance that an inspector was coming and I had things fixed up in such apple-pie order that I was sure he could make no criticism. He spent pretty much the whole day poking around, and I was laughing in my sleeve all the time to see how stumped he was, but in the end he made his report stating there were some flies in the toilet and instructing that I should buy a can of disinfectant. I suppose his traveling expenses and hotel bill and salary for that day's work was in the neighborhood of twenty-five dollars.

You do a lot of things when someone is riding you all the time that you wouldn't do under ordinary circumstances. Beans and clover seed are the farmers' principal money crops around here, and one fall in September and October we had one heavy rain after the other that practically ruined everything. Business was terrible because the farmers hadn't recovered yet from the bank failures and the slump of 1920; and one day I wrote in to the Company, telling what bad shape the farmers were in and asking if my quota couldn't be reduced for a few months until things picked up. All I got for my trouble was a letter stating that "such farmers are not the people to sell to."

Of course it was easy enough for them to write such a letter, but I always thought Mr. Ford ought to realize that in a country community when the farmers are broke the doctors and dentists and storekeepers are in about the same fix. Not being able to get my quota reduced, I had to take business wherever I could find it.

■ ■ ■

If Mr. Ford knew personally some of the things that go on I am sure he would call a halt to his branch managers riding the local agents the way they do. Like I say, when you are crowded all the time to make your quota under all sorts of business conditions, you do things you don't like to. There are some pretty tough characters in this town just as there are everywhere else; but a quota is a quota and you can't stop to pick your customers. One thing I have noticed is that the hardest boiled eggs are most likely to come up with their time payments. Only last year I sold a car to a big colored fellow and of course as he had no visible means of support I took a mortgage on it so I could replevin it in case he didn't pay, but every month he came in right on the dot with the cash. Naturally I'm not bragging about it, and I'm not saying anything was wrong; but during that time a street car conductor was held up at the end of the line a couple of times and there were some other bits of devilment of a like character.

I have talked to a lot of Ford agents around here and practically every one of them complains about the way the branch managers have stuffed their orders for parts. It often happened with me. I remember once I ordered a hundred timers and when the shipment came it was five hundred. I wrote and called attention to the mistake but got no answer. The next week I was up in the city and spoke to the branch manager about it personally. He was one of the fellows who quit the Company later on to go into another line of business. At first he tried to laugh off the five hundred timers and said a little thing like that wouldn't make any difference to a millionaire like me, and anyhow I would use them up in a few months. But that evening over a couple of drinks he got confidential.

"You Bozos in the small towns think I'm riding you," he said. "Well, maybe I am. I've got my work cut out for me the same as you have, and I've got to make good or lose my job. But if any of you think you're having a hard time, all I've got to say is that you ought to trade jobs with me about a month!"

The thing that made me quit the Ford game was the campaign they put on for farm machinery. Understand, I was in sympathy with it too, because I knew Mr. Ford was trying to make things easier for the farmers—like he says, help them do their whole year's work in twenty days. Still and all, I didn't feel I wanted to go broke even in a good cause.

The first thing I knew of Mr. Ford's plans was on a Saturday afternoon when I got a long-distance call from the city saying the branch manager was coming out next day and for me to be in my office at eleven o'clock. I usually go to church Sunday mornings, and besides I always understood Mr. Ford was against Sunday work; but an order is an order and I wasn't taking any chances on getting in bad with the branch manager. In our town there are laws on Sabbath observance, but if a business man wants to work a little no one bothers him just so he keeps the shades down.

The branch manager was a new man by the name of Biggs, and he told me that from then on I would be required to carry a line of farm machinery suitable to go with the Ford tractors. As I remember it, there were no ifs or ands; I understood it to be an order, and I knew what Biggs could do to me if I didn't obey orders. Anyhow I thought it might be a good thing to help move the tractors, which were always harder to sell than Ford cars. I asked Biggs if he wanted me to sign a contract and he said no, that wouldn't be necessary in this case, but when the salesman came along it would be indicated to me what I should buy.

■ ■ ■

Well, so far as our section of the country was concerned, the farm machinery campaign was a pretty bad flop. In the first place, it was hard to convince the farmers that they ought to buy their machines from the Ford dealers instead of from regular implement merchants. Naturally the implement merchants were down on us for trying to take away their trade, and knocked Ford cars every time they had a chance. Then it was found that 12-inch plows weren't suitable for our territory, and some of the other machines proved too heavy for the Ford tractor. Biggs sent out a lot of demonstrators and high-powered salesmen to help us move the stuff, but none of us could make a go of the line and after a while so many squawks came from the dealers that Biggs called a meeting to hear complaints. As I was the biggest agent in that part of the state the meeting was held in my office and the smaller dealers came there.

Biggs called the meeting to order and asked the different ones to air their complaints. Believe me, there were a plenty. One fellow would tell his troubles with the farm machinery line, and then another, and then half a dozen would be on their feet at once, blaming Biggs, and the Ford Motor Company, and the farm machinery company, and pretty near everyone else, for their griefs. In the midst of it Biggs hopped to his feet and pounded the table.

"If any man here can show a scratch of the pen," he yelled, "to prove he bought his farm machinery at the orders of the Ford Motor Company, I dare him to get up and say so!"

Of course no one could show a scratch of the pen because there wasn't any. Biggs hadn't made any of us sign a contract for our farm machinery. He had just *told* us to buy it, and we took it to be an order from headquarters.

I sold out my business as soon after that as I could find a buyer. I was afraid after Mr. Ford got through helping the farmers he might decide to help out the Hottentots or someone, and I didn't feel like I could afford to assist him. The fellow I sold my business to wouldn't take the farm machinery stock at any price.

Since then I have been peddling it wherever I could, but it's a hard game. I sold
one machine that cost me $800 for $300, and took the farmer's notes for it, spread
out over three years, without interest.

I am sure Mr. Ford can't know about all these things, because if he did he
couldn't have written in his book this grand sentiment:

"The principle of the service of business to the people has gone far in the
United States and it will spread through and remake the world."

Corncobs for Hair-cuts

How a Modern Farm Woman Gets on by Swap and Dicker

EVELYN HARRIS

Another side of life in the twenties is portrayed in this selection by a widowed farm woman from Maryland's Eastern Shore. Raising five children along with corn, wheat, chickens, hogs, various fruits and vegetables, she also cooks, bakes, cans preserves, makes soap, candy, ice cream, and butter. Beyond this incredible range of skills and energy, she summons remarkable ingenuity to pay untimely bills.

The author provides interesting reflections on country life—from the decline in youngsters' interest in farming to the decline in prices, which occurred despite farmers' endless work and high production. Both the inability of farmers to affect market prices and the tendency of young, rural people to move to cities reflect basic forces in American society that predominated throughout the twenties. In spite of the problems that are described below, can you see advantages to this style of life? Do they remain the same today?

I suppose I am a modern woman. I have succumbed to the "bob," drive my own car, vote to suit myself, and have the mischief of a time in getting interest and taxes together. Since the death of my husband, three years ago, I have been carrying on the farm myself. My neighbors will bear witness that my crops are above the average, my cost sheet compares favorably with that of any other farmer in the vicinity, and my sales of fruit exceed any in this locality. I am convinced that my best chance to make a living for the five children is where I can have them with me at all times and can teach them something of the business which was their father's and grandfather's.

My problem at this time is to try to discover where my chance for a profit disappeared in 1927 and how to grasp it in 1928. Total sales were equal to one-half of the mortgage. Taxes, insurance and interest took just 25 per cent of total sales, containers and labor each took 20 per cent, fertilizer and spray material 10 per cent. Up-keep on old machines and the purchase of a little more, took the balance of the 100 per cent—and I had absolutely nothing left for a living.

The radio reduced the isolation of farm and city families alike and introduced them to a strange and mysterious world that came over the airways. This is a photo of an Oregon farm family listening to the radio. Can you imagine their pleasure? Do you just listen to the radio today?

City folks think that country people get their living for nothing. But I know country women who sell all of the milk and use canned milk and imitation butter. The lady on the radio thought it much cheaper for the country woman to use three eggs than for the city woman to use them, but I'll tell her now that in the winter the country woman's eggs cost her around a dollar and a half a dozen—the price that she could get in the city if she were to sell them. We see our fresh vegetables as something which means hard labor for horse and man, much sweat of little children in gathering them, and a season of two months or three at the most, in which to eat them. To have milk means that some man or boy must get up before light, and with freezing fingers coax it from the cow. The cow, by the way, has no regard for an eight-hour day nor a forty-hour week. She runs as steadily as the calendar, and if the boss decided to milk only five days a week, the cities would be howling blue murder.

O. M. Kile, who writes quite feelingly on the subject of farms and their problems, says that "dairying utilizes *unpaid* family labor to a degree that few other lines of farming can. When this kind of labor is not available, the dairyman usually quits, as farm labor is scarce." Sometimes the wife is the unpaid labor. One man was bragging to me about making one thousand dollars last year on his cows. He advised me to get a large herd. But I saw his wife pumping water for those cows to drink; she always went into the barn to help milk, washed the buckets, helped bottle the milk, and the little boy peddled it before school. The farmer made one thousand dollars—but he had not figured feed or help or interest. That was his gross amount.

City folks have such vague ideas about a farm. They seem to imagine that everything you could possibly want is there for the asking. Bless your soul, children need clothes and food here, and although I have enough corn to make a trainload of cornflakes, my profit on that corn crop will not buy enough cornflakes for the children for one year. About forty years ago, a man with $70,000 invested in farms had as good a chance to keep his family in style as did the man with that much money invested in a going livery stable. But the money we have in farms does not give us as good return now as if we had it invested in a filling station. True, we do run a filling station after a fashion, but folks are still praying each night, "*Give* us this day our daily bread!" They don't pray for their gasoline: they still seem willing to pay for it! We have fresh eggs; I cannot swap a dozen eggs for a dozen oranges. We have chickens, yet they do not grow free. The very least on which a hen can be supported is about two dollars a year.

Once a month we need hair-cuts, which we do not raise on the farm. Children need dentists, too. Forty years ago, they did not get them. The Lord sends the snow, but it took my profit on twelve cords of wood to buy each child a very ordinary sled. He sends the ice to us free, but what is ice unless there are skates and ice-cream? My children are very fond of both, and the steel worker belongs to a union, which sets the price on my children's skates and the ice-cream freezer. Somebody around here is responsible for all sorts of entertainments, suppers and Chautauquas, and it knocks the spots out of a five-dollar bill every time I attend one.

A new definition of a pessimist came to me over the radio. "A pessimist is he who turns out the light to see how dark it is." Once in a while a farmer must do just that thing. In 1924, but one young man in this county married and went to live on a farm. He lived there two years and then had to quit. One of my problems is to try to demonstrate that a young man can live on a farm, as I have two young men, one nineteen and one fourteen, and I do so want them to stay here. But most of the boys are leaving to go to the cities.

I have three girls. They need and demand a good time, with those of their kind. The high schools in this county do not boast of many young boys. The town boys are in school, but the farm boys are not. If the girls are to live on the farms, they should have farm boys, of equal education and equal advantages, to live with them. Here in Maryland the modern mother sees with dismay that the farm owners are leaving the farms, taking their children with them, and going into the cities and towns. In their places, are the sons and daughters of farm tenants. Sometimes these children are white, sometimes not. But in most instances, they are of another type, with other standards of living and entirely different customs. For the most part, they are not inclined to take part in the social activities of either clubs or church, and these are dwindling.

Forty years ago the owners lived on the fifteen farms along our road. Their children sang in the church choir, attended the "institutes," kept alive a going Farmer's Club with a big monthly dinner held at the homes of the members; kept a good social hour weekly in the Grange, and had a good time generally. Now they are gone, and the fine hospitality of the Eastern Shore will be as hard to find as the famous box-wood, which used to frame the paths around the front yard. Most tenants use the front yard for the pigs, anyway, the front porch for a woodshed in the winter-time and a repository for various farming tools in summer. The owner, living in the town or the city (or the graveyard), cannot find enough cash after paying taxes, insurance and interest, to make repairs on the house.

In the midst of all of this you will find a few, like myself, who are trying to work against all sorts of odds. My problems are not the same as those of a woman in the city who finds education and recreation often provided by taxes, and ready for use; who can choose the neighborhood in which she wants to rear her children, and can usually figure on having enough cash to make her payments when they come due.

Now I am not a weeper, nor a sleeper, nor a creeper. I am constantly looking for a chance to prove to myself that farming is a business that can be carried on like any other business. But the advice which is given us, though well-meaning, is of no practical value. Last year the county and state urged every farmer to have his soil tested to find out whether or not it needed lime. I am not sure who paid for all of this surveying. But I took samples, had them tested, and found out it would take five hundred and sixty tons of lime for my fields. I did not buy it, for I did not have the money. Had we purchased the lime and grown more stuff, we would have been in much better shape for bankruptcy than we now are! The lime man would have had a profit, the railroads, and labor, but our surplus corn and wheat and other things would have been here yet to plague the life out of us.

On the one hand, the fertilizer folks, the lime folks, the implement folks, the men who want to lend money for the federal government say, "Make two blades grow where only one grew before," and then the whole lot of them say, "Of course you can do nothing with a surplus. The price you receive will have to be based on a world price." But so long as they can make a profit on anything at all to sell a farmer, they urge him to buy—and pay later.

Somehow, I cannot seem to be able to use the money I make this year for next year's crop. It must always go for last year's crop, with an interesting lot of interest following. I am not alone in this. Most farm work is done just that way. I am always hoping for a crop and a price *the same year*. Now, in 1925, I had a dandy price for my pears, but very few pears. In 1926, I had a dandy crop of pears, but a very small price. I cannot figure out whether I am hopefully hopeless, or hopelessly hopeful, but along in January each year, I begin to recover from my December depression, caused by fixing up my Orphan's Court statement of cash received and cash expended, and begin to plan again for good crops. Right at this time, I feel like borrowing enough money to cover each orchard with high-priced fertilizer, intensive cultivation, and a cover crop. If I could get the credit, I'd purchase another sprayer and pipe water away out to the far orchard, so as to save time in the spraying. I feel just like going to the city and buying about one thousand tons of manure, and I want to plow up sod and plant fifty acres more corn, although I know very well that I lost money on my corn last year, and if I should have the crop which I hope to get when I plant it, so would the fellow next door, and the price would be lower than ever. A person can have only a certain number of disappointments; after that they cease to be disappointments, and he does not feel them. That explains farmers, better than anything else I can think of. It also explains their apparent willingness to get along without money.

In the beginning of my story, I told of spending 100 per cent of my gross income, and did not mention living at all. That is one of my problems. For two years, it was taken care of by the death of a relative and frequent contributions of old clothing which were washed, ironed and made over for myself and the children. There seems to be no one about to die in the family this year, so I shall have to write magazine articles to make up for that, and I fear the stock of old clothing is greatly depleted. But of course, I am hoping that I shall grow more and better pears, more and better corn, more and better tomatoes, more and better wheat, more and better eggs and chicks, more and better hogs and hay.

You can see that I have faithfully followed out another of the pet schemes of the would-be farm advisers, and have a good crop of "diversification" growing here. And while it looks all right for the newspapers to preach it and the advertisers to preach it, yet that is the most expensive crop we can grow. When every other business is advised to concentrate on one or two things so as to make production costs low, does it not seem foolish to preach another doctrine to farm folk? But the newspapers tell us to do it—and the folks in the country just swear by their newspapers. One of my neighbors, much to his surprise, read of his own death in the morning paper. He at once called up his best friend and said, "Say, Jim, did you read of my death in this morning's paper?"

"Sure," said Jim, "where are you calling from?"

A farm has to specialize some, and it cannot right-about-face when market conditions change. A pants factory is not prepared to turn over and make parasols if the market on pants becomes glutted. It is foolish to tell an orchardist that he must pull out his apple trees because there are too many growing, for he cannot turn his sprayer into a reaper if he should plant wheat, and thus put the wheat farmer out of business, nor can he use his picking bags and ladders in producing eggs and milk. Neither can a man who has studied fruit for years turn easily into a grain grower.

A farmer has to be born a farmer. He just has to have an ear for the music which is to be found in the lowing of cows, an eye for the beauties to be found in the blossom of a potato or a tomato plant; and a heart strong enough to stand the prosperity of a crop and a low price the same year. But here is Mr. Virgil Jordan saying in the Forum, "Farming does not pay as a business, is not a success as an industry, and is unprofitable as an investment." Then he adds, "Farming has never been and cannot be more than a home and a job . . . a way of living and a noble occupation. . . . The only solution of the farm problem is not to devise ways by which the farmer can get more money, but to free him from the bonds of artificial debt and desire which have made him want it at all."

He is partly right. I find my desire for money, as such, is rapidly dwindling. I want a fair exchange for labor. When I have a bill due, I look around the farm for a while to see if it is possible to "swap" something I have for something I need (not want). I must purchase hair-cuts, six of them about every three weeks. The retail price on hair-cuts (I buy them by the dozen) is thirty-five cents here. I heard the wife of the barber say she wanted some corncobs to help her morning exercises in the old family kitchen. So I proposed that we exchange two wagon loads of corncobs for one dozen hair-cuts. My proposition was accepted.

Children with no father need good reading material. All of my magazines "expire" in the cold of the winter, and at a time when everything is going out and nothing coming in. I looked around for something to trade. We had splendid apples down in the cellar, real old-fashioned Maryland apples. I wrote the editors of five magazines regarding a trade, and so far four have accepted. I hope to serve them next year also. Taxes—three months overdue and interest to pay on them.

What did the state need, which I had? Locust posts and gravel I found I could exchange for taxes, and so it was done.

To pay for the needed implements in these days, the farmer must have enough dollars to pay for union labor in the manufacture, sale and transportation of those implements. The only way in which he can get more dollars to pay for replacing these implements, is to receive more for his crop. With one or two exceptions, prices are lower than they were before the War, on crops grown in the United States, but production costs are still climbing up a ladder now ten years long. The first statement quoted from Mr. Jordan would seem to stamp him as a farmer, or the president of a bank in a rural community. The second might be paraphrased by using instead of the word farmer, the word teacher, or preacher or merchant, for those fellows have a home and a job—a way of living and a noble occupation, just like a farmer, except that the home is usually up-to-date in improvements and the salary of the job has been increased to enable his wife to buy a semi-annual pair of silk hose, a monthly ticket for a show, the current magazines, and an occasional vacation in the family flivver.

There was a debate by radio on the subject of "The two-job wife." Neither of the contestants was really qualified to talk on the subject. The first was a man and the second an unmarried woman. But volumes could have been spoken on this subject by the farm woman. Her side of the yarn is so seldom heard, or read. So-called farm magazines publish thousands of words about successful men on the farms and the money they make, but unless something is said about the women and unless the photo illustrating the story contains the likeness of the wife as well as the husband, I pass it by. City news-gatherers and city editors, as a rule, can see masculine success only, for that is the way in which most men are made in the cities—self-made, as it were. The city news writer, interviewing the successful city business man, never thinks of the man as the husband of some woman. He sees him as the employer of some or many, as the case may be, so naturally, when he interviews the farmer, he never thinks of the man as only half of the business. And the other half, busy with the children and the dinner and the chickens, is not interviewed at all.

■   ■   ■

The mother on a farm has identically the same problems as the mother in the city, plus the farm duties of a woman, which have not changed since the days of long ago, except that we do not spin nor weave our cloth. But we dye and press, boil our hams, make and bake our rolls in a stove burning wood. We heat the water for baths in a tea-kettle, do our own canning and preserving. Many times we churn our own butter, pick our own chickens. To provide amusements for the children, we make our own candy and ice cream and cake. We make our own soap and do without face creams, powder and rouge.

Except for these minor things, the farm woman and the city woman "are sisters under their skins."

Petting and the Campus

ELEANOR ROWLAND WEMBRIDGE

One day very early in this century, a young woman stood in a Chicago hotel lobby and lit a cigarette. The manager quickly approached Alice Roosevelt and asked her to leave the premises immediately, with no regard for the fact that her father was President of the United States.

By the 1920s, women not only smoked openly, they were also experimenting with a variety of activities that challenged conventional notions of proper behavior. Women had already gained, through political activism, the right to vote by 1920. Changes in manners and morals followed.

While the observance of a strict Victorian moral code had always been more proclaimed than observed, many middle-class women of the twenties shocked convention by freely discussing the taboo subject of sexual impulses. Fashion trends frankly expressed sensuality and created the idealized. vision of the flapper, the thoroughly modern woman. Yet, as the following selection indicates, this new expression of sexual etiquette still had catching a man as its objective. In what ways have American courting practices changed since the era of the flapper?

Last summer I was at a student conference of young women comprised of about eight hundred college girls from the middle western states. The subject of petting was very much on their minds, both as to what attitude they should take toward it with the younger girls (being upperclassmen themselves) and also how much renunciation of this pleasurable pastime was required of them. If I recall correctly, two entire mornings were devoted to discussing the matter, two evenings, and another overflow meeting.

So far as I could judge from their discussion groups, the girls did not advise younger classmen not to pet—they merely advised them to be moderate about it, not lose their heads, not go too far—in fact the same line of conduct which is advised for moderate drinking. Learn temperance in petting, not abstinence.

Before the conference I made it my business to talk to as many college girls as possible. I consulted as many, both in groups and privately, as I had time for at the conference. And since it is all to be repeated in another state this summer, I have been doing so, when opportunity offered, ever since. Just what does petting consist in? What ages take it most seriously? Is it a factor in every party? Do "nice" girls do it, as well as those who are not so "nice"? Are they "stringing" their elders, by

A

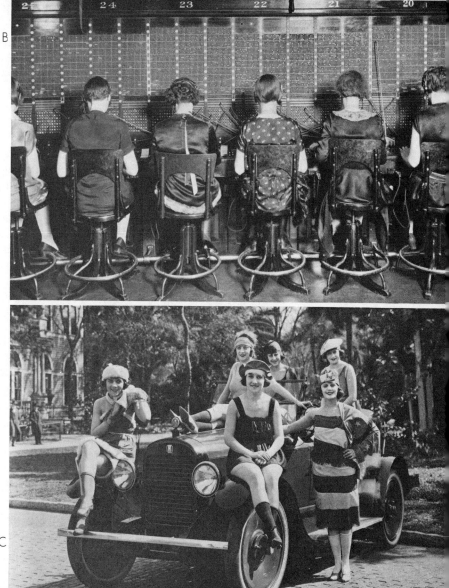

B

C

The war and the 1920s brought new opportunities and new freedom for women. During the war some women, such as these Philadelphia ordinance workers (A), took over men's jobs. More typical of those benefiting from the new occupational opportunities for women are the telephone operators (B). (Can you explain their common hair style?) But the image of women as sex objects continued and was exaggerated in the 1920s. The women posing on the auto (C) represent a typical use of attractive women to promote products. Could women be both flappers and serious workers? Did more personal freedom lead to more economic and political opportunity? Which image of women has persisted into the 1980s?

exaggerating the prevalence of petting, or is there more of it than they admit? These are samples of the questions I have asked, and have heard them ask each other in the discussions where I have listened in.

One fact is evident, that whether or not they pet, they hesitate to have anyone believe that they do not. It is distinctly the *mores* of the time to be considered as ardently sought after, and as not too priggish to respond. As one girl said—"I don't particularly care to be kissed by some of the fellows I know, but I'd let them do it any time rather than think I wouldn't dare. As a matter of fact, there are lots of fellows I don't kiss. It's the very young kids that never miss a chance."

■ ■ ■

I sat with one pleasant college Amazon, a total stranger, beside a fountain in the park, while she asked if I saw any harm in her kissing a young man whom she liked, but whom she did not want to marry. "It's terribly exciting. We get such a thrill. I think it is natural to want nice men to kiss you, so why not do what is natural?" There was no embarrassment in her manner. Her eyes and her conscience were equally untroubled. I felt as if a girl from the Parthenon frieze had stepped down to ask if she might not sport in the glade with a handsome faun. Why not indeed? Only an equally direct forcing of twentieth century science on primitive simplicity could bring us even to the same level in our conversation, and at that, the stigma of impropriety seemed to fall on me, rather than on her. It was hard to tell whether her infantilism were real, or half-consciously assumed in order to have a child's license and excuse to do as she pleased. I am inclined to think that both with her and with many others, it is assumed. One girl said, "When I have had a few nights without dates I nearly go crazy. I tell my mother she must expect me to go out on a fearful necking party. . . ."

But I imagine that the assumed childish attitude of the daughter is reflected by her mother, who longs to have her daughter popular, and get her full share of masculine attention. And if the daughter takes for granted that what her mother does not know will not hurt her, so does her mother's habit of blind and deaf supervision indicate that she too does not want to know any more than she has to. The college student is no longer preeminently from a selected class. One has only to look at the names and family status in the college registers to see that. If petting is felt to be poor taste in some families, there are many more families of poor taste than there used to be, whose children go to college. Their daughters are pretty and their sons have money to spend, and they seem prodigies of learning and accomplishment, especially to their unlettered mothers, who glow with pride over their popularity. The pleasant side of the picture is that anybody's daughter may go to college and pass on her own merits. The less agreeable side is that more refined, but timid and less numerous stocks feel obliged to model their social behavior on the crude amorousness and doubtful pleasantries which prevail at peasant parties. If anyone charges the daughters with being vulgar, the chances are that the mothers, though more shy, are essentially just as vulgar. The mothers have no accomplishments in which the daughters cannot surpass them, or no alternate social grace or cultivated recreation to suggest, if petting is denied them. Indeed that daughters are really at war with their mothers in point of view, I do not believe. On the contrary, thousands of mothers live all their emotional life in the gaiety of their daughters—having nothing else to live it in, and they suffer

quite as deeply as their daughters if maternal strictness threatens to make 143
wallflowers of them. Do not listen to what their mothers *say*, but *watch* them, if
you want to know how they feel about their daughters petting! Their protests are
about as genuine, as the daughter's, "Aren't you terrible?" when a young man
starts to pet.

The sex manners of the large marjority of uncultivated and uncritical people
have become the manners for all, because they have prospered, they are getting
educated, and there are so many of them. They are not squeamish, and they never
have been. But their children can set a social standard as the parents could not.
The prudent lawyer's child has no idea of letting the gay daughter of the broad-
joking workman get the dates away from her. If petting is the weapon Miss
Workman uses, then petting it must be, and in nine cases out of ten, not only Mrs.
Workman, but also Mrs. Lawyer agree not to see too much. At heart both women
are alike. Neither one can bear to see her daughter take a back seat in the struggle
for popularity, and neither woman has any other ambition for her daughter but a
successful husband. If by any chance, petting led *away* from popularity and
possible husbands instead of *to* them, the mothers would be whole-heartedly
against it, and if they were—petting, as a recognized recreation, would stop.

The Weary Blues

LANGSTON HUGHES

Throughout the twenties, American artists and writers produced an extraordinary collection of novels, poetry, painting, music, and plays. Some, like Ernest Hemingway, F. Scott Fitzgerald, and Gertrude Stein, settled as expatriates in Paris. Others, like Sinclair Lewis, Eugene O'Neill, Hart Crane, and Edward Hopper, reflected basic American themes.

Generally overlooked at the time were the remarkable artistic expressions coming from New York City's Harlem, which became the capital of black America during this decade. Popularly recognized for its jazz clubs and ebullient nightlife, Harlem in the twenties witnessed an artistic renaissance, as intellectuals gave expression to the historic triumphs, tragedies, and hopes of black America. James Weldon Johnson, Claude McKay, Countee Cullen, and Langston Hughes were the best known among scores of black artists. Hughes' "The Weary Blues" drew on the black musical idiom to express "that sad raggy tune . . . from a black man's soul."

Droning a drowsy syncopated tune,
　Rocking back and forth to a mellow croon,
　　I heard a Negro play.
Down on Lenox Avenue the other night
By the pale dull pallor of an old gas light
　He did a lazy sway. . . .
　He did a lazy sway. . . .
To the tune o' those Weary Blues.
With his ebony hands on each ivory key
He made that poor piano moan with melody.
　O Blues!
Swaying to and fro on his rickety stool
He played that sad raggy tune like a musical fool.
　Sweet Blues!
Coming from a black man's soul.
　O Blues!
In a deep song voice with a melancholy tone
I heard that Negro sing, that old piano moan—

　"Ain't got nobody in all this world,
　Ain't got nobody but ma self.
　I's gwine to quit ma frownin'
　And put ma troubles on the shelf."
Thump, thump, thump, went his foot on the floor.
He played a few chords then he sang some more—
　"I got the Weary Blues
　And I can't be satisfied.
　Got the Weary Blues
　And can't be satisfied—
　I ain't happy no mo'
　And I wish that I had died."
And far into the night he crooned that tune.
The stars went out and so did the moon.
The singer stopped playing and went to bed
While the Weary Blues echoed through his head.
He slept like a rock or a man that's dead.

144

Booze, Here and There

ERNEST W. MANDEVILLE

Beginning in 1920, the Eighteenth Amendment to the Constitution of the United States prohibited "the manufacture, sale or transportation of intoxicating liquors." Most Americans simply refused to obey the Volstead Act, which Congress had passed to enforce Prohibition. The struggle between "dries" and "wets" lasted until 1933, when the Twenty-first Amendment did away with this massive social experiment.

Throughout the twenties, organized crime took its modern shape from the immense profits found in bootlegging imported and homemade intoxicants. In the process, lawlessness became acceptable to most Americans as the price to be paid for continued alcoholic supplies. Federal and local authorities were regularly corrupted, courts were paralyzed, and criminals, like Al Capone, became celebrities. In the following selection, a reporter describes the drinking scene along the Eastern seaboard.

In Elmira, New York, I found over twenty saloons within five blocks on Railroad Avenue. Before prohibition this section of the town was frequented only by the "low lifes." Now, I am informed, a good part of its patronage is drawn from the sons of the wealthy and from car-loads of Cornell boys who drive over from Ithaca.

The proprietor of one of the hotels there showed me the system by which he controls the entrance to his bar. The door to the barroom is unlocked by pushing a button in the lobby. The desk clerk thus prevents free access to the stranger. Once in the barroom, you can't get out until the bartender releases the lock by pushing another button.

The bartender at another place told me that he wouldn't touch the Scotch whisky that was coming into Elmira—it was too poor stuff. He added that fine rye whisky was shipped in from the warehouses in Scranton, Pennsylvania. Beer in plenty is brought in from Sayre and Scranton. Pennsylvania is said to be the center of most of the Eastern beer supply. Elmirians also report that Auburn, New York, is one of the main liquor-distributing points for Central New York. Champagne occasionally is brought down from Lake Keuka.

Whisky brings from $70 a case up in Elmira. There are several well-known dealers who will arrange delivery, or one can buy from the traveling bootleggers who make their rounds weekly. Highballs, over the bar, are fifty and seventy-five cents, depending upon the quality of the liquor.

Railroad Avenue is also the disorderly-house section, and this business as well as the drug traffic is closely allied with booze-selling, I was told by a resident of the street, an old friend.

He also told me that the foreigners, who for the most part run these saloons, are getting rich from the business and buying quantities of expensive real estate with their earnings. This statement was borne out by the testimony of local real estate and investment men. An automobile insurance man and the head of a company which finances the time-payment purchase of automobiles told me that automobile thefts have more than doubled in the last few years. These men attribute this to the rum-running crowd, who steal cars to transport their contraband. They also said that bootleggers buy cars on time payments, so that if the car be confiscated by the authorities under the Prohibition Law the investment loss will not be so heavy.

■ ■ ■

The police of the city show the usual indifference to the Volstead Law, and the league of dry enthusiasts employs its own deputies, paying a lump sum for each conviction. Of course these men have to work in conjunction with the Federal agents. Many complaints were made to me of the methods employed by these deputies to run up their earning power. They take pot shots at innocent automobilists riding on the highways after dark who will not stop at their waving lantern. The automobilists say that they dare not stop in secluded spots, on account of the increased number of road bandits. From the waving lantern they cannot tell whether it be a law enforcer or a law-breaker. The bootleggers say that they don't mind being arrested when fairly "caught with the goods," but that these privately paid enforcers (a poor lot, they say) "frame up" the evidence against them. They allege that warrants for arrest are sworn out without any actual evidence and without previous entrance to their places. It is common talk among the drinkers of the town that the booze-selling places are always "tipped off" before a Federal raid. They always know of the time set for raiding, and manage to have nothing illegal on their premises at the time of search. The Law Enforcement League is making a strenuous effort to dry up the town. Its members attend the sittings of the Federal Court, petition the judge to extend the full penalties, and hold prayer-meetings in the corridors during the lunch hours.

A great deal of public opinion which was formerly with the drys seems to have turned against them now, because of some of the methods that they have employed.

The social events of the town are marked now by their wetness in contrast to the pre-prohibition customs. It is now quite the thing for a young couple to get roaring drunk at the best parties. Champagne punch is served at the fashionable dances. It is reported that after the social event of the year the hall and anterooms were strewn with empty bottles.

Conditions in Corning, New York, I am told, are similar to those in Elmira. Ithaca is much drier, at least as far as open selling and drinking goes. Buffalo and Syracuse are two of the widest-open cities in the State. I believe they surpass New York in openness of selling and lawlessness. Geneva saloons furnish all the liquor the drinkers want; beer at 20 cents a glass; gin at $6 a quart, and whisky for $8 to $12 according to the quality and origin. A favorite Geneva drink is raw alcohol mixed with ginger ale. This alcohol sells for $4 a pint.

People in Schenectady who are close observers of conditions tell me that the underworld has grown wealthy and powerful from the profits of booze-selling. A daughter of one of the first families in Schenectady told me that girls of her set have "hen luncheons," to which they all carry flasks of liquor and drink it in the wash-rooms. Saloons operate openly in Ballston Spa, a small town north of Schenectady. Beer and whisky are sold to any one who wants them, and the places keep open as late at night as they can do business.

■ ■ ■

The New York suburban towns that I visited were selling quite openly. At a fashionable resort within forty miles of New York City, with hundreds of the young aristocracy present, I saw more drinking and boisterous drunkenness in a single evening than I have seen in any other evening in all my up-State travel-

The "noble experiment" of Prohibition lasted from 1920 to 1933. The idealistic dreams of its supporters soon confronted the very clear fact that a massive number of Americans not only opposed the law but also were quite prepared to break it. An efficient production and distribution system, usually controlled by underworld mobsters, kept illicit booze flowing, despite some attempts to stop it. This photograph shows the seizure of a still. What do you think persuaded America to try Prohibition? Why did it fail?

148 ing—and that is *some* drinking. Walking out on the piazza for fresh air, I saw a young girl, expensively gowned, stretched out, face downwards, in the muddy driveway, dead to the world from drink.

New Year's Eve in New York City showed me more drunkenness in the early morning hours than any of the previous celebrations that I have witnessed. The little side-street places which sold beer or ale by the glass seemed to be the ones troubled by the authorities, while the big places in the Broadway white lights kept on selling, evidently without molestation. There was little secrecy that I saw. Bottles of liquor were brought in and placed on the tables; reeling drunks were much in evidence.

One proprietor of a "speak-easy" in Greenwich Village told me that there is now a growing demand for "confidential tenors." He explained that he meant an entertainer who can sing in muted *tempo* or practically in a whisper, going from table to table while performing. This is to avoid complaints from neighboring tenants, who have been registering protests that the noise of these night places causes them to be public nuisances.

Alcoholism is said to have increased twofold in New York State during the past year. I interviewed Dr. John J. McGrath, President of the Board of Trustees of Bellevue Hospital, New York City. He said: "There were more than three times as many victims of alcoholic poisoning last year than there were in 1921. During the last five years the number of alcoholic poisoning cases has been so great that the facilities of this department of the hospital have been taxed to their utmost. Each successive year for the last five years the number of alcoholics treated at Bellevue Hospital has increased; as a matter of fact, from 1,500 in 1919 to 6,000 in 1924. Formerly an alcoholic patient needed not more than two or three days in the hospital for recovery. He now requires about fifteen days and the whole-time services of a nurse. This can only be accounted for by the fact that the liquor which these unfortunate people are able to obtain is a potent poison as compared with the liquor of previous years.

"The victims are mostly poor folks," he added. "They buy terrible stuff; spend fifteen days in the hospital, and go right back at it again."

■ ■ ■

Hartford is one of the driest cities in Connecticut, which on the whole is a wet State. There are only two States in the Union which have not yet ratified the Eighteenth Amendment. They are Connecticut and Rhode Island.

Hugh M. Alcorn, State's Attorney, is a most vigorous prosecutor, and he has succeeded in closing up Hartford as far as open drinking is concerned. A story is woven about his activity. It is said that, having as a boy seen at close hand the effects of alcoholism, he has grown up to hate liquor. To right what he conceives to be a wrong he gives himself to the full. The bootleggers fear and respect his ruthless activity.

For the stranger Hartford is dry. The bootleggers, however, solve the family problem, and there is a great deal of home drinking, I am told. The efficient prosecutor is after this too. A society bootlegger was recently arrested and a list of his clients was published. They were summoned to court amid much unpleasant notoriety.

Bridgeport is very wet. Whisky is plentiful at prices slightly above those of

College football became a major spectator sport during the 1920s at a time when the professional game remained disorganized and unstable. Collegiate heroes such as Red Grange, the Galloping Ghost from Illinois, attracted adulation and newspaper space. Can you speculate on the reasons for the continued popularity of this game, most of whose fans have never played it on any organized level? In this 1929 photo, Northwestern is on its way to beating Illinois for the first time in eighteen years.

New York. The selling is quite open. New Britain and Waterbury are also wide open. Waterbury saloons run almost as in pre-prohibition days, and a new species of "club" (two flights up) sells liquor of uncertain quality to almost any visitor. In these clubs are coin slot gambling machines which are said to have an earning power of $50 each weekly and to be owned by the politicians. Druggists sell with or without prescriptions. A favorite local compound consists of rye whisky essence plus grain alcohol and synthetic gin. Flavoring extracts to which one adds alcohol are becoming very popular. "Imported" rye whisky sells for from $60 to $90 a case, while the local bootleggers offer their own make "Green Rye" for $20 a gallon.

In Danbury a close friend of mine visited one Sunday morning a bar which sold liquor openly, and he found that the bartender had gone to church.

New Haven is much stricter than Waterbury, and there is little open selling. Most of the liquor is brought in, and is said to come from Providence, but the extent of the traffic is small, I believe, in comparison with the easier-going cities. Even so, the last Yale-Harvard football game, which brought in thousands of visitors, was the scene of much open drinking while the spectators viewed the game in a drizzling rain.

Massachusetts is notoriously wet. In Boston the liquor traffic, from all indications, must be an enormous one. Prices are about twenty-five per cent higher than in New York, but the openness and extent of selling seem to be about as great.

Federal Prohibition Director Murdock, of Philadelphia, Pennsylvania, says that local bootleggers have made more than $100,000,000 in the last few years. He is very pessimistic about the hopes of stopping their traffic, which is getting more and more intrenched all the time.

I found Philadelphia to be one of the wettest cities in the East. Liquor is plentiful at very cheap prices, and little or no attempt is made to cover up the selling. James P. Britt, general counsel to the Prohibition Unit, considers the Quaker City the great booze-distributing point of the East.

Liquor was served openly in the dining-room of one prominent downtown club that I visited. At another club this was not the case. The practice was discouraged, it is said, as a mark of respect to one of its members, Governor Pinchot. Drinking was not absent in this club however. The locker-room took the place of the dining-room.

Together with my companion, who was wearing his clerical collar, I stepped into a fashionable club in suburban Philadelphia to get warm by the fire. My companion had been there only a few times, but we were inside less than five minutes before the steward offered us any spirituous drink that we might choose.

This steward told us that the club rented out its ballroom nearly every night for society dances. "Before prohibition," he said, "I never had any trouble with rowdyism or misconduct at the dances, but that has changed now. It is a problem to keep order and to prevent an open scandal. My cleaning-women tell me that they find scores of empty bottles now in the ladies' retiring-rooms after every dance."

Reaffirming the Sacco-Vanzetti Verdict

The social, economic, and cultural ferment of the twenties developed within a political context that emphasized tradition, even reaction. The progressive spirit of prewar politics gave way to the corruption of Harding's Ohio Gang and the passivity of Silent Cal Coolidge. As progressivism disappeared, political dissent and eccentricity came to be regarded with suspicion and hostility. Especially vulnerable were foreigners and recent immigrants from southern and eastern Europe, who often preached and organized in industrial centers and working-class neighborhoods. Although socialist thought had become a staple of European politics, its American history was short-lived and actively challenged by businessmen, politicians, and the press. In the years immediately following the 1917 Bolshevik Revolution in Russia, antiradical fears spread throughout the United States, and basic constitutional rights were routinely flouted by law enforcement agencies. The Red Scare of 1919–1920 included a roundup of suspected radicals, invasion and seizure of property, and deportations. Within this atmosphere, two Italian workers were charged with armed robbery and murder in a case that still excites passionate argument.

Nicola Sacco and Bartolomeo Vanzetti, active in Boston-area radical circles, were given a trial at which the hostile attitudes of prosecutor, judge, and jury seemed obvious. The two men were convicted in 1921 and executed in 1927, after a succession of appeals had been denied. Storms of protest attracted international support for the men, and they were joined by many American liberals and radicals. Yet most Americans probably agreed with the verdict of the courts.

While the lawyers look for some last legal loophole to keep Bartolomeo Vanzetti and Nicola Sacco from the electric chair, thus taking full advantage of the twelve-day respite given by the Governor to make possible last-minute appeals to the courts, the press of the country seem for the most part to be swinging toward acceptance of Massachusetts justice. Even when Governor Fuller's decision upholding the conviction of the two Italian radicals was made public, many observers withheld judgment until they could peruse the finding of the Governor's advisory committee, Judge Robert Grant, President Lowell of Harvard, and President Stratton of the Massachusetts Institute of

Technology. Scores of editors all over the country now declare that all reasonable men must accept the decision of so distinguished a triumvirate that the conviction and sentencing of Sacco and Vanzetti were fully justified. A minority, including several influential papers, feel that there still exists too much room for doubt when men's lives are at stake, and appeal either for a complete rehearing or the substitution of life imprisonment for the capital sentence. Meantime, throughout the world the Sacco-Vanzetti case is arousing more agitation than any trial since that of Dreyfus. Radicals of all kinds meet and parade in protest, petitioning letters come to Boston and Washington from all the capitals of the Old World. Our legations in a score of cities are guarded against threatened attacks. Bombs were exploded in New York subway stations, and police reserves have been called out in a dozen cities to prevent violence expected in connection with mass meetings called to protest against the execution of Sacco and Vanzetti. Well-known writers and liberal leaders have been throwing all their energy into the work of assisting in the defense of the two doomed men. As one more postponement draws out the agony, there comes from many a press writer strong protest against the judicial system which allows the death sentence to be still hanging over men in the summer of 1927 for a crime committed in the spring of 1920.

When Governor Fuller of Massachusetts gave out his decision that Sacco and Vanzetti had had a fair trial; were not entitled to a new one; and were in his opinion actually guilty and should therefore pay the extreme penalty, he stated that his advisory committee had come unanimously to the same conclusion. The committee made an independent investigation, calling witnesses and consulting with the judge and jury who first tried the case, and the counsel on both sides, besides visiting the scene of the crime and calling on the prisoners in jail. Taking up first the question of the conduct of the trial the committee say that the record gives the impression "that the judge tried to be scrupulously fair":

> "It has been said that while the acts and language of the judge seem to be correct, yet his attitude and emphasis conveyed a different impression, but the jury did not think so. They state that the judge tried the case fairly; that they perceived no bias.
>
> "Affidavits were presented to the committee and witnesses were heard to the effect that the judge, during and after the trial, had exprest his opinion of guilt in vigorous terms. Prejudice means an opinion or sentiment before the trial. That a judge should form an opinion as the evidence comes in is inevitable and not prejudicial if not in any way brought to the notice of the jury, as we are convinced was true in this case.
>
> "From all that has come to us we are forced to conclude that the judge was indiscreet in conversation with outsiders during the trial. He ought not to have talked about the case off the bench, and doing so was a grave breach of official decorum. But we do not believe that he used some of the expressions attributed to him, and we think that there is exaggeration in what the persons to whom he spoke remember. Furthermore, we believe that such indiscretion in conversation did not affect his conduct at the trial or the opinions of the jury, who so stated to the committee."

The committee finds no evidence of collusion between the District Attorney at the trial and the United States Department of Justice, as charged by spokesmen for the defense. They do not take seriously allegations "that the whole atmosphere of the courtroom and its surroundings, with the armed police and evident precautions, were such as to prejudice the jury at the outset; while the remark of the Judge to the talesmen that they must do their duty as the soldier boys did in the war was of a nature to incline them against the prisoners." On the whole, "they are of opinion that the Judge endeavored, and endeavored successfully, to secure for the defendants a fair trial; that the District Attorney was not in any

Nicola Sacco (left) and Bartolomeo Vanzetti (right) leaving the courthouse during their trial. Do they look like radicals and criminals?

way guilty of unprofessional behavior, that he conducted the prosecution vigorously, but not improperly; and that the jury, a capable, impartial and unprejudiced body, did, as they were instructed, "well and truly try and true deliverance make."

Judge Thayer, in the opinion of the committee, was fully justified in holding the new evidence insufficient for a new trial. As for the new witness, Gould, who was in "an unusually good position to observe the men in the car" used by the murderers in South Braintree and made an affidavit that the men were not the defendants—his evidence is said to be "merely cumulative," as other defense witnesses said the same thing, and to be balanced by new witnesses on the other side. These witnesses are two women who have stated that they saw Sacco near the place of the murder about the time it was committed. The committee find no reason for supposing that Captain Proctor, a fire-arms expert, made an answer designed to mislead a jury in connection with the identification of a certain bullet on exhibition, as charged by the defense. On the whole, it is found that the prosecution's bullet experts presented more convincing evidence than those for the defense. The committee do not take seriously the statement of Madeiros, a convicted murderer, that he himself was a member of the South Braintree murder gang, and that Sacco and Vanzetti were not. His statements are found extremely vague, as are also other affidavits offered by the defense to indicate that the murder was committed by a notorious Providence "gang." The committee are inclined to believe that there is something more than coincidence in the resemblance between the bullets used in the murder and those found on Sacco's person. They emphasize the fact that both Sacco and Vanzetti "were armed for quick action when arrested." They do not believe that fear of punishment as "Reds" explains all the falsehoods told by Sacco and Vanzetti in trying to explain their

Women won the vote in 1920, but it was a difficult fight and many people opposed woman suffrage fearing that all kinds of horrible things would result. Even after the woman's suffrage amendment passed, not everyone approved of giving women political power. Did women really gain equality by winning suffrage? What is the reasoning of today's groups that oppose equal rights for women?

movements. They reject the alibi offered by Sacco to prove that he was in Boston the day of the murder. Vanzetti's alibi is also held "decidedly weak." Both Sacco and Vanzetti are "guilty beyond reasonable doubt" and guilty of a crime which was undoubtedly "murder in the first degree." The report concludes:

> "It has been urged that a crime of this kind must have been committed by professionals, and it is for well-known criminal gangs that one must look; but to the committee both this crime and the one at Bridgewater do not seem to bear the marks of professionals, but of men inexpert in such crimes."

"Where before in the history of American jurisprudence," asks the Binghamton *Press*, "have three more disciplined minds given to condemned murderers the benefit of what, in effect, is a second trial?" Their decision, insists the Chicago *Tribune* "will be accepted by the American conscience." This is the attitude of a host of papers. The mere mention of their names is impossible for lack of space. Among them, however, may be mentioned such widely scattered journals as the Jersey City *Journal*, New York *Herald Tribune*, New York *Sun*, Springfield *Union*, Washington *Post*, Providence *Journal*, the Louisville *Courier-Journal*, Richmond *Times-Dispatch*, New Orleans *Times-Picayune*, St. Louis *Globe-Democrat*, Kansas City *Star*, Indianapolis *News*, St. Paul *Pioneer Press*, San Francisco *Chronicle*, Spokane *Spokesman-Review*, and Tacoma *Ledger*.

One of the three things that stand out significantly, as the New York *Times* examines the report, "is the transparent desire of the committee to run to earth the charge that the two men were convicted not on the evidence, but out of prejudice." A second is the judicial quality in the sifting of the evidence offered in the

demand for a new trial. In the third place, there is the carefully reviewed evidence
offered at the original trial. Says *The Times*:

> "Human law can do no more. There is no infallibility in our criminal procedure.
> Juries and judges have to do the best they can with the evidence of men who may be
> mistaken. But, while everybody must feel that the long and heartrending delays in the
> Sacco-Vanzetti case have been a reproach to American justice, and while it is a
> lamentable thing that the two men have been elevated all over the world into a kind of
> symbolic martyrdom, it is a great public service which President Lowell, President
> Stratton, and ex-Judge Grant have done in assuring the American people and the world
> that no intentional or notorious injustice has been done."

The strongest attacks on the Governor's decision and his committee's report
come from the Sacco-Vanzetti Defense Committee. Their detailed criticisms can
not be taken up here. We may note, however, their assertion that the Governor's
statement "betrays an appalling ignorance of the vital facts in the Sacco-Vanzetti
case," and "shows a complete failure to grasp the ideas involved." Not only, we
are told, "does the Governor omit discussion of the chief points relied on by the
defense; he also fills his opinions with half-truths, whose stupidity is as dangerous
as if they were absolute falsehoods." The detailed reply to the Grant-Lowell-
Stratton report starts off like this:

> "President Lowell of Harvard University and his associates make no pretense of
> believing any defense witnesses. They believe only prosecution witnesses, no matter
> how discredited they are.
> "In the process of explaining the State's case, the commission falls into the most
> terrible inconsistencies, contradictions, omissions, and misrepresentations."

Conspicuous among many editorial doubters is the Springfield *Republican*,
which in an editorial addressed to Governor Fuller notes the committee's admission
that Judge Thayer was guilty of "a grave breach of official decorum"—"the
malignant mischief that can be done by that phrase in the mouths of promoters of
industrial and social strife in the years to come appalls the imagination." This
Massachusetts paper insists that the "accused men should not be put to death
unless the official conduct of the judge who presided at their trial was beyond
rebuke, above reproach." *The Republican* believes there is still enough doubt
remaining "to justify commutation of sentence to life imprisonment." Similarly
the Norfolk *Virginian-Pilot* feels that the committee's report "adds to the general
uneasiness." It wonders what Messrs. Lowell and Stratton and Judge Grant
"would consider truly prejudicial conduct," and it concludes:

> "Nothing in the advisory commission's statement reinforces the conviction that
> Sacco and Vanzetti should be executed, and very much in it sustains the conviction that
> the doubt as to their guilt is of such formidable proportions as to command a stay of
> execution in the interest of a civilized application of the principles of justice.
> "It is probably true that the doubt that hangs over the Sacco-Vanzetti case is
> beyond resolving by any judicial machinery in the world. Millions believe Sacco and
> Vanzetti guilty, and millions believe them innocent, and the division is likely to survive
> anything that can be done to eliminate it. In the circumstances, *The Virginian-Pilot*
> believes the death sentence should be commuted to life imprisonment."

The New York *World* also vigorously maintains that Sacco and Vanzetti
should be given a life sentence instead of execution. It praises the advisory

committee's report as showing "fairness, consideration, shrewdness, and coolness." But it feels that the case "remains one that rests on circumstantial evidence which, while it may be highly damaging, is not fully conclusive." It insists that "Massachusetts has thus far failed to convince a very important section of American opinion that the execution of these two men is clearly justified." If Sacco and Vanzetti are guilty, argues *The World*, "the ends of justice are fully served by life imprisonment; but if perchance one or both of these men are innocent, there would still remain the chance to undo the mistake." Similar doubts are voiced by the Baltimore *Sun*, Macon *Telegraph*, Providence *News*, Topeka *State Journal*, and Denver *Rocky Mountain News*. Henry Ford, reiterating his disbelief in capital punishment, declares—

> "I believe Sacco and Vanzetti should not be executed. The sentence of death could be revoked without the verdict of guilty being annulled, and this would give opportunity to weigh new evidence that may appear in the men's favor."

William Green, President of the American Federation of Labor, who has decried radical outbursts over the Sacco-Vanzetti case, says in a letter to Governor Fuller:

> "Taking these facts into account, as well as the mental and physical anguish which Sacco and Vanzetti must have undergone during the last seven years, I appeal to you for commutation of sentence.
>
> "I base this appeal for the exercise of executive clemency upon the broad ground of humanity and social expediency, and in behalf of the millions of men and women affiliated with the American Federation of Labor."

"Two innocent men are going to their doom in order that a social system may be upheld; a tottering social order may triumph," declares that radical weekly, *The Nation*. And it adds:

> "We can not for one instant accept this verdict in the face of facts known to us for years as they have been known to multitudes of others. Nor are we convinced by the facile report of the Governor's committee of three eminent and conventional gentlemen, two chosen from the highest Boston social circles, all of one type of mind and not one of them representing the vast groups that have felt from the first that they had a vital stake in the fate of these men.
>
> "As for Governor Fuller's judgment of the case, it no more closes it than the hanging of John Brown ended the Harper's Ferry raid and condemned him to execration and oblivion. Rightly or wrongly, the case of Sacco and Vanzetti has become identified with efforts to reconstruct the social order."

The Nation insists that it is not merely the radicals who are dismayed:

> "It is not the radicals alone who fought for Sacco and Vanzetti. Noble souls have given years of their lives and their money to this cause who are neither Reds nor foreign-born Americans; nor have they belonged to those holding the anarchist view of the condemned. If there are finer types of our citizenship, or men and women of older American lineage, we should like to have them pointed out to us. To them an incredible tragedy is being finished before their eyes; a judicial murder is being committed. Does not the passionate belief of these unselfish supporters of the right merit consideration?"

Letters from Jail

BARTOLOMEO VANZETTI

During their more than six years in prison, both Sacco and Vanzetti wrote extensively, *proclaiming their innocence in rough but memorable English.*

December 11, 1926. Charlestown Prison

MY DEAR FRIEND [MRS. MAUDE PETTYJOHN]:

Our I—— B—— has told me that I will receive a letter from you. . . . I was pleased with the news, for it is quite a long time that I have heard from you, and I eagerly expected the letter, because I like your writing. Finally, I received it some days ago, and now I am trying to answer it.

Yes, trying . . .! for there is much understanding in your beautiful letter, strong beliefs, and hints to things so vast and deep, that I do not know anything about, not even how to begin my reasoning, before which however, I wish to thank you for the goodness of your letter and the pleasure that it brought to me—to us all.

Exactly talking, I am not busy in writing, but in trying to write. For, the prisoner's spell is telling its story also on me, and how so! It seems to be increasing my understanding and diminishing my power of expression. In fact, it is an experience alright; but an experience that undermines the life straight to its sources and centers so that as long as consciousness and memory are not yet weakened, you can realize something—but, as to express oneself at one's best, one has to be at one's best, while after such experiences one is no longer at his best; he can no longer express himself at the best of his power. These are the reasons why I am busy trying to write and writing very little at all. Oftentimes my mind is ravishing; oftentimes, it is blank. More often I cannot express my thoughts. Oftentimes, I manoeuver hard to write down what I wish, then, reading it, I perceive that it does not say what I mean and I tear the writings in many little pieces. Many times, I feel lazy, indolent, malignant and cynic; asking myself what is the use to write and if it pays its troubles. If I still write it is to gratify myself, when I feel to write. At least, it seems to me.

The crux of this inner drama is not only about expression—it is that I doubt my own thoughts, my opinions, my feeling, my sentiments, beliefs and ideals. I am sure of nothing, I know nothing. When I think of a thing and try to understand it, I see that in the time, in the place, and in the matter that thing is, both before and after, related to so many other things that I, following its relations, both backward and forward, see it disappear in the ocean of the unknown, and myself lost in it. It is easy to create a universal system, to human minds; that is why we are blessed by so many of universal systems, while no one knows what a bad brick is. The sense of relativity and of measure is a progress on the sense of the absolute and infinite, for the former is a capacity of discernment, the second a mental abstraction, a symbol of the "abroad" of our senses and relative knowledge.

To be sure, I am not in any better support with the words, opinions, beliefs and ideas of others than I am with my own ones. I believe to have been [born] with the faculties of acquiring ideas, forming opinions, learning words, and express myself— but not with opinions, ideas and words already in me. Believing this, I must also believe that all my actual ideas, opinions, beliefs and words came to me from some other persons. Yet . . . only that part of their saying that satisfies my ego. But, even in this, I am not entirely free, for, to be the best that I could be now, I should have been, before my very conception, conscientious, intelligent, a power more capable and intelligent than the one I am now, so to begin my beginning in the best of the ways, and to impart continually to my evolving self only truths and normalcy. Evidently, it must not have been so, for I have not the least recollection of such a feast! Whereas, I am but too well aware, alas! to have begun as a miser to have inherited all the misery of the earth and of the race, called atavism—to have been taken to church when I was wholly unconscious and irresponsible, to have been spiritually raped by the priests, when I was wholly unable to defend myself, to have been intellectually warped and poisoned by the State school, when I was unable to discriminate—to have grown within a humanity so stupid, ignorant, vile, coward, arrogant, self-conceited, brutal, greedy, ferocious and filthy and falsely proud and humble, that the best of my essence was choked in myself, or, what is still worse, distorted and aberrated. To my parents, to my mother especially, I owe not only my life that she gave me by birth and cares, but all that is good in me. Yet, even my parents, in spite of their love and good-will, they teach me many wrong ideas, false principles, and a false divinity. It is by a rinnovation of [my] own previous self, through a self reaction, an inner tragedy which costed me the bleeding of my heart's blood, that I re-began and became what I am now. I brought it to myself and ever more to many humble persons and children who gave me fragments of truth and to the genious of the race. Thus I reached the present stage of my being.

All what I have said may induce you to believe that I am a so-called "Determinist." I am not so, though I believe in the existence of a "together of things" which we pass through and which influence is a "concomittant" factor of our individuality. That "together" is made of two different orders of things, namely; of the things of nature above the human-will and power, and the things which result from the human behaviors and their worksome matters. But that is not "all," for each of us differ from the others, though many spoke of conception, maternity, atavism, etc. Well, those things too are subject to changes and conditions that alter them,—still determinism. But, why are we? Why are we as we are? Why chances make differences? Here the "determinism" spring from something else—from the unknown. If we follow it, it ultimately opens in the unknown again.

To believe that hope, faith, optimism, confidence, are good to the individual, is part of the race wisdom; an historical experience. So we all are most grateful and appreciative of your motherly incitation to them.

Yet, life, happiness, health and goodness depend from things which are what and as they are, and not what and as we believe or hope them to be. So that wrong faith, absurd hope, unfounded optimism and confidence are or may be fatal or at least very deleterious to the individual, in spite of their real help to him as animators. For they mislead us and when we face evil, cannot help us.

I believe better, to try and look the reality straight in its face, eyes into eyes. The question is not to shift from barren reality by any dreams or auto-suggestion. It is: 1st—Not to let ourselves be overwhelmed by the adversity, scared by black prospects, but face them as bravely as possible. 2nd—Try to fight them with all our force. To destroy bad realities, to create good ones, lo! that makes gods out of men and women.

It is for such reason that I indict all the new and all religions. They dope the people so to eternate slavery, unequality, exploitations, crimes, vices and death. The new religions are not better than the old ones for this. . . . By these criterion I came to understand the phylosophy of "free will" and that of "determinism." According to the latter, none is guilty. The former is more wrong and deleterious than the latter, and it explains the mercilessness of the law, the dishonesty of the State, the ferocity monstrous of the churches, and the immorality of the pure moralists. The latter, too, has its weakness and bad consequences. It tends to weaken the human will, to incline its believers to an idle fatalism, to self-indulgence and irresponsibility in a way, for if things cannot be otherwise than how they are, or go otherwise than how they go, if we are what external factors determine, you can see the consequence of such thinking. As for me, I believe to a certain extent in both, as limited and changeable phenomenum, interdependent, and dependant from some higher phenomenism. So, I have no ultimate word on them and I remain a *Voluntarist.*

You are right—maybe it would be a rest to me, not to think of the case. But the case is turning badly. The enemies are determined to burn us as soon as possible, and therefore, I am compelled to write of it, while I can. You know that I am a revolutionist; dreaming, willing a Polygenesis of life. My own story serves my purpose, points to my goal magnificently. That is why I am in spiritual travail. . . .

M—— M—— is a dear little soul. A farmer girl too. . . . Her letters are bliss to me. Now, she may be sad for me, for she wrote me about religion. . . . The dear thing asked them to pray for me, to send her prayers to me and one for me. She sent it to me. I answered as kindly as possible, that I do not believe in it, but that I respect her belief, and appreciate her intention. Maybe, I told her, it is good to me, do it if you wish, but I don't believe. She must be sad for it for it is quite a long time since I have heard from her. . . .

I see that B—— L—— is quite a scorner and a pessimist. Well, the world will never have enough scorners. Pessimism itself, in a way, is good. Darrow said, "If you are not worse than your fathers, if you have progressed a little, you shall acquit these negroes." And the jury acquitted them. Had they thought their fathers to be holy, in spite of slavery, they would not have acquitted the Negroes.

Thayer and Katzmann always appealed to the jury pretence of superiority and goodness to induce them to convict us.

Of course, the saints have a better way; but the saints are few. . . .

I too, would be with your son, in the farm, through woods, on hills and mountains. I love farming more than any other works and nature over all. But I do dislike hunting, not as a sport, but for its killing. Bears must be damaging and dangerous if people are allowed to hunt them freely. Don't you think so?

Your place must be very similar to my native place. Can you see from your home, mountain peaks eternally covered by snow? If so, your place is like mine. . . .

[BARTOLOMEO VANZETTI]

"Babe" Ruth's Record-breaking

World Series

While Americans have enjoyed recreational sports since colonial days, professional sports, dependent upon paying customers, are a recent phenomenon. Organized baseball took shape in late nineteenth-century industrial centers and caught on as an urban reminder of timeless rural play. Not until the twenties, however, did large-scale spectator sports develop as a permanent feature of American life. Million-dollar gates for boxing matches featured heavyweight champion Jack Dempsey. Overflow crowds at college football games stimulated a fledgling professional league, including George Halas' Canton Bulldogs. Golf's Bobby Jones and tennis star Big Bill Tilden became national celebrities. Above all these sports loomed baseball, America's pastime. And into baseball's universe strode a kid

from the slums of Baltimore, George Herman Ruth, "the Babe."

Ruth captured the imagination of America. His ability and the introduction of a new cork-centered baseball were the start of the home-run era. In 1917, Yankee first baseman Wally Pipp led the American League with nine homers. In 1920, Ruth hit 54. The Babe fit perfectly into the splashy decade, with his scarcely concealed tastes for fast automobiles, showgirls, and speakeasies. Above all, he possessed great individual talent. Probably the best all-around player in the game's history, Ruth quickly became an American hero, a representative figure of the rags-to-riches dreams of millions.

A description of one characteristic incident, in the 1928 World Series, follows.

The big barrage of pop bottles was about to start. First there were hoots and then a few preliminary bottles came whizzing out over the diamond toward the big, good-natured ball player. "They were what is known in artillery circles as 'ranging shots,'" W. O. McGeehan writes in the New York *Herald Tribune*. "The big barrage would come as soon as the range had been corrected." But it never came. "Babe" Ruth stopt it. For it was none other than the "home-run king," to give him but one of his many nicknames, who was the object of these beginning hostilities. The scene was Sportsman's Park in St. Louis, and the time was the thrilling seventh inning of the last game when the New York Yankees defeated the St. Louis Cardinals in the recent world series. The series, we are informed, left the field strewn with broken records, with the "Babe" towering

Babe Ruth drank too much, ate too much, enjoyed countless love affairs, and often stayed up all night pursuing all of these pastimes. Yet he was a superb athlete who dominated baseball and soon was recognized as a symbol of his time. Would he be as successful or as popular today? Is there anyone today who might compare to the Babe?

among them as the greatest record-breaker of all. In place of the old records are thirty-four bright and shining new ones, of which Ruth set nineteen, in spite of an injured knee. The achievements of this series, James R. Harrison tells us in the New York *Times*, "will live as long as the game itself." Among the most spectacular features of the event is the fact that the Yankees have now won two consecutive series in four straight games each.

That seventh inning opened with the Yankees at bat and the score 2 to 1 in favor of St. Louis. When it was over the score was 5 to 2 for New York. And the reason for the demonstration against Ruth was that Umpire Pfirman had refused to call a strike on him when the Cardinals' pitcher sent a "sneak" delivery, which is barred, we are told, in world series games.

"Monitor," in the New York *World*, describes the incident thus:

Sherdel curved over a low one, just where he likes to pitch them to the Babe, and Pfirman, the umpire at the plate, called a strike. He tossed up his famous dewdrop slow ball, curling so slowly over that the seams almost could be seen, and a second strike was called.

Ruth straightened up and looked back at Pfirman as tho in protest, and Smith, the Card's catcher, threw the ball back to Sherdel. The latter did what he has often done in the National League season, wound up his arms quickly and threw back across the plate—a perfect strike—there can be no doubt of that.

But Pfirman refused to allow it. He called it "no delivery" and the decision stood, altho all the Cardinals raved around all the four umpires for five minutes.

It seems that before the series opened the umpires agreed on a special rule against the quick return. Some of the Cards say it was not agreed on, but all four umpires, Pfirman and Rigler of the National League and Owens and McGowan of the American League, are positive. Why there should be rules for the World's Series different from the regular season, is not at all clear, but they are made.

While J. Roy Stockton in the St. Louis *Post-Dispatch* writes:

Sherdel slipt over two strikes on Ruth and then tried the quick return, putting the ball across the plate, through the strike zone. Ruth was in the batter's box, but Pfirman contended that he had called time, and turned a deaf ear to the Cardinal protests.

When another pitch came along in place of the barred one, Ruth knocked his second home run of the series. And while excited players debated the decision, Ruth went from group to group, applauding them. When the Cardinals came to bat and Ruth moved to outfield, there were boos. Then came the bottles. Ruth stood and picked up one of the missiles that had landed at his feet and "made as if to throw it with unbridled ferocity back at his tormenters. Everybody ducked. Frankly," says Mr. McGeehan, "they were frightened. The 'Babe' has a great throwing arm." Reading on:

Having shown them that a return fire was possible, and might even be deadly, he suddenly grinned his broadest grin and tossed the bottle gently toward the sidelines. Those who are familiar with Mr. Ruth's countenance will realize how broad a grin he can produce when he really puts himself out to do it. Probably among those records the experts esteem so highly there should be some mention of a new Ruthian record for the standing broad grin.

At any rate, it was so broad that everybody in the crowd saw it and caught the spirit. First—Mr. Ruth cowed them. Then he won them over to his side. The second was the greater victory. When he hit his third home run in the following inning, he was welcomed out to his position as tho he were one of the native East St. Louis boys who had just knocked half a dozen New Yorkers off the end of a dock. Even the rabid rooters of the Mound City realized that when a hero like Ruth put on such a magnificent feat, party lines were minor matters and that there were bigger things in sport than the insignia on the uniform.

Thus, in addition to his record setting, Ruth set a great example of mob control. "That man," Mr. McGeehan continues, "has amazing hidden resources and produces the proper solutions at what is familiarly known as the psychological moment."

This is a photo of Mary Sullivan Hughes on the day of her wedding, October 30, 1929, to James F. Watts. Their marriage followed a 1920s courtship and immediately preceded the Great Crash and depression. Can you find a 1920s wedding photo in your family collection?

ASSIGNMENT 4
Your Family in the Great War and Twenties

This section has introduced several major historical themes. Your assignment is to attempt to relate your family to these basic patterns of American life during the period between 1917 and 1929. Survivors of World War I, the Great War, are becoming rare. But perhaps you can do research on a member of your family who participated in the war by using family records or a hometown newspaper.

Your relatives who are now in their seventies probably have sharp memories of the twenties, and some firm opinions to go with them. Raise questions suggested by the selections you have read. What are their recollections of Ford's Model T and Model A? Were they blessed by the economic boom? Do they have any prohibition stories? What did they think about Sacco and Vanzetti? Several other topics are available to you, including the emergence of nontraditional women, black pride and oppression, the arrival of sports heroes as national celebrities, the dominance of business values despite some shady practices, and the massive movement away from farms to the cities. Select what most interests you.

If members of your own family are not readily accessible, arrange to speak to neighbors or senior citizens in your college community. Can you find an artifact from the period to take to your interview? Based on your research, with the related reading in this section, draw a conclusion as to whether your research confirms or questions the selections in this book.

BIBLIOGRAPHIC NOTE

There is a vast literature on the military aspects of World War I, but David M. Kennedy, *Over Here: The First World War and American Society* (1981), focuses on the wider impact of the war. Frederick Lewis Allen's *Only Yesterday: An Informal History of the Nineteen Twenties* (1931) is an account written by a journalist immediately after the close of the decade, but it is colorful and still worth reading. A more scholarly and better balanced account is William E. Leuchtenburg, *The Perils of Prosperity, 1914–1932* (1958). The best account of the innovative literature of the period is Frederick Hoffman, *The Twenties: American Writing in the Postwar Decade* (1955), but everyone should sample the writings of F. Scott Fitzgerald, Ernest Hemingway, H. L. Mencken, and Sinclair Lewis, among others.

The Depression

S ome events are so important that their influence cuts across class lines, affects all races and ethnic groups, and leaves no region untouched. The depression of the 1930s was such an event. No one who lived through those years in the United States could ever completely forget the bread lines, the millions of unemployed, or the forlorn and discouraged men and women who saw their mortgages foreclosed, their dreams shattered, their children hungry and afraid.

The depression was precipitated by the stock market crash in October 1929, but the actual cause of the collapse was an unhealthy economy. While the ability of the manufacturing industry to produce consumer goods had increased rapidly, mass purchasing power had remained relatively static. Most laborers, farmers, and white-collar workers, therefore, could not afford to buy the automobiles and refrigerators turned out by factories in the 1920s, because their incomes were too low. At the same time, the federal government increased the problem through economic policies that encouraged the very rich to oversave.

Herbert Hoover, a sensitive and humane engineer, had the misfortune of being President when the depression began. Even though he broke with the past and used the power of the federal government to stem the tide of depression, especially through loans to businesses and banks, his efforts proved to be too little and too late. Somewhat unfairly, his name became synonymous with failure and despair. As a result, Hoover was defeated by Franklin Roosevelt, who took office in March 1933 with the country in a state of crisis. Many banks had failed, millions were unemployed, and in the Middle West thousands of farmers seemed ready to use violence to protest their hopeless situation.

Roosevelt had a sense of confidence that was contagious. In his inaugural address he announced, "We have nothing to fear except fear itself," which was, of course, not exactly true. But he acted swiftly and decisively, if not always consistently, to right the economy. He closed all the banks and then gradually reopened those that were sound. He rushed a series of acts through Congress ranging from attempts to aid business and agriculture to emergency banking legislation to the legalization, for the first time in thirteen years, of the sale of beer and wine. Very few people who lived through the 1930s were neutral about Roosevelt. He came to be hated by many businessmen, who called him a socialist or simply "that man in the White House." Others, more radical than the President, attacked him for not going far enough in his reforms, for trying to patch up the American free enterprise system rather than replacing it with some form of socialism. More important, however, he was loved and admired by the great mass of ordinary Americans, who crowded around the radio to listen to his comforting voice in "fireside chats" that explained the complex government programs.

Many of his New Deal measures, such as the Social Security Act and the Wagner Act (aiding the cause of unionism), had far-reaching influence. None, however, solved the massive social and economic problems facing the country.

The long list of agencies and administrations, popularly known by their initials—from the AAA that aided farmers to the WPA that provided jobs for the unemployed—succeeded only to the extent of restoring a measure of self-respect and hope to some hard-hit by the depression. Financially, the country remained in a slump. It was not until the 1940s, when defense spending stimulated the economy, that the nation finally emerged from its worst economic crisis.

To many, the fact that the nation could go into such a deep slough was puzzling. The early and middle twenties, in which people became fully conscious of being part of the age of the machine, seemed to auger unending economic expansion. Two years before the stock market crash, in 1927, Henry Ford produced his fifteen-millionth automobile and then promptly switched from his all-black Model T to the more colorful and modern Model A. In the same year, the world "shrank" considerably when radio-telephone service was established between New York, London, San Francisco, and Manila, and Charles Lindbergh opened the way for rapid transatlantic travel by his solo flight from New York to Paris. The year 1927 also foreshadowed the great media explosion with the establishment of the first national radio network and the release of the first feature-length film with spoken dialogue. Within a few years, millions would be listening to radio shows like "The Shadow" and "The Lone Ranger" and flocking to their neighborhood theaters to live vicariously with their movie-star heroes and heroines—Clark Gable, Greta Garbo, Gary Cooper, Bette Davis. Technology, with its many facets, seemed to be widening horizons.

This promise of prosperity through

technology was deceptive, though. For one thing, although radios and electric refrigerators and flush toilets were being produced by the millions, a great many Americans outside the middle and upper classes still had to use iceboxes and outhouses and live much the same way their ancestors had. Furthermore, as already noted, the prosperity of the middle class was itself based on an economic lie. The depression punctured its inflated dreams.

The great majority of Americans, whether they were business executives, farmers, workingmen, housewives, or secretaries, suffered from the economic collapse. In a sense, the depression was not as devastating for the lower classes as it was for the upper and middle classes. The sharecropper in Mississippi, the unemployed black in Chicago, probably did not notice the depression as much because his life was already depressed.

There are many ways to chart the impact of the depression on the lives of Americans. One can mention the $26 billion wiped out by the stock market crash or the millions who lost their savings when the banks failed. The total industrial production in 1932 was half of what it had been in 1929. No one knows how many men and women lost their jobs; estimates of those out of work range from 12 million to 16 million at the peak of the depression, and in some cities the unemployment rate was more than 50 percent. For those who did work, the average pay in 1932 ranged from twenty to thirty cents an hour in heavy industry. In addition, one out of every four farmers lost his farm, and millions were evicted from their homes because they could not pay the rent. (There were 200,000 evictions in New York City alone in 1931.)

But none of these statistics really communicates the hopelessness and the despair of the depression years. In Chicago, men and women fought with children over the garbage dumped by trucks. A social worker noticed that the children in one city were playing a game called Eviction. "Sometimes they play 'Relief,'" she remarked, "but 'Eviction' has more action and all of them know how to play." In Philadelphia, a store owner told of one family he was keeping on credit. "Eleven children in that house," he reported. "They've got no shoes, no pants. In the house, no chairs. My God, you go in there, you cry that's all."

The search for a secure job, the fear of failure, the worry about vanished savings, lost hope and shattered dreams, and the nagging worry that it would all happen over again separated those who lived through the depression from those who were born in the 1940s and after. Parents who experienced the depression urged their children to train for a good job, to get married and settle down. But often their children, products of an age of affluence, cared little about security and sometimes rejected the material objects, the signs of success, that took on such importance for parents.

Studs Terkel of Chicago, the writer who has made an art of talking to people and arranging their thoughts into books, spoke to a young woman who remarked:

> Everytime I've encountered the Depression, it has been used as a barrier and a club, it's been a countercommunication. Older people use it to explain to me that I can't understand *anything*: I didn't live through the Depression. They never say to me: We can't understand you because we didn't live through the leisure society." All attempts at communication are totally blocked.*

Young people growing up in the 1980s perhaps have a greater appreciation of the depression mentality than those who came of age in the 1960s. Do you think it is possible to bridge the gap between the depression generation and those who came after? The following selections, most of which are autobiographical accounts and recollections of the 1930s, should help you begin to understand the experience and effects of that era. After you have read them, we will ask you to go out on your own to talk to someone who remembers the depression.

*Studs Terkel. *Hard Times: An Oral History of the Great Depression* (New York: Pantheon, 1970), p. 39.

How the E. Family Lives

ELI GINZBERG AND HYMAN BERMAN

The following is the story of "commonplace people" with few ambitions who seem never to have been influenced by the American Dream. They were working-class people who barely survived before the depression; after the crash, they faced an even tighter budget. The budgets included here indicate how inexpensive most things were in the 1930s, and how it was possible to survive, and for a time even live comfortably, on a small income. But for many even a small income was difficult to achieve, as this family found out. Could you live on their "ideal budget"? Why didn't a family like this collapse like those of Jim F—— and Mr. D——?

Mr. E., age thirty-six, is a mechanic in a large factory on the "west side" of Chicago. He is married to a childhood playmate now aged thirty-three, and has three children—Helen, aged seven, Robert, aged five, and Julia, aged 15 months. Mr. E. and his wife have had a common school education and are commonplace people who have no particular abilities or disabilities, but are fairly energetic and thrifty. Until recently they have managed to make a fairly comfortable living. About two years ago they had a fund of several hundred dollars saved up and were hoping to make a first payment on a home in one of the outlying neighborhoods. At that time Mr. E.'s health began to fail, and in a short time he was compelled to quit work. A local physician told him he had "consumption," and Mr. E. began to treat his cough with home remedies and patent medicines. Meantime there was no income, and in about five months every resource was exhausted; savings were spent, cheaper quarters found, superfluous furniture sold, credit at neighborhood stores exhausted, sick benefits from the lodge were withdrawn, and expenses trimmed at every point, even to dropping payments on life insurance. In short there was nothing to do but follow the suggestions of an interested neighbor and "appeal to the charities." They were then about $250 in debt. . . .

. . . An estimate of the family's original average of expenditures follows:

Rent (four rooms, stove heat)	$35.00
Fuel and light (coal and gas)	7.50
Food	62.25
Clothing	24.00
Household expenses (including upkeep on furniture)	8.20
Carfare	5.00
Health	5.00
Insurance	1.15
Spending money and recreation	4.00
Savings	8.50
Average monthly total expense	$160.60

Mr. E.'s earnings at 72 cents an hour, including a little extra money he earned at overtime work, had enabled him to meet this budget very easily. During his illness, of course, the standard of living rapidly fell and no organized scheme of expenditures could be found from the household account book. During the last month before they appealed to the charities, the E.'s had pared their expenses down to absolute necessities: "We barely lived," as Mrs. E. expressed it.

Their expenditures, when classified as above, were as follows:

Rent	$23.00
Fuel and light	4.50
Food	47.88
Clothing	8.00
Household expenses	3.16
Carfare	.85
Health	12.00
Insurance	0.00
Spending money and recreation	.36
Savings	0.00
Total	$99.75

Value of articles given by neighbors, friends, relatives:

Food	$10.00
Clothing	3.00
Fuel	2.00
Total	$114.75

When Mr. E. came home from the sanitarium some eight months later and went back to his work, the worker made a similar estimate to determine whether the family would be fully self-supporting, or would need further assistance. Her figures were approximately those shown in the table, but when the social worker talked over the budget problem in a friendly way with Mrs. E., the worker pointed out several changes that she proposed should be made. Among these were:

ITEM	TOTAL	GENERAL FAMILY EXPENSE	MR. E.	MRS. E.	HELEN	ROBERT	JULIA
Housing	$ 35.00	$35.00					
Food	59.81		$17.77	$14.30	$10.40	$ 8.67	$ 8.67
Clothing	29.00		9.00	7.50	5.00	3.75	3.75
Fuel and light	8.50	8.50					
Household expenses	5.00	5.00					
Carfare	5.04		3.64	1.40			
Spending money and recreation	2.50		1.00	1.00	.25	.25	
Health	7.00	7.00					
Education	.90	.75			.15		
Insurance	6.25		5.00	1.25			
Savings	10.00	10.00					
Total	$169.00	$66.25	$36.41	$25.45	$15.80	$12.67	$12.42

(1) A better grade of food could be secured with perhaps a slight decrease in 171
cost by purchasing in larger quantities rather than from day to day, and by
patronizing "cash-and-carry" shops; (2) household expenses could be materially
reduced by the same plan and by purchasing furniture, when needed, for cash
rather than on installments; (3) the worker believed that the family should have a
daily and Sunday paper or some good popular magazine; (4) the expenditures for
health had been too low previously, dental care in particular being badly needed;
(5) the family had too little insurance for safety; (6) some economies should be
effected in spending money; and (7) it ought to be possible to increase the savings
item a little. The total budget was a little larger than formerly, but Mr. E. had had
a slight increase in wages and could meet it easily. . . .

Mrs. E. confided to the worker that their income had never been large enough
to meet their real needs though they had succeeded in living within it and saving a
little. Neither she nor Mr. E. had "aspirations beyond their station in life," but
they both thought that their present living quarters were inadequate, that they
needed several new pieces of parlor furniture and some really nice clothing. They
would like to go to church more often and to make friends and also to join one or
two neighborhood organizations. Mr. E. in particular was anxious to join a
popular fraternal order to which many of the men at the shop belonged. They felt
debarred from these relations now because they could not afford suitable clothing
and proper home furnishings. For her part she had always wanted to go to the
opera and see what it was like, and she wanted to send her washing to the "wet
wash." Mr. E. had had the promise of a foreman's job before he became ill, with an
increase of pay. He and his wife had thought then that they would be able to have
everything they wished. In fact they had worked out a tentative monthly budget.
Mrs. E. was reluctant to show this "ideal" budget since they "weren't in the habit
of counting too much on the future." The estimate was:

Rent (5 rooms, steam heat)	$60.00
Fuel and light (gas and electricity)	5.00
Food	65.00
Clothing	32.00
Household expenses	12.00
Carfare	6.00
Health	5.00
Insurance	3.00
Organization and church dues	5.00
Spending money and recreation	15.00
Savings (including $30 monthly to buy a home)	42.00
Total	$250.00

I'd Rather Die

ELI GINZBERG AND HYMAN BERMAN

One of the hardest things for many people to get used to in the 1930s was the idea of being poor, for somehow Americans were not supposed to be poor. If one worked hard, got good grades, one ought to be a success. The following is the account of a father and son and how they dealt with poverty and failure. Neither seems to have been radicalized by his experience of pover-ty, as might have been expected. In fact, both tried to adjust themselves to the system that had failed them. Perhaps it was easier to be poor when most of those around you were also poor. But there was a toll to be paid for that adjustment. As you read their story, try to determine what effect the depression had on their willingness to ac-cept the American Dream.

I went to work for Travis and Son a few weeks after Dad died. It's an overall factory—run by old Dave MacGonnigal and his four boys.

Dad was a pattern-maker there and worked for Old Dave over forty-five years. If things hadn't gone the way they did, I'd never known what he went through to keep us alive all those years. After Dad's death when the bottom dropped out from under the family I couldn't find a job anywhere. Finally I applied to Old Dave MacGonnigal.

". . . Well," he said to me, "you needn't think that because you've got that high school diploma you can sit around on your tail here and talk Latin. We work here, boy. I put on overalls and work like the rest. You soldier on me and I'll fire you like a shot—understand?"

Seemed to me at the time that the job was something handed down out of heaven. I was so happy and relieved I didn't even ask the old man how much he was going to pay me. Rushed on home as fast as I could go to tell Mom.

I can tell you I didn't feel that way when the end of the first week came around. I drew six dollars and fifty cents.

I don't ever remember want or any feeling of insecurity when I was little. Dad made good money in those days—say, about $50 or $60 a week. You know, a pattern-maker has a pretty important job in an overall factory. If the patterns he lays out aren't right to the fraction of an inch the cutters will ruin a lot of goods. There's a good deal of figuring to it, complicated figuring, and he can't make mistakes. Dad never learned mathematics because he hadn't a chance to go to high school. But he'd worked out a system of his own with all sorts of funny little

172

signs and symbols. Nobody else understood it. He could take a problem of figuring up goods and have it done in a minute where some of the efficiency experts Old Dave had in from time to time would take an hour to work it. And Dad's would be nearer the right answer than the experts'. The boys in the cutting room told me all about it when I came there to work. So they paid Dad a pretty good salary, though not what he was worth.

We had our own home . . . and we had a car. My two older brothers and my sister finished high school. My oldest brother, after being a salesman for a few years . . . worked his way through Columbia University. I don't guess he could have done it by work alone. But he won one scholarship after another and finally a travelling fellowship that gave him a year in Europe. . . .

The first hard times I remember came in 1933, when I was in the eighth grade. Travis and Son shut down and for six months Dad didn't draw a penny. Things must have been pinching for two or three years before that because by that time the house was mortgaged and the money spent. I don't know much about the details. Anyhow, my brother . . . couldn't help much.

Then we were really up against it. For a whole week one time we didn't have anything to eat but potatoes. Another time my brother went around to the grocery stores and got them to give him meat for his dog—only he didn't have any dog. We ate that dog meat with the potatoes. I went to school hungry and came home to a house where there wasn't any fire. The lights were cut off. They came out and cut off the water. But each time, as soon as they left, my brother went out and cut it on again with a wrench.

I remember lying in bed one night and thinking. All at once I realized something. We were poor. Lord! It was weeks before I could get over that. . . .

. . . We lost our car and house and kept moving from one house to another. Bill collectors hunted us down and came in droves. Every now and then my brother or Dad would find some sort of odd job to do, or the other brother in Chicago would send us a little something. Then we'd go wild. I mean we'd go wild over food. We'd eat until we were sick. We'd eat four times a day and between meals. We just couldn't help ourselves. The sight and smell of food sort of made us crazy, I guess.

The winter of 1934 was the hardest time of all. . . . We were completely out of coal one time when we were living away out at the edge of town. The weather was freezing bitter then, so at night my brother and I would bundle up and go about a quarter of a mile away to a big estate on the Tennessee River. We made a hole in the fence and stole some of the wood that was piled a good distance from the house. We just walked in and got it. I don't remember that we tried to be quiet about it in particular.

After awhile things got some better. My brother in Chicago got so he could send money home and my other brother got another newspaper job. Dad went back to regular work at Travis and Son, though he only got about $20 a week. . . .

I went on through high school and made good marks. In my senior year I had an average of 98 and was elected class president and was valedictorian at graduation. I expected to go to college the next fall. Now, I can't see how on earth I could have expected to. I knew that there was no money for it. But somehow or other it just seemed to me that a way would turn up.

Mother felt the same about it. She'd say, "If you want a college education badly enough you will get it. Any boy who is determined can work his way through."

As the budget of the E. family indicated, little money was available for entertainment in the 1930s. Reading was a popular family pastime, as the increase in library circulation throughout the country in these years shows. The most popular at-home entertainment by far, however, was listening to the radio. Away from home, people liked to gather at a familiar meeting place to discuss the hard times. And, because movie tickets were relatively inexpensive—as little as fifteen cents—an evening at the movies was a popular entertainment, especially when escapist themes were dramatized. What effect has television had on changing the way Americans spend their leisure time in the 1980s?

175

That summer we had a scare. There was some sort of strike at Travis and Son. Seems that after the NRA blew up, Old Dave put the girls in the sewing room on piecework and some of them just couldn't make a living. They protested but it didn't do no good. . . . Then some organizer came and got them to go out on strike. The men went out too, and they ganged around the entrance blocking off part of the street.

Dad didn't know what to do. He walked the floor at home. He said that the girls were right, but he didn't believe they could win out because the mayor had said he'd back Old Dave to the limit. I remember Mama telling Dad, "Oh, Bob, please don't do anything foolish—! We've been through such a hard time. What on earth would we do if we had to face it again? I couldn't bear it!"

So Dad went to work the next morning. I had some errands to do for Mama so I went to town with him. Old Dave had called up and said he'd have policemen to carry Dad through the strikers. When we got there the policemen were ready all right. They told Dad they'd rush him through. He started out, with me tagging behind. Then he made me go back to the corner and started again. The strikers were bunched up at the door of the factory. They weren't saying a thing or making a move. Just men and women standing there watching.

I saw Dad stop again. He had an argument with the police. I heard him say pretty loud, "No, I'll go by myself or I won't go at all." He said it two or three times.

The policemen were mad. "Okay, Cap," I heard one of them say. "It's your look-after, not mine."

Dad walked on without them, but they sort of edged along some way behind.

All at once the strikers began yelling and meeowing. Dad walked on. When he was right at them, about a dozen men and women grabbed at him and started tearing his coat and shirt.

I started running down there and so did the police. . . . But right then the strikers got into a free-for-all fight among themselves. Dad had a lot of good friends among them and these friends jumped on the ones who'd grabbed him. They pulled them off and Dad walked on through and went into the factory. He never was bothered again. Old Dave and the others had to have the police to get in and out. Dad came and went without anybody trying to stop him.

So the strike petered out and the strikers were out of jobs. Some of them came to Dad and he tried to get them back on. But Old Dave said he wouldn't touch a one of them with a ten-foot pole.

One night late in July Dad didn't come home at his usual time. . . . The doctors never did know what was wrong with Dad. He was sixty, but there wasn't anything like cancer or tuberculosis. One of the doctors at the hospital told me he was really just worn out completely. I guess he was right.

Hard Times

STUDS TERKEL

The depression meant different things to different people. For a wealthy young Southern belle it was a disconnected telephone that symbolized a changed role. For a farmer from South Dakota it was surpluses amid starvation and using old automobile seat covers for clothing.

The following two interviews were done by Studs Terkel, a historian and writer who uses a tape recorder to discover the past as ordinary people remember it. His technique is as interesting as the stories he uncovers. Perhaps you too can learn something about the impact of the depression on your family and your neighborhood by asking questions and listening.

DIANA MORGAN

She was a "southern belle" in a small North Carolina town. "I was taught that no prince of royal blood was too good for me." (Laughs.) Her father had been a prosperous cotton merchant and owner of a general store. "It's the kind of town you became familiar with in Thornton Wilder's Our Town. *You knew everybody. We were the only people in town who had a library."*

Her father's recurring illness, together with the oncoming of hard times—the farmers and the townspeople unable to pay their bills—caused the loss of the store. He went into bankruptcy.

The banks failed about the time I was getting ready to go to college. My family thought of my going to Wellesley, Vassar, Smith—but we had so little money, we thought of a school in North Carolina. It wasn't so expensive.

It was in my junior year, and I came home for Christmas. . . . I found the telephone disconnected. And this was when I realized that the world was falling apart. Imagine us without a telephone! When I finished school, I couldn't avoid facing the fact that we didn't have a cook any more, we didn't have a cleaning woman any more. I'd see dust under the beds, which is something I'd never seen before. I knew the curtains weren't as clean as they used to be. Things were beginning to look a little shabby. . . .

The first thing I noticed about the Depression was that my great-grandfather's house was lost, about to be sold for taxes. Our own house was sold. It

177

was considered the most attractive house in town, about a hundred and fifty years old. We even had a music library. Imagine my shock when it was sold for $5,000 in back taxes. I was born in that house.

I never felt so old in my life as I felt the first two years out of college. 'Cause I hadn't found a new life for myself, and the other one was finished.

I remember how embarrassed I was when friends from out of town came to see me, because sometimes they'd say they want a drink of water, and we didn't have any ice. (Laughs.) We didn't have an electric refrigerator and couldn't afford to buy ice. There were those frantic arrangements of running out to the drugstore to get Coca-Cola with crushed ice, and there'd be this embarrassing delay, and I can remember how hot my face was.

All this time, I wasn't thinking much about what was going on in this country. . . . I was still leading some kind of social life. Though some of us had read books and discussed them, there wasn't much awareness. . . . Oh, we deplored the fact that so many of our young men friends couldn't find suitable things to do. . . .

One day a friend of my father stopped me on the street and said, "Would you like a job? A friend of mine is director of one of those New Deal programs. She'll tell you about it."

Oh, I was so excited, I didn't know what to do—the thought of having a job. I was very nervous, but very hopeful. Miss Ward came. She looked like a Helen Hokinson woman, very forbidding, formal. She must have been all of forty-five, but to me she looked like some ancient and very frightening person from another world.

She said to me, "It's not a job for a butterfly." She could just look at me and tell that I was just totally unsuitable. I said I was young and conscientious and if I were told what I was supposed to do, I would certainly try to the best of my ability. . . . She didn't give me any encouragement at all.

When she left, I cried for about an hour. I was really a wreck. I sobbed and sobbed and thought how unfair she was. So I was very much amazed to receive a telegram the next day summoning me to a meeting in Raleigh—for the directors of women's work.

There were dozens of women there, from all over the state, of all ages. It seemed to me very chaotic. Everyone was milling around, talking about weaving projects, canning, bookbinding. . . . Everyone there seemed very knowledgeable. I really didn't know what they were talking about. And nobody really told me what I was supposed to do. It just seemed that people were busy, and I somehow gathered that I was in.

So I went back home. I went to the county relief offices at the courthouse. There were people sitting on the floor of a long hallway, mostly black people, looking very depressed, sad. Some of them had children with them, some of them were very old. Just endless rows of them, sitting there, waiting. . . .

My first impression was: Oh, those poor devils, just sitting there, and nobody even saying, "We'll get to you as soon as we can." Though I didn't know a thing about social work, what was good and what wasn't good, my first impulse was that those people should be made to feel somebody was interested in them. Without asking anybody, I just went around and said, "Have you been waiting long? We'll get to you just as soon as we can."

I got the feeling the girls in the office looked very stern, and that they had a

Although everyone was affected by the depression, class and regional differences still existed. What differences can you detect in these photos of two families at dinnertime. Which picture would approximate the experience of your family during the 1930s?

punitive attitude: that the women just had to wait, as long as they were there and that you had to find out and be sure they were entitled to it before they got anything.

I didn't know a thing about sewing, bookbinding, canning . . . the approved projects. I'd never boiled an egg or sewed a stitch. But I knew seamstresses, who used to make clothes for us when we were children. I went to see them and got them to help me. I sought help from everybody who knew how to do things.

In the meantime, I would work in the relief office and I began interviewing people . . . and found out how everybody, in order to be eligible for relief, had to have reached absolute bottom. You didn't have to have a lot of brains to realize that once they reached that stage and you put them on an allowance of a dollar a day for food—how could they ever pull out of it?

Caroline, who used to cook for us, came in. I was so shocked to see her in a position where she had to go to the agency and ask for food. I was embarrassed for her to see me when she was in that state. She was a wonderful woman, with a big heart. Here she was, elderly by now, and her health wasn't good at all. And she said, "Oh the Lord's done sent you down from heaven to save me. I've fallen on hard times. How beautiful you are. You look like an angel to me." In the typical southern Negro way of surviving, she was flattering me. I was humiliated by her putting herself in that position, and by my having to see her go through this. (Weeps softly; continues with difficulty.)

For years, I never questioned the fact that Caroline's house was papered with newspapers. She was our laundress for a while, and I remember going to her house several times. Caroline was out in the yard, just a hard patch of dirt yard. With a big iron pot, with fire under it, stirring, boiling the white clothes. . . .

She was always gracious and would invite me in. She never apologized for the way anything looked. I thought to myself at the time: How odd that Caroline uses newspapers to paper walls. I didn't have any brains at eleven or twelve or whatever to think: what kind of country is this that lets people live in houses like this and necessitates their using the Sunday paper for wallpaper. I'm shocked that I can't say to you: "When I was twelve, I was horrified when I first went into this house." I was surprised, but I wasn't horrified.

The girls at the office—when the clients had all gone—it's funny you treat them this way, and you still call them clients—when they had all gone, the girls would be very friendly with me. They would ask what I wanted to know and would show me the files. I was quite impressed with their efficiency. But when they were dealing with clients, they were much more loose. I didn't see why they had to be this way. Perhaps they were afraid the people in town would think they were too easy with the welfare people.

Because even then, people were saying that these people are no good, they didn't really want to work. Oftentimes, there were telephone calls, saying so-and-so Joe Jones got a bag of food from Welfare, he got an automobile, or his wife's working or something like that. I spent my time away from the job talking to my old friends, defending the program, saying: You don't know about the situation. They would tell me I was terribly sentimental and that I had lost my perspective. That was when I first heard the old expressions: If you give them coal, they'd put it in the bathtub. They didn't even have

bathtubs to put coal in. So how did anybody know that's what they'd do with
coal if they had it?

We were threatened the whole time, because funds were constantly being questioned by the legislators. After I'd been there three months, the program *was* discontinued. By this time, I was absolutely hooked. I could almost weep thinking about it. I told Miss Ward, who had by now become my staunch friend, that this is what I want to do with myself: I want to do something to change things.

By this time, the girls in the office—Ella Mae was the one I like best— were perfectly willing to let me interview people, because they had more than they could do. Something like 150 cases each. In two months, I was employed as a case worker.

As I recall, when a person came into the office and applied for help, you filled out a form, asked all those humiliating questions: Does anybody work? Do you own your own house? Do you have a car? You just established the fact they had nothing. Nothing to eat, and children. So you give them one food order. You couldn't give them shoes, or money for medicine—without visiting and corroborating the fact that they were destitute.

So, of course, you get out as fast as possible to see those people before the $4 grocery order ran out. You know, the day after tomorrow, I used to drive out to make house calls. It was the first I'd been off Main Street. I'd never been out in the rural area, and I was absolutely aghast at the conditions in the country.

I discovered, the first time in my life, in the county, there was a place called the Islands. The land was very low and if it rained, you practically had to take a boat to get over where Ezekiel Jones or whoever lived. I remember a time when I got stuck in this rented Ford, and broke down little trees, and lay them across the road to create traction, so you could get out. Now I regard that as one of my best experiences. If somebody said to you: What would you do, having been brought up the way you were, if you found yourself at seven o'clock at night, out in the wilderness, with your car stuck and the water up to your hubcaps or something like that? Wouldn't you worry? What would you do? I could get out of there: I could break down a tree or something. It helps make you free.

I would find maybe two rooms, a dilapidated wooden place, dirty, an almost paralyzed-looking mother, as if she didn't function at all. Father unshaven, drunk. Children of all ages around the house, and nothing to eat. You thought you could do just absolutely nothing. Maybe you'd write a food order. . . .

■　■　■

This family . . . the Rural Rehabilitation program came along, the RRA. I had the joy of certifying certain families from the relief rolls to go to the land bought by the government. To have better houses, to have equipment. And I saw this family move to a different house. Saw that woman's face come alive— the one who'd been in that stupor—her children clean, her house scrubbed—I saw this family moved from a hopeless situation. . . . The man had been a sharecropper. Apparently, he had once been a very good worker. There he was with nothing, till . . . I could go on about that. . . .

I had twelve families in this program. And Ella Mae had twelve. It was a beautiful farm, maybe two, three hundred acres. With houses, not two-room shacks. Ella Mae and I were involved in the thrilling task of selecting the families. Ella Mae would say, "I think Jess Clark would be good." And Davis, the man in charge of the program, would say, "That old, lazy bum? He's not gonna be able to do nothin'. You're just romantic." So we became personally involved in seeing these people prove their own worth. . . .

Every month the program was threatened with lack of funds. We didn't know if Congress was gonna discontinue it. A lot of the public thought the money was being spent foolishly.

With the program in danger of being killed from month to month, the state administrator suggested she accept other job offers. She attended the New York School of Social Work, under federal auspices; she married; there was an absence of six months from the county.

The first thing I did when I got back, I got out of the car and rushed over to the courthouse—to know how did those people perform. Did they make it?

I talked about this one white family. There was a Negro family, nine of them living in one room. The man was not young; he was in his sixties. But he impressed me as being a strong person—who would really make it, if he had a chance. Every one of the people we had certified had done well and had begun to pay back the loans. Not one of them had been lazy and done a bad job. They were absolutely vindicated. The people were vindicated, not us.

OSCAR HELINE

For all his seventy-eight years, he has lived on this Iowa farm, which his father had cultivated almost a century ago. It is in the northwestern part of the state, near the South Dakota border. Marcus has a population of 1,263.

On this drizzly October Sunday afternoon, the main street is deserted. Not a window is open, nor a sound heard. Suddenly, rock music shatters the silence. From what appeared to be a years-long vacant store, two girls and a boy emerge. They are about thirteen, fourteen.

I ask directions. They are friendly, though somewhat bewildered. "An old man?" They are eager to help. One points north; another, south; the third, west. Each is certain "an old man" lives somewhere in the vicinity.

Along the gravel road, with a stop at each of three farmhouses: no sign, no knowledge of "an old man," nor awareness of his name. At each is a tree bearing the identical sticker: "Beware The Dog." One trots forth, pauses warily and eyes the stranger in the manner of Bull Connor and a black militant. The young farmers are friendly enough, but innocent of Oscar Heline's existence.

At the fourth farm, an elderly woman, taken away from the telecast of the Tigers—Cardinals World Series game, knows. . . . Several gravel roads back I find him.

The struggles people had to go through are almost unbelievable. A man lived all his life on a given farm, it was taken away from him. One after the other. After the foreclosure, they got a deficiency judgment. Not only did he lose the farm, but it was impossible for him to get out of debt.

He recounts the first farm depression of the Twenties: "We give the land back to the mortgage holder and then we're sued for the remainder—the deficiency judgment— which we have to pay." After the land boom of the early Twenties, the values declined constantly, until the last years of the decade. "In '28, '29, when it looked like we could see a little blue sky again, we're just getting caught up with the back interest, the Thirties Depression hit. . . ."

The farmers became desperate. It got so a neighbor wouldn't buy from a neighbor, because the farmer didn't get any of it. It went to the creditors. And it wasn't enough to satisfy them. What's the use of having a farm sale? Why do we permit them to go on? It doesn't cover the debts, it doesn't liquidate the obliga- tion. He's out of business, and it's still hung over him. First, they'd take your farm, then they took your livestock, then your farm machinery. Even your household goods. And they'd move you off. The farmers were almost united. We had penny auction sales. Some neighbor would bid a penny and give it back to the owner.

Grain was being burned. It was cheaper than coal. Corn was being burned. A county just east of here, they burned corn in their courthouse all winter, '32, '33. You couldn't hardly buy groceries for corn. It couldn't pay the transportation. In South Dakota, the county elevator listed corn as minus three cents. *Minus* three cents a bushel. If you wanted to sell 'em a bushel of corn, you had to bring in three cents. They couldn't afford to handle it. Just think what happens when you can't get out from under. . . .

We had lots of trouble on the highway. People were determined to withhold produce from the market—livestock, cream, butter, eggs, what not. If they would dump the produce, they would force the market to a higher level. The farmers would man the highways, and cream cans were emptied in ditches and eggs dumped out. They burned the trestle bridge, so the trains wouldn't be able to haul grain. Conservatives don't like this kind of rebel attitude and aren't very sympathetic. But something had to be done.

I spent most of my time in Des Moines as a lobbyist for the state cooperatives. Trying to get some legislation. I wasn't out on the highway fighting this battle. Some of the farmers probably didn't think I was friendly to their cause. They were so desperate. If you weren't out there with them, you weren't a friend, you must be a foe. I didn't know from day to day whether somebody might come along and cause harm to my family. When you have bridges burned, accidents, violence, there may have been killings, I don't know.

There were some pretty conservative ones, wouldn't join this group. I didn't want to particularly, because it wasn't the answer. It took that kind of action, but what I mean is it took more than that to solve it. You had to do constructive things at the same time. But I never spoke harshly about those who were on the highway.

Some of the farmers with teams of horses, sometimes in trucks, tried to get through. He was trying to feed his family, trying to trade a few dozen eggs and a few pounds of cream for some groceries to feed his babies. He was desperate, too. One group tried to sell so they could live and the other group tried to keep you from selling so they could live.

The farmer is a pretty independent individual. He wants to be a conservative individual. He wants to be an honorable individual. He wants to pay his debts. But it was hard. The rank-and-file people of this state—who were brought up as

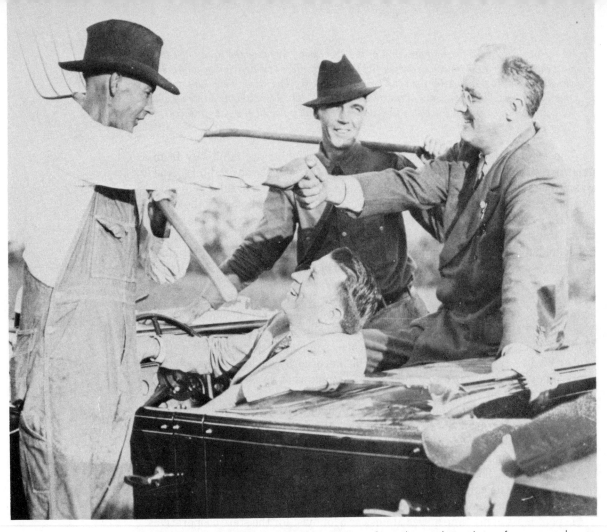

Franklin Roosevelt drew much of his support from the working class—farmers and industrial laborers. In return for their confidence, he initiated a wide-based program of relief and reform that, nevertheless, failed to lift the country out of the depression. Why, in light of his failures, did he continue to largely receive their support?

conservatives, which most of us were—would never act like this. Except in desperation.

There were a few who had a little more credit than the others. They were willing to go on as usual. They were mostly the ones who tried to break the picket lines. They were the ones who gained at the expense of the poor. They had the money to buy when things were cheap. There are always a few who make money out of other people's poverty. This was a struggle between the haves and the have-nots.

The original bankers who came to this state, for instance. When my father would borrow $100, he'd get $80. And when it was due, he'd pay back the $100 and a premium besides that. Most of his early borrowings were on this basis. That's where we made some wealthy families in this country.

We did pass some legislation. The first thing we did was stop the power of the judges to issue deficiency judgments. The theory was: the property would come back to you someday.

The next law we passed provided for committees in every county: adjudication committees. They'd get the person's debts all together and sit down with his creditors. They gave people a chance. People got time. The land banks and insurance companies started out hard-boiled. They got the farm, they got the judgment and then found out it didn't do them any good. They had to have somebody to run it. So they'd turn around and rent it to the fella who lost it. He wasn't a good renter. The poor fella lost all his capacity for fairness, because he couldn't be fair. He had to live. All the renters would go in cahoots. So the banks and companies got smart and stopped foreclosing.

Through a federal program we got a farm loan. A committee of twenty-five of us drafted the farm legislation of this kind thirty-five years ago. We drew it up with Henry Wallace. New money was put in the farmers' hands. The Federal Government changed the whole marketing program from burning 10-cent corn to 45-cent corn. People could now see daylight and hope. It was a whole transformation of attitude. You can just imagine . . . *(He weeps.)*

It was Wallace who saved us, put us back on our feet. He understood our problems. When we went to visit him, after he was appointed Secretary, he made it clear to us he didn't want to write the law. He wanted the farmers themselves to write it. "I will work with you," he said, "but you're the people who are suffering. It must be your program." He would always give his counsel, but he never directed us. The program came from the farmers themselves, you betcha.

Another thing happened: we had twice too many hogs because corn'd been so cheap. And we set up what people called Wallace's Folly: killing the little pigs. Another farmer and I helped develop this. We couldn't afford to feed 45-cent corn to a $3 hog. So we had to figure a way of getting rid of the surplus pigs. We went out and bought 'em and killed 'em. This is how desperate it was. It was the only way to raise the price of pigs. Most of 'em were dumped down the river.

The hard times put farmers' families closer together. My wife was working for the country Farm Bureau. We had lessons in home economics, how to make underwear out of gunny sacks, out of flour sacks. It was cooperative labor. So some good things came out of this. Sympathy toward one another was manifest. There were personal values as well as terrible hardships.

Mrs. Heline interjects: "They even took seat covers out of automobiles and re-used them for clothing or old chairs. We taught them how to make mattresses from surplus cotton. We had our freedom gardens and did much canning. We canned our own meat or cured it in some way. There was work to do and busy people are happy people."

The real boost came when we got into the Second World War. Everybody was paying on old debts and mortgages, but the land values were going down. It's gone up now more than ever in the history of the country. The war. . . . (A long pause.)

It does something to your country. It's what's making employment. It does something to the individual. I had a neighbor just as the war was beginning. We had a boy ready to go to service. This neighbor one day told me what we needed was a damn good war, and we'd solve our agricultural problems. And I said, "Yes, but I'd hate to pay with the price of my son." Which we did. (He weeps.) It's too much of a price to pay. . . .

In '28 I was chairman of the farm delegation which met with Hoover. My family had always been Republican, and I supported him. To my disappointment. I don't think the Depression was all his fault. He tried. But all his plans failed, because he didn't have the Government involved. He depended on individual organizations.

It's a strange thing. This is only thirty-five years ago—Roosevelt, Wallace. We have a new generation in business today. Successful. It's surprising how quickly they forget the assistance their fathers got from the Government. The Farm Bureau, which I helped organize in this state, didn't help us in '35. They take the same position today: we don't need the Government. I'm just as sure as I'm sitting here, we can't do it ourselves. Individuals have too many different interests. Who baled out the land banks when they were busted in the Thirties? It was the Federal Government.

What I remember most of those times is that poverty creates desperation, and desperation creates violence. In Plymouth County—Le Mars—just west of us, a group met one morning and decided they were going to stop the judge from issuing any more deficiency judgments. This judge had a habit of very quickly O.K.'ing foreclosure sales. These farmers couldn't stand it any more. They'd seen their neighbors sold out.

There were a few judges who would refuse to take the cases. They'd postpone it or turn it over to somebody else. But this one was pretty gruff and arrogant: "You do this, you do that, it's my court." When a bunch of farmers are going broke every day and the judge sits there very proudly and says: "This is my court . . . "; they say: "Who the hell are you?" He was just a fellow human being, same as they were.

These farmers gathered this one particular day. I suppose some of 'em decided to have a little drink, and so they developed a little courage. They decided: we'll go down and teach that judge a lesson. They marched into the courtroom, hats on, demanded to visit with him. *He* decided he would teach *them* a lesson. So he says: "Gentlemen, this is my court. Remove your hats and address the court properly."

They just laughed at him. They said, "We're not concerned whose court this is. We came here to get redress from your actions. The things you're doing, we can't stand to have done to us any more." The argument kept on, and got rougher. He wouldn't listen. He threatened them. So they drug him from his chair, pulled him down the steps of the courthouse, and shook a rope in front of his face. Then, tarred and feathered him.

The Governor called out the National Guard. And put these farmers behind barbed wire. Just imagine . . . (he weeps) . . . in this state. You don't forget these things.

Choosing a Dream

MARIO PUZO

Not everyone looking back on the depression years remembers the poverty and the despair; some recall the good times, the dreams, and the aspirations. In this selection, Mario Puzo, author of The Godfather, *describes what it was like to grow up in the Hell's Kitchen section of New York City. Being Italian was more important for him than was being poor. In fact, he does not remember being deprived in the 1930s; and his recollection is that his family always managed to eat well.*

Puzo's dream was to become an artist or a writer, rather than a railroad worker. Therefore, the American Dream of success did not end just because of the downturn in the economy. Indeed, for Puzo, as for so many others, World War II provided a way for him to escape his family and his neighborhood.

As a child and in my adolescence, living in the heart of New York's Neapolitan ghetto, I never heard an Italian singing. None of the grown-ups I knew were charming or loving or understanding. Rather they seemed coarse, vulgar, and insulting. And so later in my life when I was exposed to all the clichés of lovable Italians, singing Italians, happy-go-lucky Italians, I wondered where the hell the moviemakers and storywriters got all their ideas from.

At a very early age I decided to escape these uncongenial folk by becoming an artist, a writer. It seemed then an impossible dream. My father and mother were illiterate, as were their parents before them. But practising my art I tried to view the adults with a more charitable eye and so came to the conclusion that their only fault lay in their being foreigners; I was an American. This didn't really help because I was only half right. I was the foreigner. They were already more "American" than I could ever become.

But it did seem then that the Italian immigrants, all the fathers and mothers that I knew, were a grim lot; always shouting, always angry, quicker to quarrel than embrace. I did not understand that their lives were a long labor to earn their daily bread and that physical fatigue does not sweeten human natures.

And so even as a very small child I dreaded growing up to be like the adults around me. I heard them saying too many cruel things about their dearest friends, saw too many of their false embraces with those they had just maligned, observed with horror their paranoiac anger at some small slight or a fancied injury to their pride. They were, always, too unforgiving. In short, they did not have the careless magnanimity of children.

In my youth I was contemptuous of my elders, including a few under thirty. I thought my contempt special to their circumstances. Later when I wrote about these illiterate men and women, when I thought I understood them, I felt a condescending pity. After all, they had suffered, they had labored all the days of their lives. They had never tasted luxury, knew little more economic security than those ancient Roman slaves who might have been their ancestors. And alas, I thought, with new-found artistic insight, they were cut off from their children because of the strange American tongue, alien to them, native to their sons and daughters.

Already an artist but not yet a husband or father, I pondered omnisciently on their tragedy, again thinking it special circumstance rather than a constant in the human condition. I did not yet understand why these men and women were willing to settle for less than they deserved in life and think that "less" quite a bargain. I did not understand that they simply could not afford to dream; I myself had a hundred dreams from which to choose. For I was already sure that I would make my escape, that I was one of the chosen. I would be rich, famous, happy. I would master my destiny.

And so it was perhaps natural that as a child, with my father gone, my mother the family chief, I, like all the children in all the ghettos of America, became locked in a bitter struggle with the adults responsible for me. It was inevitable that my mother and I became enemies.

As a child I had the usual dreams. I wanted to be handsome, specifically as cowboy stars in movies were handsome. I wanted to be a killer hero in a world-wide war. Or if no wars came along (our teachers told us another was impossible), I wanted at the very least to be a footloose adventurer. Then I branched out and thought of being a great artist, and then, getting even more sophisticated, a great criminal.

My mother, however, wanted me to be a railroad clerk. And that was her *highest* ambition; she would have settled for less. At the age of sixteen when I let everybody know that I was going to be a great writer, my friends and family took the news quite calmly, my mother included. She did not become angry. She quite simply assumed that I had gone off my nut. She was illiterate and her peasant life in Italy made her believe that only a son of the nobility could possibly be a writer. Artistic beauty after all could spring only from the seedbed of fine clothes, fine food, luxurious living. So then how was it possible for a son of hers to be an artist? She was not too convinced she was wrong even after my first two books were published many years later. It was only after the commercial success of my third novel that she gave me the title of poet.

My family and I grew up together on Tenth Avenue, between Thirtieth and Thirty-first streets, part of the area called Hell's Kitchen. This particular neighborhood could have been a movie set for one of the Dead End Kid flicks or for the social drama of the East Side in which John Garfield played the hero. Our tenements were the western wall of the city. Beneath our windows were the vast black iron gardens of the New York Central Railroad, absolutely blooming with stinking boxcars freshly unloaded of cattle and pigs for the city slaughterhouse. Steers sometimes escaped and loped through the heart of the neighborhood followed by astonished young boys who had never seen a live cow.

Italians, like other immigrant groups, tended to cluster in ethnic ghettos. This one, on New York's Lower East Side, is much like the one Puzo inhabited in the 1930s, but "Little Italy" existed in dozens of large American cities. In what ways might a person raised in an ethnic ghetto be significantly different from someone who grew up without ethnic reinforcement?

The railroad yards stretched down to the Hudson River, beyond whose garbagey waters rose the rocky Palisades of New Jersey. There were railroad tracks running downtown on Tenth Avenue itself to another freight station called St. Johns Park. Because of this, because these trains cut off one side of the street from the other, there was a wooden bridge over Tenth Avenue, a romantic-looking bridge despite the fact that no sparkling water, no silver flying fish darted beneath it; only heavy dray carts drawn by tired horses, some flat-boarded trucks, tin lizzie automobiles and, of course, long strings of freight cars drawn by black, ugly engines.

What was really great, truly magical, was sitting on the bridge, feet dangling down, and letting the engine under you blow up clouds of steam that made you disappear, then reappear all damp and smelling of fresh ironing. When I was seven years old I fell in love for the first time with the tough little girl who held my hand and disappeared with me in that magical cloud of steam. This experience was probably more traumatic and damaging to my later relationships with women than one of those ugly childhood adventures Freudian novelists use to explain why their hero has gone bad.

■ ■ ■

My father supported his wife and seven children by working as a trackman laborer for the New York Central Railroad. My oldest brother worked for the railroad as a brakeman, another brother was a railroad shipping clerk in the freight office. Eventually I spent some of the worst months of my life as the railroad's worst messenger boy.

My oldest sister was just as unhappy as a dressmaker in the garment industry. She wanted to be a school teacher. At one time or another my other two brothers also worked for the railroad—it got all six males in the family. The two girls and my mother escaped, though my mother felt it her duty to send all our bosses a gallon of homemade wine on Christmas. But everybody hated their jobs except my oldest brother who had a night shift and spent most of his working hours sleeping in freight cars. My father finally got fired because the foreman told him to get a bucket of water for the crew and not to take all day. My father took the bucket and disappeared forever.

Nearly all the Italian men living on Tenth Avenue supported their large families by working on the railroad. Their children also earned pocket money by stealing ice from the refrigerator cars in summer and coal from the open stoking cars in the winter. Sometimes an older lad would break the seal of a freight car and take a look inside. But this usually brought down the "Bulls," the special railroad police. And usually the freight was "heavy" stuff, too much work to cart away and sell, something like fresh produce or boxes of cheap candy that nobody would buy.

The older boys, the ones just approaching voting age, made their easy money by hijacking silk trucks that loaded up at the garment factory on Thirty-first Street. They would then sell the expensive dresses door to door, at bargain prices no discount house could match. From this some graduated into organized crime, whose talent scouts alertly tapped young boys versed in strongarm. Yet despite all this, most of the kids grew up honest, content with fifty bucks a week as truck drivers, deliverymen, and white-collar clerks in the civil service.

I had every desire to go wrong but I never had a chance. The Italian family structure was too formidable.

I never came home to an empty house; there was always the smell of supper cooking. My mother was always there to greet me, sometimes with a policeman's club in her hand (nobody ever knew how she acquired it). But she was always there, or her authorized deputy, my older sister, who preferred throwing empty milk bottles at the heads of her little brothers when they got bad marks on their report cards. During the great Depression of the 1930s, though we were the poorest of the poor, I never remember not dining well. Many years later as a guest of a millionaire's club, I realized that our poor family on home relief ate better than some of the richest people in America.

My mother would never dream of using anything but the finest imported olive oil, the best Italian cheeses. My father had access to the fruits coming off ships, the produce from railroad cars, all before it went through the stale process of middlemen; and my mother, like most Italian women, was a fine cook in the peasant style.

My mother was as formidable a personage as she was a cook. She was not to be treated cavalierly. My oldest brother at age sixteen had his own tin lizzie Ford and used it to further his career as the Don Juan of Tenth Avenue. One day my mother asked him to drive her to the market on Ninth Avenue and Fortieth Street, no more than a five-minute trip. My brother had other plans and claimed he was going to work on a new shift on the railroad. Work was an acceptable excuse even for funerals. But an hour later when my mother came out of the door of the tenement she saw the tin lizzie loaded with three pretty neighborhood girls, my Don Juan brother about to drive them off. Unfortunately there was a cobblestone lying loose in the gutter. My mother dropped her black leather shopping bag and picked up the stone with both hands. As we all watched in horror, she brought the boulder down on the nearest fender of the tin lizzie, demolishing it. Then she picked up her bag and marched off to Ninth Avenue to do her shopping. To this day, forty years later, my brother's voice still has a surprised horror and shock when he tells the story. He still doesn't understand how she could have done it.

My mother had her own legends and myths on how to amass a fortune. There was one of our uncles who worked as an assistant chef in a famous Italian-style restaurant. Every day, six days a week, this uncle brought home, under his shirt, six eggs, a stick of butter, and a small bag of flour. By doing this for thirty years he was able to save enough money to buy a fifteen-thousand-dollar house on Long Island and two smaller houses for his son and daughter. Another cousin, blessed with a college degree, worked as a chemist in a large manufacturing firm. By using the firm's raw materials and equipment he concocted a superior floor wax which he sold door to door in his spare time. It was a great floor wax and with his low overhead, the price was right. My mother and her friends did not think this was stealing. They thought of it as being thrifty.

The wax-selling cousin eventually destroyed his reputation for thrift by buying a sailboat; this was roughly equivalent to the son of a Boston brahmin spending a hundred grand in a whorehouse.

As rich men escape their wives by going to their club, I finally escaped my mother by going to the Hudson Guild Settlement House. Most people do not know that a settlement house is really a club combined with social services. The Hudson Guild, a five-story field of joy for slum kids, had ping pong rooms and billiard rooms, a shop in which to make lamps, a theater for putting on amateur plays, a gym to box and play basketball in. And then there were individual rooms where your particular club could meet in privacy. The Hudson Guild even suspended your membership for improper behaviour or failure to pay the tiny dues. It was a heady experience for a slum kid to see his name posted on the billboard to the effect that he was suspended by the Board of Governors.

■ ■ ■

The Hudson Guild was also responsible for absolutely the happiest times of my childhood. When I was about nine or ten they sent me away as a Fresh Air Fund kid. This was a program where slum children were boarded on private families in places like New Hampshire for two weeks.

192   As a child I knew only the stone city. I had no conception of what the countryside could be. When I got to New Hampshire, when I smelled grass and flowers and trees, when I ran barefoot along the dirt country roads, when I drove the cows home from pasture, when I darted through fields of corn and waded through clear brooks, when I gathered warm brown speckled eggs in the hen-house, when I drove a hay wagon drawn by two great horses—when I did all these things—I nearly went crazy with the joy of it. It was quite simply a fairy tale come true.

The family that took me in, a middle-aged man and woman, childless, were Baptists and observed Sunday so religiously that even checker playing was not allowed on the Lord's day of rest. We went to church on Sunday for a good three hours, counting Bible class, then again at night. On Thursday evenings we went to prayer meetings. My guardians, out of religious scruple, had never seen a movie. They disapproved of dancing, they were no doubt political reactionaries; they were everything that I came later to fight against.

And yet they gave me those magical times children never forget. For two weeks every summer from the time I was nine to fifteen I was happier than I have ever been before or since. The man was good with tools and built me a little playground with swings, sliding ponds, seesaws. The woman had a beautiful flower and vegetable garden and let me pick from it. A cucumber or strawberry in the earth was a miracle. And then when they saw how much I loved picnics, the sizzling frankfurters on a stick over the wood fire, the yellow roasted corn, they drove me out on Sunday afternoons to a lovely green grass mountainside. Only on Sundays it was never called a picnic, it was called "taking our lunch outside." I found it then—and now—a sweet hypocrisy.

■ ■ ■

From this Paradise I was flung into Hell. That is, I had to help support my family by working on the railroad. After school hours of course. This was the same railroad that had supplied free coal and free ice to the whole Tenth Avenue when I was young enough to steal with impunity. After school finished at 3 P.M. I went to work in the freight office as a messenger. I also worked Saturdays and Sundays when there was work available.

I hated it. One of my first short stories was about how I hated that job. But of course what I really hated was entering the adult world. To me the adult world was a dark enchantment, unnatural. As unnatural to the human dream as death. And as inevitable.

The young are impatient about change because they cannot grasp the power of time itself; not only as the enemy of flesh, the very germ of death, but time as a benign cancer. As the young cannot grasp really that love must be a victim of time, so too they cannot grasp that injustices, the economic and family traps of living, can also fall victim to time.

■ ■ ■

America may be a fascistic, warmongering, racially prejudiced country today. It may deserve the hatred of its revolutionary young. But what a miracle it once was! What has happened here has never happened in any other country in any

Many Italian-Americans of your parents' and grandparents' generations saw Frank Sinatra and Joe DiMaggio as symbols of the American Dream come true. Few Italians achieved this kind of wealth and fame; most had to settle for much less. What function do celebrities perform for their ethnic groups?

other time. The poor who had been poor for centuries—hell, since the beginning of Christ—whose children had inherited their poverty, their illiteracy, their hopelessness, achieved some economic dignity and freedom. You didn't get it for nothing, you had to pay a price in tears, in suffering, but why not? And some even became artists.

Not even my gift for retrospective falsification [remembering the good and not the bad] can make my eighteenth to twenty-first years seem like a happy time. I hated my life. I was being dragged into the trap I feared and had foreseen even as a child. It was all there, the steady job, the nice girl who would eventually get knocked up, and then the marriage and fighting over counting pennies to make ends meet. I noticed myself acting more unheroic all the time. I had to tell lies in pure self-defense, I did not forgive so easily.

But I was delivered. When World War II broke out I was delighted. There is no other word, terrible as it may sound. My country called. I was delivered from my mother, my family, the girl I was loving passionately but did not love. And delivered WITHOUT GUILT. Heroically. My country called, ordered me to defend it. I must have been one of millions, sons, husbands, fathers, lovers, making their innocent getaway from baffled loved ones. And what an escape it was. The war made all my dreams come true. I drove a jeep, toured Europe, had love affairs, found a wife, and lived the material for my first novel. But of course that was a just war as Vietnam is not, and so today it is perhaps for the best that the revolutionary young make their escape by attacking their own rulers.

Then why five years later did I walk back into the trap with a wife and child and a civil service job I was glad to get? After five years of the life I had dreamed

193

about, plenty of women, plenty of booze, plenty of money, hardly any work, interesting companions, travel, etc., why did I walk back into that cage of family and duty and a steady job?

For the simple reason, of course, that I had never really escaped, not my mother, not my family, not the moral pressures of our society. Time again had done its work. I was back in my cage and I was, I think, happy. In the next twenty years I wrote three novels. Two of them were critical successes but I didn't make much money. The third novel, not as good as the others, made me rich. And free at last. Or so I thought.

Then why do I dream of those immigrant Italian peasants as having been happy? I remember how they spoke of their forebears, who spent all their lives farming the arid mountain slopes of Southern Italy. "He died in that house in which he was born," they say enviously. "He was never more than an hour from his village, not in all his life," they sigh. And what would they make of a phrase like "retrospective falsification"?

No, really, we are all happier now. It is a better life. And after all, as my mother always said, "Never mind about being happy. Be glad you're alive."

When I came to my "autobiographical novel," the one every writer does about himself, I planned to make myself the sensitive, misunderstood hero, much put upon by his mother and family. To my astonishment my mother took over the book and instead of my revenge I got another comeuppance. But it is, I think, my best book. And all those old-style grim conservative Italians whom I hated, then pitied so patronizingly, they also turned out to be heroes. Through no desire of mine. I was surprised. The thing that amazed me most was their courage. Where were their Congressional Medals of Honor? Their Distinguished Service Crosses? How did they ever have the balls to get married, have kids, go out to earn a living in a strange land, with no skills, not even knowing the language? They made it without tranquillizers, without sleeping pills, without psychiatrists, without even a dream. Heroes. Heroes all around me. I never saw them.

But how could I? They wore lumpy work clothes and handlebar moustaches, they blew their noses on their fingers and they were so short that their high-school children towered over them. They spoke a laughable broken English and the furthest limit of their horizon was their daily bread. Brave men, brave women, they fought to live their lives without dreams. Bent on survival, they narrowed their minds to the thinnest line of existence.

It is no wonder that in my youth I found them contemptible. And yet they had left Italy and sailed the ocean to come to a new land and leave their sweated bones in America. Illiterate Colombos, they dared to seek the promised land. And so they, too, dreamed a dream.

■ ■ ■

But maybe the young are on the right track this time. Maybe they know that the dreams of our fathers were malignant. Perhaps it is true that the only real escape is in the blood magic of drugs. All the Italians I knew and grew up with have escaped, have made their success. We are all Americans now, we are all successes now. And yet the most successful Italian man I know admits that though the one human act he never could understand was suicide, he understood it when he became a success. Not that he ever would do such a thing; no man with

Puzo speaks of the immigrant generation of Italians as "happy," although their lives were grim. Can you detect anything in this photo of an Italian-American religious festival in 1915 that suggests what he means? Is happiness, in Puzo's sense, part of the American Dream of success?

Italian blood ever commits suicide or becomes a homosexual in his belief. But suicide has crossed his mind. And so to what avail the finding of the dream? He went back to Italy and tried to live like a peasant again. But he can never again be unaware of more subtle traps than poverty and hunger.

There is a difference between having a good time in life and being happy. My mother's life was a terrible struggle and yet I think it was a happy life. One tentative proof is that at the age of eighty-two she is positively indignant at the thought that death dares approach her. But it's not for everybody that kind of life.

Thinking back I wonder why I became a writer. Was it the poverty or the books I read? Who traumatized me, my mother or the Brothers Karamazov? Being Italian? Or the girl sitting with me on the bridge as the engine steam deliciously made us vanish? Did it make any difference that I grew up Italian rather than Irish or black?

No matter. The good times are beginning, I am another Italian success story. Not as great as DiMaggio or Sinatra but quite enough. It will serve. Yet I can escape again. I have my retrospective falsification (how I love that phrase). I can dream now about how happy I was in my childhood, in my tenement, playing in those dirty but magical streets—living in the poverty that made my mother weep. True, I was a deposed dictator at fifteen but they never hanged me. And now I remember, all those impossible dreams strung out before me, waiting for me to choose, not knowing that the life I was living then, as a child, would become my final dream.

ASSIGNMENT 5

A Project in
Oral History:
Impact of
the Depression

This project in oral history has several objectives. First, you should utilize your interviewing techniques by talking to a resident of the community in which you are living. Select a person, aged fifty or older, and attempt to recover some of the history of the depression years.

You might follow a line of questioning similar to this: Do you remember the stock market crash? What did you think of Herbert Hoover? Did you or your family lose any money in the market or in bank failures? What was your attitude toward Franklin Roosevelt? Did you ever listen to him on the radio? What else did you listen to on the radio? Were you or someone in your family unemployed? Do you know anyone who worked for the CCC or WPA? What kinds of experiences did he or she have? Did you move from one house to another? What did you do for fun? Did people have more fun in those days? Were the movies important in any way? What about the importance of the automobile? What did economic hardship do to family life? Did anyone you knew lose faith in the American system? Does the fact that you lived through the depression influence your ideas and attitudes today?

Try not to let a preconceived idea of how the discussion should flow interfere with the direction the conversation will spontaneously take. Use your common sense and be flexible. Interrupt as little as possible, except when you have to jog the interviewee's memory. Your role is to listen.

Use the same techniques and questions when you interview members of your own family on their depression experiences. Then, write a preliminary report on your findings, to be incorporated later into your research paper.

BIBLIOGRAPHIC NOTE

For a lively introduction to the depression era, see W. E. Leuchtenburg, *Franklin D. Roosevelt and the New Deal, 1932–1940* (1963). Enormous detail and texture emerges from the continuing biographical studies on Roosevelt and his times by Frank Freidel and Arthur Schlesinger, Jr. For specific information on aspects of life then, you should consult David Shannon, ed., *The Great Depression* (1960), a collection of contemporary bits and pieces, and the very graphic book by Dorothea Lange and P. S. Taylor, *An American Exodus: A Record of Human Erosion in the Thirties* (1969). Studs Terkel's *Hard Times* (1970), a selection from which has been included in this chapter, provides not only excellent firsthand accounts of life in the thirties but a model of the techniques used in oral history as well. Another collection of oral interviews, Ann Banks' *First Person America* (1980), provides, for the first time, life histories collected between 1938 and 1942 by the Federal Writers Project.

PART SIX

World War II

Strange as it must seem to a generation of Americans accustomed to an overwhelming American presence throughout the world, the United States sat on the sidelines as World War II approached. Although the likelihood of a second world war increased throughout the 1930s, not many Americans appeared to notice. The armed struggle between Japan and China seemed far away to an American middle class that was preoccupied with preserving itself amid a severe economic depression. Even the ominous regime that Adolf Hitler led to power in Germany in 1933 could parade its barbarism throughout the decade without arousing much American censure. Germany abandoned the League of Nations in 1933, and by 1935, in flagrant scorn of the armaments provisions of the Treaty of Versailles, had rebuilt a vast army and air force. Then in March 1936 it flouted international opinion by forcibly reoccupying the Rhineland. Yet just six months later, a team of Americans participated with athletes from around the world in the Berlin Olympics, thus tacitly acknowledging Hilter's international respectability. Popular American myopia continued from 1936 to 1939 as the German *Luftwaffe* enjoyed a dress rehearsal for World War II in the service of Francisco Franco's Fascists in the Spanish Civil War. Even the 1938 German seizure of Austria passed without effective objection. President Franklin D. Roosevelt joined most other

197

world leaders in praising the Munich Pact, the high point of appeasement.

From the American perspective, these were matters for the Europeans to settle. In effect, the United States government played the role of a minor power throughout the 1930s, neither participating in the recurring European diplomatic crises nor seeking to generate popular support for international collaboration. Many American political leaders reflected the popular belief that American involvement in World War I had been a mistake, that Europeans, insufficiently grateful for American aid in the earlier war, were about to battle again and were trying to maneuver the United States into another of their seemingly endless conflicts.

On September 1, 1939, the war began in earnest when Germany invaded Poland, and England and France kept their alliance with Poland by declaring war on Germany. Americans worried and wondered; still, most thought that the United States was safe and could stay out of war. Then Hitler's *Blitzkrieg*, in the spring of 1940, shattered the western front: Norway, Denmark, and the Low Countries fell; France was taken with astonishing ease; now England stood alone against the Nazi war machine. Although most Americans clearly sympathized with Britain and the Allied powers, the strong public opposition during 1940 and 1941 to full belligerency limited the role of the United States. It did send arms and supplies to England, and the navy expanded the scope of its activities in Atlantic and Caribbean waters. Yet most Americans still hoped that the United States could avoid joining the fight.

These hopes were destroyed on December 7, 1941, the day of the surprise Japanese attack on Pearl Harbor that quickly brought the United States into war against the Axis powers of Germany, Italy, and Japan. Although the careful observer of the long-deteriorating relationship between Japan and the United States might have predicted the outbreak of hostilities, the attack on Pearl Harbor shocked all Americans. To this day millions of people can recall exactly what they were doing when the news flashed over the radio. Pearl Harbor united and activated the people of this country in a way seldom experienced before or since. Patriotism ran high as the nation prepared to defeat the Axis. All the debates about intervention or isolation were swept away: innocent and peace-loving America had been attacked by the forces of evil.

World War II, like the depression, was a transcendent event that affected all Americans and their families. Over 400,000 Americans lost their lives in the war and more than 670,000 were wounded. For many families the war meant utter tragedy—the death in faraway places of sons, husbands, fathers, brothers, and other loved ones. Even many of the military men who survived would be haunted all their lives by the memory of the terror and slaughter and the untimely deaths of comrades and friends.

Paradoxically, many men and women found military service the high point of their lives. The terror faded with time and only the memory of adventure, comradeship, and the glory of being involved in an epic common cause remained. Strange names like Truk, Leyte, Anzio, El Alamein, and Midway assumed permanent, almost fond memories for those who were there. Catapulted out of small-town lives and mundane jobs into exotic places, many men and women in the armed services felt released from the normal restraints and responsibilities of marriage, family, and work. Despite occasional or frequent danger, many had the time of their lives, whether in the Moroccan desert or on shore patrol duty at Atlantic City, New Jersey.

An even more common shared experience—of soldier and civilian alike—was uprooting. Although Americans have historically been a mobile people, the impact of World War II on mobility was extraordinary. Military service naturally relocated millions. All men between the ages of eighteen and forty-five had to register for the draft; many others enlisted. There were 500,000 in the armed forces by 1940; 3,800,000 by 1942; and over 12 million by 1945. By the end of the war one out of every five American males between the ages of eighteen and forty-five had served in the armed forces. Many of those not in the services found work in war industries, jobs that frequently meant having to move. Statistics indicate a substantial migration away from New England and the upper Plains states; in another exodus hundreds of thousands left the South, from all along the arc stretching from West Virginia toward Mississippi and Oklahoma. Across the nation nearly 10 million people left farms during the decade of the 1940s. Increasing numbers crowded into the major cities of New York and northern New Jersey, Chicago, Cleveland, Detroit, Baltimore, and Miami. In particular, people sought the sun-drenched new world of California.

Millions of these Americans moved eagerly into a war-based economy, and the nation's policy makers discovered a hedge against another major economic disaster. Gone finally was the depression of the 1930s, with full employment returning for the first time since the 1920s. The American economy, fed by public and private capital, thus entered its still-continuing dependence on the production of war or war-related materials. For unemployed workers the return to full production was a great opportunity after the lean thirties, and surely sufficient reason to uproot a family. Employment in major industries, which had dropped to 23 million in the depths of the depression, ballooned to over 42 million in 1943. Unemployment, near 13 million in 1933, fell to 670,000 in 1944. Spending for national defense became a way of life for the American government. For working people, war jobs suggested the possibility that good wages and steady work would mean a decent home and a better education for their children.

Among the beneficiaries of the wartime demand for labor were black Americans. Repeating a pattern established during World War I, a mass of black Americans streamed out of the rural South to the urban North to find jobs at decent wages. The war did not end racial tension and violence, but it did raise hopes for justice and equal opportunity. Many of the black American servicemen sent abroad, even while relegated to units racially segregated by American military precedent, found psychological release from the oppression of racism for the first time.

Yet the opportunities that the war provided for American blacks were severely circumscribed. Jammed into the black ghettos of central cities, which rarely provided adequate housing, transportation, education, or cleanliness, many black families became trapped. At the war's end, black men and women fell victim in large numbers to the "last hired, first fired" principle of black employment. And returning black servicemen found that the high democratic idealism of wartime struggle had little relevance to postwar life in the slums of Northern cities or the dusty towns of the rural South.

Racism's twisted cruelty was more overtly expressed when the government of the United States arbitrarily incarcerated most Americans of Japanese descent. Soon after Pearl Harbor, about 125,000 Japanese-Americans (over 70 percent of them American citizens) were forcibly removed from their West Coast homes and imprisoned in concentration camps in the interior. Their property was seized with little or no compensation, and the process was upheld by the Supreme Court. No similar treatment was considered necessary either for German-Americans or Italian-Americans. The objectives of total victory justified all expedients, notwithstanding some uneasiness, and minor protests, about putting American citizens in concentration camps. As in most wars, however, the fervor of patriotic righteousness devoured its minority of dissenters.

This fervor was constantly promoted on the American homefront. Grade-school children went on scrap drives, saved tin foil, bought savings stamps, and helped in the family "victory garden," a backyard fruit-and-vegetable patch designed to free food production for the war effort and to encourage full participation in the national struggle. High-school students might join paramilitary drill teams or wrap bandages as Red Cross volunteers. Housewives went into factories in large numbers, working on assembly lines, in arsenals, or in offices. Local service clubs formed air-raid-warden squads or organized war-bond drives. In town meetings and along flag-festooned parade routes, big cities and small towns proclaimed their united support for total victory.

From Hollywood came a flood of war movies, simplistic but appealing stories of heroism and virtue struggling against treachery—and winning. The many warriors of Sunset Strip—John Wayne, Alan Ladd, Randolph Scott, Brian Donleavy—reassured Americans of the nobility of their cause and the inevitability of their victory. Betty Grable, Veronica Lake, and Rita Hayworth made their own contributions to morale.

For the American middle class the sense of national unity effectively compensated for wartime hardship, not the least of which was strict rationing of a broad variety of foods and consumer goods, which encouraged some black market activities. Horsemeat appeared on some dinner tables. Leg paint replaced nylon stockings. Yellow-colored margarine pretended to be butter. Automobile production stopped, tires and gasoline were in limited supply. Yet the army of middle-class consumers hardly uttered a protest. Organized labor abandoned its precious right to strike. The harmony of common purpose pervaded the land.

Yet the phenomenon of united war effort should not obscure the diversity of experience, the enormously complex impact that World War II had on American society. In particular, the social history of families reflected substantial changes. The uprooting and resettlement of so many families obviously shattered long-settled patterns of residence. Millions of fathers were taken from the home. Social flux affected marriages, the birth rate, divorces. The number of marriages rose sharply during wartime, many of them entered into in haste under the pressures of imminent separation. The nation's population increased by 6.5 million during the war years. Yet in 1946, the year after the war ended, divorces soared to 610,000, the highest level in American history to that point.

Thus the American nuclear family, traditional backbone of the social structure, underwent significant alteration. Opportunity and good fortune on the road to middle-class happiness beckoned many. Others were permanently affected by the sights and sounds of distant places and returned home with new ideas. The war left irreparable scars on those many families whose lost sons would remain forever young in the frozen uniformed photos on the mantlepiece.

Two Experiences in the Combat Zone

CHARLES E. KELLY and JAMES J. FAHEY

Have you ever talked to soldiers about their wartime experiences? Some will tell you a great deal, but for others the horror is still too great, the memories too personal. The war changed many people who fought in it. It uprooted them from their hometowns and neighborhoods and introduced them to new lands and customs. For some, the army provided a chance for adventure and the close comradeship that comes with shared danger. (After the war, veterans' organizations became their social clubs.) For many, the war meant that they would never be the same again.

As you read the following selections, think about the way that World War II influenced your family and your community. Was any member of your family in the war? What effect has that experience had on his or her attitudes toward war and peace and patriotism?

KELLY: HEROISM IN WAR

Leaving the Salerno beach fifty feet behind me, I pumped my knees up and down in a sort of dog trot, moving straight ahead. That first rush took me past a dead G.I., lying peacefully, as if asleep, with his head on his pack, his rifle by his side. I pulled my eyes away and told myself, *Don't let that worry you.*

Then came a big drainage ditch with G.I.'s lying down inside of it. "Come on! It ain't deep! Jump!" I jumped, only to find the water and slime up to my eyes. The bottom was oozy; my feet sank into it, and I was weighted down by ammunition. I let go of my automatic rifle, but as soon as I dropped it, I felt lonely and lost, and ducked my head under to find it. Groping around, I got my hand on it. There was a small tree handy and, using one of its branches, I pulled myself out of the muck, and so to the other side.

There is no rhyme or reason to how the mind of a soldier in battle works. There I was charging into Italy, passing dead men and coming close to drowning in a ditch, and, after cleaning my rifle as best I could, all I could think about was whether or not the photographs in my wallet had been ruined.

Look at the faces of these young men who have just registered for the draft. How do you explain their enthusiasm? Do you agree with the theory that, whatever sorrow and hardship it brought, World War II was the last time that the United States was united on anything? Can it be true that people "enjoy" war? Is this only a male instinct?

I took them out, tried to wipe them off on the grass, and waved them back and forth to stir up a little air to dry them.

Machine-gun bullets were boring into the ground in front of me and, at intervals, when the blup-blup of their impact came too close together, I hit the dirt. Those machine guns blazed away at us and mopped up our staff sergeant. He went down with bullets in his head.

I kept right on moving forward, and the next time I looked around to check my position, I was alone. The orders I'd heard back on shipboard had gone out of my mind. All I remembered was hearing somebody say, "When you get on the beach, keep moving forward."

Hopping over a wall and following a little path, I jumped over another wall into a clump of thorn bushes. Machine-gun bullets were streaking up and down the path I had just left, so I lay down in those bushes and played dead until the fire slackened. Finally I found a break through the thorns and, at the end of the break, a row of our men dug in. They were from two of our outfits, all mixed up together.

Once more, I started looking for my outfit. After a while I got tired of going along doubled up and stooping over, so I stood up and started walking. I decided I was thirsty and stopped at a farmhouse well to get a drink. There were grapes and peaches around, and I stuffed some of them into me. I passed deserted farms and houses until they all ran together in my mind and I couldn't tell one from the other. Finally I figured I had walked about eight hours, and must be about twelve miles inland. Turning around, I saw a highway, and started to walk along it heading back in the direction from which I had come. Then, in the distance, German medium Mark IV tanks hove in sight. I dived into a ditch, squinted along my

BAR—Browning automatic rifle—and began to fire as they came close, but the slugs from my gun made no impression on them. I was aiming at the tanks' slit openings, but there is so much noise and racket inside one of those things that the Heinies probably didn't hear me. They rumbled and clanked by, and I kept on walking down the highway, coming at last to a little creek, where I drank, took off my shoes and bathed my feet. My toes were stuck together from the sea water I'd waded through back at the Salerno beach. I washed my socks to get the salt out of them and put the same socks back on, keeping my extra ones in reserve.

I put in about fifteen minutes trying to remember the things I was supposed to have had firmly fixed in my head when we landed on the beach. Finally I remembered what our detail was supposed to do. I could see the mountain Lieutenant O'Leary had told us about. He had called it Mountain Forty-two and we were supposed to take it. So I started toward it.

After climbing for a while, I came to a winery and found the first battalion of our regiment dug in there and all around it in the open fields. I wanted to ask them where my outfit was, but their trigger fingers were too itchy; they were shooting at sounds and dimly seen movements, and it wasn't any time to be dropping in unannounced to tear a social herring with them. So I dug in behind a bush and went to sleep.

It would have been nice to fill my canteen with water before I started again, but my canteen had picked up a bullet hole somewhere along the way. I hadn't known about that bullet before, although it must have given quite a jerk when it ripped through. I tried to rub the sleep from my eyes and walk down the highway. Both sides had infiltrated into and behind each other, so that you had to be on the alert each minute and watch every moving thing on each side of you.

German bullets were zipping around like high-velocity bees, but I finally found my outfit dug in, in spattered, shallow holes. They greeted me with, "Where the hell have you been?"

When I reported to Lieutenant O'Leary, he said, "I was sure they'd got you."

Every once in a while a shell landed near us, but they didn't do any real damage.

After a time we started down the road, and ran into a little Italian boy, who said, "Germans. Germans. Germans." My pal, La Bue, spoke to him in Italian, but the kid was frightened and didn't make much sense.

While La Bue was bickering with him, Lieutenant O'Leary shouted, "Here come some Heinie scout cars! Get off the road!"

We dived for cover and the scout cars opened fire. Bullets and fragments of shells bounced from our rifles, and two of us were hit. All of a sudden, one of our boys got his bazooka on his shoulder and let go with a tremendous, crashing "Boom!" and immediately afterward one of our men jumped up on a wall beside the road, leaped like a frog to the top of one of those panzer wagons and dropped his hand grenade into it. That particular scout car stopped then and there. The others speeded up, trying to get past us, when a company of our antitankers we hadn't seen up to that time went into action with its 57-mm. cannon. It was chancy stuff, for if that 57-mm. had missed its target, it would have gotten us. But as it was, everything worked out nice and clean and efficient. The bazooka kept on booming, and, quicker than it seemed possible, that whole small reconnaissance detachment was knocked out.

The place was a shambles. Scout cars were going up in flames. Tires were burning with a rubbery stink, and bodies were burning too. One German leaped out and started to run. When we went after him, he put his revolver to his head and killed himself. We had thought that only the Japs did that, and for a moment I was surprised and shocked.

Then a deep-rooted G.I. habit asserted itself. A moment before, hell had been popping on that stretch of road. Now, two seconds later, all we thought of was souvenirs. Milky Holland found a German Lüger. Looking back at it, I can remember no feeling about the German dead except curiosity. We were impersonal about them; to us they were just bundles of rags.

About two hours afterward, things were so quiet that some of us sneaked off into the near-by town, but we weren't relaxed and casual, and we took our rifles and sidearms with us. The townspeople were out waving at us and offering us water, wine and fruit. La Bue, a kid named Survilo and I had a yen to see the inside of an Italian jail. A woman had told us it was where they kept the Fascist sympathizers. The leading Fascist citizen of the town was in there, mad as blazes and yelling his head off behind the bars. La Bue listened to him for a while, then got mad himself and tried to reach through the bars and tickle him with the end of a bayonet. The Fascist really sounded off then.

When we came out, we saw some pretty Italian girls. La Bue made a date with one of them—the procedure following the same line as if we had been back in Pittsburgh's North Side. He asked her if she could get a couple of friends for us. Smiling, she said she could, and, feeling that we had accomplished something important, we went back to our bivouac.

But, just as they sometimes do in the North Side of Pittsburgh, our plans laid an egg. Platoon Sgt. Zerk Robertson pointed to a town named Altavilla, five or six miles away, and said, "See that town over there? That's where I'm going, and I want some volunteers to go with me. I'm taking the second platoon and some sixty-millimeter mortars." La Bue looked at me, and I looked at him, and we

An American car strafed by Japanese planes during the attack on Pearl Harbor, December 7, 1941. Why did the Pearl Harbor attack come as such a shock to Americans?

Was fighting in the Pacific more bitter because of the hardships induced by the rugged terrain? Was racism a factor as well?

thought of our dates, but there wasn't anything we could do about it, and presently we were walking out along the highway.

FAHEY: FEAR IN THE SOUTH PACIFIC

July 15, 1943: We returned from our prowl up the Slot in search of Jap ships but nothing happened. I guess the Japs are licking their wounds. . . .

. . . Fighting the Japs is like fighting a wild animal. The troops said that the Japs are as tough and fierce as they come; the Jap is not afraid to die, it is an honor to die for the Emperor, he is their God.

A lot of the fighting is done at night and you can smell the Japs 25 yards away. The jungle is very hot and humid and drains the strength quickly. The jungle is also very thick; you could be right next to a Jap and yet you could not see him. The

206

Japs also have Jap women with them. The Japs watch from coconut trees in the daytime and then when it becomes dark they sneak into your foxhole and cut your throat or throw in a hand grenade. A 200 lb. soldier was pulled from his foxhole and killed in short time. You also hear all sorts of noises made by the animals and you think it is the Japs. This is too much for some men and they crack up.

They say the Japs also have some Imperial Marines who are 6 ft. 4″ tall. The Japs are experts at jungle fighting and they know all the tricks. You would hardly believe the tricks they use. In the darkness, for instance, they like to throw dirt in your eyes and then attack you. Many of our troops get killed learning their tricks. The Japs take all kinds of chances, they love to die. Our troops are advancing slowly, it is a very savage campaign. Very few Japs surrender, they die fighting, even when the situation is hopeless.

State of the Nation

JOHN DOS PASSOS

The war meant movement—both the movement of troops to training camps and the migration of war workers and their families to industrial and port cities. Perhaps your family participated in this wartime migration.

In the selection that follows, John Dos Passos, best-selling author of U.S.A. *and other novels, describes some of the tensions and difficulties caused by wartime migration into a Southern city. Was the war the real cause of this tension or were there deeper causes? Does war lead to progress and prosperity, or does it cause the opposite? Are there any traces of social and economic change brought about in your own community as a result of war?*

The bus rumbles down the sunny empty highway through the rusty valleys and the bare rainwashed fields and the scraggly woods and the hills the color of oakleaves that are the landscape of winter in the southeast states. Inside, the air is dense with packed bodies and stale cigarette smoke. There's a smell of babies and an occasional sick flavor from the exhaust. The seats are all full. Somewhere in the back a baby is squalling. A line of men and women stands swaying in the aisle. Behind me two men are talking about jobs in singsong voices pitched deep in their chests.

"What's it like down there?" one is asking the other.

"Ain't too bad if you kin stand that bunch of loudmouthed foremen . . . If you look crosseyed at one of them guards he'll reach out and yank off your badge and you're through and that's all there is to it."

"Well, I've worked in about all of 'em."

"Say, ain't I seen you somewheres before?"

"I dunno. Might have been on this bus. I been on this bus a thousand times."

■ ■ ■

A TOWN OUTGROWS ITSELF

We are in the city now. The bus is swinging out of the traffic of the crowded main street round the low gray building of the bus station, and comes to a stop in the middle of a milling crowd: soldiers, sailors, stout women with bundled up babies, lanky backwoodsmen with hats tipped over their brows and a cheek full of chewingtobacco, hatless young men in lightcolored sports shirts open at the neck, countrymen with creased red necks and well-washed overalls, cigarsmoking stocky men in business suits in pastel shades, girls in bright dresses with carefully curled hair piled up on their heads and highheeled shoes and bloodred fingernails, withered nutbrown old people with glasses, carrying ruptured suitcases, broad-shouldered men in oilstained khaki with shiny brown helmets on their heads, negroes in flappy jackets and pegtop pants and little felt hats with turned-up brims, teenage boys in jockey caps, here and there a flustered negro woman dragging behind her a string of white-eyed children. Gradually the passengers are groping their way down the steep steps out of the bus and melting into the crowd.

Out on the streets every other man seems to be in work clothes. There are girls in twos and threes in slacks and overalls. Waiting for the light at a crossing a pinkfaced youth who's dangling a welder's helmet on a strap from the crook of his arm turns laughing to the man who hailed him. "I jes' got tired an' quit." Ragged families from the hills and the piney woods stroll staring straight ahead of them along the sidewalks towing flocks of little kids with flaxen hair and dirty faces. In front of a window full of brightcolored rayon socks in erratic designs a young man with glasses meets two girls in slacks. "We missed you yesterday," they say. "I was sick. I didn't go in. Anyway, I've got me a new job . . . more money."

The mouldering old Gulf seaport with its ancient dusty elegance of tall shuttered windows under mansard roofs and iron lace overgrown with vines, and scaling colonnades shaded by great trees, looks trampled and battered like a city that's been taken by storm. Sidewalks are crowded. Gutters are stacked with litter that drifts back and forth in the brisk spring wind. Garbage cans are overflowing. Frame houses on tree-shaded streets bulge with men in shirtsleeves who spill out onto the porches and trampled grassplots and stand in knots at the streetcorners. There's still talk of lodginghouses where they rent "hot beds." (Men work in three shifts. Why shouldn't they sleep in three shifts?) Cues wait outside of movies and lunchrooms. The trailer army has filled all the open lots with its regular ranks. In cluttered backyards people camp out in tents and chicken-houses and shelters tacked together out of packingcases.

In the outskirts in every direction you find acres and acres raw with new building, open fields skinned to the bare clay, elevations gashed with muddy roads and gnawed out by the powershovels and the bulldozers. There long lines of small houses, some decently planned on the "American standard" model and some mere boxes with a square brick chimney on the center, miles of dormitories, great squares of temporary structures are knocked together from day to day by a mob of construction workers in a smell of paint and freshsawed pine lumber and tobacco juice and sweat. Along the river for miles has risen a confusion of new yards from which men, women, and boys ebb and flow three times a day. Here and there are whole city blocks piled with wreckage and junk as if ancient cranky warehouses and superannuated stores had caved in out of their own rottenness under the impact of the violence of the new effort. Over it all the Gulf mist, heavy with smoke of soft coal, hangs in streaks, and glittering the training planes endlessly circle above the airfields.

To be doing something towards winning the war, to be making some money, to learn a trade, men and women have been pouring into the city for more than a year now; tenants from dusty shacks set on stilts above the bare eroded earth in the midst of the cotton and the scraggly corn, small farmers and trappers from halfcultivated patches in the piney woods, millhands from the industrial towns in the northern part of the state, garage men, fillingstation attendants, storekeepers, drugclerks from crossroads settlements, longshore fishermen and oystermen, negroes off plantations who've never seen any town but the county seat on Saturday afternoon, white families who've lived all their lives off tobacco and "white meat" and cornpone in cranky cabins forgotten in the hills.

For them everything's new and wonderful. They can make more spot cash in a month than they saw before in half a year. They can buy radios, they can go to the pictures, they can go to beerparlors, bowl, shoot craps, bet on the ponies. Everywhere they rub elbows with foreigners from every state in the Union. Housekeeping in a trailer with electric light and running water is a dazzling luxury to a woman who's lived all her life in a cabin with half-inch chinks between

Some 27 million people moved during the war, mostly to urban areas to be near factories turning out war goods. To meet the severe housing shortage that developed, trailer camps, like this one in Nashville, sprang up. How might native townspeople have reacted to this influx of newcomers?

the splintered boards of the floor. There are street cars and busses to take you
anywhere you want to go. At night the streets are bright with electric light. Girls
can go to beautyparlors, get their nails manicured, buy readymade dresses. In the
backwoods a girl who's reached puberty feels she's a woman. She's never worried
much about restraining her feelings when she had any. Is it any wonder that they
can't stay home at dusk when the streets fill up with hungry boys in uniform?

"It's quite dreadful," says the man with his collar around backwards, in
answer to my question. He is a thinfaced rustylooking man in black with dark-
ringed dark eyes who sits rocking in a rocking chair as he talks. "We are quite
exercised about the problems these newcomers raise for the city . . . Juvenile
delinquency, illegitimate babies, venereal disease . . . they are what we call the
riffraff. I've seen them in their homes when I was travelling about the state
inspecting C.C.C. camps for the government. They live in an astonishing state of
degradation, they have no ambition. They put in a few measly crops, hoe their
corn a little, but they have no habits of regular work. Most of them would rather
freeze than chop a little wood. Most of the time they just sit around taking snuff
and smoking. You see little children four and five years old smoking stubs of
cigars. It's *Tobacco Road* and what was that other book? . . . *Grapes of Wrath*.
People say those books are overdrawn, but they are not . . . They aren't exaggerated a bit. No wonder there's absenteeism . . . They've never worked regularly in their lives . . . They live in a daze. Nothing affects them, they don't want
anything. These awful trailer camps and filthy tent colonies, they seem dreadful
to us, but they like it like that. They think it's fine. They don't know any
different."

"Don't you think malnutrition might have something to do with their state of
mind?" He was strangely inattentive to my question. A smell of frying fish had
begun to fill the bare front room of the rectory. Somewhere out back a little bell
had tinkled. The man with his collar around backwards began to stir uneasily in
his chair. "I'm afraid I'm keeping you from your supper," I said, getting to my
feet. "Yes," he said hastily. I thanked him and said goodbye. As I was going out
the door he added, "Of course the people who come to my church, whom you were
asking about, are foremen, skilled mechanics, good union men, they are a much
better element. These other people are riffraff."

Waiting for the bus at the streetcorner in front of one of the better trailer
camps that has clean white gravel spread over the ground, and neat wooden
platforms beside each shiny trailer for use as a front stoop, I get to talking to a
young man in a leather jacket. He's just worked four hours overtime because the
other fellow didn't get there to relieve him at his machine. He's tired. You can tell
by his breath that he's just had a couple or three beers. He's beefing because of the
state regulations limiting the sale of whiskey and cutting out juke boxes in beer
parlors. When a man's tired, he says, he needs relaxation. Works better next day.
What's the use of dancing if you can't have a drink? What's the use of drinking if
you can't dance? If this sort of thing keeps up he's going to pick up and move some
place where things are wide open. Meanwhile several busses so jammed with
soldiers from the airfield there's no more room, have passed us by. Hell, he
groans, might as well go get him another beer, and he trots back into the silent
"Dine and Dance" joint across the street.

■　■　■

Casual love affairs or marriages entered into hastily before soldiers left for overseas duty were common during the war. Crowded housing conditions, pregnancies, and forced separations often further strained relations. What other factors might have contributed to the high postwar divorce rate?

"And now they've unloaded the race problem on us," mumbled the Mediator. "We were gettin' along all right until they stirred that up on us. We were givin' the colored folks the best break we could."

"Ain't never no trouble," said the roofer, "unless somebody stirs it up."

"Washington kicked off and the politicians down here are runnin' with the ball . . . White supremacy's a gold mine for 'em."

"As if we didn't have enough troubles organizin' this pile of raw muleskinners into decent union men and citizens," cried out the man in the stetson hat, "without having these longhaired wiseacres come down from Washington to stir up the race question . . . You know as well as I do that there isn't a white man in the South who isn't willing to die for the principle of segregation." He paused. All the men in the room silently nodded their heads. "Hell, we were jogglin' along all right before they sprung that on us. Sure, we have colored men in the unions in the building trades; the bricklayers even had colored officers in some of their locals."

"It's a thing you just have to go easy on," spoke up the Mediator. "Most white mechanics down here 'ud rather have a colored helper than a white helper, but when a colored man gets a notch up above them, they don't like it . . . Ain't a white man in the South'll stand for it. We tried that once in reconstruction days . . . I know of two of those niggers that fair practices board ordered upgraded who are dead niggers today. A piece of iron just fell on 'em."

"If they'd only just concentrate on givin' the negro a square deal within his own sphere most of the liberalminded people in the South would go along."

"There are small towns out here where all the young white men have gone to the army or war industry, and where the old men are all deputy sheriffs with guns slapped on their hips." The Mediator was talking in his slow drawling voice. "The people in those little towns are scared. If some day a drunken nigger made a pass at a white woman all hell 'ud break loose. Now there ain't nothin' going to happen, we know there ain't nothin' goin' to happen, but, mister, you tell your friends up North that this ain't no time to rock the boat."

"We've got our friends in the industrial unions to thank for that," said the young man in the stetson hat, spitting out his words savagely. "They came down here when we had the whole coast organized solid and put in their oar. They beat us at an election in this one yard . . . they got the negroes to vote for 'em, but they couldn't get 'em to join their union. What kind of labor politics is that? They've only got nine hundred members to this day, out of thousands. That's not majority rule . . . That doesn't sound like democracy to me."

A few days before in a mining town in the northern part of the state I'd had lunch with a young college man from North Carolina, who had given me in a slow serious voice the industrial union side of the race question. They knew it was a difficult matter, he'd said, but they had decided to face it squarely. At first the employers down here had hired negro labor to break the white unions, but now that the negroes were joining up the employers were trying to hire all white men. On the whole the negroes had stuck to their locals through hard times better than the whites. In locals where they'd faced the issue squarely . . . equal rights for all . . . there had been very little trouble, even in locals made up of country boys from the farms. He told me of one local right in the black belt where they had tried it without having any real trouble, but the strain on the organizer, who was a Southern boy, had been terrific. He'd gone to a hospital with a nervous breakdown. I laughed. He didn't. It wasn't easy, he went on unsmilingly, but prejudice was something that tended to die away if nobody stirred it up. The cure was firmness and courage—meet it head on.

I told him about a meeting I'd drifted into in the basement of a colored church in a war industry town in the North. It was a meeting to protest against the separate dormitory the government was erecting for colored people. Quietlooking elderly negroes were sitting on cane chairs round an oldfashioned coal stove listening to the booming oratory of a preacher from the city. In a voice stirring as a roll of drums he invoked the Four Freedoms and asked how this country could fight for democracy in the rest of the world while there was still discrimination and segregation for thirteen million of our citizens at home. A lawyer had talked about the Constitution and said that now was the time for negroes to rise up and insist that they would no longer be treated as secondclass citizens. If they were called upon to send their sons and brothers to die for their country they had the right to demand equal rights everywhere throughout the broad land. Very much stirred, the listeners had whispered fervent amens at every pause. A young labor organizer had gotten up and said that such injustices made him ashamed to be a white man.

I was asking whether, perhaps, if only as a matter of tactics, it would not be better to work for fair play, equal wages, equal living conditions, first. Wasn't trying to break up segregation that way an infringement of the liberty of white men who didn't want to mix with negroes? After all, white men had rights, too.

"We have found," the young man said quietly, "that to get fair play for poor whites we've got to fight for equal rights for poor negroes. Of course we have to use tact, a great deal of tact. But in the unions, at least, the question has to be met head on."

TWENTY-FIVE YEARS BEHIND THE TIMES

And all the while, by every bus and train the new people, white and black, pour into the city. As fast as a new block of housing is finished, it's jampacked. As soon as a new bus is put into service, it's weighed down with passengers. The schools are too full of children. The restaurants are too full of eaters. If you try to go to see a doctor, you find the waitingroom full and a long line of people straggling down the hall. There's no room in the hospitals for the women who are going to have babies. "So far we've been lucky," the health officers say with terror in their voices, "not to have had an epidemic. But we've got our fingers crossed."

Lines of men wait outside of every conceivable office. If you get to see the mayor in the City Hall, you find him, a certain desperation under his bland exterior, desperately calling up Washington to try to pry loose some sewer pipe. The housing project has attended to the plumbing within its domain. The army has attended to these matters within its camps, but nobody has thought of how the new projects are to be linked up with the watermains and sewers of the city.

If you go to see the personnel director of one of the big yards—he used to be a football coach—you find him fuming because he can't get the old team spirit into his employees. "What can you do when workingmen are making such big wages they don't give a damn?"

If you ask a labor man why management and labor can't get together to take some action about absenteeism and labor turnover, he snaps back at you: "Management down here won't talk to labor. The men running these yards are twenty-five years behind the times."

"I try to tell the president of one of these concerns," says the Government Man, "that he ought to set up a modern labor relations department and he just gives me a kind of oily grin and says, 'Oh go 'long—you get it all out of a book.'"

The Government Man's office is under continual siege. Today two very pretty girls in overalls with magnificent hairdos and long sharp red polished nails have been waiting all morning to tell their story. Meanwhile, they tell it to a sympathetic telephone girl. They are welders. They want a release from this company so that they can go somewhere else where they can get more money. The mean old company won't see it their way. Can't the government do something about it? A group of farmboys is complaining that the local police won't let them run their cars without getting local plates. They can't get local plates until they get paid at the end of the week. Without their cars they can't get to work. Can't the government do something about it? In the hall some very black negroes are hunched in a group leaning against the white marble sheathing of the wall of the officebuilding. They are appealing to Caesar. At the personnel office they've been told that if they quit

A

B

The stereotyped character "Rosie the Riveter" is a product of the war production work of millions of American women. For a few years, the most physically demanding factory work became sanctioned for women. A 1943 photograph (A) shows prospective welders attending school at a Los Angeles shipyard. How do you think the image of "women's work" changed after the war? However, American servicemen still clung to the sexy image of women conjured up by pinups, such as Rita Hayworth.

216 their jobs they'll have to leave town. They want Uncle Sam to say if it's true. No, it's not true, not yet.

"It's incredible," says the Government Man when his office is finally clear. "Labor turnover in this town has reached twenty-five percent a quarter. That means every man Jack of 'em changed his job in a year. It's rugged individualism, all right. What they do is come into town and get some training, then when they've qualified for the lowest rate of skilled work they go and get 'em a job somewhere else. They can say they've had experience and can get in at a higher rate. After they've worked there a while, they move to some other outfit and get taken on in a higher category still, and they don't know a damn thing about the work because they spend all their time on the bus travelling around. It's the same thing with the foremen and executives. Before any one of them has a chance to learn his work he's snatched off somewhere else. I can't keep anybody in my office. Don't know anything about organizing industry, but they all get big jobs in management. It's upgrading for fair. It's very nice, but nobody stays any place long enough to learn his job. It's a nightmare."

And still . . . the office is in a tall building. We both happen to look out the window at the same time. Across a welter of sunblackened roofs we can see in the slanting afternoon sunlight the rows of great cranes and the staging and the cradled hulls and beyond, in the brown strip of river, packed rows of new tankers, some splotched with yellow and red, some shining with the light gray of their last coat of paint. In spite of turmoil and confusion, ships are getting built, ships, ships, ships.

Of Thee I Sing

The American Dream in Wartime

MARTHA WEINMAN LEAR

There have been few times in American history when the American people have been as united as they were during World War II. The American Dream was real, the enemy was always wrong, we were always right. It was easy to be patriotic, to believe in all that America stood for. Among those most loyal were individuals and families who had recently immigrated to the land of liberty to realize their hopes of freedom.

This selection describes the effect of an immigrant father's patriotism in the shaping of his daughter's sense of what was valuable in life. Notice that patriotism and the American Dream held distinct and different roles for men and women.

They still tell in our family how the 14-year-old, my father, came off the boat with a rope around his waist to hold up his pants. When he bent to kiss the ground, the rope loosened and his pants fell down. "America!" he cried.

My God, how he believed. He carried his faith into the country like baggage and hung onto it, with that fierce urgent immigrant's grip, through the sweatshops, through the Crash, through the wars, the political scandals, the Coughlins, the Ku Klux Klanners, the lynchings, whatever. They were all temporary aberrations from the eternal goodness of America, which was second only to the goodness of God.

American cops were honest (though intimidating; he never overcame that Old-Country tremor; once, when he was stopped for speeding, he went white and I thought he would faint), American politicians were omniscient and incorruptible, American millionaires were benevolent, The American Dream was real and it was upon him. It was not jingoism, never anything like that, and it was surely no belief in capitalism, of which he knew nothing. It was simply a celebration of that *safety* that shone like sun upon his home, his children, his religion, his pennies in the bank.

Once he took us from Boston to see the Statue of Liberty. It was important, he said, for the children to understand what America meant. We stood at the top of that colossus in the bay and he gestured outward with the pride of a host.

"This is the melting pot of the world," he said.

"What does it melt?" I asked.

The Boy Scouts have been an important organization for the teaching of male sex roles, patriotism and loyalty, service to the community, and other values cherished by the middle class throughout the twentieth century. Are they as important today in the community where you grew up as they once were? If not, why not? What other organizations are important in the process of socialization?

"People," he said.

He could never understand other immigrants' complaints about the hardness of life. "You should thank God to work here," he said. "There could never be a Hitler here."

And to his children, whenever we whined about anything we couldn't have, or refused to finish the food set before us: "Shame. Think of the poor children in Europe." We were fattened on visions of the poor children in Europe.

World War II was a holy war. F.D.R. was a saint. (When he invited us in for a fireside chat, no one was allowed to speak. When he died, we cried. I don't know why, except that our elders cried. What better reason?) Truman was a *very* good person. Ike was Homeric, beyond politics. The Checkers speech was suspect, and it was true that the man was not likable, but out of this possible breach of faith my father salvaged a peculiarly American ethic. "A man deserves another chance," he said. "You can see he's sorry." Joe McCarthy was bad, but American goodness triumphed. "Have you no sense of decency, sir?" Joseph Welch intoned, and my father applauded wildly and thumped the table. "Decency!" he said. He was so proud that Joseph Welch came from Boston.

Our earliest perceptions of what it meant to be American were filtered through his own. We moved with him in a magnetic field of verities: God blesses America. A chicken in every pot. The land of plenty. The land of opportunity. Streets paved with gold (he lived poor and died poor but assumed, cheerfully, that he simply had not found the right streets. "Money doesn't buy happiness," he said). The cradle of liberty. Our boys in blue. Our cause is just. The land of the free and the home of the brave. Brothers under the skin. All men are created equal. Anyone can grow up to be President.

My father voted Democratic by rote, and by some cultural imperative that he only dimly understood; I never knew a Republican until I got to college. But he loved the *sound* of "two-party system," it tinkled like a soft clear bell in his ear, and in fervent lectures to his friends around our kitchen table, over the coffee, after the pinochle, he defended the right of Republicans to exist.

"Freedom means that you can pick from different things," he said. "I do not agree with what you say, but I will defend with my life . . . How does the rest of it go? You know, that saying by George Washington."

"Nathan Hale, Daddy," I said (and so believed for many years).

He beamed triumphantly around the table. "There! You see what it means to get an American education? Where else could she get an education like that."

Thus his faith informed us, and we never had reason to doubt. It was everywhere corroborated. Each morning in school we prayed as mechanically as we brushed our teeth, invoking God's blessing upon this land. We stood, facing the flag, put our hands to our hearts and chirped: " . . . one nation, indivisible, with liberty and justice for all."

One girl brought a note from home requesting that she be excused from reciting the Pledge of Allegiance. This was wartime. She was suspended for a week, and when she returned—on condition that she recite the Pledge—we ostracized her. "Traitor!" we shrieked in the school cafeteria. I cannot imagine what we thought it meant. A teacher reprimanded us. "It's not her fault that her parents are traitors," she said.

At assemblies we sang "America the Beautiful," rendering it, as we had been taught, up-tempo and with a great operatic rolling of the R's: " . . . And cr-r-rown thy good with br-r-rother-r-rhood/Fr-r-rom sea to shining sea!" And then, after school, we would go out into the streets of Roxbury, where the black kids were forever beating up on the Jewish kids and the Irish kids on the black kids and the police on them all. We heard no dissonance. We sensed no irony.

We went to the movies and watched our brave boys yield nothing to the Nazi torturers beyond name, rank and serial number. We hissed the Jap savages impaling infants on their bayonets. In downtown Boston we watched the grown women, the 17-year-olds, strolling on the arms of acned boys in uniform, and ached to be old enough to stroll with them. To comfort them.

We made brownies and sent them to our friends' older brothers. I won a good-citizenship contest and got to sit in the window of Filene's specialty shop, selling war bonds, wearing an Uncle Sam hat and a red, white and blue ribbon across my chest which said: "Miss Roxbury for Victory."

The son of my parents' friends was killed in action. We sat and mourned with them, and with the pregnant young widow, and someone pointed to her belly and said: "He died so his child and his grandchildren would live in peace." It was comforting. It was beyond doubt.

220   Our school was an architectural entity split down the middle by slapped-up walls and double-locked doors, with honor students standing guard: girls' side, boys' side. On our side, we learned.

"Cleanliness is next to godliness," the home-economics teacher told us. And on the blackboard she wrote:

"The way to a man's heart is through his stomach."

We sewed pink-and-white gingham aprons. We balanced imaginary food budgets. We made chicken pot pie. We learned how to set tables and how to lift coffee stains from tablecloths.

Our American-history teacher, who had absorbed her history from others as we absorbed it from her, without question, retired to get married (imagine, we said to each other, getting married *so old*; she was 27). We gave her a farewell party. The principal, who always wore a tiny American flag in his lapel, came and told us: "Most of you girls will grow up to be wives and mothers. For a woman, there is no higher calling. . . ."

Americans have always had faith that their schools would turn out good citizens as well as teach the three Rs and open the doors to opportunity. An equal education for all was part of the American Dream. Can you tell something about the social, economic, and ethnic background of these children? Do you suppose these youngsters were always this alert and happy? What do today's different-looking classrooms reflect in contrast to what you see in this photo? Have the schools failed over the last generation?

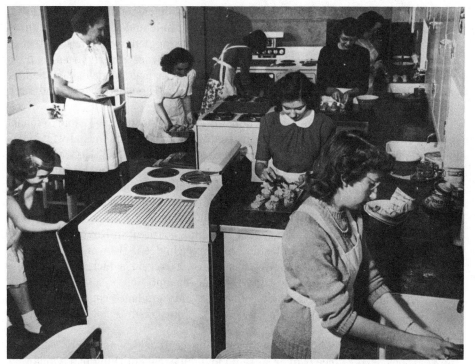

What can you tell about sex roles and the future expectations of the students in these home economics and shop classes? How have your schools reinforced traditional values? Why do you think it has been so threatening for a boy to take home economics or a girl shop? How is the situation different today?

The slyness with which we prepared for that calling astounds me still. It was, after all, a war game. Battle plans, camouflages, hide-and-seek. We thought it was marvelous. We pouted, Hollywood-style. We giggled, even the smartest of us, like twits. We wriggled when we walked and wore contrivances to push whatever was there up to make a cleavage and out to make pencil-sharp points, and made our lips glisten dark and lush, like Rita Hayworth's lips, and said: "No . . . *Don't!*"

The first of the engagements was announced after the war. She came to school bearing on her ring finger a glinting chip that was almost lost in the baby fat of her knuckle, and we all stared as though it were the Hope diamond. He was the boy next door. They had a blueprint for life: she would drop out after this junior year and work until she had saved enough for a trousseau. He would finish high school. Then they would marry—she had planned, already, every detail of her wedding gown; she described the bits of lace and the placement of seed pearls and we all closed our eyes envisioning—and settle into an apartment in Roxbury and save for a home in Brookline. They would have four children. He would go into the insurance business, and his goal was to earn $10,000 a year, which would buy one hell of a house. We all blinked at the force of his ambition.

My own ambition was to study journalism. My guidance counselor advised against it. "Be an English teacher," he said. "Journalism is not for women. It makes them tough."

We were graduated in a fine postwar euphoria. It said beneath my picture in the yearbook: "Her voice is ever soft and low, an excellent thing in a woman." I was pleased.

I gave the Class Speech and spoke, soft and low, of the sacrifices that had been made for democracy and of our mission, now, to go forth into the world and assure that they would not have been made in vain: to be good Americans, to marry good Americans, to raise good Americans. My parents cried a little. The graduation ceremony ended with "God Bless America," and it echoed so that, as we filed out into the sun, we could hear nothing but America singing.

The cataclysmic assaults upon faith and myth, innocence, invincibility all came after my father's death. I cannot imagine what he would think today, but I suspect that he would still hear America singing. It was a sound so sweet that he could never have borne to relinquish it.

A Choice of Weapons

GORDON PARKS

The United States Armed Forces were segregated during World War II. At that time black soldiers had to face subtle and direct prejudice everywhere they went. There were many racial incidents and one major race riot in Detroit in these years. The following is an account of some of the problems faced by one black man, Gordon Parks. He writes of his bitter experiences as a press corps member assigned to an all-black air force unit during the war. What did black men and women learn from the war? How did their experiences contribute to the civil rights movement of the 1950s and 1960s? Would you have had as much patience as Gordon Parks demonstrated?

The hot air smelled of gasoline and planes when I arrived at Selfridge Field the next morning. Though it was early the sprawling air base was alive with men and all kinds of machines, from jeeps to P-40 fighter ships. A sergeant met me at the gate in a command car; and, as we halted at company headquarters, a squadron of fighter ships thundered up into the hot sky. I stood marveling at the climbing ships, finding pleasure in the fact that black boys were inside them. And, thinking back to Richard Wright's *Native Son*, I recalled the Negro boy's remark when he witnessed a similar sight: "Look at those white boys fly," he had said in a special sort of awe. Now I was thinking the same thing about these black boys as they flashed above the earth like giant birds.

■ ■ ■

We spent our weekends in Detroit. And Paradise Valley, a Negro section of the city, opened its arms wide to the nattily uniformed pilots and officers. They were already heroes to these people who had never seen black boys with wings on their chests before. There was no shortage of women; they came from miles around—"in furs, Fords and Cadillacs," Tony used to crow in delight. The problem was to pick wisely from the multitude. Tony was cocky, proud and brazen with good humor; and he was like a one-eyed dog in a sausage factory after two weeks at the base. A very unpretty woman approached him one night at a bar, but Tony, his sights fixed on something more choice, ignored her. Hours later, when we were leaving the bar loaded and broke, the woman passed us and got into a beautiful new Cadillac.

Tony stopped in his tracks. Then, walking up to the woman, he tipped his hat. "Baby," he said, "you look like King Kong, but this car and those furs you've got on are a natural gas. Move over, honey. Let Tony baby drive this thing back to camp." She smiled, moved over and we journeyed out to Selfridge in style.

As the training went into fall, the men's attitude began to change. The fun was about over now. And the talk of women and the joking gave way to more serious things. Racial tensions began to have an effect on their actions and thinking. There were several incidents of white enlisted men on the base not saluting Negro officers. And black soldiers in combat were writing back about being segregated in barracks and mess halls in the war zones. The Negro newspapers were filled with stories about the black men being turned from the factory gates when war plants cried desperately for more help. The Pittsburgh *Courier* carried a long piece about Negro soldiers being assigned to menial labor. And there was a front-page article about an army band playing "God Bless America" when the white soldiers boarded the troopships; then, when Negroes went up the gangplank, the band switched to "The Darktown Strutters' Ball."

And one Sunday night a race riot erupted in Detroit. Fighting spread all over the city; twenty-five Negroes and nine whites were killed and hundreds of both races were injured. The black man was beginning to meet humiliation with violence. White supremacy had become as much an enemy as "blood" and "race" doctrines of the Nazis. Vindictiveness was slowly spreading through the air base. One could feel it in the air, in the mess halls, the barracks and the ready huts.

Once, after I returned from a trip to Washington, I found a note Tony had left for me. It read:

Dear Gordon,
Sorry to miss you but I'm on my way to Steubenville with Judy Edwards' body. As you probably heard, poor Judy spun in and I had to take his body all the way to Detroit because "there are no facilities" for handling Negro dead up there at Oscoda. It's about three hundred miles from Oscoda to Detroit, and in a goddamn Army ambulance you can imagine how long it took us to get there. Even as I write this to you, my feelings keep swinging from a murderous rage to frustration. How could anybody do anything like this?

His body was lying wrapped in a tarpaulin in the back of the ambulance; and I had trouble accepting the fact that he was dead, for every time I looked back there, the body seemed to move. I now wonder if the doctors at the hospital had examined him, since this would have required them to touch him too. By the time night had fallen I felt so badly that all I could say was "Judy, I'm sorry. . . .I'm sorry. . . ." We have all suffered some brutal indignities from the whites in this country but this was the final indignity of all. All during the trip I was in an emotional state, alternately talking to the driver and quietly crying for Judy, for his family, for the country and for myself. I felt shame and revulsion for having to wear the uniform I had on. The driver seemed to be caught up in the same mood. We were two of the loneliest soldiers in the world.

I won't tell his folks about this trip because it will just hurt them more. At least to them he was a hero and I'll make sure that when I arrive in Steubenville everyone knows it. The whole dirty business will come into even sharper focus when they lower him into the grave. He'll get an honor guard (a white one), the rifle fire and all the trappings. See you when I get back.

Tony

I stuffed the letter into my pocket and walked over to the airstrip. The night was clear and cold and the stars seemed lower than usual. The fighter ships lined up on the quiet field were ghostly. I walked along beside them, noted the names

stenciled in white block letters on the cockpits: Gleed, Pruitt, Tresville, Knox,
Bright, Walker and many others. How many of these names will be on little white
crosses this time next year? I wondered. At least the 332nd would go into battle
with pilots who had faced the enemy before. This would be more of a chance than
the 99th Squadron was allowed; for, unlike the white pilots, they had gone into
their first battle without one seasoned pilot to lead them. The costly pattern of
segregation had arranged a lonely death for some of these men—even over enemy
territory. Hitler's Luftwaffe must have laughed when they screamed into the
formations of the *schwarz* boys—knowing there wasn't an experienced fighter
amongst them.

■ ■ ■

A little after mid-December an order came from the Pentagon halting all
furloughs. We knew what this meant. Any day now we would be going overseas.
A new tempo hit the base; the men rushed about, restless, patting one another's
backs, awaiting moving orders. They came one morning about a week before
Christmas. That afternoon Colonel Davis called me to headquarters. "We're
about to pull out," he said, "and your traveling papers are not in order."

"What's wrong with them?" I asked.

"You'll have to take that up with Washington. I'd advise you to fly there. We'll
probably be leaving before they can get word back here to you."

I packed the battle gear that had been issued to me that morning, took a bus to
Detroit, then a plane to Washington; I arrived there late that evening. Stryker
had left the OWI [Office of War Information] by now and had gone to work in New
York for the Standard Oil Co. In fact, just about everyone I knew there had gone;
the rest were preparing to leave. Besides, it was a weekend and no officials were
around. I didn't know where to turn. The one man I did reach had developed a
strange case of laryngitis, and was unable to talk, he said. Finally in desperation I
tried to reach Elmer Davis, head of the OWI, but he was away on a trip. I fretted
through Saturday and Sunday. Then the first thing Monday morning I went to see
Ted Poston, a friend of mine in the OWI press section. He had heard the rumors.
And Ted put things in their true perspective: "There's some Southern gentlemen
and conservative Republicans on Capitol Hill who don't like the idea of giving this
kind of publicity to Negro soldiers."

I was shocked—and so was Ted—but there wasn't much we could do about it.
The next day I reached Elmer Davis by telephone and told him my story. He
listened attentively. When I finished he said, "Don't worry, Gordon, I'll be in
touch with the Pentagon this afternoon. You report there tomorrow. I'm sure
everything will be all right."

That night, on the Howard University campus, I met Captain Lee Rayford
and Lieutenant Walter Lawson, two pilots from the 99th Fighter Squadron. They
had returned to the States after completing their required number of missions.
Captain Rayford was the holder of the Purple Heart, the Distinguished Flying
Cross, the Croix de Guerre, the Air Medal, and the Yugoslav Red Star. He had
been shot up over Austria by a Messerschmitt 109. Both of them could have
remained Stateside as instructors. Instead they had volunteered to go back to the
war zone. We ate dinner together, and since they had to go to the Pentagon the
next day we agreed to meet and go together.

We had no sooner boarded the bus and seated ourselves behind the driver than his voice came at us, metallic and demanding. "If you fellas wanta ride into Virginyuh, you gotta go to the rear." We looked at one another questioningly, deciding in our silence not to move. The driver stood up and faced us, a scrawny disheveled man with tobacco-stained teeth and a hawk nose. The armpits of his uniform were discolored from sweat. "You all heard what I said. This bus ain't goin' nowhere till you all go to the back where you belong."

"We intend going to Virginia in the seats we're in," Lee said with finality.

"Okay, if you ain't back there in one minute I'm callin' the MP's and havin' you put off."

"You'd better start calling right now," Lee replied.

Two white Air Force captains and a major were seated across the aisle from us and I noticed that they stirred uncomfortably. Several other whites were scattered in the near-empty bus and an elderly Negro woman sat at the rear. I watched her through the rear-view mirror. She had half risen from her seat; there was courage, dignity and anger in every line of her small body. Her look demanded that we stay there, and I was determined not to disappoint her. The bus had become dead quiet while the driver stood glowering at us.

"Fellows." One of the young white captains was speaking now. "We know how you feel about this," he said, his voice cloaked in false camaraderie, "but the major has an appointment at the Pentagon in a half hour. He wonders if you would mind moving back so that we can be on our way?"

My two friends were outranked. But there were no bars on my shoulders. The American eagle on my officer's cap was as large and significant as his or the major's. I took a good look at the old woman in the rear. She was standing now, gripping the seat ahead of her. Then, borrowing the captain's icy politeness, I stood and addressed the major. "Sir," I said, "as you can see, these men are fighter pilots. They have completed their missions but they have volunteered for more duty at the front. Would you like to order your fellow officers to the rear? They have no intention of moving otherwise." My anger was rising, so I sat back down.

The bus driver stood watching us until the major finally spoke to him. "Drive on," he said. "Can't you tell when you're licked?" The driver cursed under his breath, threw himself into the seat and slammed in the gears and we lurched off toward Virginia. "Hallelujah!" the Negro woman shouted from the rear. "Hallelujah!" Her voice rang with pathos and triumph. "Thank God we don't have to sit in the back of our P-38's," Lawson sighed as we got off the bus.

■ ■ ■

Our plane took off in a blinding rainstorm—and it landed in another one at Norfolk, Virginia. A taxi took me to the ferry landing where I would cross over into Newport News. I sat there in the waiting room for an hour on top of my battle gear among a boisterous group of white enlisted men. Four Negro soldiers were huddled in a nearby corner. Two of them were propped against each other sleeping. Most of the white boys seemed to be making a festivity of these last hours. But there was a sort of emptiness attached to their laughing and drinking. Obviously they were headed for some departure point. It's all to hide the fear, I thought. Their faces were so young.

We filed out when the ferry whistled. It was still raining and we stood near the edge of the dock watching the boat fasten into the slip. Through the wetness I noticed a sign reading COLORED PASSENGERS and another one reading WHITES ONLY. The four black soldiers moved automatically to the colored side, and so did I. How ironic, I thought; such nonsense would not stop until we were in enemy territory.

After all the outgoing passengers were off and the trucks and cars had rumbled past, we started forward. Then I saw a Negro girl step from the ferry. She had been standing in the section marked for cars; now she was in the direct line of the white enlisted men, who stampeded to the boat screaming at the tops of their voices. I saw the girl fall beneath them into the mud and water. The four Negro soldiers also saw her go down. The five of us rushed to her rescue. She was knocked down several times before we could get to her and pull her out of the scrambling mob.

"You lousy white bastards!" one of the Negro soldiers yelled. "If I only had a gun!" Tears were in his eyes, hysteria in his voice. A long knife was glistening in his hands.

"Soldier!" I shouted above the noise, letting him get a look at my officer's cap. "Put that knife away!"

He glared at me fiercely for a second. "But you saw what they did!"

"Yes, I saw, but we're outnumbered ten to one! You can't fight all of them. Get on the boat!" He looked at me sullenly for another moment, then moved off. We cleaned the mud from the girl's coat and she walked away without a word. Only proud anger glistened on her black face. Then the four of us joined the soldier I had ordered away. He was standing still tense beneath the sign reading "colored passengers."

"Sorry, soldier," I said. "We wouldn't have had a chance against a mob like that. You realize that, don't you?"

"If I gotta die, I'd just as soon do it where I got real cause to." His tone was resolute. I had to answer. I was tempted to hand him the bit about the future and all that, but the future was too uncertain. The yelling was even louder now on the other side of the boat. "Sons-of-bitches," he muttered under his breath.

"Good luck," I said to them as we parted on the other shore. "So long," they said—except the one I had spoken to—then they moved off into the darkness and rain again. I turned away, feeling I had somehow let him down.

"Colored move to the rear!" The voice met me again when I got on the bus with some of the white enlisted men. Sick of trouble, I made my way to the back and sat down; I was the only Negro aboard. Some of the whites were standing, but I had four empty seats around me. "Gordy! My God, it's Gordy!" a voice rang out above the noise. And suddenly a soldier was rushing back toward me. "Bud!" I shouted, getting to my feet only to be knocked back to my seat by his bear hug. It was Bud Hallender, a husky man I had played basketball with back in St. Paul. Now he was down beside me, slapping my back and wringing my hands.

"You all cain't ride back there with that nigra! Move back up front where you belong!" Bud ignored the command; now he was telling the others I was the co-captain of his basketball team, his friend.

"You all hear me? You cain't ride back there with that nigra!"

"Go screw yourself!" Bud shouted back. "Drive on or we'll throw you off this goddamned crate and drive it ourselves!" Laughter rocked the bus. The driver

228 plopped down into his seat without another word and drove off toward the heart of town. And Bud and I talked excitedly of a time and place where things had been different. Finally, at the terminal we wished each other a jovial goodbye.

■ ■ ■

Tony and I went out for some fresh air the next night. "It's hard to believe but we've had trouble right here on this base," he said as we walked along, "so we'd better stay in this area."

"What kind of trouble?"

"The same old jazz. One of our ground crewmen was beaten up by some white paratroopers night before last. Then they've tried to segregate us at the base's movie house. Everyone's in a hell of a mood." We became suddenly quiet as we circled the area.

A shot sounded nearby and the two of us stopped in our tracks. Then there was another shot. Someone seemed to be returning the fire. "We'd better get in. Sounds like trouble," Tony said. Our barracks had already gone dark when we entered it. Several men were at the windows with guns looking out cautiously into the night. When all was quiet again, the lights went back on and the gambling and the letter writing and the drinking started again. New orders came the following morning. We would take to the boat two days earlier than had been proposed. I was happy about this. There seemed to be less danger at sea than on this troubled base.

Colonel Davis sent for me just before noon. I hurried anxiously to his office. No more trouble, I hoped; it was too close to sailing time. But when he looked up at me his face was calm. It was, after all, some routine matter he would speak about, I thought.

"I'm sorry. Your papers are not in order. A final call from the Pentagon has come through. You will not be able to embark with us."

"This is ridiculous," I said. "Can't you do something? Someone in Washington is trying to prevent coverage of your group overseas, Colonel. This is the first Negro fighter group. It's history. It has to be covered. Can't you protest in some way, Colonel?"

"There's nothing, absolutely nothing I can do. The orders are from the Pentagon. They cannot be rescinded. I'm terribly sorry."

I had lost. And suddenly anesthetized to the colonel and all that was around him, I turned and started out. "You are aware that you are sworn to the strictest of secrecy about what you have seen or learned here," he was saying as he followed me to the door. "You realize the dangers of any slip."

"Yes, I understand, Colonel."

"It is even possible to detain you until we are overseas under such conditions. But I am sure you won't discuss our movements with anyone."

"I won't. Don't worry. I want to forget the whole thing as quickly as possible." I rushed back toward the barracks, angry and disgusted. I couldn't bring myself to say goodbye to the pilots again. I packed quickly and waited for the command car the colonel had ordered for me.

The pilots were readying themselves for the boat when the car arrived; and I slipped through the rear door without even a backward glance. At five o'clock the next morning, after wiring Sally, I boarded a plane for Washington. I would

This all-black infantry battalion represents only a small fraction of the half-million blacks who saw overseas service in World War II. How did wartime experiences at home and abroad help fuel the civil rights struggles of the 1960s?

change planes there and go on to New York, where I would wait for my wife and children. The thought of even stopping in this city irked me. I wouldn't live there again if they gave me the White House rent free, I thought as the plane roared down the runway.

We began circling over Washington at dawn; and far below I could see the landing field, lying like small strips of cardboard under a wispy path of cloud. Further out in the distance the monuments of the city shone milk-white in the winter sunlight and the water in the mall sparkled like an oblong jewel between the sculptured trees; there was the Capitol standing quiet and strong on one end and the Lincoln Memorial set on the high quarter of the opposite slope. What a beautiful sight to be wed to such human ugliness, I thought. And as we dropped lower I could see the tops of the stores, theaters, and restaurants whose doors were still closed to me.

I thought back to the fighter pilots. They would soon be far out to sea, sailing toward war and death, ignoring at least temporarily, their differences with the land they were leaving to defend. This was the price for a questionable equality.

Life in the Camps

The locking up of Japanese-Americans in concentration camps during World War II was in many ways a logical extension of the anti-Oriental racism that had existed on the West Coast since the arrival of the first Chinese immigrants in the 1840s. Japanese laborers began to arrive in California in the decade following the Exclusion Act of 1882, which barred further Chinese immigration. Despite their record of good citizenship and hard work in menial tasks, the first generation of Japanese-Americans endured similar discrimination: the "Gentlemen's Agreement" of 1907 ended Japanese immigration. Many of the Nisei, the second generation of Japanese-Americans, born and brought up in the United States in the period between the two world wars, became substantial businesspeople and property owners. Nevertheless, in the wake of Japan's attack on Pearl Harbor in December 1941, an outpouring of bigotry and fear persuaded officials in California and Washington to "relocate" the Nisei. Ultimately ten "relocation camps" were established in remote areas, from California to Arkansas. Losing their homes and businesses, the Nisei and their children, charged with no crimes and denied legal recourse, became prisoners of war in their own country. The following letters reflect life in the camps.

• • • Left Fresno at 8:55 this morning and reached the Assembly Center at about 9:10 A.M. We first stopped at the registrar's office to be checked and registered. Our bags and pockets were searched, to my surprise. For what? I don't know. Luckily we all passed. I mean nothing was taken from us. Then our baggage was inspected from corner to corner. What a feeling I had when they went through our personal belongings. . . .

When I first entered our room, I became sick to my stomach. There were seven beds in the room and no furniture nor any partitions to separate the males and the females of the family. I just sat on the bed, staring at the bare wall. For a while I couldn't speak nor smile. Well, after getting over with my shock, I started to get the baggage in. . . .

Then we wanted to know where our rest rooms were. This was too much for me. There is no privacy. I just can't explain how it is, but it's worse than a country privy. After it's been used a couple of times, there is a whole stack of flies. Once you open the door the flies can be seen buzzing around; it is like a nest of bees. We just couldn't go in there, so we excavated. The hospital being facilitated with flush

230

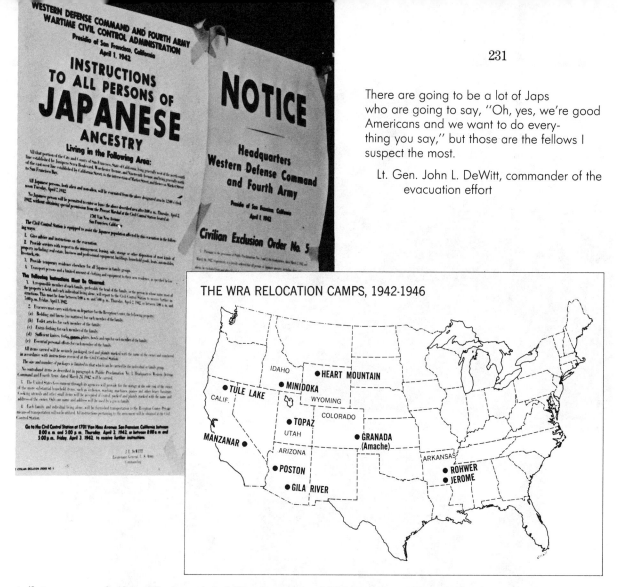

There are going to be a lot of Japs who are going to say, "Oh, yes, we're good Americans and we want to do everything you say," but those are the fellows I suspect the most.

Lt. Gen. John L. DeWitt, commander of the evacuation effort

THE WRA RELOCATION CAMPS, 1942-1946

toilets, we sneaked in. Then we tried the showers, which are not so bad except that there is no privacy. Well that's that for the day's happening.

As to what I think of camp life; I think it's hell. That's the only word I could think of to describe it.

■ ■ ■

Every Nisei . . . was extremely annoyed when he was reminded by some visiting Caucasian that he had been placed in the assembly center "for his own protection." Also, without exception, everyone was highly indignant at the practice of focusing floodlights from twelve watchtowers on camp every night from twilight to dawn. When informed by the administration that the search lights had been installed to protect us from outsiders who might leap over the fence to injure us, his usual retort was: "Why should the lights be focused on the barracks and not on the outer fence as a logical procedure?" Similarly, there was keen resent-

232

What we hate to recall is not so much the hardships that the war and evacuation brought to us but the vast sense of alienation we suffered when we were like the man without a country.

Kats Kunitsugu, "Evacuation—the Pain Remains," *Pacific Citizen*, Dec. 20—27, 1968.

ment against the barbed-wire fence surrounding camp and many a time I watched a novice throwing rocks at it to discover if the wires were actually charged.

No systematic study was made of the attitudes of little children but the narrating of a few stray incidents might be of some aid in identifying them. One afternoon in late June, I heard a great commotion behind my barrack and on investigation perceived a group of twelve boys about six to ten years of age shouldering wooden guns and attacking a "Japanese fort" while lustily singing "Anchors Aweigh." . . . Similarly, in the blackout of May 24, little children raced down our street yelling at the top of their lungs: "Turn off your lights! The Japs are coming!"

A Nisei mother once told me with tears in her eyes of her six-year-old son who insisted on her "taking him back to America." The little boy had been taken to Japan about two years ago but was so unhappy there that she was compelled to return to California with him. Soon afterwards they were evacuated to Santa Anita, and the little boy in the absence of his Caucasian playmates was convinced that he was still in Japan and kept on entreating his mother to "take him back to America." To reassure him that he was in America she took him to the information center in her district and pointed to the American flag but he could not be consoled because Charlie and Jimmie, his Caucasian playmates, were not there with him in camp.

It is also interesting to note that whenever little children sang songs these were not Japanese folksongs but typically American songs like "God Bless America," "My Country 'Tis of Thee," "My Old Kentucky Home," "Row, Row, Row Your Boat," "Jesus Loves Me," and other songs known to every American child. The "Americanness" of the Sansei may serve to identify the character of their Nisei parents.

When 1,500 work orders were sent out by the Personnel Office to U.S. citizens above the age of sixteen a day before the camouflage project was opened, approximately 800 were reported to have refused to work. Some excused themselves by claiming that they were allergic to the dye on burlap strips or to the lint which fell off from them, but at least half of that number was said to have refused on principle. They felt that they were really "prisoners of war" and that the U.S. government had no right to appeal to them to aid in the war effort on a patriotic note. The battle cry during the camouflage strike of June 16−17 seemed to be: Give us the treatment accorded other American citizens and we will gladly cooperate in completing the number of nets requested by the U.S. Army. . . .

Childhood Innocence

in Time of War

N. SCOTT MOMADAY

Momaday, a Kiowa Indian, spent the war years in the Southwest. Born in 1934, he was only eleven years old when the war was over, but he recalls the patriotism and the movies and the play battles, even though his friends sometimes mistook him for a Japanese. The war was distant and romantic for him. It was only later that he realized its significance and its tragedy.

The second world war had nothing to do with my parents and me at first, certainly nothing of which I could be aware. But I see now that the war eventually determined our circumstances in numerous ways, and it became for me a kind of constant abstraction on the far edge of my mind. There came a time, indeed, when I could not have conceived of a world which was not somehow articulated in terms of "the war." For one thing there were markets, more or less directly related to "the war effort," of which we heard incessantly; jobs were everywhere, it seemed, and for my parents, who had begun their married life in hard times, there were opportunities. For another thing there was a kind of patriotic sympathy to those days, the romantic integrity of a cause, which was perceptible to me even then; I was becoming conscious of such things. And this, too, was a real spur to my imagination.

We moved to the Staked Plains (which country my Kiowa forebears knew well), where my father worked for an oil company as a draftsman. My mother found a job with the Civilian Personnel Office, then with the Office of the Provost Marshal, at the Hobbs Army Air Base.

Hobbs, New Mexico, was then a raw, undistinguished town on the flat, hot apron of the Staked Plains. It had not the color or the character of Gallup, although it had something of the same vigor and strength. New Mexican towns of the north are different one from another, or they are set in different landscapes; but in the south they seem all of a kind. Hobbs and Artesia and Carlsbad are thus related in their appearance and in their spirit, I believe, which is the hard spirit of the high,

236

World War II stirred the patriotic fervor of many Americans—a sentiment that endured long after the war ended. What has happened to cause some contemporary Americans to distrust this sentiment?

arboreal desert. And in this respect they are like the towns of west Texas: Lamesa, Midland, Plainview. There were many dusty dirt streets in Hobbs in my day, a good many wary old plainsmen and their sunbonneted wives, a "Niggertown," and a bakery that dispatched its breads in a horse-drawn wagon.

I see now that one experiences easily the ordinary things of life, the things which cast familiar shadows upon the sheer, transparent panels of time, and he perceives his experience in the only way he can, according to his age. There is a quality to the experience of any given place that is especially available to a child. I came to know Hobbs in a certain way, and in that way I knew it very well. I was in the third grade.

My best friend was Billy Don Johnson, a reddish, robust boy of great good humor and intense loyalty. He had a slight speech impediment, and he liked nothing better than to sing, for anyone who would hear him out, "Onward, Christian Soldiers," which he rendered with remarkable feeling. At such times he squeezed himself into a terrible concentration, and his round red face bore the holy, irresistible aspect of an angel, a cherub gone slightly to seed. Even in the third grade his physique was impressive, thick and solid and low-slung. We all knew that his destiny lay in the middle of the line and a split second after the ball was snapped. I believe that he made All State in his senior year. The Hobbs Eagles are a traditional powerhouse in New Mexico high school football. We went religiously to their home games and were caught up in the frenzy of those brassy autumn nights. On the sidelines we expressed our pitiful adoration of our heroes, and we tackled each other viciously from behind.

It seems to me that half the boys of Hobbs were named Billy.

In the early forties Hobbs was fixed on the far fringe of the war, and yet there were moments of great immediacy, when it seemed to us that we were very close to the front. On Saturday afternoons at the Reel Theatre we cheered to those wonderful newsreels in which, out of nowhere, a Zero or an Me-109 suddenly swerved into our sights. It was the very maneuver, grand, irrevocable, fatal, we had been waiting for. The whole field of vision shuddered with our fire; the 50-caliber tracers curved out, fixing brilliant arcs upon the span, and struck; then there was a black burst of smoke, and the target went spinning down to death. Or, better, it simply disintegrated before our eyes, an instantaneous transformation of man and machine into thin air. Along with reading and writing we were taught to hate our enemies. Every day, after we had pledged allegiance to the flag, we sang— Billy Don louder than the rest—"Let's remember Pearl Harbor, as we do the Alamo," and I remember a picture postcard on which the cartoon faces of Hitler, Mussolini, and Tojo were represented on squares of toilet paper above the legend WIPE THEM OUT.

As a child, especially, my features belied the character of my ancient ethnic origin. (There are early photographs of me which might have been made thirty thousand years ago on the Bering Strait land bridge; just wide of the prehistoric camera's eye there stands a faithful dog of the chow strain, dragging a travois. My mother recalls that one day in Bayou le Batre, a pretty moppet was heard to say in my defense, "Well, I don't care if he *is* a Chinaman. *I* like him anyway." And as recently as my undergraduate days someone sitting next to me on the side of a swimming pool asked me from what part of Asia I had come. "Northern Mongolia," I replied.) In Hobbs, New Mexico, in 1943, I was suspected of that then dreadful association. Nearly every day on the playground someone would greet me with, "Hi'ya, Jap," and the fight was on. Now and then two or more patriots would gang up on me, and that's when Billy Don stepped in. As a team we compiled a formidable record.

I fell hopelessly in love with a girl named Kathleen. She had blond, curly hair and pale blue eyes that were wonderfully sad, and she wore ribbons and clean, crisp dresses. She kept to the company of other girls, and I followed her about at a discreet distance, wanting in some fresh stirring within me to snatch her up and carry her away to the mountains, wherever they were. What a pity, I now believe, that I did not at least tell her that she was pretty, though I suppose she knew. And when the stirring became a modest turbulence I fell in love again, with a dark, lithe girl whose name was Eugenia. She was several years my senior, and I went to school to her, as boys have gone to school to women always. She inspired dark rumors, for that was her calling, I believe. The older boys, whom my peers and I admired and emulated, spoke of her leeringly in terms that I could not yet fully understand, and so I adored her. I bought her a purse which cost three dollars, the whole of my Christmas allowance. That generosity, that extravagance which remains in some sense the ultimate in me, was lost upon her. She reacted not with gratitude—much less did she swoon—but with a kind of easy knowingness. And in that affair I learned how to be a fool, a lesson that I have learned again and again.

By the time American troops landed at Salerno, the Italians had surrendered. American soldiers, expecting nothing more than a pleasant walk up the Italian coast, met stiff German resistance instead. Does the experience of shared danger in battle tend to produce exaggerated patriotism?

Billy Don was my true friend, and I was very much at home in his house. His parents were wonderful, down-to-earth people, and they were very good to me; it was in their nature, and they should not have known how to be otherwise. Theirs was a large family, of which Billy Don was the youngest, and there was a lot of activity in their house. Mrs. Johnson was a large, jovial woman who cooked heroic meals. On the nights that I spent there we woke up, Billy Don and I, to the most wonderful smells, bacon and chops, breads and gravy, coffee and cakes. Billy Don liked to sleep late, and it was difficult to get him awake. I kneaded him, poked him in the ribs, pulled him upright, and he sat interminably on the edge of the bed, dealing with his shoes and socks. But after such a breakfast he ran on all day like a clock. We prowled the streets of Hobbs, without which there was no order in the universe, looking round all the corners for our destiny.

For a time Billy Don's father kept a little truck farm near the air base, about eight miles from the town. Sometimes we went there to chase the pigs about and to play at war out in that sweltering sand country. We dug trenches and slithered like vipers through the brittle brush, dragging our toy rifles across the minefield, hurling grenades against the glassy dunes, the thousand bunkers that lay between us and our glory, pausing only to treat our wounds and to grab at lizards and horned toads or to drink Kool-Aid from our canteens. One day, in July, when we were prisoners of war, we set out on a march from the pigpen there, which was our concentration camp, towards the town. We went on and on through infernal regions, through the morning and afternoon. We went on until our heroism evaporated and the game was given up and our mouths were full of cotton, and there was nothing to do but go on. I believe that we walked fifteen miles in the desert that day. We limped into Hobbs more dead than alive; Billy Don dropped out at his house, and I went on to mine. When I arrived I spent the very last bit of my strength getting upon my bed. And even before my mother could place the cool, damp washcloth to my forehead I fell into the deepest sleep that I have ever known.

I was not much interested in the process of learning at school. I can only barely remember the sort of work that was put to us; it was a thing that was not congenial to my mind. The evil of recitation was real; I hated to be called upon. And even worse was the anticipation of it. I knew of no relief that was equal to that of the bell. My eyes were very weak, and I had about that time to wear eyeglasses. Eyeglasses conformed in no way at all to any notion that I had of myself, and I did away with them at every opportunity. Tommy, a shrimp of a boy, the menace of whose gaze was effectively exaggerated by means of round, thick, smudgy lenses, told on me consistently. I hoped that he would die.

My mother read to me, or she told me stories in which I had the leading part. And my father told me the old Kiowa tales. These were many times more exciting than anything I found at school; they, more than the grammars and arithmetics, nourished the life of my mind.

In my day there were two classifications of boys at Hobbs, the toughs and the sissies. I was big and strong, and so I most often aligned myself with the toughs. It was convenient to do so, for I had then a stake in the dominant society, and the world of children is simply informed by the principle of domination. On the other hand, some of the boys that I liked best were sissies, and I got on with them very well in the main. The truth is, I moved more easily across the dividing line, back

240

Mothers, during the war, were made to feel honored that their sons were in the service. Some even proudly displayed gold stars for those who had been killed in action. This is a 1942 photograph of a Portuguese-American woman from New Bedford, Massachusetts, with pictures of her sons, all of whom were in the service.

and forth, than did most of my fellows, and I learned to deal in crude diplomacies, strategies of choice and adjustment.

The movies of those days were a great and dubious influence upon us; we were utterly seduced by them. On those Saturday afternoons at the Reel Theatre we were drawn into worlds of infinite possibility. Our taste ran to high adventure, and we cared much more for Sergeant York than for Mrs. Miniver, of course, but we devoured everything that came our way. It is strange how indelible are some of those impressions in my mind after many years—Lon Chaney, Jr., looking with both horror and infinite sadness at the full moon, for example. And for a boy bearing hard upon adolescence, how is it possible to forget Ingrid Bergman in *Casablanca*, say, or Hedy Lamarr in *White Cargo?* And we would not let go of the movies, but we lived in them for days afterwards. I remember that after we had seen *The Black Swan*, there were sword fights in the streets, and we battered each other mercilessly. Most of the swords were flimsy affairs, curtain weights and yardsticks; but mine was a length of doweling that I had pushed through a gelatin mold; it was a superior weapon, and with it I terrorized the neighborhood. Once, through a picket fence, I saw the Mummy moving across a moonlit yard, dragging his ancient foot. For good or bad, something of my belief was fashioned there, once and for all, among the shadows.

For a time my aunt Ethel and her son, John, lived at Hobbs and were our next-door neighbors. John was five years older than I, and I loved and admired him greatly. In the years of our association, which were largely confined to my childhood, he taught me many things by example, and he was always very tolerant of me, in spite of the difference in our ages. I must have been a bother to him on occasion, but he never let me know it. To the life between us I had little enough to contribute, but once, at Hobbs, I was given a chance to help him, and I did, and I have been grateful for that chance ever since. This is how it happened: I was coming home from school and I saw that there were eight or ten older boys on the lawn of the public library, John among them. He was standing apart from the others, and they were shouting at him. As I approached they surrounded him, and one of them hurled himself at John's back, grabbing him about the neck. John did not fall, but he threw the boy around and struck him in the face and the boy fell to the ground, his nose bleeding. I could not believe what was happening, and I was very much afraid and did not know what to do. And suddenly there was an awful quiet, a hard stillness, and I could feel the rage running there, and I wanted to run away; something was going to happen, something bad, in the next moment. Then John said softly, evenly, "Come here. Stand at my back, will you?—where I can't see." And I understood that he was talking to me, and I went to him and stood at his back, to see that no one jumped on him again. And then together we moved out of the circle and nothing happened and we got away. I never knew what the fight was about, but I never doubted that my cousin John was in the right.

I had about that time discovered the dark joy of masturbation. For a time the burden of guilt lay heavily on me, and I read in everyone's eyes that I had been found out, that I was perverted and depraved, though these large concepts were certainly crude and tentative in my mind. It was John who assuaged my guilt in this matter. He knew more than I did, but not so much more that he hadn't a genuine interest in my society, my education, and the salvation of my soul.

We gave each other model airplane kits for Christmas. My gift was so far inferior to John's that I was ashamed and cried. Not only did he give me the fine model airplane, but he assembled it for me as well.

■ ■ ■

It happened that we moved to a community called Los Llanos at the Hobbs Army Air Base and lived there for a year, but I continued in the same school, riding the bus each day. I was growing up. About that time my parents gave me a bicycle, and I rode everywhere on the base. I came to have a different sense of the war there. Hobbs was a B-17 base, and I formed a good impression of those "Flying Fortresses," which came in and went out incessantly. The war was being won from the bomb-bay doors of those planes; they were the workhorses of our air force, and they bore the brunt of the battle over Europe. They were superseded in the late stages of the war by the B-29s; it was a kind of upstaging that I have always resented a little. Some of those planes were badly damaged; they had acquired an awful character under fire, and they had flown home to die. I played in the catwalks of their carcasses—and my games were then a benediction—and extended their missions into the dreams of a child.

I try now to think of the war, of what it was to me as a child. It was almost nothing, and nothing of my innocence was lost in it. It was only later that I realized what had happened, what ancient histories had been made and remarked and set aside in a fraction of my lifetime, in an instant. And *there* is the loss of innocence, in retrospection, in the safe distance of time. There are the clocks of shame; we tell the lie of time, and our hearts are broken.

ASSIGNMENT 6

An Interview:
Your Family and
World War II

Like the depression of the 1930s, World War II was an event of such major consequence that it touched the lives of nearly everyone. Yet, as the readings attempt to illustrate, the effects of the war on people were not as uniform as might be expected. At the same time that soldiers were dying on distant Pacific islands, men unemployed through most of the thirties found steady work.

Your assignment is to interview members of your family about their experiences in the war, at home and abroad. For many people, this may well dredge up feelings of pain and terror; you must therefore be sensitive in deciding what is an appropriate line of questioning. Try to discover the ways in which the war affected your family and how existence in the early 1940s contrasted with life in the 1930s. Your investigation should come to some conclusion on the changes that the war brought in terms of economic and social conditions, place of residence, political convictions, opportunities gained, and hardships suffered. Then, after completing your interviews, write a brief preliminary report on your findings, to be incorporated later into your research paper.

BIBLIOGRAPHIC NOTE

The literature on World War II military campaigns and specific battles is enormous. You should be able to find accounts of any particular wartime military episode that is related to your family's experiences by consulting such official sources as the 75-volume *United States Army in World War II* series; the 7 volumes of *The Army Air Forces in World War II*; the 15 volumes of the *History of United States Naval Operations in World War II*; and the *History of U.S. Marine Corps Operations in World War II* in 5 volumes with supplements. A useful reference is *World War II Almanac, 1931–1945* (1981), edited by Robert Goralski. Two of the best accounts of soldiers' experiences in combat are *The Story of G.I. Joe* (1945) by Ernie Pyle, a wartime correspondent, and *The Naked and the Dead* (1948) by Norman Mailer, the well-known American novelist.

The history of the homefront is still inadequately written. But see Richard Polenberg's collection, *America at War: The Home Front, 1941–1945* (1968), and his *War and Society: The United States 1941–1945* (1972). Fun to read is Richard R. Lingeman's *Don't You Know There's a War On?* (1970). A scholarly monograph is John Morton Blum's *"V" Was for Victory: Politics and American Culture During World War II* (1976). Several excellent works have appeared on the Japanese-American internment camps, including Roger Daniels' *Concentration Camps USA* (1972).

PART SEVEN

The Sixties

America, always fascinated with the concept of youth, experienced in the 1960s a decade saturated with the hopes and fears of the young. Yet what began with a rush of fresh idealism in 1960 ended in 1970 with the death of four college students at Kent State University. The sophisticated style and promise of John Fitzgerald Kennedy, the youngest man ever elected President, gave way to the discredited presidency of Richard M. Nixon amidst a war so unpopular that it tore the nation's social fabric.

When the sixties began, the nation seemed basically self-confident, with an overwhelming belief that the essential problems of society had already been solved. Whatever the remaining obstacles were that prevented specific minority groups from achieving the American Dream would soon be removed through liberal legislation. Kennedy called on Americans to get moving; neither he nor anyone else foresaw the events that were to follow.

Before the decade ended, all values and institutions would be challenged, and frequently rejected. Violence, including assassination (or attempts at assassination), aimed at major American leaders became almost commonplace. Cities burned, children questioned their parents, students challenged professors, Presidents were forced from the White House, millions went into the streets, drugs, rock music, and strange dress styles were everywhere. When the ferment finally died, the United States had moved farther and faster than President Kennedy could possibly have imagined.

The New Frontier promised to use the federal government to solve the perennial problems of civil rights and poverty. Acting through the processes of Congress and the courts, the belief was that liberal reform would finally bring satisfaction to those few groups that had not benefited from America's material abundance. Abroad, the United States embarked on a crusade against communism and the poverty that seemed to produce communism. A Peace Corps of dedicated and highly educated Americans, mostly in their twenties and thirties, traveled the globe to bring technological skills and instruction in the American way of life to remote villages and squalid ghettos. At the same time, American military muscle challenged the communists everywhere. As Kennedy promised in his inaugural address, ". . . we shall pay any price, bear any burden, meet any hardship, support any friend, oppose any foe to assure the survival and the success of liberty."

A dissident left wing emerged slowly and shakily in response to the perceived inadequacies of liberal reform and the cold war crusade. Most of Kennedy's New Frontier promises were still being debated in Congress when he was assassinated on November 22, 1963. President Lyndon B. Johnson promised "guns and butter," a "war" on poverty at home, and a war on communism in Southeast Asia.

While American poverty proved more intractable than Washington politicians would admit, the increasing scope of American involvement in Vietnam soon commanded the attention of the politically involved young. Chapters of Students for a Democratic Society spread from campus to campus. From their first convention, in 1962, "an agenda for a generation" was set forth. Principally written by Tom Hayden, this so-called Port Huron Statement outlined major discontents, particularly the narrowness of bureaucracy and careerism, reflexive anticommunism, and alienation of individuals from supportive communities. Other college students channeled their energies into the civil rights movement. Later preoccupations included energy and ecological issues. A young consumer-rights advocate named Ralph Nader attracted widespread support. By the middle of the decade, the sources and objectives of dissent had exploded in different directions, destroying the political consensus.

While Martin Luther King remained the titular leader of the black struggle, more militant voices demanded immediate and fundamental change. The Black Power campaign that emerged early in 1966, out of the Student Non-Violent Coordinating Committee (SNCC), created racial separation in this once-integrated protest movement. Black discontent flared in several inner cities, where violence and rioting led to the burning down of whole sections of black ghettos.

The rapid development of protest against the Vietnam war seemed to provide a unifying umbrella for dissent, but, in fact, it did not. The antiwar movement quickly became nonideological, with no broader social purpose beyond the end of the conflict. Such an emotional mass movement included a place for Americans of all political and social views, age groups, classes, and vocations. By the late sixties, articulate supporters of the war were hard to find. The popular antiwar cause, which brought hundreds of thousands into the streets, once seemed the prelude to revolution. However, as the war dragged on until 1975, the one-cause movement had already disappeared. Its principal effect had been to absorb the energy of the dissident spirit of the sixties. It left behind some scattered sectarian pockets and a counterculture that often confused revolution with narcissism.

Images of the sixties' counterculture often suggest cultural revolution. While some changes in manners and mores did emerge, there were few significant political or economic results. Indeed, major corporations found an expanded youth market for "counterculture" products in a new conservative political climate.

To many of the young, however, America seemed to be made up of older people who had followed the rules and ended up miserable. Stifling suburbs filled up with products that brought no pleasure to sexually repressed pill-poppers and alcoholics. The middle-aged middle class, in this popular stereotype, usually discovered too late that this was all the payoff they would receive.

The mass challenge to basic American values became epidemic as political consensus splintered. At times, violence replaced rationality. Counterculture weapons included rock music, drugs, casual sex, free-form dress, and the rejection of traditional work. Underground newspapers circulated on campuses, in radical communities in the major cities, and in isolated rural communes. News reports, commentary and analysis, music reviews, and survival advice were phrased in an idiom that few middle-aged Americans could (or cared to) penetrate. The young understood their special language in print, and in music that was loud and primitive and seemed to fill the air everywhere.

One political outgrowth of the sixties that has survived is the woman's movement, which seems to have secured a permanent place in American social and political life. Measured against the prejudices and obstacles that confronted women just two decades ago, the movement has obviously had an impact in changing attitudes and institutional practices.

In the same sense, the perspective of two decades permits us to look at the sixties with some objectivity. While neither the inflated hopes nor the exaggerated fears of those years materialized, the social, political, and economic lives of most people were affected. A sixties cliché, "raised consciousness," seems appropriate in any attempt to assess the period's significance. Most people who lived through the sixties will never again be able to think as they had before about race, politics, foreign affairs, gender, religion, equal opportunity—or music, for that matter.

Inaugural Address, Jan. 20, 1961

JOHN FITZGERALD KENNEDY

John Fitzgerald Kennedy entered the White House at the age of forty-three, the youngest man ever elected President of the United States. Memories of his rugged good looks, youthful enthusiasm, and charming, sophisticated style have preserved JFK's place among America's heroes. Most Americans born before 1955 can immediately remember their whereabouts on November 22, 1963, the day of Kennedy's assassination, just as an earlier generation could recall the events of December 7, 1941, Pearl Harbor day.

Kennedy's inaugural address, beauti-fully delivered in his arresting Boston accent, summoned Americans to "struggle against the common enemies of man— tyranny, poverty, disease and war itself."

The enthusiasms and expectations aroused by Kennedy and his New Frontier contrasted sharply with the ferment that was soon to erupt. He had addressed a nation generally believed to be united by political, social, and cultural values. By the end of the decade, almost all American values and institutions had been thoroughly challenged.

[Delivered in person at the Capitol]

Vice President Johnson, Mr. Speaker, Mr. Chief Justice, President Eisenhower, Vice President Nixon, President Truman, Reverend Clergy, fellow citizens:

We observe today not a victory of party but a celebration of freedom—symbolizing an end as well as a beginning—signifying renewal as well as change. For I have sworn before you and Almighty God the same solemn oath our forebears prescribed nearly a century and three quarters ago.

The world is very different now. For man holds in his mortal hands the power to abolish all forms of human poverty and all forms of human life. And yet the same revolutionary beliefs for which our forebears fought are still at issue around the globe—the belief that the rights of man come not from the generosity of the state but from the hand of God.

We dare not forget today that we are the heirs of that first revolution. Let the word go forth from this time and place, to friend and foe alike, that the torch has been passed to a new generation of Americans—born in this century, tempered by war, disciplined by a hard and bitter peace, proud of our ancient heritage—and unwilling to witness or permit the slow undoing of those human rights to which this nation has always been committed, and to which we are committed today at home and around the world.

Let every nation know, whether it wishes us well or ill, that we shall pay any price, bear any burden, meet any hardship, support any friend, oppose any foe to assure the survival and the success of liberty.

This much we pledge—and more.

To those old allies whose cultural and spiritual origins we share, we pledge the loyalty of faithful friends. United, there is little we cannot do in a host of cooperative ventures. Divided, there is little we can do—for we dare not meet a powerful challenge at odds and split asunder.

To those new states whom we welcome to the ranks of the free, we pledge our word that one form of colonial control shall not have passed away merely to be replaced by a far more iron tyranny. We shall not always expect to find them supporting our view. But we shall always hope to find them strongly supporting their own freedom—and to remember that, in the past, those who foolishly sought power by riding the back of the tiger ended up inside.

To those peoples in the huts and villages of half the globe struggling to break the bonds of mass misery, we pledge our best efforts to help them help themselves, for whatever period is required—not because the communists may be doing it, not because we seek their votes, but because it is right. If a free society cannot help the many who are poor, it cannot save the few who are rich.

John F. Kennedy was the first President to make effective use of television. He probably won the close election of 1960 against Richard Nixon because he appeared more relaxed and perhaps more like a television personality during the televised debates that took place during the campaign. While President, he made use of the new medium to communicate with the American people. Are there dangers in the Presidential use of television?

To our sister republics south of our border, we offer a special pledge—to convert our good words into good deeds—in a new alliance for progress—to assist free men and free governments in casting off the chains of poverty. But this peaceful revolution of hope cannot become the prey of hostile powers. Let all our neighbors know that we shall join with them to oppose aggression or subversion anywhere in the Americas. And let every other power know that this Hemisphere intends to remain the master of its own house.

To that world assembly of sovereign states, the United Nations, our last best hope in an age where the instruments of war have far outpaced the instruments of peace, we renew our pledge of support—to prevent it from becoming merely a forum for invective—to strengthen its shield of the new and the weak—and to enlarge the area in which its writ may run.

Finally, to those nations who would make themselves our adversary, we offer not a pledge but a request: that both sides begin anew the quest for peace, before the dark powers of destruction unleashed by science engulf all humanity in planned or accidental self-destruction.

We dare not tempt them with weakness. For only when our arms are sufficient beyond doubt can we be certain beyond doubt that they will never be employed.

But neither can two great and powerful groups of nations take comfort from our present course—both sides overburdened by the cost of modern weapons, both rightly alarmed by the steady spread of the deadly atom, yet both racing to alter that uncertain balance of terror that stays the hand of mankind's final war.

So let us begin anew—remembering on both sides that civility is not a sign of weakness, and sincerity is always subject to proof. Let us never negotiate out of fear. But let us never fear to negotiate.

Let both sides explore what problems unite us instead of belaboring those problems which divide us.

Let both sides, for the first time, formulate serious and precise proposals for the inspection and control of arms—and bring the absolute power to destroy other nations under the absolute control of all nations.

Let both sides seek to invoke the wonders of science instead of its terrors. Together let us explore the stars, conquer the deserts, eradicate disease, tap the ocean depths and encourage the arts and commerce.

Let both sides unite to heed in all corners of the earth the command of Isaiah—to "undo the heavy burdens . . . (and) let the oppressed go free."

And if a beach-head of cooperation may push back the jungle of suspicion, let both sides join in creating a new endeavor, not a new balance of power, but a new world of law, where the strong are just and the weak secure and the peace preserved.

All this will not be finished in the first one hundred days. Nor will it be finished in the first one thousand days, nor in the life of this Administration, nor even perhaps in our lifetime on this planet. But let us begin.

In your hands, my fellow citizens, more than mine, will rest the final success or failure of our course. Since this country was founded, each generation of Americans has been summoned to give testimony to its national loyalty. The graves of young Americans who answered the call to service surround the globe.

Now the trumpet summons us again—not as a call to bear arms, though arms we need—not as a call to battle, though embattled we are—but a call to bear the burden of a long twilight struggle, year in and year out, "rejoicing in hope, patient in tribulation"—a struggle against the common enemies of man: tyranny, poverty, disease and war itself.

Can we forge against these enemies a grand and global alliance, North and South, East and West, that can assure a more fruitful life for all mankind? Will you join in that historic effort?

In the long history of the world, only a few generations have been granted the role of defending freedom in its hour of maximum danger. I do not shrink from this responsibility—I welcome it. I do not believe that any of us would exchange places with any other people or any other generation. The energy, the faith, the devotion which we bring to this endeavor will light our country and all who serve it—and the glow from that fire can truly light the world.

And so, my fellow Americans: ask not what your country can do for you—ask what you can do for your country.

My fellow citizens of the world: ask not what America will do for you, but what together we can do for the freedom of man.

Finally, whether you are citizens of America or citizens of the world, ask of us here the same high standards of strength and sacrifice which we ask of you. With a good conscience our only sure reward, with history the final judge of our deeds, let us go forth to lead the land we love, asking His blessing and His help, but knowing that here on earth God's work must truly be our own.

NOTE: The President spoke at 12:52 P.M. from a platform erected at the east front of the Capitol. Immediately before the address the oath of office was administered by Chief Justice Warren.

The President's opening words "Reverend Clergy" referred to His Eminence Richard Cardinal Cushing, Archbishop of Boston; His Eminence Archbishop Iakovos, head of the Greek Archdiocese of North and South America; the Reverend Dr. John Barclay, pastor of the Central Christian Church, Austin, Tex.; and Rabbi Dr. Nelson Glueck, President of the Hebrew Union College, Cincinnati, Ohio.

The Peace Corps, 1961 – 1970

Kennedy-style idealism is best represented by the Peace Corps. By the end of 1962, about 5,000 volunteers were located in thirty countries, where they served as school-teachers, physicians, poets, agronomists, professors, technicians, surveyors, linguists, and so on. Thousands of Americans ultimately volunteered and served, and between 1961 and 1965, the Peace Corps received bipartisan political support and unqualified public praise.

" There are, of course, a good many hundreds of millions of people scattered throughout the world and you will come in contact with only a few, but the great impression of what kind of country we have and what kind of people we are will depend on their judgment in these countries of you.

"You will be the personification of a special group of young Americans, and if you can impress them with your commitment to freedom, to the advancement of the interests of people everywhere, to your pride in your country and in its best traditions and what it stands for, the influence may be far-reaching and will go far beyond the immediate day to day tasks that you may do in the months that are ahead."

*President John F. Kennedy
in remarks to the first group
of Volunteers to be sent overseas. August 28, 1961.*

"The Peace Corps represents the best in the American ideal because it helps the peoples of the world follow the American example of peacefully reordering their society within the philosophical concept that man is capable of determining his destiny.

"The Peace Corps is a reflection of our diverse, pluralistic society. The peoples of Latin America, Africa, and Asia see young men and women of different color, different religious faiths, different economic and social backgrounds and different geographic and cultural heritages, leave our shores with a common purpose—that somehow Americans must help the less fortunate of the world attain a higher degree of human dignity. To do less would be a travesty of the American ideal of which I speak today.

"We must encourage this great work, not because the program must be sold.
The Peace Corps is already sold to more American volunteers than the Peace Corps can train, and to more interested countries than the Peace Corps can supply with volunteers. In a word, the program can stand on its own merits and on its own record of success. The question before us is are we willing to permit the Peace Corps to carry out the historic mandate of the American tradition of helping others secure human dignity."

Rep. William F. Ryan, Nov. 13, 1963.

". . . the moment a Peace Corps Volunteer begins to feel that he is *not* special, that is the moment he begins to lose his effectiveness. And the moment the Peace Corps loses the mystique of a special calling is the moment we might as well turn it over to any of the other government agencies in Washington that have tried for four years to absorb us. . . .

"You *are* special citizens. You are special citizens because you are *volunteers*, and a volunteer is a person who in a free, democratic society, decided to serve that society—who by a conscious act of his or her free will, has left the ranks of the bystanders and spectators to become a participant. A volunteer is a person with a large ego—and he should be. He is a person with a split personality—wondering on the one hand if he really can make a difference, and knowing on the other hand that he *must* make a difference.

"When you begin to think you are average, my only advice to you is simply: go back to your split-level homes, turn on your television sets, drink your beer— somebody else with a special sense of his individual worth will step up to serve in the Peace Corps."

Bill Moyers, then Special Assistant to President Johnson, former Deputy Director of the Peace Corps, March 1965.

The Peace Corps and

Pax Americana

MARSHALL WINDMILLER

By the late 1960s, popular disillusionment with United States foreign policy came to include even the Peace Corps, which was denounced as an extension of American imperialism. Though this level of criticism never predominated, its articulation in respectable academic circles indicated the political distance traveled by many Americans since the Kennedy inauguration.

The name "Peace Corps" is good for public relations but poor as description of the organization's activities and mission. It does not make peace between warring nations; neither does it play a conciliating role between nations that are on the brink of war. If its name were to be taken seriously, then one would have to assume that the only nations likely to go to war are the poor nations, for it is there that the Peace Corps is sent. It does not go to the USSR, to Germany, to France, or to China to make those peoples less likely to engage in war. Neither does it go to make peace between Israel and Egypt.

The Peace Corps, of course, is aware of all this, but insists that it is promoting peace nevertheless. "What is its contribution to peace?" asked Associate Director Harris Wofford. "The basic proposition, of course, is that peace is not merely the absence of war but the presence of justice, and that twentieth-century justice requires universal education and development. As carriers of twentieth-century technology and agents of peaceful change, Volunteers are, thus, indeed contributing to peace."

This approach raises several questions. Does the introduction of new technology contribute to justice, or to the creation of economically privileged technical elites? Does the peaceful change encouraged by the Peace Corps lead to significant advances toward justice, or does it merely deflate revolutionary pressures in those areas where violent overthrow of the existing order may, in fact, be the only pragmatic alternative? In other words, is the peace-making contribution of the Peace Corps essentially its capacity to prevent a particular kind of war, namely, revolutionary war?

252

Whatever the answers to these questions . . . there does not seem to be any evidence that any carefully thought-out theory of change played much of a role in the conception and early design of the Peace Corps. Indeed, it appears to have come into existence as much by accident as by design when John F. Kennedy seized upon the idea as a gimmick in the presidential election campaign of 1960.

■   ■   ■

"This would be a volunteer corps—and volunteers would be sought among talented young women as well—and from every race and walk of life. For this nation is full of young people eager to serve the cause of peace in the most useful way. . . ."

Then, in conclusion, Kennedy went back to anti-Communism: "I am convinced that our young men and women, dedicated to freedom, are fully capable of overcoming the efforts of Mr. Khrushchev's missionaries who are dedicated to undermining that freedom."

As the Kennedy speech makes clear, the Peace Corps was originally conceived as an instrument with which to fight Communism, although it was also meant to be more than that. According to the act of Congress which established it, the Corps has three purposes. The first is to help developing countries meet their needs for trained manpower. The second is to promote a better understanding of other peoples by Americans, and the third is to help other peoples understand Americans. According to the Peace Corps, these are essentially non-political goals, and the Corps is not an instrument of American foreign policy. "A volunteer is on his own, and we won't have it any other way," Director Jack Vaughn said at UCLA in 1966. "He is not an instrument of American foreign policy." And two years later Vaughn told the Senate Foreign Relations Committee: "It was established in the early days of the Peace Corps that this movement would not be a part of U.S. foreign policy. This position has been reiterated and I think faithfully followed. So, instead, the Peace Corps is a movement of our society."

This is nonsense. The Peace Corps is no more a movement than is the United States Information Agency or the CIA, but it is just as much an instrument of U.S. foreign policy as they are. All of its overseas programs are planned in careful consultation with Embassy and AID representatives (the U.S. Ambassador in each country must approve all projects), and there is an elaborate multi-agency review procedure in Washington with vetoes all along the line. Moreover, it was sold to Congress primarily as a propaganda device with which to fight Communism and improve America's image abroad. Hubert Humphrey made this clear when he carried the Peace Corps bill on the floor of the Senate and read into the Record a document prepared for him by the Peace Corps. "There is no better way to counteract anti-American propaganda," it said, "than by providing contact between Americans and citizens of other countries. . . . The bright, young, dedicated Americans who will constitute the Peace Corps are the finest fruits of our way of life and the best ambassadors this country can produce. Simply by living and working abroad . . . they can do more to serve the image of this country abroad than all the counter-propaganda that money can buy."

But the most compelling argument against the international Peace Corps, in my opinion, is that it diverts attention from the more important problem of containing United States expansionism by reforming its internal political structure. It is the moral and political underdevelopment of the United States coupled with enormously destructive nuclear capability that demands the highest priority. To advance the development of the United States through economic and political reform may be the greatest service that young Americans can perform for the poor people of the third world, because it may be the only way to make sure that they will not ultimately become the victims of another Vietnam war.

It is against this background that one must consider what ought to be done with the Peace Corps. Is there some way whereby the overall impact on history of the organization can be altered so that it makes a greater contribution to peace and to the liquidation of poverty than it does to the expansion of American power? . . .

Knox County, Kentucky

The Other America

JOHN FETTERMAN

When the dimensions of poverty in this country were finally exposed in the 1960s, the region called "Appalachia" came to symbolize all the worst aspects of the problem. Knox County, in eastern Kentucky, is in that region. Although the area contains fabled amounts of prized energy resources, especially coal, the sad and debilitating evidences of poverty and suffering are evident everywhere. Corporate mining interests are largely at fault. The profits reaped from the area have gone elsewhere, leaving both land and people scarred by their encounter with "progress."

The following article exposes some of the social and economic costs of this progress. Is welfare the solution to such technologically induced poverty? Given our economic system of private enterprise for profit, can poverty ever be eliminated?

There are eight million mountaineers left in Appalachia. Many are leaving. But some are staying—in determination or in despair. Knox County is not the worst of the mountain counties. Nor is it the best. It is merely the county where one day they dedicated a courthouse and where one day a decision was made to visit a place called Stinking Creek.

The Kentucky Department of Commerce and the Knox County Chamber of Commerce have caused to be published a bold little booklet extolling "Industrial Resources, Barbourville, Kentucky." It reveals that the 1960 census credited Knox County with 25,258 living souls, of whom 3,211 live in Barbourville, the county seat. It further advises that 1,187 men and 1,511 women are available as a labor supply.

Barbourville, the booklet says, is 493 miles from Chicago, 388 miles from Detroit, and 829 miles from New York. The study makes the statement, "The inhabitants of Knox County are primarily engaged in agriculture."

We shall see.

The booklet also makes other information available to interested industrial planners:

• The average weekly earnings during 1961 were $51.89 for all industries and $47.20 for manufacturing. During the same period the state average was $83.44 for all industries and $96.07 for manufacturing.

255

- In 1960, per capita income for Knox County was $501; per capita income for Kentucky was $1,573, far below the national average of $2,223. Knox County ranked 119th among Kentucky's 120 counties and Kentucky ranked 46th among the 50 states.

- The largest employer in Barbourville is a firm which manufactures brassieres and employs around 150 people.

- Knox County operates on an annual budget of something over $125,000.

- The net assessed value of property in Knox County was given as $14,331,725.

But Knox County is not primarily in the agricultural business, nor is it in the timber business or the coal business, or the brassiere business: Knox County, like all counties of Appalachia, is in the welfare business. And business is great.

Of the 6,500 dwelling units, only 10 percent have plumbing, and about 6 percent of the 20,625 acres of crop land is in good condition. More than 64 percent of the population receives some kind of welfare assistance—not counting medical aid. About half of the lunches in the school lunch programs are served free, because the children cannot pay the price of ten cents.

■ ■ ■

In Knox County the collecting of welfare benefits has far outstripped the manufacture of brassieres as the backbone of the economy.

Perhaps the most basic and interesting of all the phenomena of the welfare county is the surplus-commodity program. Its administration is simple. A family gets itself approved, is issued a card, and from then on it collects its fair share of the nation's food bounty once a month.

In Knox County, as this is written, 8,461 people enjoy these benefits. The surplus commodities are distributed in a dingy little building on the eastern outskirts of the city to ragtag descendants of men who would fight to the death rather than "be beholden to any man."

In a year, a quarter of a million Kentuckians were given 56,000,000 pounds of surplus foodstuffs that had an estimated wholesale value of around $13,000,000. The recipient families draw a monthly average of around 100 pounds of powdered milk, rice, meal, flour, lard, dried eggs, butter, canned beef and pork, cheese, beans, peanut butter, and occasional cans of fruit.

The commodity food programs are administered on the local level and are regarded with horror by students of political science for the simple reason that the control of food can lead to the control of votes. Charges and denials, innuendoes and inefficiency, are handmaidens of the program.

As for the commodities themselves, most are of high quality. Unattractively packaged by the United States Department of Agriculture in brown boxes or stenciled tin cans, the contents are first rate. The beef and pork, cooked in big iron skillets on wood-burning stoves, is delicious. And so is the cheese, which the occasional visitor "bums" for a lunch up a hollow. The peanut butter is also very good. Many mountaineers dislike the rice and do not know how to prepare it. But they all know what to do with the lard, since frying in deep grease is standard procedure.

But children grow tired of the "commodity food," and rebel. Some mountaineers use the food to trade. Some feed it to the hogs. Others wisely use the commodities as a way to vary their diet of biscuits, coffee, garden beans, corn, and boiled or fried pork.

Some people live in rural America today very much the way they have lived for a century. Except for an ancient automobile and one or two other items, their lives are almost untouched by the modern world.

Stinking Creek is . . . a part of Knox County. It is neither the best nor the worst part. It is typical of nothing, because every hollow of the thousands in eastern Kentucky bears its own particular characteristics dictated by the nature and size of the creek that drains it, the families that settled it, and the particular array of welfare programs that sustain it.

■ ■ ■

Stinking Creek is not a community. It is an area of steep slopes and narrow bottoms sprinkled with homes that range from neat painted clapboard houses—some of them even boasting an inside bathroom—to tottering, sagging little shacks. Each home is a little society unto itself, and many families find they have little in common with their neighbors. They differ in their religion, morals, ethics, and their attitudes toward the welfare program. Family bloodlines are complicated; and although there is a deep feeling of attachment to one's "kin," there is little sense of community unity.

The head-hanging shyness and suspiciousness often credited to the mountaineer are merely his generations-old habit of keeping his nose out of other people's business. Outward signs of love—even between husband and wife—are rare. When affection is shown, it almost always is for the "baby" of the family or for the oldest member.

Mountain homes, those of the very poor, follow a pattern. A room in front, one or two double beds, and a sagging couch in front of a television set being paid for from welfare checks; another room directly behind, full of beds, dark and musty and always with the feeling of dampness; a small room or a lean-to used as a kitchen with a wood- or coal-burning stove, a rickety table, wooden shelves for storing things, and a collection of often-repaired chairs. There are door facings at all the doors, but rarely are there doors. Some doorways modestly boast faded strips of cotton material that can be pulled together for a semblance of privacy.

There is a smell of poverty that is characteristic of many houses along Stinking Creek: a flat, weary, penetrating aroma of seasoned and rotting wood, unwashed clothing and bodies. But the smell of poverty is strangely similar to the smell of prosperous mountain farm homes. Some find it overwhelmingly insufferable. Others find in the flat, strong smell of human bodies a sense of permanence, of enduring things. After several days in the hollows, an elevator filled with ladies in town for a convention is unbearable. The entrapped reek of oils and perfumes and powders can be more nauseating than anything encountered in Stinking Creek— or in any hollow.

An outhouse has a stench of its own, of course. But these are neither an invention of, nor peculiar to, the mountains. Outhouses by the thousands are found in other rural areas across our nation—and even in our cities—and they are often regarded as "quaint." It is customary, however, to gasp in disgust at a two-holer in Appalachia as though it were a temple erected to some god of moral degeneration.

The mountaineer is what he is simply because he was born what he is. Each hollow has its moonshine peddlers and loose women and lazy men and complaining women. And each hollow has its courageous men and determined women who battle hopeless odds to bring their broods to a better life. But the best way to know something of Stinking Creek—and thereby something of Appalachia—is to meet and talk with and learn to know some of the people who live there. Not to study them with the idea of categorizing them into meaningless groups, but to sit and listen.

■   ■   ■

Those who would attempt to separate the citizens of Stinking Creek into two groups could do no better than repeat the words of Golden Slusher:

"What don't work is drawin'."

The majority are "drawin'." They draw welfare checks or commodities or both, and these are the basis of their economic security. The balance are working—for the time being.

Golden Slusher was working. It was a blowing, snowy day, and the warmth from his small coal fireplace was welcome. Slusher is a muscular, quiet man in his forties, and not a talker. But he is hospitable and willing to share his fireplace on a wintry day. The Slushers had no children. Mrs. Slusher, a small, wiry, dark-haired woman, sat silently back near the edge of the circular yellow glow from the fireplace. Nearer the fire sat Mrs. Slusher's mother, Mrs. Betty Smallwood, who is eighty-six and who sits and rocks and silently recollects, and complains of her heart.

Golden Slusher knows better than to try to farm as his ancestors did. The soil on the ridges above Pigeon Creek is thin and sandy and heavy with gravel. It contains little clay, and cannot retain moisture. The plant-food content is low. There is no level land along the banks of Pigeon Creek.

Golden Slusher is a logger. He arises before dawn, goes to the woods over in Bell County, hitches up the mules he keeps there, and all day strains his still-

American abundance and the sense of unlimited resources has sometimes led to the destruction of the landscape and the careless use of natural resources. This is a photo of a strip mine in West Virginia. Can you think of a scene near your home where the natural environment has been destroyed? Is this the price of progress?

powerful muscles to drag out the logs that keep him alive—and off the welfare rolls.

"I ain't drawin'. I'm loggin'," he repeats.

But not many men have his stamina.

It is always easiest to talk with the old people, of whom there are many. They know the creek well, and have a serenity from long years of living with the hills, and an instinctive politeness. Most of the old men once worked in the deep mines. The mines killed many of them and maimed many more. To those who worked and lived, the mines left memories that will not die until the last old man dies.

There are many such old men on Stinking Creek. Ed Sizemore and Frank Patterson are two of them.

Ed Sizemore . . . had his own private coal mine. It was only a small out-cropping of coal on the hillside behind his house. But Ed could take a wheelbarrow back there, pick around in the hole he had dug, and return with his own private coal supply. But he doesn't do that much anymore because his back hurts. "If I bend my back it gives me such miseries I can't stand it," he said. He went to work in the mines when he was fourteen, and stayed there until about a year ago.

His present age is a matter of dispute between him and the federal government. Ed is trying to get social security.

Stinking Creek runs directly behind Ed Sizemore's house. A huge boulder sits on the bank to deflect the torrent when the creek is swollen from the spring rains. So far, the boulder has saved his house from each succeeding flood. "It turns the tide right back into the creek," Ed said.

He massaged the small of his back through his loosely fitting overalls, and tried to tell of his difficulties with federal authority. "I don't get a dime from the government," he said. Hurt filled his pale blue eyes. He shuffled his blocky figure beneath the folds of the overalls. "Oh, I got a little compensation when I got hurt.

I'm going in front of the doctors agin 'fore long. One's a social-security doctor, too. I got plenty in that social security. Buddy, I worked years and years before social security ever thought of coming in. I was working when the man brought that card up to me for me to sign.

"I said, 'What is it?' It was all green to me.

"I put up most of my life in a mine. I made my living in a hill and raised fourteen kids. Under the union I made good—twenty-five or thirty a day. Under a scab mine you had to really work to get ten a shift.

"Hit'll be a year the sixteenth of this month since I was hurt. I'm old enough to retire, as far as that goes. They sent and got fifty-four as my age. I'm 'way older than that. My mother ought to know my age. Well, I was sixty-two years old two years ago, but they wouldn't have it that way. I just let it go for then. I seen I couldn't do no better.

"The govermint ought to see to a man when he's down and out. But they are hardest on the man who put it in, in the world. He can put it in, but he can't get it out. And nobody in this whole county helped me."

Ed Sizemore remembers the mines well, but not with fondness. Like most old miners, he had a horror that his sons would follow him into the mines. One son did. "Me and one of my boys worked a seam together oncet. I tried and tried to get him not to go back in. He finally quit and went to Detroit. He runs a 'dozer up there."

Ed Sizemore was injured while "robbing" a mine, a practice that has left many a body entombed forever beneath the mountains. As the old deep miners worked farther and farther into a seam, they left pillars of coal to support the treacherous roof of the mine. After the coal was all taken out, the miners would begin to "rob" the mine—take out the supporting pillars. Starting with the pillar farthest back in the mine, they would salvage all that was left, working their way back to the mine mouth and ready to flee for the opening at the first sign of a fault in the roof.

Mining, Ed said, was dangerous enough without having to rob the seams. "The electric cable, for one thing, could kill you deader than thunder, and it did kill some. I done most my mining in Leslie County. You'd lay on your side or get on your knees, anyway you can get to get at the coal. We was robbing. Getting the last of it."

Ed Sizemore cocked his head to look across the creek, and was silent for a long time. Perhaps he was reliving the day when the mine roof came crashing down and put the miseries in his back. But when he turned back, he did not mention robbing a mine again.

His first wife died twenty-three years ago, and that was when he bought his forty acres on Stinking Creek. He quickly remarried. "I couldn't rest easy working in the mines with the kids home by theirself. So I married her. She help me raise them.

"This is a good spot to live. In forty-seven I had this whole bottom in sweet taters big as your two fists from a goose egg up. They just rot in the ground, but I had enough left for the winter. I had two big mares, and I had some old time getting them up that hill out of the tide when the rains come."

The smell of beans cooking had been coming from the house. Now Ed's wife, a pleasant woman with a broad smile, came to the kitchen door, made an almost imperceptible signal, and Ed Sizemore eased toward the house.

"Come back any time you take a notion," he said.

Frank Patterson . . . was sitting on a log in the sunshine up by the road near his house. The spot is the last place you can turn a car without climbing all the way to the head of hollow, and the road was muddy from a recent rain. Frank's unblinking eyes were fixed on the camera. He shoved his hat back a bit on his head and said evenly, "Put under that picture, 'Frank Patterson who's lived eighty-two years!'"

In eighty-two years, he has done about everything a man can do on Stinking Creek. He let his eyes sweep across the hills. "I used to farm all those hills 'till I got wore out . . . and the hills got wore out . . . no timber . . . no nothin'."

The Pattersons are a big family—or a big "generation," as mountain people term it. They came to the hollow early, crossing the shallow place in the Cumberland River, then turning northeastward into the Stinking Creek watershed. The first Patterson was "old man" John Patterson, Frank's grandfather.

"There wasn't no record kept of nobody," Frank said. "But John Patterson was the first in. He fought in the old Revolution War and didn't die 'til after I was married. John was old enough to be using a walking cane, and I was about twenty when he died. He was a big tall fellow. Weighed about one seventy-five. He farmed and hunted. John had eight children. My notion is he came from Tennessee. John married a Golden, Polly Ann Golden. They used to live up the hill there."

The old man, John Patterson, who had come to live upon his land given him for his service against the British, did leave a large "generation." There are many Pattersons in the hollow.

Frank is the oldest Patterson now. And the family records are in his head.

"My daddy was James, or Jim. Jim lived to eighty-four, and my mother was a Taylor. There were nine of us children." Frank and a sister are the only survivors of that family.

As was the custom, the family land was divided among the children, then among the children's children, until the vast mountain holdings dwindled to tiny plots.

"My mother aired [was heir to] three hundred acres of land, and we divided it up. John had one hundred acres at Messer and sold it out. I own this little bit of property here where I'm livin'."

Frank waved a bony hand toward the bottom below his house, a wide space beside the creek where a square, concrete block one-room school now sits. The name of the school is Erose.

"The county paid me $150 for that bottom. I tried to get out of selling it, but they forced me to. That was going on thirty year ago."

Mrs. Patterson is a small woman, gray and prim, friendly and frank. Her tiny body appears to be buried in layers of cotton petticoats, skirts, and an apron. Her dark eyes are alert and inquisitive. The best single word to describe her, perhaps, is "sweet." If a woman were needed to personify the perfect mountain grandmother, Mrs. Patterson would make an excellent candidate. The Pattersons were sitting on the porch of their sturdy, ancient house. The yard is surrounded by its "palings," a fence of slender slats that encircles and protects the yard.

■ ■ ■

Mrs. Patterson spoke softly and slowly, sometimes pausing to knit her pale brow in concentration, as though she wanted to make sure there would be no inaccuracies: "Lord, I'm seventy-five, and I was Mary Jane Mills. My generation of Mills' lived in Clay County."

Frank interrupted. "I think we got eighty grandchildren."

Mrs. Patterson's voice was patient and firm: "We got sixty-eight grandchildren and thirty-three great-grandchildren. We got a big generation." Mrs. Patterson smoothed her cotton apron. "It don't hurt nobody to tell what you think," she said, "I think there's a lot around here that'll write and try to get more added on their check. Some are getting $64 and up that away. We hain't. They claimed we drawed too much to get commodities. You ain't allowed to sell a calf unless you turn it in and they cut your check down. And we ain't got no way to get out of here to buy. I just shop around these little places—I call them peanut stores."

She said most of the young people are gone. "People have just quit lookin' for work around here and went off hunting for jobs. There ain't nothin' around here to work at. We got two children still live here on the creek. The rest scattered over the whole known world, 'peers like to me. Some in Clay County, some in Bell County, some in Dayton, some in Cleveland."

So Mrs. Patterson runs her four-room house for only her husband now, and they live in apparent mountain comfort on their old-age benefits. "We draw $55 apiece every month."

"We git some out of there," Frank said, waving toward the small garden just outside the paling fence. "I own, in all, sixty acres." There is coal under the land, but Frank, like most mountaineers, considers it a curse rather than a blessing. "There's plenty coal here," he said. "There's a seven-foot vein. But most of the coal around here was sold out years ago. They sold mineral rights sixty years ago at least.

"Here we are sittin' on millions in coal, oil, and gas. They claim there's a pocket of oil and gas forty miles square in here. Over on Red Bird you can hear that gas a-squealin' before you get within half a mile of it. They struck oil, and it run just like water 'till they plugged it up.

"It don't do this country no good."

Demonstrating in Mississippi

ANNE MOODY

The civil rights promise of the New Frontier was welcomed by black America. Five years before Kennedy's election, the successful Montgomery bus boycott struck a serious blow against Southern racism, as had the Supreme Court's decision outlawing segregated schools in 1954. The civil rights movement gradually coalesced around the charismatic Reverend Martin Luther King, Jr., although several black organizations soon developed tactics that differed from King's evolutionary nonviolent approach.

During the Kennedy administration, sit-ins, freedom rides, and well-publicized school and university integration events were invariably accompanied by violent white reaction. With Kennedy's civil rights legislation tied up in Congress, the President pursued an approach too cautious for most black leaders. Organizers of the massive March on Washington in August 1963 received a lukewarm reception at the White House and Kennedy was not present to hear King's "I Have a Dream" speech.

In the Deep South, demonstrations mounted. The following selection is the autobiographical account of a black college student during the violent summer of 1963. From a perspective of two decades later, do you think the results were worth the violence and danger?

A few weeks after I got involved with the Tougaloo chapter of the NAACP, they organized a demonstration at the state fair in Jackson. Just before it was to come off, Medgar Evers came to campus and gave a big hearty speech about how "Jackson was gonna move." Tougaloo sent four picketers to the fair, and one of them was Dave Jones. Because he was chosen to be the spokesman for the group, he was the first to be interviewed on TV. That evening when the demonstration was televised on all the news programs, it seemed as though every girl in the dorm was down in the lounge in front of the set. They were all shooting off about how they would take part in the next demonstration. The girl Dave was now seeing was running all around talking about how good he looked.

Dave and the other demonstrators had been arrested and were to be bailed out around eight that night. By eight-thirty a lot of us were sitting outside on the dormitory steps awaiting their arrival, and they still hadn't shown up. One of the girls had just gone inside to call the NAACP headquarters in Jackson, when suddenly two police cars came speeding through the campus. Students came

The protests of the early 1960s were focused on civil rights, particularly on the traditionally racist institutions of the South. Courageous and energetic people, many of them young, threw themselves into demonstrations and voting drives. Only later would the focus shift to racist patterns in the North and elsewhere, and by then the nation's attention had drifted to other concerns and crises. To what extent was the civil rights movement successful in altering the social and political life of the South? Has the economic situation changed? What prevented further change? In what ways is the political consciousness of the 1960s related to your sense of politics today? Why does the enormous Washington demonstration which heard Martin Luther King's "I Have a Dream" speech in 1963 seem so out of character today?

running from every building. Within minutes the police cars were completely surrounded, blocked in from every direction. There were two cops in the front seat of each car. They looked frightened to death of us. When the students got out of the cars, they were hugged, kissed, and congratulated for well over an hour. All during this time the cops remained in their seats behind locked doors. Finally someone started singing "We Shall Overcome," and everyone joined in. When we finished singing, someone suggested we go to the football field and have a big rally. In minutes every student was on the football field singing all kinds of freedom songs, giving testimonies as to what we were going to do, and praying and carrying on something terrible. The rally ended at twelve-thirty and by this time, all the students were ready to tear Jackson to pieces.

The following evening Medgar Evers again came to campus to, as he put it, "get some of Tougaloo's spirit and try and spread it around all over Jackson." He gave us a good pep talk and said we would be called upon from time to time to demonstrate.

■ ■ ■

In mid-September I was back on campus. But didn't very much happen until February when the NAACP held its annual convention in Jackson. They were having a whole lot of interesting speakers: Jackie Robinson, Floyd Patterson, Curt Flood, Margaretta Belafonte, and many others. I wouldn't have missed it for anything. I was so excited that I sent one of the leaflets home to Mama and asked her to come.

Three days later I got a letter from Mama with dried-up tears on it, forbidding me to go to the convention. It went on for more than six pages. She said if I didn't stop that shit she would come to Tougaloo and kill me herself. She told me about the time I last visited her, on Thanksgiving, and she had picked me up at the bus station. She said the sheriff had been by, telling her I was messing around with that NAACP group. She said he told her if I didn't stop it, I could not come back there any more. He said that they didn't need any of those NAACP people messing around in Centreville. She ended the letter by saying that she had burned the leaflet I sent her. "Please don't send any more of that stuff here. I don't want nothing to happen to us here," she said. "If you keep that up, you will never be able to come home again."

I was so damn mad after her letter, I felt like taking the NAACP convention to Centreville. I think I would have, if it had been in my power to do so. The remainder of the week I thought of nothing except going to the convention. I didn't know exactly what to do about it. I didn't want Mama or anyone at home to get hurt because of me.

I had felt something was wrong when I was home. During the four days I was there, Mama had tried to do everything she could to keep me in the house. When I said I was going to see some of my old classmates, she pretended she was sick and said I would have to cook. I knew she was acting strangely, but I hadn't known why. I thought Mama just wanted me to spend most of my time with her, since this was only the second time I had been home since I entered college as a freshman.

Things kept running through my mind after that letter from Mama. My mind was so active, I couldn't sleep at night. I remembered the one time I did leave the house to go to the post office. I had walked past a bunch of white men on the street on my way through town and one said, "Is that the gal goin' to Tougaloo?" He acted kind of mad or something, and I didn't know what was going on. I got a creepy feeling, so I hurried home. When I told Mama about it, she just said, "A lotta people don't like that school." I knew what she meant. Just before I went to Tougaloo, they had housed the Freedom Riders there. The school was being criticized by whites throughout the state.

I had become very friendly with my social science professor, John Salter, who was in charge of NAACP activities on campus. All during the year, while the

NAACP conducted a boycott of the downtown stores in Jackson, I had been one of Salter's most faithful canvassers and church speakers. During the last week of school, he told me that sit-in demonstrations were about to start in Jackson and that he wanted me to be the spokesman for a team that would sit-in at Woolworth's lunch counter. The two other demonstrators would be classmates of mine, Memphis and Pearlena. Pearlena was a dedicated NAACP worker, but Memphis had not been very involved in the Movement on campus. It seemed that the organization had had a rough time finding students who were in a position to go to jail. I had nothing to lose one way or the other. Around ten o'clock the morning of the demonstrations, NAACP headquarters alerted the news services. As a result, the police department was also informed, but neither the policemen nor the newsmen knew exactly where or when the demonstrations would start. They stationed themselves along Capitol Street and waited.

To divert attention from the sit-in at Woolworth's, the picketing started at J. C. Penney's a good fifteen minutes before. The pickets were allowed to walk up and down in front of the store three or four times before they were arrested. At exactly 11 A.M. Pearlena, Memphis, and I entered Woolworth's from the rear entrance. We separated as soon as we stepped into the store, and made small purchases from various counters. Pearlena had given Memphis her watch. He was to let us know when it was 11:14. At 11:14 we were to join him near the lunch counter and at exactly 11:15 we were to take seats at it.

Seconds before 11:15 we were occupying three seats at the previously segregated Woolworth's lunch counter. In the beginning the waitresses seemed to ignore us, as if they really didn't know what was going on. Our waitress walked past us a couple of times before she noticed we had started to write our own orders down and realized we wanted service. She asked us what we wanted. We began to read to her from our order slips. She told us that we would be served at the back counter, which was for Negroes.

"We would like to be served here," I said.

The waitress started to repeat what she had said, then stopped in the middle of the sentence. she turned the lights out behind the counter, and she and the other waitresses almost ran to the back of the store, deserting all their white customers. I guess they thought that violence would start immediately after the whites at the counter realized what was going on. There were five or six other people at the counter. A couple of them just got up and walked away. A girl sitting next to me finished her banana split before leaving. A middle-aged white woman who had not yet been served rose from her seat and came over to us. "I'd like to stay here with you," she said, "but my husband is waiting."

The newsmen came in just as she was leaving. They must have discovered what was going on shortly after some of the people began to leave the store. One of the newsmen ran behind the woman who spoke to us and asked her to identify herself. She refused to give her name, but said she was a native of Vicksburg and a former resident of California. When asked why she had said what she had said to us, she replied, "I am in sympathy with the Negro movement." By this time a crowd of cameramen and reporters had gathered around us taking pictures and asking questions, such as Where were we from? Why did we sit-in? What organization sponsored it? Were we students? From what school? How were we classified?

I told them that we were all students at Tougaloo College, that we were represented by no particular organization, and that we planned to stay there even after the store closed. "All we want is service," was my reply to one of them. After they had finished probing for about twenty minutes, they were almost ready to leave.

At noon, students from a nearby white high school started pouring in to Woolworth's. When they first saw us they were sort of surprised. They didn't know how to react. A few started to heckle and the newsmen became interested again. Then the white students started chanting all kinds of anti-Negro slogans. We were called a little bit of everything. The rest of the seats except the three we were occupying had been roped off to prevent others from sitting down. A couple of the boys took one end of the rope and made it into a hangman's noose. Several attempts were made to put it around our necks. The crowds grew as more students and adults came in for lunch.

We kept our eyes straight forward and did not look at the crowd except for occasional glances to see what was going on. All of a sudden I saw a face I remembered—the drunkard from the bus station sit-in. My eyes lingered on him just long enough for us to recognize each other. Today he was drunk too, so I don't think he remembered where he had seen me before. He took out a knife, opened it, put it in his pocket, and then began to pace the floor. At this point, I told Memphis and Pearlena what was going on. Memphis suggested that we pray. We bowed our heads, and all hell broke loose. A man rushed forward, threw Memphis from his seat, and slapped my face. Then another man who worked in the store threw me against an adjoining counter.

Down on my knees on the floor, I saw Memphis lying near the lunch counter with blood running out of the corners of his mouth. As he tried to protect his face, the man who'd thrown him down kept kicking him against the head. If he had worn hard-soled shoes instead of sneakers, the first kick probably would have killed Memphis. Finally a man dressed in plain clothes identified himself as a police officer and arrested Memphis and his attacker.

Pearlena had been thrown to the floor. She and I got back on our stools after Memphis was arrested. There were some white Tougaloo teachers in the crowd. They asked Pearlena and me if we wanted to leave. They said that things were getting too rough. We didn't know what to do. While we were trying to make up our minds, we were joined by Joan Trumpauer. Now there were three of us and we were integrated. The crowd began to chant, "Communists, Communists, Communists." Some old man in the crowd ordered the students to take us off the stools.

"Which one should I get first?" a big husky boy said.

"That white nigger," the old man said.

The boy lifted Joan from the counter by her waist and carried her out of the store. Simultaneously, I was snatched from my stool by two high school students. I was dragged about thirty feet toward the door by my hair when someone made them turn me loose. As I was getting up off the floor, I saw Joan coming back inside. We started back to the center of the counter to join Pearlena. Lois Chaffee, a white Tougaloo faculty member, was now sitting next to her. So Joan and I just climbed across the rope at the front end of the counter and sat down. There were now four of us, two whites and two Negroes, all women. The mob started smearing us with ketchup, mustard, sugar, pies, and everything on the counter. Soon Joan and I were joined by John Salter, but the moment he sat down he was hit on the jaw with what appeared to be brass knuckles. Blood gushed from his face and someone threw salt into the open wound. Ed King, Tougaloo's chaplain, rushed to him.

At the other end of the counter, Lois and Pearlena were joined by George Raymond, a CORE field worker and a student from Jackson State College. Then a Negro high school boy sat down next to me. The mob took spray paint from the counter and sprayed it on the new demonstrators. The high school student had on a white shirt; the word "nigger" was written on his back with red spray paint.

We sat there for three hours taking a beating when the manager decided to close the store because the mob had begun to go wild with stuff from other counters. He begged and begged everyone to leave. But even after fifteen minutes of begging, no one budged. They would not leave until we did. Then Dr. Beittel, the president of Tougaloo College, came running in. He said he had just heard what was happening.

About ninety policemen were standing outside the store; they had been watching the whole thing through the windows, but had not come in to stop the mob or do anything. President Beittel went outside and asked Captain Ray to come and escort us out. The captain refused, stating the manager had to invite him in before he could enter the premises, so Dr. Beittel himself brought us out. He had told the police that they had better protect us after we were outside the store. When we got outside, the policemen formed a single line that blocked the mob from us. However, they were allowed to throw at us everything they had collected. Within ten minutes, we were picked up by Reverend King in his station wagon and taken to the NAACP headquarters on Lynch Street.

After the sit-in, all I could think of was how sick Mississippi whites were. They believed so much in the segregated Southern way of life, they would kill to preserve it. I sat there in the NAACP office and thought of how many times they had killed when this way of life was threatened. I knew that the killing had just begun. "Many more will die before it is over with," I thought. Before the sit-in, I had always hated the whites in Mississippi. Now I knew it was impossible for me to hate sickness. The whites had a disease, an incurable disease in its final stage. What were our chances against such a disease? I thought of the students, the young Negroes who had just begun to protest, as young interns. When these young interns got older, I thought, they would be the best doctors in the world for social problems.

■ ■ ■

Mass rallies had [soon] come to be an every night event, and at each one the NAACP had begun to build up Medgar Evers. Somehow I had the feeling that they wanted him to become for Mississippi what Martin Luther King had been in Alabama. They were well on the way to achieving that, too.

After the rally on Tuesday, June 11, I had to stay in Jackson. I had missed the ride back to campus. Dave Dennis, the CORE field secretary for Mississippi, and his wife put me up for the night. We were watching TV around twelve-thirty, when a special news bulletin interrupted the program. It said, "Jackson NAACP leader Medgar Evers has just been shot."

We didn't believe what we were hearing. We just sat there staring at the TV screen. It was unbelievable. Just an hour or so earlier we were all with him. The next bulletin announced that he had died in the hospital soon after the shooting. We didn't know what to say or do. All night we tried to figure out what had happened, who did it, who was next, and it still didn't seem real.

First thing the next morning we turned on the TV. It showed films taken shortly after Medgar was shot in his driveway. We saw the pool of blood where he had fallen. We saw his wife sobbing almost hysterically as she tried to tell what had happened. Without even having breakfast, we headed for the NAACP headquarters. When we got there, they were trying to organize a march to protest Medgar's death. Newsmen, investigators, and reporters flooded the office. College and high school students and a few adults sat in the auditorium waiting to march.

■ ■ ■

The Sunday following Medgar's funeral, Reverend Ed King organized an integrated church-visiting team of six of us from the college. Another team was organized by a group in Jackson. Five or six churches were hit that day, including Governor Ross Barnett's. At each one they had prepared for our visit with armed policemen, paddy wagons, and dogs—which would be used in case we refused to leave after "ushers" had read us the prepared resolutions. There were about eight of these ushers at each church, and they were never exactly the usherly type. They were more on the order of Al Capone. I think this must have been the first time any of these men had worn a flower in his lapel. When we were asked to leave, we did. We were never even allowed to get past the first step.

A group of us decided that we would go to church again the next Sunday. This time we were quite successful. These visits had not been publicized as the first ones were, and they were not really expecting us. We went first to a Church of Christ, where we were greeted by the regular ushers. After reading us the same resolution we had heard last week, they offered to give us cab fare to the Negro extension of the church. Just as we had refused and were walking away, an old lady stopped us. "We'll sit with you," she said.

We walked back to the ushers with her and her family. "Please let them in, Mr. Calloway. We'll sit with them," the old lady said.

"Mrs. Dixon, the church has decided what is to be done. A resolution has been passed, and we are to abide by it."

"Who are we to decide such a thing? This is a house of God, and God is to make all of the decisions. He is the judge of us all," the lady said.

The ushers got angrier then and threatened to call the police if we didn't leave. We decided to go.

"We appreciate very much what you've done," I said to the old lady.

As we walked away from the church, we noticed the family leaving by a side entrance. The old lady was waving to us.

Two blocks from the church, we were picked up by Ed King's wife, Jeanette. She drove us to an Episcopal church. She had previously left the other two girls from our team there. She circled the block a couple of times, but we didn't see them anywhere. I suggested that we try the church. "Maybe they got in," I said. Mrs. King waited in the car for us. We walked up to the front of the church. There were no ushers to be seen. Apparently, services had already started. When we walked inside, we were greeted by two ushers who stood at the rear.

"May we help you?" one said.

"Yes," I said. "We would like to worship with you today."

"Will you sign the guest list, please, and we will show you to your seats," said the other.

I stood there for a good five minutes before I was able to compose myself. I had never prayed with white people in a white church before. We signed the guest list and were then escorted to two seats behind the other two girls in our team. We had all gotten in. The church service was completed without one incident. It was as normal as any church service. However, it was by no means normal to me. I was sitting there thinking any moment God would strike the life out of me. I recognized some of the whites, sitting around me in that church. If they were praying to the same God I was, then even God, I thought, was against me.

When the services were over the minister invited us to visit again. He said it as if he meant it, and I began to have a little hope.

Statement on Vietnam

The following statement, issued by the Student Non-Violent Coordinating Committee (SNCC), represented an early linking of the civil rights movement and the antiwar struggle. SNCC, the center of the Black Power movement, equated the aspirations of black Americans with the Viet-namese, and urged civil disobedience. Most civil rights organizations had separated themselves from their white supporters. On college campuses, however, once-dominant civil rights concerns turned increasingly to antiwar activities.

January 6, 1966

The Student Non-Violent Coordinating Committee assumes its right to dissent with United States foreign policy on any issue, and states its opposition to United States involvement in the war in Vietnam on these grounds:

We believe the United States government has been deceptive in its claims of concern for the freedom of the Vietnamese people, just as the government has been deceptive in claiming concern for the freedom of the colored people in such other countries as the Dominican Republic, the Congo, South Africa, Rhodesia and in the United States itself.

We of the Student Non-Violent Coordinating Committee have been involved in the black people's struggle for liberation and self-determination in this country for the past five years. Our work, particularly in the South, taught us that the United States government has never guaranteed the freedom of oppressed citizens, and is not yet truly determined to end the rule of terror and oppression within its own borders.

We ourselves have often been victims of violence and confinement executed by U.S. government officials. We recall the numerous persons who have been murdered in the South because of their efforts to secure their civil and human rights, and whose murderers have been allowed to escape penalty for their crimes. The murder of Samuel Younge in Tuskegee, Alabama is no different from the murder of people in Vietnam, for both Younge and the Vietnamese sought and are seeking to secure the rights guaranteed them by law. In each case, the United States Government bears a great part of the responsibility for these deaths.

Samuel Younge was murdered because United States law is not being enforced. Vietnamese are being murdered because the United States is pursuing an

To many Americans, it seemed as if the war in Vietnam would never end. Do you recall the demonstrations and the often violent confrontations? Why was the reaction so different during World War II?

aggressive policy in violation of international law. The United States is no respector of persons or law when such persons or laws run counter to its needs and desires. We recall the indifference, suspicion and outright hostility with which our reports of violence have been met in the past by government officials. We know for the most part that elections in this country, in the North as well as the South, are not free. We have seen that the 1965 Voting Rights Act and the 1964 Civil Rights Act have not yet been implemented with full federal power and concern. We question then the ability and even the desire of the United States government to guarantee free elections abroad. We maintain that our country's cry of "preserve freedom in the world" is a hypocritical mask behind which it squashed liberation movements which are not bound and refuse to be bound by the expediency of the United States cold war policy.

We are in sympathy with and support the men in this country who are unwilling to respond to the military draft which would compel them to contribute their lives to United States aggression in the name of the "freedom" we find so false in this country.

We recoil with horror at the inconsistency of this supposedly free society where responsibility to freedom is equated with responsibility to lend oneself to military aggression. We take note of the fact that 16% of the draftees from this country are Negro, called on to stifle the liberation of Vietnam, to preserve a "democracy" which does not exist for them at home.

We ask: Where is the draft for the Freedom fight in the United States?

We therefore encourage those Americans who prefer to use their energy in building democratic forms within the country. We believe that work in the civil rights movement and other human relations organizations is a valid alternative, knowing full well that it may cost them their lives, as painfully as in Vietnam.

Address on U.S. Policy in Vietnam Delivered Before a Joint Session of the Tennessee State Legislature, March 15, 1967

LYNDON BAINES JOHNSON

President Lyndon Baines Johnson's dreams of a Great Society died as his commitment to the war in Vietnam increased. Johnson doggedly but unsuccessfully sought to rally support by defining American objectives in reasonable and traditional terms.

L ieutenant Governor Gorrell, Speaker Cummings, Governor Ellington, distinguished members of the legislature, and my friends:
It is always a very special privilege and pleasure for me to visit Tennessee.

For a Texan, it is like homecoming, because much of the courage and the hard work that went into the building of the Southwest came from the hills and the fields of Tennessee. It strengthened the sinews of thousands of men—at the Alamo, at San Jacinto, and at the homes of our pioneer people.

This morning, I visited the Hermitage, the historic home of Andrew Jackson. Two centuries have passed since that most American of all Americans was born. The world has changed a great deal since his day. But the qualities which sustain men and nations in positions of leadership have not changed.

274

The antiwar movement and demonstrations of the 1960s often caused confrontation between middle-class Americans and other Americans carrying guns and tear gas. Many of these respectable citizens were even beaten up and thrown in prison. There seemed to be fundamental conflict in a divided America. What were the results of this confrontation and conflict? What is the relationship between the protests of younger and older generations?

In our time, as in Andrew Jackson's, freedom has its price.

In our time, as in his, history conspires to test the American will.

In our time, as in Jackson's time, courage and vision, and the willingness to sacrifice, will sustain the cause of freedom.

This generation of Americans is making its imprint on history. It is making it in the fierce hills and the sweltering jungles of Vietnam. I think most of our citizens have—after a very penetrating debate which is our democratic heritage—reached a common understanding on the meaning and on the objectives of that struggle.

Before I discuss the specific questions that remain at issue, I should like to review the points of widespread agreement.

It was 2 years ago that we were forced to choose, forced to make a decision between major commitments in defense of South Vietnam or retreat—the evacuation of more than 25,000 of our troops, the collapse of the Republic of Vietnam in the face of subversion and external assault.

Andrew Jackson would never have been surprised at the choice we made.

We chose a course in keeping with American tradition, in keeping with the foreign policy of at least three administrations, with the expressed will of the Congress of the United States, with our solemn obligations under the Southeast

Asian Treaty, and with the interest of 16 million South Vietnamese who had no wish to live under Communist domination.

As our commitment in Vietnam required more men and more equipment, some voices were raised in opposition. The administration was urged to disengage, to find an excuse to abandon the effort.

These cries came despite growing evidence that the defense of Vietnam held the key to the political and economic future of free Asia. The stakes of the struggle grew correspondingly.

It became clear that if we were prepared to stay the course in Vietnam, we could help to lay the cornerstone for a diverse and independent Asia, full of promise and resolute in the cause of peaceful economic development for her long-suffering peoples.

But if we faltered, the forces of chaos would scent victory and decades of strife and aggression would stretch endlessly before us.

The choice was clear. We would stay the course. And we shall stay the course.

I think most Americans support this fundamental decision. Most of us remember the fearful cost of ignoring aggression. Most of us have cast aside the illusion that we can live in an affluent fortress while the world slides into chaos.

I think we have all reached broad agreement on our basic objectives in Vietnam.

First, an honorable peace, that will leave the people of South Vietnam free to fashion their own political and economic institutions without fear of terror or intimidation from the North.

Second, a Southeast Asia in which all countries—including a peaceful North Vietnam—apply their scarce resources to the real problems of their people: combating hunger, ignorance, and disease.

I have said many, many times, that nothing would give us greater pleasure than to invest our own resources in the constructive works of peace rather than in the futile destruction of war.

Third, a concrete demonstration that aggression across international frontiers or demarcation lines is no longer an acceptable means of political change.

There is also, I think, a general agreement among Americans on the things that we do not want in Vietnam.

We do not want permanent bases. We will begin with the withdrawal of our troops on a reasonable schedule whenever reciprocal concessions are forthcoming from our adversary.

We do not seek to impose our political beliefs upon South Vietnam. Our Republic rests upon a brisk commerce in ideas. We will be happy to see free competition in the intellectual marketplace whenever North Vietnam is willing to shift the conflict from the battlefield to the ballot box.

So, these are the broad principles on which most Americans agree.

On a less general level, however, the events and frustrations of these past few difficult weeks have inspired a number of questions about our Vietnam policy in the minds and hearts of a good many of our citizens. Today, here in this historic chamber, I want to deal with some of those questions that figure most prominently in the press and in some of the letters which reach a President's desk.

Many Americans are confused by the barrage of information about military engagements. They long for the capsule summary which has kept tabs on our previous wars, a line on the map that divides friend from foe.

Precisely what, they ask, is our military situation, and what are the prospects of victory?

The first answer is that Vietnam is aggression in a new guise, as far removed from trench warfare as the rifle from the longbow. This is a war of infiltration, of subversion, of ambush. Pitched battles are very rare, and even more rarely are they decisive.

Today, more than 1 million men from the Republic of Vietnam and its six allies are engaged in the order of battle.

Despite continuing increases in North Vietnam infiltration, this strengthening of allied forces in 1966, under the brilliant leadership of General Westmoreland, was instrumental in reversing the whole course of this war.

—We estimate that 55,000 North Vietnamese and Vietcong were killed in 1966, compared with 35,000 the previous year. Many more were wounded, and more than 20,000 defected.

—By contrast, 9,500 South Vietnamese, more than 5,000 Americans, and 600 from other allied forces were killed in action.

—The Vietnamese Army achieved a 1966 average of two weapons captured from the Vietcong to every one lost, a dramatic turn around from the previous 2 years.

—Allied forces have made several successful sweeps through territories that were formerly considered Vietcong sanctuaries only a short time ago. These operations not only cost the enemy large numbers of men and weapons, but are very damaging to his morale.

Well, what does all of this mean? Will the North Vietnamese change their tactics? Will there be less infiltration of main units? Will there be more of guerrilla warfare?

The actual truth is we just don't know.

What we do know is that General Westmoreland's strategy is producing results, that our military situation has substantially improved, that our military success has permitted the groundwork to be laid for a pacification program which is the longrun key to an independent South Vietnam.

Since February 1965, our military operations have included selective bombing of military targets in North Vietnam. Our purposes are three:

—To back our fighting men by denying the enemy a sanctuary;

—To exact a penalty against North Vietnam for her flagrant violations of the Geneva accords of 1954 and 1962;

—To limit the flow, or to substantially increase the cost of infiltration of men and materiel from North Vietnam.

All of our intelligence confirms that we have been successful.

Yet, some of our people object strongly to this aspect of our policy. Must we bomb, many people ask. Does it do any military good? Is it consistent with America's limited objectives? Is it an inhuman act that is aimed at civilians?

On the question of military utility, I can only report the firm belief of the Secretary of Defense, the Joint Chiefs of Staff, the Central Intelligence Agency, General Westmoreland and our commanders in the field, and all the courses of information and advice available to the Commander in Chief and that is that the bombing is causing serious disruption and is bringing about added burdens to the North Vietnamese infiltration effort.

We know, for example, that half a million people are kept busy just repairing damage to bridges, roads, railroads, and other strategic facilities, and in air and coastal defense and repair of powerplants.

I also want to say categorically that it is not the position of the American Government that the bombing will be decisive in getting Hanoi to abandon aggression. It has, however, created very serious problems for them. The best indication of how substantial is the fact that they are working so hard every day with all their friends throughout the world to try to get us to stop.

The bombing is entirely consistent with America's limited objectives in South Vietnam. The strength of Communist main-force units in the South is clearly based on their infiltration from the North. So I think it is simply unfair to our American soldiers, sailors, and marines, and our Vietnamese allies to ask them to face increased enemy personnel and firepower without making an effort to try to reduce that infiltration.

Now as to bombing civilians, I would simply say that we are making an effort that is unprecedented in the history of warfare to be sure that we do not. It is our policy to bomb military targets only.

We have never deliberately bombed cities, nor attacked any target with the purpose of inflicting civilian casualties.

We hasten to add, however, that we recognize, and we regret, that some people, even after warning, are living and working in the vicinity of military targets and they have suffered.

We are also too aware that men and machines are not infallible and that some mistakes do occur.

But our record on this account is, in my opinion, highly defensible.

Look for a moment at the record of the other side.

Any civilian casualties that result from our operations are inadvertent, in stark contrast to the calculated Vietcong policy of systematic terror.

Tens of thousands of innocent Vietnamese civilians have been killed, tortured, and kidnaped by the Vietcong. There is no doubt about the deliberate nature of the Vietcong program. One need only note the frequency with which Vietcong victims are village leaders, teachers, health workers, and others who are trying to carry out constructive programs for their people.

Yet, the deeds of the Vietcong go largely unnoted in the public debate. It is this moral double bookkeeping which makes us get sometimes very weary of our critics.

But there is another question that we should answer: Why don't we stop bombing to make it easier to begin negotiations?

The answer is a simple one:

—We stopped for 5 days and 20 hours in May 1965. Representatives of Hanoi simply returned our message in a plain envelope.

—We stopped bombing for 36 days and 15 hours in December 1965 and January 1966. Hanoi only replied: "A political settlement of the Vietnam problem can be envisaged only when the United States Government has accepted the four-point stand of the Government of the Democratic Republic of Vietnam, has proved this by actual deeds, has stopped unconditionally and for good its air raids and all other acts of war against the Democratic Republic of Vietnam."

—And only last month we stopped bombing for 5 days and 18 hours, after many prior weeks in which we had communicated to them several possible routes to peace, any one of which America was prepared to take. Their response, as you know, delivered to His Holiness the Pope, was this: The United States "must put an end to their aggression in Vietnam, end unconditionally and definitively the bombing and all other acts of war against the Democratic Republic of Vietnam, withdraw from South Vietnam all American and satellite troops, recognize the South Vietnamese National Front for Liberation, and let the Vietnamese people settle themselves their own affairs."

That is where we stand today.

They have three times rejected a bombing pause as a means to open the way to ending the war and going to the negotiating table.

The tragedy of South Vietnam is not limited to casualty lists.

There is much tragedy in the story of a nation at war for nearly a generation. It is the story of economic stagnation. It is the story of a generation of young men—the flower of the labor force—pressed into military service by one side or the other.

No one denies that the survival of South Vietnam is heavily dependent upon early economic progress.

My most recent and my most hopeful report of progress in this area came from an old friend of Tennessee, of the Tennessee Valley Authority—David Lilienthal, who recently went as my representative to Vietnam to begin to work with the Vietnamese people on economic planning for that area.

He reported—and with some surprise, I might add—that he discovered an extraordinary air of confidence among the farmers, and the village leaders, and the trade unionists and the industrialists. He concluded that their economic behavior suggests and I quote him, "that they think that they know how this is all going to come out."

Mr. Lilienthal also said that the South Vietnamese were among the hardest working people that he had seen in developing countries around the world, that "to have been through 20 years of war and still have this amount of 'zip' almost ensures their long-term economic development."

Mr. Lilienthal will be going with me to Guam Saturday night to talk with our new leaders about the plans that he will try to institute there.

Our AID programs are supporting the drive toward this sound economy.

But none of these economic accomplishments will be decisive by itself. And no economic achievement can substitute for a strong and free political structure.

We cannot build such a structure—because only the Vietnamese can do that.

And I think they are building it. As I am talking to you here, a freely elected Constituent Assembly in Saigon is now wrestling with the last details of a new constitution, one which will bring the Republic of Vietnam to full membership among the democratic nations of the world.

We expect that constitution to be completed this month.

In the midst of war, they have been building for peace and justice. That is a remarkable accomplishment in the annals of mankind.

Ambassador Henry Cabot Lodge, who has served us with such great distinction, is coming to the end of his second distinguished tour of duty in Saigon.

To replace him, I am drafting as our Ambassador to the Government of Vietnam, Mr. Ellsworth Bunker—able and devoted, full of wisdom and experience acquired on five continents over many years.

As his Deputy, I am nominating and calling from Pakistan, Mr. Eugene Locke, our young and very vigorous Ambassador to Pakistan.

To drive forward with a sense of urgency in our work in pacification, I am sending the President's Special Assistant, Mr. Robert Komer.

To strengthen General Westmoreland in the intense operations that he will be conducting in the months ahead, I am assigning to him additional topflight military personnel, the best that this country has been able to produce.

So you can be confident that in the months ahead we shall have at work in Saigon the ablest, the wisest, the most tenacious, and the most experienced team that the United States of America can mount.

In view of these decisions and in view of the meetings that will take place this weekend, I thought it wise to invite the leaders of South Vietnam to join us in Guam for a part of our discussions, if it were convenient for them. I am gratified to be informed that they have accepted our invitation.

I should also like for you to know that the representatives of all the countries that are contributing troops in Vietnam will be coming to Washington for April 20 and 21 meetings for a general appraisal of the situation that exists.

Now this brings me to my final point, the peaceful and just world that we all seek.

We have just lived through another flurry of rumors of "peace feelers."

Our years of dealing with this problem have taught us that peace will not come easily.

The problem is a very simple one: It takes two to negotiate at a peace table and Hanoi has just simply refused to consider coming to a peace table.

I don't believe that our own position on peace negotiations can be stated any more clearly than I have stated it many times in the past—or than the distinguished Secretary of State, Mr. Rusk, or Ambassador Goldberg, or any number of other officials have stated it in every forum that we could find.

I do want to repeat to you this afternoon—and through you to the people of America—the essentials now, lest there be any doubts.

—United States representatives are ready at any time for discussions of the Vietnam problem or any related matter, with any government or governments, if there is any reason to believe that these discussions will in any way seriously advance the cause of peace.

—We are prepared to go more than halfway and to use any avenue possible to encourage such discussions. And we have done that at every opportunity.

We believe that the Geneva accords of 1954 and 1962 could serve as the central elements of a peaceful settlement. These accords provide, in essence, that both South and North Vietnam should be free from external interference, while at the same time they would be free independently to determine their positions on the question of reunification.

We also stand ready to advance toward a reduction of hostilities, without prior agreement. The road to peace could go from deeds to discussions, or it could start with discussions and go to deeds.

We are ready to take either route. We are ready to move on both of them.

But reciprocity must be the fundamental principle of any reduction in hostilities. The United States cannot and will not reduce its activities unless and until there is some reduction on the other side. To follow any other rule would be to violate the trust that we undertake when we ask a man to risk his life for his country.

We will negotiate a reduction of the bombing whenever the Government of 281 North Vietnam is ready and there are almost innumerable avenues of communication by which the Government of North Vietnam can make their readiness known.

To this date and this hour, there has been no sign of that readiness.

Yet, we must—and we will—keep on trying.

As I speak to you today, Secretary Rusk and our representatives throughout the world are on a constant alert. Hundreds and hundreds of quiet diplomatic conversations, free from the glare of front-page headlines, or of klieg lights, are being held and they will be held on the possibilities of bringing peace to Vietnam.

Governor Averell Harriman, with 25 years of experience of troubleshooting on the most difficult international problems that America has ever had, is carrying out my instructions that every possible lead, however slight it may first appear, from any source, public or private, shall be followed up.

Let me conclude by saying this: I so much wish that it were within my power to assure that all those in Hanoi could hear one simple message—America is committed to the defense of South Vietnam until an honorable peace can be negotiated.

If this one communication gets through and its rational implications are drawn, we should be at the table tomorrow. It would be none too soon for us. Then hundreds of thousands of Americans—as brave as any who ever took the field for their country—could come back home.

And the man who could lead them back is the man that you trained and sent from here, our own beloved, brilliant General "Westy" Westmoreland. As these heroes came back to their homes, millions of Vietnamese could begin to make a decent life for themselves and their families without fear of terrorism, without fear of war, or without fear of Communist enslavement.

That is what we are working and what we are fighting for. We must not—we shall not—and we will not—fail.

Thank you.

NOTE: The President spoke at 12:05 P.M. in the House Chamber of the State Capitol at Nashville. In his opening words he referred to Lieutenant Governor Frank C. Gorrell, Speaker James H. Cummings of the State House of Representatives, and Governor Buford Ellington, all of Tennessee.

Born on the Fourth of July

RON KOVIC

Ron Kovic's autobiography traces the development of a "typical" American boy's evolution from gung-ho marine to opponent of the war—a war that left him permanently paralyzed.

For me it began in 1946 when I was born on the Fourth of July. The whole sky lit up in a tremendous fireworks display and my mother told me the doctor said I was a real firecracker. Every birthday after that was something the whole country celebrated. It was a proud day to be born on.

■ ■ ■

Every Saturday afternoon we'd all go down to the movies in the shopping center and watch gigantic prehistoric birds breathe fire, and war movies with John Wayne and Audie Murphy. Bobbie's mother always packed us a bagful of candy. I'll never forget Audie Murphy in *To Hell and Back*. At the end he jumps on top of a flaming tank that's just about to explode and grabs the machine gun blasting it into the German lines. He was so brave I had chills running up and down my back, wishing it were me up there. There were gasoline flames roaring around his legs, but he just kept firing that machine gun. It was the greatest movie I ever saw in my life.

Castiglia and I saw *The Sands of Iwo Jima* together. The Marine Corps hymn was playing in the background as we sat glued to our seats, humming the hymn together and watching Sergeant Stryker, played by John Wayne, charge up the hill and get killed just before he reached the top. And then they showed the men raising the flag on Iwo Jima with the marines' hymn still playing, and Castiglia and I cried in our seats. I loved the song so much, and every time I heard it I would think of John Wayne and the brave men who raised the flag on Iwo Jima that day. I would think of them and cry. Like Mickey Mantle and the fabulous New York Yankees, John Wayne in *The Sands of Iwo Jima* became one of my heroes.

We'd go home and make up movies like the ones we'd just seen or the ones that were on TV night after night. We'd use our Christmas toys—the Matty Mattel machine guns and grenades, the little green plastic soldiers with guns and flamethrowers in their hands. My favorites were the green plastic men with bazookas. They blasted holes through the enemy. They wiped them out at thirty

feet just above the coffee table. They dug in on the front lawn and survived
countless artillery attacks. They burned with high-propane lighter fluid and a
quarter gallon of gasoline or were thrown into the raging fires of autumn leaves
blasting into a million pieces.

■ ■ ■

The army had a show on Channel 2 called "The Big Picture," and after it was
over Castiglia and I crawled all over the back yard playing guns and army, making
commando raids all summer into Ackerman's housing project blasting away at the
imaginary enemy we had created right before our eyes, throwing dirt bombs and
rocks into the windows, making loud explosions like hand grenades with our
voices then charging in with our Matty Mattel machine guns blazing. I bandaged
up the German who was still alive and had Castiglia question him as I threw a
couple more grenades, killing even more Germans. We went on countless missions and patrols together around my back yard, attacking Ackerman's housing
project with everything from bazookas to flamethrowers and baseball bats. We
studied the Marine Corps Guidebook and Richie brought over some beautiful
pamphlets with very sharp-looking marines on the covers. We read them in my
basement for hours and just as we dreamed of playing for the Yankees someday,
we dreamed of becoming United States Marines and fighting our first war and we
made a solemn promise that year that the day we turned seventeen we were both
going down to the marine recruiter at the shopping center in Levittown and sign
up for the United States Marines Corps.

■ ■ ■

High school was just about over for me and the rest of the guys. We had been
on the block together for almost twelve years, running and moving from Toronto
Avenue to Lee Place to Hamilton Avenue. No one could remember how we all
first got together back then, but we had become friends, "as close as real
brothers," Peter told me one afternoon, and we wanted to believe it would always
be that way.

President Kennedy got killed that last year and we played football in the huge
snowdrifts that had settled on the Long Island streets that afternoon. We played
in silence, I guess because you're supposed to be silent when someone dies. I truly
felt I had lost a dear friend. I was deeply hurt for a long time afterward. We went
to the movies that Sunday. I can't remember what was playing, but how ashamed
I was that I was even there, that people could sit through a movie or have the
nerve to want to go to football games when our president had been killed in Dallas.
The pain stuck with me for a long time after he died. I still remember Oswald
being shot and screaming to my mother to come into the living room. It all seemed
wild and crazy like some Texas shootout, but it was real for all of us back then, it
was very real. I remember Johnson being sworn in on the plane and the fear in the
eyes of the woman judge from Texas. And then the funeral and the casket. I guess
all of us, the whole country, watched it like a big football game. Down the street
the black horses came and his little boy saluting the way he did, the perfect way he
did. Soon after he died there was a memorial picture of him that went up in the
candy store down the block. At the bottom of it it said he had been born in 1917 and

had died in 1963. It stayed up in the candy store on the wall for a long time after we all went to the war.

That spring before I graduated, my father took me down to the shopping center in Levittown and made me get my first job. It was in a supermarket not far from the marine recruiting station. I worked stacking shelves and numbing my fingers and hands unloading cases of frozen food from the trucks. Working with Kenny each day after school, all I could think of, day after day, was joining the marines. My legs and my back ached, but I knew that soon I would be signing the papers and leaving home.

I didn't want to be like my Dad, coming home from the A&P every night. He was a strong man, a good man, but it made him so tired, it took all the energy out of him. I didn't want to be like that, working in that stinking A&P, six days a week, twelve hours a day. I wanted to be somebody. I wanted to make something out of my life.

I was getting older now, I was seventeen, and I looked at myself in the mirror that hung from the back of the door in my room and saw how tall and strong I had suddenly become. I took a deep breath, flexing my muscles, and stared straight into the mirror, turning to the side and looking at myself for a long time.

In the last month of school, the marine recruiters came and spoke to my senior class. They marched, both in perfect step, into the auditorium with their dress blue uniforms and their magnificently shined shoes. It was like all the movies and all the books and all the dreams of becoming a hero come true. I watched them and listened as they stood in front of all the young boys, looking almost like statues and not like real men at all. They spoke in loud voices and one of them was tall and the other was short and very strong looking.

"Good afternoon men," the tall marine said, "We have come today because they told us that some of you want to become marines." He told us that the marines took nothing but the best, that if any of us did not think we were good enough, we should not even think of joining. The tall marine spoke in a very beautiful way about the exciting history of the marines and how they had never lost and America had never been defeated.

"The marines have been the first in everything, first to fight and first to uphold the honor of our country. We have served on distant shores and at home, and we have always come when our country has called. There is nothing finer, nothing prouder, than a United States Marine."

When they were finished, they efficiently picked up their papers and marched together down the steps of the stage to where a small crowd of boys began to gather. I couldn't wait to run down after them, meet with them and shake their hands. And as I shook their hands and stared up into their eyes, I couldn't help but feel I was shaking hands with John Wayne and Audie Murphy. They told us that day that the Marine Corps built men—body, mind, and spirit. And that we could serve our country like the young president had asked us to do.

We were all going in different directions and we had our whole lives ahead of us, and a million different dreams. I can still remember the last stickball game. I stood at home plate with the sun in my face and looked out at Richie, Pete, and the rest. It was our last summer together and the last stickball game we ever played on Hamilton Avenue.

One day that summer I quit my job at the food store and went to the little red, white, and blue shack in Levittown. My father and I went down together. It was

September by the time all the paperwork was completed, September 1964. I was
going to leave on a train one morning and become a marine.

I stayed up most of the night before I left, watching the late movie. Then "The Star-Spangled Banner" played. I remember standing up and feeling very patriotic, chills running up and down my spine. I put my hand over my heart and stood rigid at attention until the screen went blank.

■ ■ ■

I remember we all sort of stopped and watched for a moment. Then all of a sudden the cracks were blasting all around our heads and everybody was running all over the place. We started firing back with full automatics. I emptied a whole clip into the pagoda and the village. I was yelling to the men. I kept telling them to hold their ground and keep firing, though no one knew what we were firing at. I looked to my left flank and all the men were gone. They had run away, all run away to the trees near the river, and I yelled and cursed at them to come back but nobody came. I kept emptying everything I had into the village, blasting holes through the pagoda and ripping bullets into the tree line. There was someone to my right lying on the ground still firing.

I had started walking toward the village when the first bullet hit me. There was a sound like firecrackers going off all around my feet. Then a real loud crack and my leg went numb below the knee. I looked down at my foot and there was blood at the back of it. The bullet had come through the front and blew out nearly the whole of my heel.

I had been shot. The war had finally caught up with my body. I felt good inside. Finally the war was with me and I had been shot by the enemy. I was getting out of the war and I was going to be a hero. I kept firing my rifle into the tree line and boldly, with my new wound, moved closer to the village, daring them to hit me again. For a moment I felt like running back to the rear with my new million-dollar wound but I decided to keep fighting out in the open. A great surge of strength went through me as I yelled for the other men to come out from the trees and join me. I was limping now and the foot was beginning to hurt so much, I finally lay down in almost a kneeling position, still firing into the village, still unable to see anyone. I seemed to be the only one left firing a rifle. Someone came up from behind me, took off my boot and began to bandage my foot. The whole thing was incredibly stupid, we were sitting ducks, but he bandaged my foot and then he took off back into the tree line.

For a few seconds it was silent. I lay down prone and waited for the next bullet to hit me. It was only a matter of time, I thought. I wasn't retreating, I wasn't going back, I was lying right there and blasting everything I had into the pagoda. The rifle was full of sand and it was jamming. I had to pull the bolt back now each time trying to get a round into the chamber. It was impossible and I started to get up and a loud crack went off next to my right ear as a thirty-caliber slug tore through my right shoulder, blasted through my lung, and smashed my spinal cord to pieces.

I felt that everything from my chest down was completely gone. I waited to die. I threw my hand back and felt my legs still there. I couldn't feel them but they were still there. I was still alive. And for some reason I started believing, I started believing I might not die, I might make it out of there and live and feel and

The war in Vietnam was bloody and horrible. All war is, of course, filled with the dead and dying, but the American people saw this war on television in color. How did the Vietnam War change American attitudes toward the role it had played and should play in world affairs?

go back home again. I could hardly breathe and was taking short little sucks with the one lung I had left. The blood was rolling off my flak jacket from the hole in my shoulder and I couldn't feel the pain in my foot anymore, I couldn't even feel my body. I was frightened to death. I didn't think about praying, all I could feel was cheated.

All I could feel was the worthlessness of dying right here in this place at this moment for nothing.

■ ■ ■

Hundreds of rounds begin to crash in now. I stare up at the sky because I cannot move. Above the hole men are running around in every direction. I see their legs and frightened faces. They are screaming and dragging the wounded past me. Again and again the rounds crash in. They seem to be coming in closer and closer. A tall man jumps in, hugging me to the earth.

"Oh God!" he is crying. "Oh God please help us!"

The attack is lifted. They are carrying me out of the hole now—two, three, four men—quickly they are strapping me to a stretcher. My legs dangle off the sides until they realize I cannot control them. "I can't move them," I say, almost in a whisper. "I can't move them." I'm still carefully sucking the air, trying to calm myself, trying not to get excited, not to panic. I want to live. I keep telling myself, Take it slow now, as they strap my legs to the stretcher and carry my wounded body into an Amtrac packed with other wounded men. The steel trapdoor of the Amtrac slowly closes as we begin to move to the northern bank and back across the river to the battalion area.

Men are screaming all around me. "Oh God get me out of here!" "Please help!" they scream. Oh Jesus, like little children now, not like marines, not like the posters, not like that day in the high school, this is for real. "Mother!" screams a man without a face. "Oh I don't want to die!" screams a young boy cupping his intestines with his hands. "Oh please, oh no, oh God, oh help! Mother!" he screams again.

We are moving slowly through the water, the Amtrac rocking back and forth. We cannot be brave anymore, there is no reason. It means nothing now. We hold on to ourselves, to things around us, to memories, to thoughts, to dreams. I breathe slowly, desperately trying to stay awake.

The steel trapdoor is opening. I see faces. Corpsmen, I think. Others, curious, looking in at us. Air, fresh, I feel, I smell. They are carrying me out now. Over wounded bodies, past wounded screams. I'm in a helicopter now lifting above the battalion area. I'm leaving the war. I'm going to live. I am still breathing, I keep thinking over and over, I'm going to live and get out of here.

They are shoving tubes and needles in my arms. Now we are being packed into planes. I begin to believe more and more as I watch the other wounded packed around me on shelves that I am going to live.

I still fight desperately to stay awake. I am in an ambulance now rushing to some place. There is a man without any legs screaming in pain, moaning like a little baby. He is bleeding terribly from the stumps that were once his legs, thrashing his arms wildly about his chest, in a semiconscious daze. It is almost too much for me to watch.

■ ■ ■

I am in this place for seven days and seven nights. I write notes on scraps of paper telling myself over and over that I will make it out of here, that I am going to live. I am squeezing rubber balls with my hands to try to get strong again. I write letters home to Mom and Dad. I dictate them to a woman named Lucy who is with the USO. I am telling Mom and Dad that I am hurt pretty bad but I have done it for America and that it is worth it. I tell them not to worry. I will be home soon.

The day I am supposed to leave has come. I am strapped in a long frame and taken from the place of the wounded. I am moved from hangar to hangar, then finally put on a plane, and I leave Vietnam forever.

Take a Memo, Mr. Smith

ROBIN MORGAN

The national campaign for women's rights has passed through several distinct phases over the last 150 years. In 1848, Elizabeth Cady Stanton and Lucretia Mott organized a convention at Seneca Falls, New York, the first major effort to gain equal political rights for women. About twenty years later, after women had not been granted the vote by the Fifteenth Amendment which enfranchised black men, the Woman's Suffrage Association was founded. The political activity of primarily middle-class women finally led in 1920 to the passage of the Nineteenth Amendment, which finally granted women national voting rights.

The contemporary women's movement emerged from the turbulence of the sixties. Unlike the earlier movement, this phase emphasized a comprehensive change in the relationship between the sexes. Decrying the rigid gender roles that existed even within the protest movement itself, leading activists demanded equal rights in all spheres of women's activities. The following selection, by Robin Morgan, an early leader in the women's movement, equates the struggle of American women with that of oppressed blacks.

Take a memo, Mr. Smith: Madame Nguyen Thi Binh leads the Vietnamese National Liberation Front delegation to the Paris peace negotiations; Indonesian women demonstrate to demand a legal voice in their husbands' taking of second wives; Sweden passes a law creating enforced shorter work hours for men, providing that this extra time is spent in child-raising and household duties; Chiang Ch'ing seems to be more in evidence than Mao; the Episcopal Church considers admitting women to the priesthood; and on and on. And in the United States, the Women's Liberation Movement is becoming more vocal, visible, and active every day.

Women's Liberation in the United States is composed mostly of women from the larger Movement, veterans of civil-rights summers, peace demonstrations, and college sit-ins who became fed up with being handed the same old second-class status *in* the Movement as *out* of it. Women's Liberation has sometimes been accused of more often attacking male chauvinism among Movement men than among Establishment males. But surely even a male reactionary on this issue can realize that it is *really* mind-blowing to hear some young male "revolutionary"— supposedly dedicated to building a new, free social order to replace this vicious one

288

under which we live—turn around and absent-mindedly order his "chick" to shut up and make supper or wash his socks—*he's* talking now. We're used to such attitudes from the average American clod, but from this brave new radical?

In September of 1968, Women's Liberation was ready for its first major action, zapping the Miss America Pageant at Atlantic City. Not resting on any laurels after that, Women's Liberation gave birth to WITCH (Women's International Terrorist Conspiracy from Hell). Aware that witches were the original guerrilla fighters against oppression, and that any woman who was intelligent, articulate, nonconformist, aggressive, or sexually liberated was usually burned at the stake, WITCH took off on, of course, Halloween. WITCH would seem to be the striking arm of the Women's Liberation Movement, and as such is firing women's imagination in totally unrelated places where covens have sprung up and witch guerrilla actions have occurred.

Meanwhile, back in the ghetto-harem of our society, all sorts of different women are digging the Women's Movement. College women are organizing to protest patronizing dorm rules, and to demand courses in women's history. High-school women are demanding the right to take "shop" instead of or as well as "home ec" if they choose, to wear slacks to school, to have an equal voice in high-school student politics. Pacifist women are getting weary of the delicate-smiley-flower image— Grace Paley[1] was the first woman to burn a draft card— and of functioning only as "support groups" for men in the Movement. Women in The Resistance[2] have formed a Women's Liberation group; they've had it with typing and groundless coffee-making, and with being used as sex-object bait for GIs. Black women don't dig the male-supremacy trend in their struggle—black women's liberation groups are forming out of SNCC as well as the Panthers, spurred on, one hears, by Eldridge Cleaver's new jokes about "Pussy Power." Welfare women are already making their voices heard loud and clear.

Like any young movement, we have our problems, and not only the usual ones, like lack of bread, like police harassment; we must also cope with the derision of our oppressors as well as their anger. Yet we know that the sexual mores of this culture dehumanize both men and women. We have energy and ideas and dedication and a double knowledge: that women alone cannot be free unless the system itself is destroyed, freeing *all* people. But we know, too, that no revolution can succeed unless once and for all women can call their bodies their own, unless all our minds are liberated from sexual stereotypes, unless each life is self-determining—truly, not tokenly, free. Join us, sisters!

And a word to the brothers.

You few "male radicals": Civilize your own "communities" (other men); as blacks said to whites, rap with your brothers about the so-called petty ways they continually make women suffer. You're beautiful, and we need you, and you need us. *The revolution begins at home.*

"Male liberals": Watch that you practice what you preach about "digging Women's Liberation." We see through that bullshit when your Hemingway mystique of super-maleness begins to brutalize us.

---

[1] One of the few public women leaders at that time in the peace movement (which was comprised in the rank and filing cabinet mostly of women), and herself a distinguished writer.
[2] The Resistance was a working coalition of anti-war groups, primarily those concerned with supporting draft resisters.

290 And you smug "male reactionary" bigots: Dig it—women are *not* inherently passive or peaceful. We're not inherently anything except human.

Take a memo, Mr. Smith: Like every other oppressed people rising up today, we're out for our freedom—*by any means necessary.*

November 1968

A

B

Some of the advertising copy of a generation ago, particularly that directed toward men, presented a clear picture of women as sexual objects. The advertisement of men's shirts (A) is a blatant example. More subtle is the advertisement for shaving cream (B) that suggests that a man who uses the product will be the cause of intense sexual rivalry among women—with the man's wife making a poor showing in the match. How does such advertising illustrate the point that women of the 1940s and 1950s lacked an identity of their own?

The roles acceptable to many women have changed enormously in your own lifetime. In the 1960s, feminists took to the streets to make their concerns known to the public. But how much has the woman's movement changed national attitudes? Are the majorettes or the feminists more typical of the young women you know? Is it possible to be both a costumed sex symbol and a believer in equality for women?

Triumph and Failure of a Cultural Revolution

GODFREY HODGSON

Probably nothing divided the college-age generation from their parents' generation during the sixties more than drugs and music. Popular music often reflects the concerns and values of the times. In the sixties, this reflection reached unprecedented heights. The folk songs of protest sung by Judy Collins, Joan Baez, and Bob Dylan, among many others, accompanied the idealism and commitment characteristic of the early part of the decade. The arrival of the Beatles and the Rolling Stones began a quick evolution of folk-type music into the hard and blaring rock that carried the messages of the counterculture.

In the following selection, a cultural historian traces the development of drug use and popular music through the decade. He concludes that the political and social interests of the music and the musicians soon gave way to empty hedonism and pretense. Would you agree?

We tell ourselves we are a counterculture. And yet are we really so different from the culture against which we rebel?

Jon Landau, *Rolling Stone*, 1971.

The heyday of the counter culture coincided with the buildup of the Vietnam War from the President's decision to escalate in the spring of 1965 to the Tet offensive of 1968. It also coincided with the climax of racial confrontation, from Selma to the death of Martin Luther King. But if the twin crises in foreign policy and the cities were the occasion of the youth rebellion, the actual process of recruitment to the counter culture probably owed more to three factors that had little enough to do with politics except as symbols—to drugs, to rock music, and to the underground media: the sacrament, the liturgy and the gospel of a religion that failed.

The youth culture liked to remind older Americans that they, too, were insatiable consumers of various stimulants and depressants. That was why young people were so fond of the Rolling Stones' song *Mother's Little Helper*:

292

And though she's not really ill,
There's a little yellow pill.
She goes running for the shelter
Of her "mother's little helper."

There was no getting away from the fact that, lashed on by advertising agencies, distillers, brewers, cigarette manufacturers and pharmaceutical companies, the ordinary American had long thought it perfectly normal to be more or less addicted to alcohol, nicotine, barbiturates and tranquilizers. American physicians were prescribing more and more drugs, and sometimes, indeed, behaving almost as if they were drug salesmen. Neither the U.S. Army nor the CIA, those two pillars of the "straight" society, saw anything wrong with using LSD long before it had become a fashion in the counter culture. The drug culture of the 1960s certainly did not grow out of a society that was totally new to the idea of chemical aids to the pursuit of happiness.

■ ■ ■

This is not, however, either a treatise on pharmacology or a moral tract. From a historical point of view, four drugs or groups of drugs are relevant to the spread of the counter culture: marijuana, the hallucinogens, the amphetamines, and heroin. The use of all of these increased dramatically during the second half of the 1960s.

The amphetamines ("speed") can be dismissed with merciful brevity. "Speed kills," the lore of the drug subculture warned, and it did not exaggerate.

Each of the other three drugs, or groups of drugs, had a special symbolic importance: the hallucinogens, especially "acid" (LSD), for the "hippies," that is, for those who were fully committed to the counter culture; marijuana for the great army of lukewarm converts and partial sympathizers; heroin for its enemies.

From the early days of the Beat Movement, the idea that hallucinogenic drugs could create a new consciousness had been "at the crux of the futurist revolt." In America, it was never in the cards that such an idea could long survive as the prerogative of an initiate elite. If Ginsberg had been the prophet of using chemistry to change consciousness, and Leary the salesman of the idea, its Henry Ford was "Owsley"—a University of California student, grandson of a United States senator from Kentucky, with the sonorous name of Augustus Owsley Stanley III. It was on February 21, 1965, ten days before Operation Rolling Thunder began, and the month before the first teach-in, that Owsley's primitive acid factory in Berkeley was raided. In March he moved to Los Angeles and went into mass production of lysergic acid monohydrate. The business was profitable by any standards: he is said to have paid twenty thousand dollars for the first shipment, of five hundred grams, which was converted into one and a half million tabs at one to two dollars apiece *wholesale*!

With massive supplies of acid guaranteed by this pioneering venture in hip capitalism, the next three years—those same three years of schism from 1965 to 1968, when the war and the urban crisis seemed to be tearing the country in two—saw the illusion that chemistry could free the human mind spin through the full cycle from frenzied hope and bombastic prophecy to panic, paranoia and catastrophe.

In the spring of 1965 the word went out that they had discovered peace and love in San Francisco. To a depressing extent, this was an illusion resulting from the chemical effects of lysergic acid. People tried it, one researcher has concluded, as "a relief from boredom, an enhancement of sentience, a source of fusion, an escape from the sheltered life, an initiation, a way to express anger or withdrawal, an answer to loneliness, a substitute for sex, a moving psychological, philosophical or religious experience, and, most importantly [for] fun." It was all of those things, no doubt. It was also a supreme example of the power of fashion in American life.

The speed with which the craze took hold is a tribute to the needs of a generation that "had everything." It was also a remarkable illustration of the fine-tuned efficiency of the American social machine for distributing *any* new idea, fashion or product.

■ ■ ■

The omens were not favorable. The Summer of Love in 1967 turned into a nightmare. The runaways poured into the Haight-Ashbury and the East Village from every campus and suburb in the United States: the bored, the delinquent, the psychotic, and the mere followers of fashion. They were followed by tourists, journalists, sociologists and undercover agents. And they met bad acid, bad vibrations, uptight cops, Mafia peddlers, chiselers, stranglers, hepatitis and VD.

There was a phrase the acid freaks used about a bad trip: they called it a "horror show." By 1968 the psychedelic paradise itself was turning into a horror show. The older and more serious seekers were horrified at what publicity was doing to their private cult. They began to move out physically from the hippie ghettoes, and to experiment with less instant paths to truth, with communal living, macrobiotic diets, group therapy and transcendental meditation.

One way station on the road out of Haight-Ashbury that summer was Esalen, in the Big Sur country, which emerged as a kind of ashram where a bizarre assembly of sadhus and disciples searched for peace and wisdom with the help of LSD, folk and rock music, naked bathing, Tai Chi exercises and the *Gestalt* therapy of Dr. Fritz Perls as interpreted by Paul Goodman. But even on the sunny cliffs of Big Sur, the quest for truth and beauty was haunted by bad vibrations. One disciple recalls a sinister evening at Esalen that summer when one of the flower children around the campfire was heard to be muttering "Blood! Blood! Blood! Hate! Hate!" And no less a symbol of the dark potentialities of Dionysian rebellion than Charles Manson was lurking around Esalen that same summer.

"If I had to summarize in one word what has happened to the street scene in the last two years," said one literate hippie in 1969, "it would be 'decay.' It's not so much love any more, it's survival." That was the year of the Woodstock festival. Three hundred thousand turned up, and the media discovered the "Woodstock Nation." But in fact, by 1969, the use of hallucinogens had already started to level off among college students in the trend-setting regions, California and the Northeast. Not long afterward college students elsewhere and high school students followed suit. As a pilgrimage in search of new freedom, the great acid trip was over before the end of the sixties.

It was during precisely these same three years, from 1965 to 1968, that marijuana first caught on as a mass habit, first among students and then among young people generally. The first studies of drug use among college students date from 1965. In that year a survey of graduating seniors from Brooklyn College found that only 4.2 per cent had ever used marijuana, and in a sample of graduate students at "a large urban university in Southern California," where the habit was most deeply established, the proportion who had ever tried marijuana was still only 10.7 per cent.

By 1969 the lowest reported incidence of marijuana use in *high schools*, in conservative Utah, was higher than the rate for graduate students in Los Angeles only four years before. By the last week of 1969, a survey of full-time college students on fifty-seven campuses in the United States conducted by The Gallup Organization and reported in *Newsweek* found that 31.9 per cent said that they had used marijuana.

Surveys of students at individual universities reported even higher rates of response: 44 per cent, for example, at Michigan in the autumn of 1969, and 48 per cent at four Massachusetts colleges, one of them Harvard, the following spring. The higher the social class from which young people came and the higher the standing of the college they attended the more likely they were to have tried marijuana. The Massachusetts study found that only 26 per cent of young people between sixteen and twenty-three in jobs had smoked marijuana, as against 48 per cent of those who were in college. And a 1970 survey of students at a wide variety of educational institutions in the Denver-Boulder area of Colorado found that the percentage who had used the drug declined roughly in proportion to the academic and social standing of the college: from 35 per cent at the University of Colorado at Boulder, to 16 per cent at Loretto Heights College, a small local girls' college. While the craze for LSD was beginning to die down, the marijuana habit was steadily spreading to new groups of the youth population.

This remarkable change in taste, involving as it did, at last, the symbolic rejection of many of society's strongest values, was essentially spontaneous. The great majority of those who used marijuana were first given it, for free, by a friend. No large commercial organization for handling the trade and distribution ever seems to have developed. Some 80 per cent of the weed was brought in over the Mexican border. The rest was grown locally, either wild, or in cultivation in Oregon and California communes, city window boxes or, once, with heroic bravado, in the median strip on Park Avenue in New York.

Some small-scale "hip capitalists" did organize shipments of grass from Mexico and of hashish from the Near East and India. But the stereotype of the evil pusher luring adolescents into the grip of addiction for his own profit was always, as far as marijuana was concerned, a myth.

Even an official publication put out by the Nixon administration in 1971, at the height of its crusade to stamp out drugs, conceded, "In general adolescents are introduced to marijuana by others in their groups. There is little evidence to confirm the belief that 'pushers' are needed to 'turn on' a novice. His friends do it for him."

Once a boy or girl had tried marijuana, he or she was automatically a potential recruit for the culture of opposition, not because of the pharmacological effects of the drug but because of its cultural associations and above all because it remained illegal. . . . [T]he human chain effect by which millions of young people were introduced to it by their friends became a powerful recruiting network for the counter culture.

Heroin had never been central to the ideas of the counter culture, as the hallucinogenic drugs were. Nor was it ever anything like as popular as marijuana. The major prophets disapproved of it (though they disapproved more vocally of punishing people for using it), and few hippies used it. A study of the drug subculture in the East Village in 1967, at the height of the acid craze, for example, found that where 100 per cent of those sampled had used marijuana and 90 per cent had used acid, only 13 per cent had ever experimented with heroin. No mass survey of college students ever found that as many as 0.5 per cent admitted to having ever tried heroin.

As an opiate, heroin is a "depressant," a "downer," like alcohol. At best, it induces not excitement or visions but a sense of relaxed satiation. Nobody would ever take it in search of enlightenment; nobody could seriously argue that it expanded the field of human consciousness.

■ ■ ■

Not the least of the ways in which America was divided in this period was by the emotional harmonics of the word "drugs." To millions of younger people, drugs meant first and foremost marijuana, which in turn meant nothing much more than fun. To some few of the intellectuals of the counter culture, drugs meant the hallucinogens, which seemed to offer the hope of achieving a "new consciousness." But to by far the largest number of Americans, drugs meant heroin. And heroin symbolized all they most hated and feared.

■ ■ ■

Throughout the sixties, the changing phases of popular music did coincide uncannily with changing political moods. First came the unworldly moralizing and naïve political idealism of the folk-music movement: Judy Collins, Joan Baez, Pete Seeger, and [Bob] Dylan the folk singer were at the height of their popularity between 1963 and 1965, the years of high hopes for the New Frontier and the Great Society.

Then, in 1965, came rock. The words of the folk songs had been full of radical implications. The singers themselves were men and women of the Left. They sang about peace and war, poverty and injustice, and sometimes, as in *The Times They Are A-Changin'*, they looked forward to the coming of revolution.

The rock singers sometimes sang about revolution, too. But the word meant something different for them from the literal, political revolution of such New York Marxist folk singers as Pete Seeger and Phil Ochs. The music itself was to be the revolution. In the first dizzy years of rock, in 1965 and 1966, and above all in 1967, the promise that intoxicated initiates was that of a wider revolution of consciousness and culture, of which political revolution would come as a by-product.

Rock music is American on both sides of the family if you trace its pedigree far enough. Its technical elements have come down through the commercial rock-and-roll and rhythm-and-blues of the 1950s from the two deepest fountains of

Bob Dylan was one of several American folk singers who inspired young Americans and summed up their dreams and discontents. Is there any singer today who has an impact on the ideas of the young?

American popular music, black blues and white country music. But, in 1965, two traditions fused to create the rock music of the late sixties: one come back to America from Britain, and one out of San Francisco.

Beginning, like so much else, in 1963, first the Beatles, and then a succession of other British pop groups, of whom the Rolling Stones eventually became almost as important as the Beatles themselves, re-exported American popular music to America and proved that their kind of it could be a commercial success on a far bigger scale than the originals it came from. Folk music, rock-and-roll, and urban blues all sold to fractional markets: to campus and coffee house and to the black "race" market. The Beatles' formula, compounded of driving rhythm, sophisticated musical craftsmanship, fresh and often exquisite melody, and literate, irreverent lyrics about real life, unlocked the American youth market as a whole. After the Beatles had made the breach, a host of imitators, British and American, poured through it.

Technical and economic factors contributed to the staggering commercial success of rock music. The improvement in electronic amplifying; the development of eight- and sixteen-track tape recorders; the spread of FM radio; the marketing shift from 45-rpm singles to 33-rpm albums (itself predicated on the new prosperity which meant that even teen-agers were used to spending four dollars on an album once a week or more and could afford elaborate stereo equipment); the rise of such aggressive new recording companies as the Ertegun brothers' Atlantic Records to compete with the stodgy giants of the industry—these made the rock boom possible.

But in the end the phenomenal success of the Beatles was due to psychological compatibility. They came from an Irish working-class background in Liverpool, where irreverence toward all established authority, and especially toward national and military authority, is endemic. They grew up knowing some of the things that young Americans were discovering with pained surprise in the 1960s: that industrial society uses people as well as makes them more affluent, that there is a good deal of hypocrisy about politicians' patriotism, that a lot of middle-class virtue is a sham. When a generation of young Americans emerged from Birmingham and Dallas, Mississippi and Vietnam, into disillusionment and cynicism, the Beatles were waiting there with a grin on their faces. They were as disillusioned and cynical as anyone, but they were cheerful about it; they had never expected that life would be any different.

It would be hard to exaggerate the influence the Beatles had on the generation of Americans who grew up in the sixties. But the Beatles were influenced by America, too, and in particular by the other stream that went into creating the vitality of rock music. That was the San Francisco influence.

In San Francisco in 1965, 1966 and 1967, Jon Landau of *Rolling Stone* has written, "rock was not only viewed as a form of entertainment." It was "an essential component of a 'new culture,' along with drugs and radical politics." That hardly does justice to the fervid claims that were made on behalf of the new music. The leading San Francisco band, The Grateful Dead, was at the very center of the general ferment in the Bay Area in those years. It had played at Ken Kesey's legendary "acid tests." Augustus Owsley Stanley III had personally bought the band its equipment out of his LSD profits. And the Dead had actually lived in a commune in Haight-Ashbury until driven out by the sheer squalor into which that neighborhood declined after 1967. The other San Francisco bands, such as the Jefferson Airplane, shared this "underground" style. In 1967, for their own various reasons, the three unarguable superstars of the new music—Bob Dylan, the Beatles, and the Rolling Stones—all stopped touring America. In their absence, after the Monterey festival of that summer, it was the "underground," San Francisco style that emerged triumphant. Soon even the Beatles were imitating the San Francisco underground style: a peculiar blend of radical political rhetoric, of allusions to the drug culture, and of the excited sense of imminent, apocalyptic liberation. After 1967 the equation between rock music and "revolution" became firmly anchored in the minds of all those who listened to the one or hankered after the other.

It was perhaps always an absurd idea that a new kind of music could change society as Hamelin was changed by the Pied Piper. It was in any case a short-lived idea. The episode which, more than any other, revealed the sheer nastiness that was the antithesis to the claim that rock music was liberating came at the Rolling Stones' concert at Altamont, California, in the last month of the sixties.

It was part of the Stones' carefully polished image to be "their satanic majesties," the naughtiest boys in the world. That winter, they toured the United States. Audiences and critics agreed that their music was as exciting as ever. To end the tour, they planned to give a free concert in San Francisco. It was to be a royal gesture, and at the same time their acknowledgment of the city's role in the culture that had crowned them.

The coronation was as satanic as any press agent could have wished. "Hustlers of every stripe," wrote the relatively sympathetic Michael Lydon in *Ramparts*, "swarmed to the new scene like piranhas to the scent of blood." And so did three hundred thousand for them to prey off. Lydon saw "the dancing beaded girls, the Christlike young men and smiling babies familiar from countless stories on the Love Generation." But another side of the culture was unmistakable, too: "speed freaks with hollow eyes and missing teeth, dead-faced acid-heads burned out by countless flashes, old beatniks clutching gallons of red wine, Hare Krishna chanters with shaved heads and acned cheeks."

Four people died. One, a young man with long hair and a metal cross around his neck, was so stoned that he walked unregarding into an irrigation ditch and drowned. Another was clubbed, stabbed and kicked to death by the Hell's Angels. What were those dangerous pets of the San Francisco *avant-garde* supposed to be doing at the concert? It turned out that they had been hired as "security guards" by the Rolling Stones, on the advice of none other than The Grateful Dead, the original troubadours of love, peace and flowers. "Regrettable," commented the Rolling Stones' manager, "but if you're asking me for a condemnation of the

One characteristic of the 1960s were groups of young people gathering to protest, to sing, to listen, and to share experiences. Their dress and hair style disturbed those of an older generation, but their search for meaning was not new. What do you make of this scene?

Angels . . ." It sounded eerily like President Nixon discussing Lieutenant Calley's conviction for the massacre at My Lai.

"Altamont showed everyone," wrote one of the most levelheaded of the rock critics, Jon Landau, in *Rolling Stone*, "that everything that had been swept under the rug was now coming into the open: the greed, the hustle, the hype. . . ." Only four months earlier, the national media, always quick to seize on some dramatic but complex event and shape its ambiguities into the oversimplified symbol of a new trend, had celebrated the Woodstock Festival as the birth of a new "nation." Then, after Altamont, the boom jibed brutally over onto a new tack. Where the news magazines, the networks and the commentators had managed to ignore the hype, the hustle and even the mud, and had portrayed Woodstock as a midsummer night's dream of idyllic innocence, Altamont was painted as Walpurgisnacht, a witches' sabbath.

Those who were most sympathetic to the counter culture had been aware of its deep and dangerous ambiguities even long before Woodstock. It was as if, wrote Andrew Kopkind, a wholehearted convert to the alternative life style, "some monstrous and marvelous metaphor had come alive, revealing itself only in terms of its contradictions: paradise and concentration camp"—it was quite typical of the fashion of the time in radical journalism to compare a wet weekend with the Final Solution—"sharing and profiteering, sky and mud, love and death. The urges of the ten years' generation roamed the woods and pastures, and who could tell whether it was rough beast or speckled bird slouching through its Day-Glo manger to be born?" For Landau, more realistically, Woodstock was not a new birth but an ending. It was "the ultimate commercialization" of the underground culture at the very moment when it seemed to be in process of being transformed into a mass culture, and perhaps indeed into *the* mass culture. Since it demonstrated "just how strong in numbers the rock audience had become, and just how limited its culture was," he thought Woodstock "a fitting end to the sixties" and the satanic events at Altamont only a parody and an anticlimax.

One reason why it was absurd to equate rock music with revolution, political or cultural, was because it was so very much a commercial product and one that was marketed with single-minded cynicism by individual entrepreneurs and corporate business alike. Behaving in this instance, for once, just as pragmatically as Marxist lore would have predicted, the entertainment industry put up with whatever the musicians and their admirers chose to inflict on it. It tolerated outrageous arrogance, boorishness and unreliability. It raised no demur at long hair on stage and clouds of marijuana in recording studios. It even shelled out royalties far higher than the deferential blacks and crooners who ground out the hits of the past had ever been paid. It would have put up with far more—just so long as the records kept selling. And sell they did.

■ ■ ■

The years from 1965 to 1968 were years of polarization for America partly because they were years of unity for the counter culture. In the beginning, those who played rock music or took LSD, even those who smoked marijuana, bought a rock album or read an underground newspaper, felt themselves part of the same great army as those who went to jail for resisting the draft or dropped out to work for radical political change. Indeed the cultural revolutionaries and the political radicals often were the same people, in the beginning. They had a single enemy, as they saw it in the first, innocent days, whether they called it capitalism, or the System, or Pig Nation, or Amerika. There was a conviction that all rebellions, however trivial or bizarre, were parts of one grand war of liberation against the infanticidal thing that Carl Oglesby, the politician, called Leviathan, and Allen Ginsberg, the poet, called Moloch.

It was in 1967 that the underground papers first began to talk about "the Revolution." The confusion between the political and the cultural was compounded by the popularity of this metaphor. At its silliest, it led to the sad delusion that you could change society by smoking marijuana and listening to amplified electric guitars (provided they were loud enough). Neither Ginsberg's mantras nor the Fugs' chords budged the walls of the Pentagon. It was a revolution that existed only in rhetoric, a linguistic escalation born of the radicals' shame at their impotence to do anything in practice either to help the blacks or to end the war, let alone to change any society but their own.

In political terms, the counter culture's claim to be revolutionary was always tenuous. Even in its political aspect, it was a subjective culture, more interested in the ethics and feelings of its members than in changing the outside world; more concerned for the morality of American policies toward Vietnam, for example, than by the future fate of the actual Vietnamese. Even the political radicals, we saw, had often been formed by a sense of alienation from a society that seemed to have gone tragically wrong in moral terms, rather than by adherence to even the broadest of programs for action.

The schism between political radicals and cultural rebels opened very gradually. As early as 1965 the underground papers were already showing signs of boredom with political issues. In the same year, Dylan, admittedly always a pathfinder, turned from his political ballads to the smoke rings of his mind. Increasingly, those who were serious about political change became exasperated by the dreamy narcissism of those who sought a personal salvation, while those whose hearts were set on a new consciousness and a new style of living were repelled by the obsessional commitments, the squalid compromises, of those whose goal was revolution.

That was one axis: between the search for salvation and the hope of revolution. But there was another sense in which both the heavily committed political radicals and those who took seriously the search for a private salvation were tiny minorities surrounded by the half-serious multitudes of their occasional followers. While an inner minority plunged deeper and deeper into alienation from society either through commitment to political extremism or through withdrawal to the north woods of Oregon or to some Oregon of the mind, for the majority the counter culture soon degenerated into a complex of fashions and attitudes. The fashions and the attitudes were not without powerful symbolic content. It was not for nothing that the mystic signs for peace and love became the most banal decorative motifs. You could even say that if the counter culture failed to change American society in any more definite way, it did make both militarism and racism unfashionable. Still, by the end of the decade, for a majority the counter culture had degenerated into a mere youth cult. Its values were often no longer determined by the aspiration to build a freer society so much as by an Oedipal hostility to the older generation.

302   In a song written by Jim Morrison of The Doors in 1967, and much praised at the time, "the killer" comes to a door (or to a Door?) and looks inside:

"Father?"
"Yes, son?"
"I want to kill you.
"Mother, I want to. . . ."*

"I think kids should kill their parents," said Abbie Hoffman.

The one idea that seemed never to occur to either side in these Freudian wars of the suburbs was how much the parents and the children were alike. The children said they loathed the uniformity of the suburbs, where your personality was defined by the size and style of your house and by the make and year of your car. But they allowed the record industry and the fashion trade to define their collective personality every bit as rigidly as Detroit had ever done for their parents. Their long hair, their blue denim, were every bit as much a uniform as the crew cuts and chinos of the fifties. Even their alienation from their parents may have owed more than they realized to their similarity. If children felt that their parents didn't understand them, it may have been less because of any deep clash of values than because the parents were often too busy having a good time or getting on in the world to spare much time for their children.

Tom Wolfe described how it felt to be a middle-class teen-ager in the fifties, cruising in Dad's car on the new highway on the edge of town, looking for some action:

The first wave of the most extraordinary kids in the history of the world . . . with all this Straight 6 and V-8 power underneath and all this neon glamour overhead, which somehow tied in with the technological superheroics of the jet, TV, atomic subs, ultrasonics—Postwar American suburbs, glorious world! . . . To be Superkids! The world's first generation of the little devils—feeling immune, beyond calamity. One's parents remembered the sloughing common order, War & Depression—but Superkids remembered only the emotional surge of the great payoff, when nothing was common any longer—the Life! A glorious place, a glorious age, I tell you!

The children who were born in those same postwar suburbs and were of college age in 1965 to 1968 did not, perhaps, feel themselves beyond calamity, even though they enjoyed a greater immunity from the sloughing common order than their parents had. They certainly had the conviction that they were "the most extraordinary kids in the history of the world." They were Superkids, Mark II.

By the end of the sixties it was plain enough that whatever the people who flocked to rock concerts or read underground newspapers wanted, it would be doing violence to the language to call it revolution. Their problem was the no-problem society—not of the United States but of the relatively privileged part of American society from which they came. They were bored because there was no problem about money, no problem about sex, no problem about college, and no great problem if you dropped out; only the inescapable bleakness of being young and insignificant, a pebble on the infinite beach of America, but a pebble bombarded with information about the gratifications of others. They turned to the life style of the counter culture for all the things they had missed in the sheltered, affluent suburbs where they grew up: excitement, purpose, a feeling of community, and some measure of individual worth. When Mick Jagger swayed in the spotlight and promised them, "We're gonna get some satisfaction," dams burst. A frightening intensity of emotion flooded normally sulky faces. It was hardly the fault of the musicians if all they had to give was excitement without purpose, an illusion of community, when the individual's yearnings were lost in the contrived explosions of mass hysteria. It wasn't revolution; it was only show business. But, then, bored, lonely, angry though they might intermittently be with a world they never made, the Superkids of the second generation wanted to change it as little as their parents had. Telegraph Avenue was indeed the child of Madison Avenue.

Colleges and universities across the United States felt the impact of the sixties in a variety of ways. On many campuses, demonstrations for and against both local and national events, policies and personalities upset normal routine, often in riotous ways. Students and some faculty members demanded curricular changes that would reflect more "relevant" and current topics, like ethnic studies and foreign policy. In addition, campuses were used for the planning of political activities in the community, including civil rights, antiwar, and feminist protests.

On a different level, campuses also became centers of the counterculture, with all of its untraditional experimentation in sex, drugs, and music.

After reading the selections in this section, compare their conclusions with the experiences of your own campus. Your college library should have student newspapers from the sixties. Most of the faculty will certainly have sharp memories if you ask them about the period. Try to determine how the college was changed. This can be determined by comparing old and new catalogues and talking to deans and chairpersons. Were new programs, courses, and requirements established? Do they survive? What elements of social change introduced then have become permanent aspects of campus life? The office of the dean of students would be a good place to ask this question. In general, what attitudes do the people you talk to have regarding the decade? Write a brief essay comparing the themes of the writers in this section with the conclusions drawn from your own research on the campus.

ASSIGNMENT 7
Testing the Sixties on Campus

The best place to begin the process of sorting out the bewildering cultural, social, and political upheavals of the 1960s is Godfrey Hodgson, *America in Our Time* (1976), part of which is reprinted here. Other books worth consulting are: William O'Neill, *Coming Apart: An Informal History of America in the 1960's* (1971); Morris Dickstein, *Gates of Eden: American Culture in the Sixties* (1977); and Frances FitzGerald, *Fire in the Lake: The Vietnamese and the Americans in Vietnam* (1972).

BIBLIOGRAPHIC NOTE

The Seventies

The seventies were a confusing and bewildering decade for most Americans. The decade opened with massive protests, on college campuses and in the cities, in support of equality and against the war in Vietnam. Symbolically, it closed with the election of Ronald Reagan, who promised to reduce government regulation and reverse the social welfare and reform policies of the New Deal, the New Frontier, and the Great Society.

The war in Vietnam illustrated vividly the tragedy of American foreign policy. Moreover, it revealed that even a great country was limited and ineffective in controlling events in developing nations. Yet at the same time during the decade, American-based multinational corporations gained increasing power in the world's marketplace. On the other hand, many immigrants, both legal and illegal, flocked to our shores drawn by the promise of America. The American Dream was not dead, but American power in the world was not as great as it had once been.

Vietnam, Watergate, the Iranian hostage crisis, and many other incidents cast doubt on the belief that the United States was always right or even that American democracy worked. Yet each crisis stimulated a new patriotic response. By the end of the decade, the Moral Majority, who sought a return to traditional family values, patriotism, and religion, was among the best organized social movements in the

305

twentieth century, and no one could predict what its real influence would be.

Still, many Americans were plagued by a vague anxiety and depression. Some called the seventies the "me decade," that is, people looked after themselves and forgot about social causes. Describing the malaise that affected the country as a "culture of narcissism," historian Christopher Lasch wrote, "Plagued by anxiety, depression, vague discontents, a sense of inner emptiness, the 'psychological man' of the twentieth century seeks neither individual self-aggrandizement nor spiritual transcendence, but peace of mind." Some statistics suggest that there was a return to religion, with an increase in attendance at church and synagogue. At the same time, self-help books and those promising a get-rich-quick scheme led the best seller lists.

The truth was that America was a large and diverse country, and no single generalization can encompass the vast differences that made up the nation. Despite jet liners that spanned the country in a few hours and television programs, fast food chains, and shopping centers that were identical in all parts of the land, the country seemed more divided than it had been in decades. There were moments of intense patriotism, as when the United States hockey team beat the Soviet Union in the Olympics or when the hostages returned home from Iran, but at other times, city seemed pitted against suburb, black against white, sun belt against frost belt, and the poor against the well-to-do. "The Balkanization of America," one critic called it. While there was a rise in ethnic and racial identity and pride, it did not always translate into pride in country.

There was, however, one thing that Americans could usually agree on: they could produce the best machines and solve any technical problem that came along. They had faith in technology, and they were confident that somehow they could out-invent and out-produce the rest of the world. Several events during the decade cast doubt on that belief, however. In the late seventies, it became apparent that Germany and Japan could make better, more efficient, and more dependable automobiles—a fact that was difficult for Americans to accept, for they had always assumed that the auto was their invention. Although Americans could feel pride in being the first to put a man on the moon and the first to devise a space shuttle, no amount of technical expertise seemed to solve the problems of the cities. As pollution hung heavily over most urban areas, there were even a few who wondered if twentieth-century technology would eventually choke everyone to death.

Similarly, Americans had always believed that they lived in a land of abundance, where soil, water, and raw materials were inexhaustible and waste did not matter. In the 1970s, however, two energy crises, brought on by events in the Middle East, caused long lines at the gas stations and cast doubts about our inexhaustible resources. In addition to the gasoline crisis, a shortage of water during some years, even in the Northeast, highlighted the fact that the land and air needed to be protected. For most Americans, these brief episodes probably did not change their faith in American abundance, but a major accident in 1979 at the Three Mile Island Nuclear Power Plant in Pennsylvania frightened everyone and, at least temporarily, cast doubt on the thesis that nuclear power could solve all the energy needs of the future.

A major source of distress in the

1970s was the performance of the economy, which combined relatively low productivity, high unemployment (especially for women, blacks, and youth), and double-digit inflation—a combination that was not supposed to occur, according to the economists. "Stagflation" was the name given to the confusing economic performance, and it was obvious that the world economy and a global marketplace influenced the situation and the lives of every American. On a personal level, it meant that purchasing a home (certainly a part of the American Dream) was out of the question for many people—a result of skyrocketing prices and high interest rates. It also meant that more and more women joined the workforce because a second income was needed to make ends meet. Consequently, jobs became difficult to find for millions of young people.

Women, blacks, and other minorities seemed to make progress during the decade, but there was also a backlash against both the civil rights and women's liberation movements. Despite the war on poverty in the 1960s, a great many people still remained poor, and many of those were over sixty-five, a part of the population that increased rapidly in size during the 1970s.

From the perspective of the early 1980s, the future seems hard to predict, though certain contemporary social trends do provide some clues. Our problems will certainly be compounded by the continuing growth in the number of Americans. Though the birth rate has declined, average life expectancy has increased because of advances in modern medicine. This has resulted not simply in more Americans but in an older society on the average. As a result, some contend, American society may well become more conserva-

tive, less willing to be innovative.

Innovation may be exactly what is needed, however, to meet such pressing social problems as decaying urban areas. The problem of the cities stems largely from another social trend of recent years—middle-class flight from cities to suburbs. For some, such class mobility is the realization of the American Dream. But for those left behind—the poor, many of whom suffer as well from discrimination—it represents a nightmare. Unable to support such basic social services as sanitation, education, hospital care, and police protection because of a declining tax base, the inner-city poor are likely to suffer even more in the future from disease, ignorance, and crime if the trend continues.

In the past, the escape route from such poverty was through education, in order to find a better-paying job. But that route is no longer as open as it once was. Aside from the fact that education has become prohibitively expensive, the economy seems less able today to provide suitable jobs for those who do have an education. The result may be a frozen class structure and a greater spread of income between rich and poor. Ironically, the apparent solution to this problem, more economic expansion, brings with it another whole set of problems—pollution, ecological imbalance, and the exhaustion of finite resources. Material progress is also usually accompanied by various social problems, such as alcoholism and a rise in consumer debt. We may have to trade some potential for upward mobility, then, for a more secure, natural and social environment.

The decades ahead will not be easy ones if contemporary trends are an indication of the future. But Americans are, as a rule, an optimistic lot. For many, the past has been good, and the present is filled with reminders of how far they have come. And few of the dissatisfied seriously entertain the idea of emigrating. However awesome its problems, America remains today, in dream if not in reality, what it meant to most of its immigrants: the New World Eden, with riches to be sought and where humanity would someday perfect itself.

The material in this section seeks to provide you with a basis for defining your relationship with contemporary society. As you read through the articles that sketch the events and trends of the last decade, try to analyze them in terms of how they may affect your own life today or sometime in the future. What leaves you optimistic and what depresses you? Do you agree with some who find the present stimulating and challenging? Or are the critics who predict strife and technological depersonalization more accurate? How has America fared since you were born?

An 18-Year-Old Looks

Back on Life

JOYCE MAYNARD

For many people, the 1970s were a time of disillusionment and despair. This essay, written in 1972 when the author was eighteen, expresses some of that attitude—a feeling of being left out, of spending countless hours watching television and looking forward to retirement. Joyce Maynard represents a generation too young to have been involved in the civil rights and antiwar movements and too old for the more practical and career-oriented activities that con-cerned those who came of age in the late 1970s. Of course, she also represents an upper-class upbringing, and her attitudes differ from those born poor. Is your experience different from hers? Is television as important for your generation as it was for Maynard? Perhaps the computer and other electronic means of communication dominate and control your life in ways that she could not imagine.

Every generation thinks it's special—my grandparents because they remember horses and buggies, my parents because of the Depression. The over-30's are special because they knew the Red Scare of Korea, Chuck Berry and beatniks. My older sister is special because she belonged to the first generation of teen-agers (before that, people in their teens were *adolescents*), when being a teen-ager was still fun. And I—I am 18, caught in the middle. Mine is the generation of unfulfilled expectations. "When you're older," my mother promised, "you can wear lipstick." But when the time came, of course, lipstick wasn't being worn. "When we're big, we'll dance like that," my friends and I whispered, watching Chubby Checker twist on "American Bandstand." But we inherited no dance steps, ours was a limp, formless shrug to watered-down music that rarely made the feet tap. "Just wait till we can vote," I said, bursting with 10-year-old fervor, ready to fast, freeze, march and die for peace and freedom as Joan Baez, barefoot, sang "We Shall Overcome." Well, now we can vote, and we're old enough to attend rallies and knock on doors and wave placards, and suddenly it doesn't seem to matter any more.

My generation is special because of what we missed rather than what we got, because in a certain sense we are the first and the last. The first to take technology

309

An American born in the 1950s who lives to be seventy may watch more than 50,000 hours of television in his or her lifetime. People, regardless of age or class, seem mesmerized by its offerings—no matter how thin. What common need does TV seem to satisfy? What function does it serve for you?

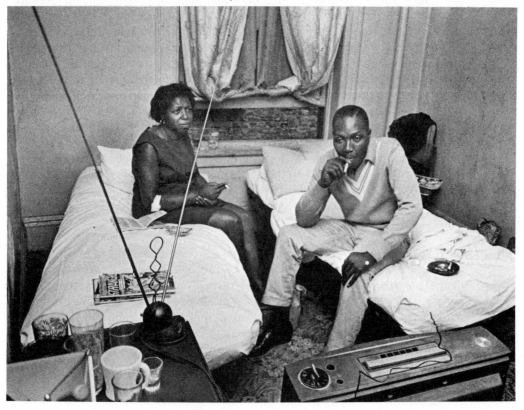

for granted. (What was a space shot to us, except an hour cut from Social Studies to gather before a TV in the gym as Cape Canaveral counted down?) The first to grow up with TV. My sister was 8 when we got our set, so to her it seemed magic and always somewhat foreign. She had known books already and would never really replace them. But for me, the TV set was, like the kitchen sink and the telephone, a fact of life.

We inherited a previous generation's hand-me-downs and took in the seams, turned up the hems, to make our new fashions. We took drugs from the college kids and made them a high-school commonplace. We got the Beatles, but not those lovable look-alikes in matching suits with barber cuts and songs that made you want to cry. They came to us like a bad joke—aged, bearded, discordant. And we inherited the Vietnam war just after the crest of the wave—too late to burn draft cards and too early not to be drafted. The boys of 1953—my year— will be the last to go.

So where are we now? Generalizing is dangerous. Call us the apathetic generation and we will become that. Say times are changing, nobody cares about prom queens and getting into the college of his choice any more—say that (because it sounds good, it indicates a trend, gives a symmetry to history) and you make a movement and a unit out of a generation unified only in its common fragmentation. If there is a reason why we are where we are, it comes from where we have been.

Like overanxious patients in analysis, we treasure the traumas of our childhood. Ours was more traumatic than most. The Kennedy assassination has become our myth: Talk to us for an evening or two—about movies or summer jobs or Nixon's trip to China or the weather—and the subject will come up ("Where were *you* when you heard?"), as if having lived through Jackie and the red roses, John-John's salute and Oswald's on-camera murder justifies our disenchantment.

We haven't all emerged the same, of course, because our lives were lived in high-school corridors and drive-in hamburger joints as well as in the pages of Time and Life, and the images on the TV screen. National events and personal memory blur so that, for me, Nov. 22, 1963, was a birthday party that had to be called off and Armstrong's moonwalk was my first full can of beer. If you want to know who we are now; if you wonder how we'll vote, or whether we will, or whether, 10 years from now, we'll end up just like all those other generations that thought they were special—with 2.2 kids and a house in Connecticut—if that's what you're wondering, look to the past because, whether we should blame it or not, we do.

■ ■ ■

If I had spent at the piano the hours I gave to television, on all those afternoons when I came home from school, I would be an accomplished pianist now. Or if I'd danced, or read, or painted . . . But I turned on the set instead, every day, almost, every year, and sank into an old green easy chair, smothered in quilts, with a bag of Fritos beside me and a glass of milk to wash them down, facing life and death with Dr. Kildare, laughing at Danny Thomas, whispering the answers— out loud sometimes—with "Password" and "To Tell the Truth." Looking back over all those afternoons, I try to convince myself they weren't wasted. I must have learned something; I must, at least, have changed.

What I learned was certainly not what TV tried to teach me. From the reams of trivia collected over years of quiz shows, I remember only the questions, never the answers. I loved "Leave It to Beaver" for the messes Beaver got into, not for the inevitable lecture from Dad at the end of each show. I saw every episode two or three times, witnessed Beaver's aging, his legs getting longer and his voice lower, only to start all over again with young Beaver every fall. (Someone told me recently that the boy who played Beaver Cleaver died in Vietnam. The news was a shock—I kept coming back to it for days until another distressed Beaver fan wrote to tell me that it wasn't true after all.)

I got so I could predict punch lines and endings, not really knowing whether I'd seen the episode before or only watched one like it. There was the bowling-ball routine, for instance: Lucy, Dobie Gillis, Pete and Gladys—they all used it. Somebody would get his finger stuck in a bowling ball (Lucy later updated the gimmick using Liz Taylor's ring) and then they'd have to go to a wedding or give a speech at the P.T.A. or have the boss to dinner, concealing one hand all the while. We weren't supposed to ask questions like "Why don't they just tell the truth?" These shows were built on deviousness, on the longest distance between two points, and on a kind of symmetry which decrees that no loose ends shall be left untied, no lingering doubts allowed. (The Surgeon General is off the track in worrying about TV violence, I think. I grew up in the days before lawmen became peacemakers. What carries over is not the gunfights but the memory that every-thing always turned out all right.) Optimism shone through all those half hours I spent in the dark shadows of the TV room—out of evil shall come good.

Most of all, the situation comedies steeped me in American culture. I emerged from years of TV viewing indifferent to the museums of France, the architecture of Italy, the literature of England. A perversely homebound American, I pick up paperbacks in bookstores, checking before I buy to see if the characters have foreign names, whether the action takes place in London or New York. Vulgarity and banality fascinate me. More intellectual friends (who watch no TV) can't understand what I see in "My Three Sons." "Nothing happens," they say. "The characters are dull, plastic, faceless. Every show is the same." I guess that's why I watch them—boring repetition is, itself, a rhythm—a steady pulse of flashing Coca-Cola signs, McDonald's Golden Arches and Howard Johnson roofs.

I don't watch TV as an anthropologist, rising loftily above my subject to analyze. Neither do I watch, as some kids now tune in to reruns of "The Lone Ranger" and "Superman" (in the same spirit they enjoy comic books and pop art) for their camp. I watch in earnest. How can I do anything else? Five thousand hours of my life have gone into this box.

■　■　■

Ask us whose face is on the $5 bill and we may not know the answer. But nearly everyone my age remembers a cover of Life magazine that came out in the spring of 1965, part of a series of photographs that enter my dreams and my night-mares still. They were the first shots ever taken of an unborn fetus, curled up tightly in a sack of veins and membranes, with blue fingernails and almost transparent skin that made the pictures look like double exposures. More than the moon photographs a few years later, that grotesque figure fascinated me as the map of a new territory. It was often that way with photographs in Life—the issue that reported on the "In Cold Blood" murders; a single picture of a boy falling from an airplane and another of a woman who had lost 200 pounds. (I remember the faces of victims and killers from seven or eight years ago, while the endless issues on Rome and nature studies are entirely lost.)

Photographs are the illustrations for a decade of experiences. Just as, when we think of "Alice in Wonderland," we all see Tenniel's drawings, and when we think of the Cowardly Lion, we all see Bert Lahr, so, when we think of Lyndon Johnson's airborne swearing-in as President in 1963, we have a common image furnished by magazines, and when we think of fetuses, now, those cabbages we were supposed to have come from and smiling, golden-haired cherubs have been replaced forever by the cover of Life. Having had so many pictures to grow up with, we share a common visual idiom and have far less room for personal vision. The movie versions of books decide for us what our heroes and villains will look like, and we are powerless to change the camera's decree. So, while I was stunned and fascinated by that eerie fetus (where is he now, I wonder, and are those pictures in his family album?) I'm saddened too, knowing what it did to me. If I were asked to pinpoint major moments in my growing up, experiences that changed me, the sight of that photograph would be one.

■ ■ ■

Everyone is raised on nursery rhymes and nonsense stories. But it used to be when you grew up, the nonsense disappeared. Not for us—it is at the core of our music and literature and art and, in fact, of our lives. Like characters in an Ionesco play, we take absurdity unblinking. In a world where military officials tell us "We had to destroy the village in order to save it," Dylan lyrics make an odd kind of sense. They aren't meant to be understood; they don't jar our sensibilities because we're used to *non sequiturs*. We don't take anything too seriously these days. (Was it a thousand earthquake victims or a million? Does it matter?) The casual butcher's-operation in the film "M*A*S*H" and the comedy in Vonnegut and the album cover showing John and Yoko, bareback, are all part of the new absurdity. The days of the Little Moron joke and the elephant joke and the knock-knock joke are gone. It sounds melodramatic, but the joke these days is life.

(You're not supposed to care too much any more.) Reactions have been scaled down from screaming and jelly-bean-throwing to nodding your head and maybe— if the music really gets to you (and music's the only thing that does any more)— tapping a finger. (We need a passion transfusion, a shot of energy in the veins. It's what I'm most impatient with, in my generation—this languid, I-don't-give-a-s— —ism) that stems in part, at least, from a culture of put-ons in which any serious expression of emotion is branded sentimental and old-fashioned. The fact that we set such a premium on being cool reveals a lot about my generation; the idea is not to care. You can hear it in the speech of college students today: cultivated monotones, low volume, punctuated with four-letter words that come off sounding only bland. I feel it most of all on Saturday morning, when the sun is shining and the crocuses are about to bloom and, walking through the corridors of my dorm, I see there isn't anyone awake.

■ ■ ■

We feel cheated, many of us—the crop of 1953—which is why we complain about inheriting problems we didn't cause. (Childhood notions of justice, reinforced by Perry Mason, linger on. Why should I clean up someone else's mess? Who can I blame?) We're excited also, of course: I can't wait to see how things turn out. But I wish I weren't quite so involved, I wish it weren't my life that's being turned into a suspense thriller.

When my friends and I were little, we had big plans. I would be a famous actress and singer, dancing on the side. I would paint my own sets and compose my own music, writing the script and the lyrics and reviewing the performance for the New York Times. I would marry and have three children (they don't allow us dreams like that any more) and we would live, rich and famous (donating lots to charity, of course, and periodically adopting orphans), in a house we designed ourselves. When I was older I had visions of good works. I saw myself in South American rain forests and African deserts, feeding the hungry and healing the sick, with an obsessive selflessness, I see now, as selfish, in the end, as my original plans for stardom.

Now my goal is simpler. I want to be happy. And I want comfort—nice clothes, a nice house, good music and good food, and the feeling that I'm doing some little thing that matters. I'll vote and I'll give to charity, but I won't give myself. I feel a sudden desire to buy land—not a lot, not as a business investment, but just a small plot of earth so that whatever they do to the country I'll have a place where I can go—a kind of fallout shelter, I guess. As some people prepare for their old age, so I prepare for my 20's. A little house, a comfortable chair, peace and quiet—retirement sounds tempting.

Global Reach

The Power of the Multinational Corporation

RICHARD J. BARNET AND RONALD E. MULLER

There was a time when America was relatively untouched by events in other parts of the world. But recent history has demonstrated that a revolution in the Middle East, an uprising in Africa, or a famine in Asia affects us in many ways. However, it is not necessary to experience a major catastrophe in order to demonstrate that we are living on a shrinking planet. We buy Toyotas and Volkswagens, clothes made in Hong Kong or Taiwan, and, at the same time, America ships products, from Coca Cola to McDonald's hamburgers, around the world.

In the following essay, Barnet and Muller sketch some ramifications of the growth of multinational corporations and the international marketplace that influence all our lives—whatever we do and wherever we live.

THE WORLD MANAGERS

The men who run the global corporations are the first in history with the organization, technology, money, and ideology to make a credible try at managing the world as an integrated unit. The global visionary of earlier days was either a self-deceiver or a mystic. When Alexander the Great wept by the riverbank because there were no more worlds to conquer, his distress rested on nothing more substantial than the ignorance of his mapmaker. As the boundaries of the known world expanded, a succession of kings, generals, and assorted strong men tried to establish empires of ever more colossal scale, but none succeeded in making a lasting public reality out of private fantasies. The Napoleonic system, Hitler's Thousand Year Reich, the British Empire, and the Pax Americana left their traces, but none managed to create anything approaching a global organization for administering the planet that could last even a generation. The world, it seems, cannot be run by military occupation, though the dream persists.

The managers of the world's corporate giants proclaim their faith that where conquest has failed, business can succeed. "In the forties Wendell Willkie spoke about 'One World,'" says IBM's Jacques G. Maisonrouge. "In the seventies we are inexorably pushed toward it." Aurelio Peccei, a director of Fiat and organizer of

316

Pommes Frites och Hamburgare hör ihop.

Liten dryck 1:25.

Big Mac 4:75   Stor Pommes Frites 2:00

Nu när den svenska höstpotatisen kommer ur jorden, blir Pommes Friten på topp igen. Om man gör den som vi.

Av bästa svenska potatis tar vi de stora och jämna. Skalar, skär och sköljer den noggrant. Blancherar i rätt antal minuter och låter den vila i 2 timmar.

Strax innan den serveras, friterar vi den frasigt gyllene och saltar den lätt. Och bäst av allt — den kostar inte mer än 1:25 för en liten och 2:- för en stor portion.

Men om Du kan hålla Dig, sänker vi priset på vår goda Pommes Frites hela nästa vecka.

Prova Pommes Frites till Hamburgaren nästa gång — det är jättegott ihop.

McDonald's

Hamburgarerestaurang
Kungsgatan 4   Sveavägen 71
Öppet alla dagar 11.00–24.00
Fredag och lördag 11.00–01.00

In almost every city in the world, the traveler is confronted with examples of the influence of American life and products—Coca-Cola, McDonald's hamburgers, American music, films, and blue jeans. Of course, the products of Germany and Japan are familiar in all parts of the United States. This is an advertisement for McDonald's in Swedish. What influence does the international marketplace have on your life?

the Club of Rome, states flatly that the global corporation "is the most powerful agent for the internationalization of human society." "Working through great corporations that straddle the earth," says George Ball, former Under Secretary of State and chairman of Lehman Brothers International, "men are able for the first time to utilize world resources with an efficiency dictated by the objective logic of profit." The global corporation is ushering in a genuine world economy, or what business consultant Peter Drucker calls a "global shopping center," and it is accomplishing this, according to Jacques Maisonrouge, "simply by doing its 'thing,' by doing what came naturally in the pursuit of its legitimate business objectives."

The global corporation is the first institution in human history dedicated to centralized planning on a world scale. Because its primary purpose is to organize and to integrate economic activity around the world in such a way as to maximize global profit, the global corporation is an organic structure in which each part is expected to serve the whole. Thus in the end it measures its successes and its failures not by the balance sheet of an individual subsidiary, or the suitability of particular products, or its social impact in a particular country, but by the growth in global profits and global market shares. Its fundamental assumption is that the growth of the whole enhances the welfare of all the parts. Its fundamental claim is efficiency.

Under the threat of intercontinental rocketry and the global ecological crisis that hangs over all air-breathing creatures, the logic of global planning has become irresistible. Our generation, the first to discover that the resources of the planet may not last forever, has a particular reverence for efficiency. The global corporations, as Maisonrouge puts it, make possible the "use of world resources with a maximum of efficiency and a minimum of waste . . . on a global scale." Rising out of the post–World War II technological explosion which has transformed man's view of time, space, and scale, global corporations are making a bid for political acceptance beyond anything ever before accorded a business organization. The first entrepreneurial class with the practical potential to operate a planetary enterprise now aspires to become global managers.

"For business purposes," says the president of the IBM World Trade Corporation, "the boundaries that separate one nation from another are no more real than the equator. They are merely convenient demarcations of ethnic, linguistic, and cultural entities. They do not define business requirements or consumer trends. Once management understands and accepts this world economy, its view of the marketplace—and its planning—necessarily expand. The world outside the home country is no longer viewed as series of disconnected customers and prospects for its products, but as an extension of a single market."

The rise of the planetary enterprise is producing an organizational revolution as profound in its implications for modern man as the Industrial Revolution and the rise of the nation-state itself. The growth rate of global corporations in recent years is so spectacular that it is now easy to assemble an array of dazzling statistics. If we compare the annual sales of corporations with the gross national product of countries for 1973, we discover that GM is bigger than Switzerland, Pakistan, and South Africa; that Royal Dutch Shell is bigger than Iran, Venezuela, and Turkey; and that Goodyear Tire is bigger than Saudi Arabia. The average growth rate of the most successful global corporations is two to three times that of most advanced industrial countries, including the United States. It is estimated that global corporations already have more than $200 billion in physical assets under their control. But size is only one component of power. In international affairs Mao's dictum that political power grows out of the barrel of a gun shocks no one. To those who question their power, corporate statesmen like to point out that, like the Pope, they have no divisions at their command. The

sources of their extraordinary power are to be found elsewhere—the power to
transform the world political economy and in so doing transform the historic role
of the nation-state. This power comes not from the barrel of a gun but from
control of the means of creating wealth on a worldwide scale. In the process of
developing a new world, the managers of firms like GM, IBM, Pepsico, GE,
Pfizer, Shell, Volkswagen, Exxon, and a few hundred others are making daily
business decisions which have more impact than those of most sovereign governments on where people live; what work, if any, they will do; what they will eat,
drink, and wear; what sorts of knowledge schools and universities will encourage;
and what kind of society their children will inherit.

Indeed, the most revolutionary aspect of the planetary enterprise is not its
size but its worldview. The managers of the global corporations are seeking to put
into practice a theory of human organization that will profoundly alter the nation-
state system around which society has been organized for over 400 years. What
they are demanding in essence is the right to transcend the nation-state, and in
the process, to transform it. "I have long dreamed of buying an island owned by no
nation," says Carl A. Gerstacker, chairman of the Dow Chemical Company, "and
of establishing the World Headquarters of the Dow company on the truly neutral
ground of such an island, beholden to no nation or society. If we were located on
such truly neutral ground we could then really operate in the United States as
U.S. citizens, in Japan as Japanese citizens and in Brazil as Brazilians rather than
being governed in prime by the laws of the United States. . . . We could even pay
any natives handsomely to move elsewhere."

A company spokesman for a principal competitor of Dow, Union Carbide,
agrees: "It is not proper for an international corporation to put the welfare of any
country in which it does business above that of any other." As Charles P.
Kindleberger, one of the leading U.S. authorities on international economics,
puts it, "The international corporation has no country to which it owes more
loyalty than any other, nor any country where it feels completely at home." The
global interests of the world company are, as the British financial writer and
Member of Parliament Christopher Tugendhat has pointed out, separate and
distinct from the interests of every government, including its own government of
origin. Although, in terms of management and ownership, all global corporations
are either American, British, Dutch, German, French, Swiss, Italian, Canadian,
Swedish, or Japanese (most, of course, are American), in outlook and loyalty they
are becoming companies without a country.

It is not hard to understand, however, why American corporate giants, even
those whose presidents must still make do with an office in a Park Avenue
skyscraper instead of a Pacific island, feel that they have outgrown the American
Dream. The top 298 U.S.-based global corporations studied by the Department of
Commerce earn 40 percent of their entire net profits outside the United States. A
1972 study by Business International Corporation, a service organization for
global corporations, shows that 122 of the top U.S.-based multinational corporations had a higher rate of profits from abroad than from domestic operations. In
the office-equipment field, for example, the overseas profit for 1971 was 25.6
percent, compared with domestic profits of 9.2 percent. The average reported
profit of the pharmaceutical industry from foreign operations was 22.4 percent as
against 15.5 percent from operations in the United States. The food industry
reported profits from overseas of 16.7 percent as compared with U.S. profits of

11.5 percent. (Extraordinarily high profit on relatively low overseas investment is not uncommon. In 1972, for example, United Brands reported a 72.1 percent return on net assets, Parker Pen 51.2 percent, Exxon 52.5 percent.) By 1973, America's seven largest banks were obtaining 40 percent of their total profits from abroad, up from 23 percent in 1971.

Department of Commerce surveys show that dependence of the leading U.S.-based corporations on foreign profits has been growing at an accelerating rate since 1964. In the last ten years it has been substantially easier to make profits abroad than in the U.S. economy. The result has been that U.S. corporations have been shifting more and more of their total assets abroad: about one-third of the total assets of the chemical industry, about 40 percent of the total assets of the consumer-goods industry, about 75 percent of those of the electrical industry, about one-third of the assets of the pharmaceutical industry are now located outside the United States. Of the more than $100 billion invested worldwide by the U.S. petroleum industry, roughly half is to be found beyond American shores. Over 30 percent of U.S imports and exports are bought and sold by 187 U.S.-based multinational corporations through their foreign subsidiaries. It is estimated by the British financial analyst Hugh Stephenson that by the mid-1970's, 90 percent of overseas sales of U.S.-based corporations "will be manufactured abroad by American-owned and controlled subsidiaries." "Investment abroad is investment in America" is the new slogan of the global corporations.

Melting Pot

The Latest Pursuers of the American Dream

ACEL MOORE AND MURRAY DUBIN

The American Dream still works for some people in the United States, as this article about a group of recent Korean immigrants in Philadelphia illustrates. If the Koreans can succeed, why do other groups not follow their path out of poverty?

Andrew Im is a Korean. Five years ago, he lived in a second-floor apartment above his Kensington wig shop. Today, he owns a chain of dry cleaners and lives on the Main Line.

Im, 42, is one of a growing number of Korean businessmen and merchants doing business in what are generally considered black commercial areas. On Lancaster Avenue, between 38th and 48th Streets, there are 14 Korean merchants. There are about 20 in the area around Germantown and Chelten Avenues. They are on 52d Street, Ridge Avenue, Columbia Avenue and on the western edge of South Philadelphia.

The rapid influx of Asian merchants (some are Vietnamese, most are Korean) has not been greeted with cheers from black merchants. Instead, there has been suspicion and worry.

"They must be getting SBA loans," says Narva Harris, co-owner of a children's store on 52d Street in West Philadelphia.

"How do these people get financing?" wonders Lenerte Roberts, a real-estate broker at 52d and Arch Streets. "Blacks can't get financing . . . You know, the Cubans have taken over Miami."

It is not only in Philadelphia where groups of Oriental merchants are succeeding conspicuously. Baltimore, New York and other cities in the Northeast have Korean business communities. Blacks in Baltimore were so suspicious of Koreans that they asked U.S. Rep. Parren Mitchell (D., Md.), head of the Congressional Black Caucus, whether they were getting any special federal government help. They weren't.

CONTRADICTS RUMORS

Im, who works in his dry cleaning store on Lancaster Avenue near 40th Street, is amused by the rumors of special aid.

"I work six days a week 6:30 a.m. to 6:30 p.m. I come in on Sunday. I employ

321

A great many immigrants, both legal and illegal, still come to the United States inspired by the dream of success. Why do you think that some, such as this Korean father and son (top), have adapted so well to American life? Why do so many, like this diverse group (bottom), still want to become American citizens?

If I work at my own cleaners, then I save hiring two more. Less overhead. No, I don't take vacations," says Im.

"A black called me 'Korean Jew.' They see me early, they see me late. I make a profit."

Mahn Su Park, who publishes the Korean Guardian newspaper at 4719 N. Broad St., is less amused by the rumors.

"The American people are stupid. They don't see the facts," he says. "If you and your wife work two jobs each, that's four jobs. You don't need a lot of money to start a business. We trust each other, we lend money."

In fact, Im and several other affluent Koreans have begun the Korean Credit Union.

"They pay back like this," Im says, snapping fingers.

Im and Park agree that Koreans coming into the United States usually work at low-paying jobs first, just like European immigrants before them. They usually have some money when they come over and are able to save enough more to soon start a small business. The Korean street vendor with the fruit stand today is the grocery-store owner of tomorrow.

IMMIGRATION LAW

The story of the Philadelphia area's 15,000 Koreans is, in part, a story of U.S. immigration laws.

In 1898, the immigration law was changed to exclude almost all Orientals. That change allowed only 100 people a year from each country. However, Koreans did start trickling in in the late 1940s and early 1950s, mainly because U.S. soldiers began bringing them home as wives.

The law allowed these Korean women to become citizens in three years and then legally petition for close relatives to come over. Those relatives could also become citizens in three years and petition for more relatives to come over. And so on.

In 1968, the law was changed to permit 20,000 immigrants from any Eastern Hemisphere country to enter yearly, with a ceiling of 170,000.

The immigration service keeps statistics on people while they remain aliens but stops once they become citizens. Those statistics, which reflect population trends, show that the only Eastern Hemisphere aliens that outnumbered the Koreans are Indians and Vietnamese.

Raymond Morris, district director of the Immigration and Naturalization Service, says, "There are more Indians here, but they've had a head start because they've been here as students. The Koreans are the fastest growing group in this area. . . .

"They are frugal and live cheaply. The Koreans have no entree into most of the unions and into many kinds of jobs. The little stores are the only things left to them."

"You know, the Chinese go where the language is spoken, but the Koreans live everywhere," he says.

He, like the black merchants, is curious about how Koreans raise the capital for their business ventures.

■ ■ ■

324 Let us return to Andrew Im to learn where his capital came from.

Like many middle-class Koreans, he was taught English in high school in Seoul. His father owns a factory that made laundry soap, not a line of work that interested him. In 1968, he joined more than 15,000 Koreans who took advantage of the change in the immigration law and came to the United States.

He started in the Los Angeles area, trying college first (he had been an accounting major in college in Korea). He didn't like it. Then he worked in a factory, but it went bankrupt. He followed the factory boss to Harrisburg, but didn't like it. Then he went to New York and worked as a bookkeeper for a construction company. Boring.

So he bought some Korean wigs on consignment and sold them, door to door, wig shop to wig shop. He traveled. He did well. He bought more wigs. In 1972, he opened a wig store at Germantown and Lehigh Avenues.

In three years, he had seven stores. He rented the stores, painted and fixed them himself and bought the wigs on consignment. By 1975, he realized that there were more wig stores than hoagie shops in the area and that the market would soon be glutted. So he sold out and began looking for another line of work.

In 1975, he bought the Lancaster Avenue dry cleaners. He had a five-year bank loan, and he says he has already paid it back. He lives with his wife, four daughters and his mother in Bala Cynwyd.

So, that's where Im's capital came from.

"There are no godfathers, no big money men financing everything," he says. "I like to play golf. I only played once in 1977, because I'm too busy. . . ."

Obviously, not all Korean businessmen are as successful as Im. Many are struggling, still living above their shops, but no Korean businesses in the area seem to have failed.

Im says that only about 20 percent of the area's 15,000 Koreans are in businesses, but that it seems like more because the Koreans are so visible. He adds that there are so many in black areas simply because the rents are cheaper. He says he has no problems with his black customers or his competitors.

Im, president of the Korean Businessmen's Association, admits that the Korean community is tightly knit, buying property and stores from anyone but selling only to Koreans. He is trying to help diversify the businesses that Koreans choose.

"I read Sunday papers every week and look at job opportunities so that we can avoid too many wig shops," he says.

Interestingly enough, Im only employs one Korean, his brother. "It takes three months to train someone and they won't last," he says. "Koreans want to own a store, not work in it."

Whites Say I Must Be

on Easy Street

NELL IRVIN PAINTER

Affirmative action programs in the 1960s and 1970s gave blacks, women, and other minorities new opportunities. But these programs did not eliminate prejudice nor did they change attitudes that had built up over many years. Affirmative action also created a backlash and many resentments, as Nell Painter, a writer and historian, points out in this article.

I've always thought affirmative action made a lot of sense, because discrimination against black people and women was prolonged and thorough. But I've been hearing talk in the last several years that lets me know that not everyone shares my views. The first time I noticed it was shortly after I had moved to Philadelphia, where I used to live. One evening I attended a lecture—I no longer remember the topic—but I recall that I arrived early and was doing what I did often that fall. I worked at polishing my dissertation. In those days I regularly carried chapters and a nicely sharpened pencil around with me. I sat with pencil and typescript, scratching out awkward phrases and trying out new ones.

Next to me sat a white man of about 35, whose absorption in my work increased steadily. He watched me intently—kindly—for several moments. "Is that your dissertation?" I said yes, it was. "Good luck in getting it accepted," he said. I said that it had already been accepted, thank you.

Still friendly, he wished me luck in finding a job. I appreciated his concern, but I already had a job. Where? At Penn, for I was then a beginning assistant professor at the University of Pennsylvania. "Aren't you lucky," said the man, a little less generously, "you got a job at a good university." I agreed. Jobs in history were, still are, hard to find.

While cognizant of the job squeeze, I never questioned the justice of my position. I should have a job, and a good one. I had worked hard as a graduate student and had written a decent dissertation. I knew foreign languages, had traveled widely and had taught and published. I thought I had been hired because I was a promising young historian. Unlike the man beside me, I didn't think my teaching at a first-rate university required an extraordinary explanation.

A group of Haitians patiently wait to go ashore in Miami after sailing over a thousand miles in a forty-five-foot boat. Why do these people want so desperately to come to the United States? Does the American Dream work for them?

"I have a doctorate in history," he resumed, "but I couldn't get an academic job." With regret he added that he worked in school administration. I said I was sorry he hadn't been able to find the job he wanted. He said: "It must be great to be black and female, because of affirmative action. You count twice." I couldn't think of an appropriate response to that line of reasoning, for this was the first time I'd met it face to face. I wished the lecture would start. I was embarrassed. Did this man really mean to imply that I had my job at his expense? The edge of competition in his voice made me squirm.

He said that he had received his doctorate from Temple, and yet he had no 327
teaching job, and where was my degree from? "Harvard," I said. It was his time
not to reply. I waited a moment for his answer, then returned to my chapter.

Now I live in North Carolina, but I still hear contradictory talk about affirmative action. Last spring I was having lunch with some black Carolina undergradu-
ates. One young woman surprised me by deploring affirmative action. I wondered
why. "White students and professors think we only got into the University of
North Carolina because we're black," she complained, "and they don't believe
we're truly qualified." She said that she knew that *she* was qualified and fully
deserved to be at Carolina. She fulfilled all the regular admissions requirements.
It was the stigma of affirmative action that bothered her; without it other
students wouldn't assume she was unqualified.

Another student said that the stigma of affirmative action extended to black
faculty as well. She had heard white students doubting the abilities of black
professors. Indeed, she herself tended to wait for black professors to disprove her
assumption that they did not know their fields. She was convinced that without
affirmative action, students would assume black faculty to be as good as white.

That's what I've been hearing from whites and blacks. White people tell me I
must be on easy street because I'm black and female. (I do not believe I've ever
heard that from a black person, although some blacks believe that black women
have an easier time in the white world than black men. I don't think so.) White
people tell me, "You're a twofer." On the other side of the color line, every black
student knows that he or she is fully qualified—I once thought that way myself. It
is just the other black people who need affirmative action to get in. No one, not
blacks, not whites, benefits from affirmative action, or so it would seem.

Well, I have, but not in the early 1960's, when I was an undergraduate in a
large state university. Back then, there was no affirmative action. We applied for
admission to the university like everyone else; we were accepted or rejected like
everyone else. Graduate and undergraduate students together, we numbered
about 200 in a student body of nearly 30,000. No preferential treatment there.

Yet we all knew what the rest of the university thought of us, professors
especially. They thought we were stupid because we were black. Further, white
women were considered frivolous students; they were only supposed to be in
school to get husbands. (I doubt that we few black women even rated a stereotype. We were the ultimate outsiders.) Black students, the whole atmosphere
said, would not attend graduate or professional school because their grades must
be poor. Women had no business in postgraduate education because they would
waste their training by dropping out of careers when they married or became
pregnant. No one said out loud that women and minorities were simply and
naturally inferior to white men, but the assumptions were as clear as day: whites
are better than blacks; men are better than women.

I am one of the few people I know who will admit to having been helped by
affirmative action. To do so is usually tantamount to admitting deficiency. To hear
people talk, affirmative action exists only to employ and promote the otherwise
unqualified, but I don't see it that way at all. I'm black and female, yet I was hired
by two history departments that had no black members before the late 60's, never
mind females. Affirmative action cleared the way.

■　■　■

Thirty-five years ago, John Hope Franklin, then a star student, now a giant in the field of American history, received a doctorate in history from Harvard. He went to teach in a black college. In those days, black men taught in black colleges. White women taught in white women's colleges. Black women taught in black women's colleges. None taught at the University of Pennsylvania or the University of North Carolina. It was the way things were.

Since then, the civil rights movement and the feminist movement have created a new climate that permitted affirmative action, which, in turn, opened areas previously reserved for white men. Skirts and dark skins appeared in new settings in the 1970's, but in significant numbers only after affirmative action mandated the changes and made them thinkable. Without affirmative action, it never would have occurred to any large, white research university to consider me for professional employment, despite my degree, languages, publications, charm, grace, *despite* my qualifications.

My Philadelphia white man and my Carolina black women would be surprised to discover the convergence of their views. I doubt that they know that their convictions are older than affirmative action. I wish I could take them back to the early 60's and let them see that they're reciting the same old white-male-superiority line, fixed up to fit conditions that include a policy called affirmative action. Actually, I will not have to take those people back in time at all, for the Reagan Administration's proposed dismantling of affirmative action fuses the future and the past. If they achieve their stated goals, we will have the same old discrimination, unneedful of new clothes.

Graciela Mendoza Pẽna

Valencia

Mexican Farm Worker

JUNE NAMIAS

Graciela Mendoza Peña Valencia was born in 1944 in a Mexican border town. She came to Los Angeles at the age of fourteen but soon returned to Mexico. Then she commuted to work in El Paso. She is one of perhaps seven million Mexican-Americans living or working in the United States. In addition, there may be as many as three million illegal Mexican aliens in the country. Similarly, there are other illegal immigrants, thousands or perhaps millions, who come every year from Latin America and the Caribbean. We do know that over one million "undocumented workers" were arrested in 1977. The illegal immigrants usually work for low wages, often for cash. Because they need to be anonymous, they rarely collect social security, health, or welfare benefits. They come lured by the American Dream—but they often live underneath America.

February 27, 1976
Salinas, California

My uncle wrote to my parents they have money for me to stay with them in Los Angeles. Is my mother's brother. I was fourteen. That first day I come from Mexico, I come on the bus. The first time I take my valise he said, "OK, first you take bath because I don't want dirt from Mexico." He take me to meet inspection. I don't say nothing. I feel something gonna happen to me after that but I don't say nothing. Sometimes I go to the bathroom and cry because I feel I want to stay in Mexico, not in United States.

I work in the house, but she promised I in school at nights. And this why my mother send me, to study more some English. But when I come here, he not put me in the school or nothing. He said, "I give you money to buy clothes," and he don't give me nothing. I remember the first time the old pants they buy me. Next he give me clothes from my aunt. They don't fit. Old clothes. Sometimes I feel something because I don't have nothing to eat.

Mexican farm workers were among the underclass of once-invisible Americans who emerged in recent protest movements. Led by the charismatic Caesar Chavaz, long-exploited Chicanos struggled for better working conditions and respect. Are they following the similar path of earlier ethnic groups toward middle-class American life and values?

No, because she keep the letters. Once I go to send letter, she opened my letter and read it out. I said, "Mother, I don't want to stay here because they make me this," and she throw the letter. She said, "Oh, your mother don't like you, because you not going to be nothing."

My neighbor, in the backyard she hanging clothes and I saw her and I said, "Maybe I go tell my problems and maybe she gonna help me go back to Mexico." And I go and she help me. She said I could move in and stay with her. I don't have to work in the house, nothing. The first time I go there she give me clean blankets and she give me food. I feel so good, and she take me to the school.

Both my uncle and my aunt found me there in the school. They call the police and the Immigration and they go for me. I was scared because I don't do nothing. Only they take me like this [putting her hands around her wrists]. They put handcuffs on me in the schoolroom. The principal come and speak to them and they take me to the Immigration office in Los Angeles. My uncle said I leave all the kids alone. I say, "No, she went to the store. When she came back I leave the house." I go and tell the neighbor everything. It's the same I tell police. That's why Immigration make my uncle take me to Mexico.

He drive me to Mexico. He not speak to me nothing. She, nothing. At my house they speak to my parents and I don't know what because I in another room. My father protect me. He say, "If she don't want to stay there, it's OK for me. Why they treat not like his family?" And he is mad because it is the brother. My mother feel sorry about, she told me, "You not helped your family."

I say this because I don't want other people to try the family way and friends that they turn bad.

Soon I start to work in Mountain Pass Company. I was sixteen. About three hundred or four hundred work there. Really two or three months we work hard. They need more people. I would cross the border every day. I had to pay a dollar for a day for the two rides from Ciudad Juárez every day to Saint Anthony. Sometimes I leave about 4:30 or 5:00 in the morning. Sometimes I come 10:00 in the night. If I work three or four hours I come back early, or sometimes late. One time I come to my home at 12:00 in the night because I don't have a ride.

We can chilis and tomatoes. The tomato comes with the skin; you cut all tomatoes up. You take all the skin and put in a little can. They put the tomatoes in hot water so I can take off the skin. You have a plastic apron. All your hair back with something. But sometimes the tomato is still soft and spill at your face and clothes. They pay the hour, $1.25. Sometimes I get $150 a week. It is more to clean the chili than the tomatoes. You have to do the same thing, skin the chili. They make the little chilis with four chilis in the can. I do this about two years. Then they said, "Wait for the next year."

I worked in houses in El Paso for four dollar a day. I worked about two years. Sometimes they pay me four dollars, but you need to pay for the trip. Two buses in Mexico and two buses in El Paso. Sometimes is a dollar because is cheap down there. About sixteen cents the trip in Mexico.

I want to come to United States. My parents say, "Wait, you are too young." I wait. Then I am twenty. I saw they needed people to pick strawberries. I went with my friend to contractor in El Paso. The contractor said, "You have never picked strawberries?"

332   "No."

"Oh! That's easy. Have big trees. You just pick the fruit off the trees."

I come here and I see those strawberries on the floor, oh! It's more hard. I came with my friend. When I come here the first day, I saw the big rooms. I feel like I'm going in jail. Only the little beds, no chair, no nothing, only the bed. For a bedspread you got a gray color. I was in a room with twelve people. But you know the big man who rents the camp? They give us a little room for the three, for my two friends and me, because he say, all the three are good people.

It was hot in the fields. First, I never worked in the sun all day, the second because it is too hard. First day I take a break at 12:00 for eat. I want to stay, lay down on the ground because I feel tired. The sun make you all red in the face and everything. That time I don't have no hat or nothing.

I don't work now. Last year I work at celery, in the shed packing. Now, there's more good places to work. If you come here alone first, it's more complicated. When I know the place and everything, I bring my brothers and my mother and my sister. She marry a good man, they got a big house. My brother's got a new car. I was the first one to do farm work in this country. Second, my sisters; next, my brothers. Because if you here first you don't know nothing. When they come here, my husband have a good job and he help my brothers. It's more good to come like that than alone.

I like it here. I am happy with my kids, my husband, the house. My uncle could see it! He say I never do nothing.

Listen America!

JERRY FALWELL

Many believe that the family is the corner-stone of American society, but today some observers suggest that the family, as we have known it, will soon disappear. Statistics seem to support this theory. In 1970, 523,000 couples admitted to the census taker that they were living together without being married. In 1980, the number had almost tripled to 1,560,000. At the same time, those divorced and not yet remarried increased from 47 per 1,000 in 1970 to 100 per 1,000 in 1980. Over 12 million children (20 percent of all children) were living in a household with only one parent in 1980. About one-sixth of the births in the United States in 1979 were to unwed mothers, up from one-tenth in 1970, and in some cities the rate was over 40 percent. The most remarkable statistic in many ways is that, in 1980, 17,800,000 (23 percent of all households) consisted of one person living alone, an increase of 64 percent since 1970.

The changes in the family and in other areas in American life have been the cause of a countermovement that is calling for a return to traditional family values, patriotism, and faith in God. One leader in this countermovement is Jerry Falwell, a Protestant minister and founder of the Moral Majority. In this brief excerpt from his book, Listen America!, *he explores some of his fears and hopes for America.*

I believe the 1980s will be a decade of destiny. During the crucial years of the 1980s it will be determined whether we continue to exist as a free people. It is now past time for the moral people of America to fight against those forces that would destroy our nation. No other nation on the face of the earth has been blessed by God Almighty like the people of the United States of America, but we have taken this for granted for too many years.

It is time that we faced reality. We are in trouble as a nation. We are very quickly moving toward an amoral society where nothing is either absolutely right or absolutely wrong. Our absolutes are disappearing, and with this disappearance we must face the sad fact that our society is crumbling.

I cannot keep silent about the sins that are destroying the moral fiber of our nation. As a minister of the Gospel, I have seen the grim statistics on divorce, broken homes, abortion, juvenile delinquency, promiscuity, and drug addiction. I have witnessed firsthand the human wreckage and the shattered lives that statistics can never reveal in their totality.

With the dissolving of our absolutes, America now has a high crime rate that costs the taxpayer $2 billion a year. In the past 10 years violent crimes have increased 174 per cent in America. Murder is up 129 per cent. Aggravated assault is up 139 per cent. A serious crime is committed every 3.5 seconds. One robbery is committed every 83 seconds. One murder is committed every 27 minutes.

Drug addiction and alcoholism are in pandemic proportions. Suicide is growing at a frightening pace. More than 400,000 heroin addicts live in the United States (60,000 in California alone), and 22 million Americans smoke marijuana. The No. 1 drug and health problem is alcohol, and there are more than 9 million alcoholics in the United States. Retail sales of alcohol in one recent year totaled $32.5 billion.

We have teen-agers who are experimenting with sex in the most vile form, while teen-age pregnancies, incest, and sexual child abuse are rampant problems. Gonorrhea is now contracted by more than 2 million Americans each year. It is the most common infection recorded by public-health officials, and it is increasing so rapidly among the nation's young people that medical authorities are desperately searching for a vaccine against it. About 65,000 women become infertile each year because of its infection.

Dr. Harold M. Voth, M.D., made this statement at the Eagle Forum on October 23, 1977: "It comes as no surprise to me that suicide is a national symptom. These youngsters are lost and are filled with anguish and finally, overcome by despair, they terminate the most precious gift of all—life itself. It is heartbreaking to listen to the outpourings of the young who see what life has to offer but who cannot grab hold and make their own lives go forward. The causes lie within them, and those disturbances were created by imperfect family life. Loneliness is becoming a national illness. People are not just lonely because they are alone. They are lonely because they are empty inside, and that comes from not having had good family life as children."

According to a recent study undertaken by The Johns Hopkins School of Hygiene and Public Health, nearly two thirds of U.S. females (63.3 percent) have premarital sexual intercourse by 19 years of age. It is predicted that teen-age pregnancies are expected to escalate in the 1980s. Early in 1979 the Stanford Research Institute estimated annual welfare costs at $8.3 billion, including all cash-support payments and food outlays by the federal, state, and local governments to households containing teen-aged mothers or women who first become pregnant in their teens.

A thriving new industry floods into the nation's homes through pornographic literature and television programs. Film producers and magazine writers now exploit innocent little children in an attempt to make money from child pornography. It is a fact that more than 20 million sex magazines are sold at our American newsstands every year. The United States will soon be the pornographic capital of the world with 780 X-rated theaters.

America's families are in trouble. America's homes are the stabilizing factors in our society, yet the family is disintegrating at an alarming rate. Nearly 1 out of 2 marriages is ending in divorce, as the divorce rate is now 46 percent. According to the United States Census Bureau more than 1.3 million unmarried couples are living together.

Two thousand American children die annually from child abuse (over 70 percent from injuries inflicted by stepfathers—the result of divorce). *Each day* more than 4,000 unborn babies are destroyed by abortion (over 1 million annual-

Richard Nixon, especially in the campaign of 1972, appealed to the traditional morality of the American middle class against the young and the intellectuals of all ages who opposed the war and who rebelled against the middle-class life style. Ironically, his own Vice-President, Spiro Agnew, was soon forced from office because of bribes and other irregularities. Within two years Nixon himself resigned the Presidency because of the Watergate scandals. Do Americans expect their elected officials to be purer and more moral than they are? Were Nixon and Agnew aberrations or, as some claim, only different because they were caught?

ly). The IRS has made abortion clinics "charitable" organizations, therefore exempt from taxes.

Sin has permeated our land. The Bible states that the pleasures of sin are but for a season. (Heb. 11:25) Those men and women in our United States who are indulging in the grossest of permissive and sexual sins are under the judgment of God. Their pleasure will be but for a very short season. Issues that have to do with the very health and perpetuity of this republic must be dealt with. Solomon wrote in Proverbs, "Righteousness exalteth a nation; but sin is a reproach to any people." (Pr. 14:34) The strength of America has been in her righteousness, in her walk with God. Now we see national sins that are permeating our nation, and we find that our citizens are without remorse, without regret or repentance, and we are not far from judgment of God upon this great nation of ours. With our erosion from the historic faith of our fathers, we are seeing an erosion in our stability as a nation.

■ ■ ■

I am convinced that we need a spiritual and moral revival in America if America is to survive the twentieth century. The time for action is now; we dare not wait for someone else to take up the banner of righteousness in our generation. We have already waited too long. The great American Senator Jesse Helms said: "Each of us has a part to play in bringing about the great spiritual awakening that must come upon this land before we are brought to our knees by the chastisements of God. Each of us must place our hope and reliance in God, and in that hope and reliance turn our energies to restoring a government and society that serve us as sons of God. . . . Faith and courage are not dispensed by civil governments or revolutions, but by the spirit of God. Americans as a people must once again rise up and reclaim their nation from the slothful, divisive, prodigal, and treacherous individuals who have bartered away our freedoms for a mess of pottage . . . we must return to the author of liberty to enjoy again what once we had so abundantly."

We should thank God every day that we were born in a free land. We must pray that God will help us to assume the obligation to guarantee that freedom to the generations that will follow. In a time when freedom is becoming less and less a privilege to the peoples of the world, we cannot value our American citizenship too highly. No one in the world knows the freedoms that Americans know. Those who so often criticize our country with their anti-American, antimilitary, anti-capitalist attitudes must forever realize that the very freedom that allows them to do this is the freedom they are trying to destroy. Let them take anti-Soviet slogans and march up and down the streets of Moscow; they would swiftly disappear.

Right living must be re-established as an American way of life. We as American citizens must recommit ourselves to the faith of our fathers and to the premises and moral foundations upon which this country was established. Now is the time to begin calling America back to God, back to the Bible, back to morality! We must be willing to live by the moral convictions that we claim to believe. There is no way that we will ever be willing to die for something for which we are not willing to live. The authority of Bible morality must once again be recognized as the legitimate guiding principle of our nation. Our love for our fellow man must ever be grounded in the truth and never be allowed to blind us from the truth that is the basis of our love for our fellow man.

The Future of the Family

ALVIN TOFFLER

In the following essay, Alvin Toffler speculates on some ways the family may be altered in the future. If the family really is the cornerstone of democracy what will happen to the country if the family does change?

The family has been called the "giant shock absorber" of society—the place to which the bruised and battered individual returns after doing battle with the world, the one stable point in an increasingly flux-filled environment. As the super-industrial revolution unfolds, this "shock absorber" will come in for some shocks of its own.

Social critics have a field day speculating about the family. The family is "near the point of complete extinction," says Ferdinand Lundberg, author of *The Coming World Transformation*. "The family is dead except for the first year or two of child raising," according to psychoanalyst William Wolf. "This will be its only function." Pessimists tell us the family is racing toward oblivion—but seldom tell us what will take its place.

Family optimists, in contrast, contend that the family, having existed all this time, will continue to exist. Some go so far as to argue that the family is in for a Golden Age. As leisure spreads, they theorize, families will spend more time together and will derive great satisfaction from joint activity. "The family that plays together, stays together," etc.

A more sophisticated view holds that the very turbulence of tomorrow will drive people deeper into their families. "People will marry for stable structure," says Dr. Irwin M. Greenberg, Professor of Psychiatry at the Albert Einstein College of Medicine. According to this view, the family serves as one's "portable roots," anchoring one against the storm of change. In short, the more transient and novel the environment, the more important the family will become.

It may be that both sides in this debate are wrong. For the future is more open than it might appear. The family may neither vanish *nor* enter upon a new Golden Age. It may—and this is far more likely—break up, shatter, only to come together again in weird and novel ways.

The most obviously upsetting force likely to strike the family in the decades immediately ahead will be the impact of the new birth technology. The ability to pre-set the sex of one's baby, or even to "program" its IQ, looks and personality traits, must now be regarded as a real possibility. Embryo implants, babies grown *in vitro*, the ability to swallow a pill and guarantee oneself twins or triplets or, even more, the ability to walk into a "babytorium" and actually purchase embryos—all this reaches so far beyond any previous human experience that one needs to look at the future through the eyes of the poet or painter, rather than those of the sociologist or conventional philosopher.

It is regarded as somehow unscholarly, even frivolous, to discuss these matters. Yet advances in science and technology, or in reproductive biology alone, could, within a short time, smash all orthodox ideas about the family and its responsibilities. When babies can be grown in a laboratory jar what happens to the very notion of maternity? And what happens to the self-image of the female in societies which, since the very beginnings of man, have taught her that her primary mission is the propagation of and nurture of the race?

Few social scientists have begun as yet to concern themselves with such questions. One who has is psychiatrist Hyman G. Weitzen, director of Neuropsychiatric Service at Polyclinic Hospital in New York. The cycle of birth, Dr. Weitzen suggests, "fulfills for most women a major creative need . . . Most women are proud of their ability to bear children . . . The special aura that glorifies the pregnant woman has figured largely in the art and literature of both East and West.

What happens to the cult of motherhood, Weitzen asks, if "her offspring might literally not be hers, but that of a genetically 'superior' ovum, implanted in her womb from another woman, or even grown in a Petri dish?" If women are to be important at all, he suggests, it will no longer be because they alone can bear children. If nothing else, we are about to kill off the mystique of motherhood.

■ ■ ■

If a couple can actually purchase an embryo, then parenthood becomes a legal, not a biological matter. Unless such transactions are tightly controlled, one can imagine such grotesqueries as a couple buying an embryo, raising it *in vitro*, then buying another in the name of the first, as though for a trust fund. In that case, they might be regarded as legal "grandparents" before their first child is out of its infancy. We shall need a whole new vocabulary to describe kinship ties.

Furthermore, if embryos are for sale, can a corporation buy one? Can it buy ten thousand? Can it resell them? And if not a corporation, how about a non-commercial research laboratory? If we buy and sell living embryos, are we back to a new form of slavery? Such are the nightmarish questions soon to be debated by us. To continue to think of the family, therefore, in purely conventional terms is to defy all reason.

Faced by rapid social change and the staggering implications of the scientific revolution, super-industrial man may be forced to experiment with novel family forms. Innovative minorities can be expected to try out a colorful variety of family arrangements. They will begin by tinkering with existing forms.

One simple thing they will do is streamline the family. The typical pre-industrial family not only had a good many children, but numerous other dependents as well—grandparents, uncles, aunts, and cousins. Such "extended" families were well suited for survival in slow-paced agricultural societies. But such families are hard to transport or transplant. They are immobile.

Industrialism demanded masses of workers ready and able to move off the land in pursuit of jobs, and to move again whenever necessary. Thus the extended family gradually shed its excess weight and the so-called "nuclear" family emerged—a stripped-down, portable family unit consisting only of parents and a small set of children. This new style family, far more mobile than the traditional extended family, became the standard model in all the industrial countries.

Super-industrialism, however, the next stage of ecotechnological development, requires even higher mobility. Thus we may expect many among the people of the future to carry the streamlining process a step further by remaining childless, cutting the family down to its most elemental components, a man and a woman.

■ ■ ■

A compromise may be the postponement of children, rather than childlessness. Men and women today are often torn in conflict between a commitment to career and a commitment to children. In the future, many couples will sidestep this problem by deferring the entire task of raising children until after retirement.

This may strike people of the present as odd. Yet once childbearing is broken away from its biological base, nothing more than tradition suggests having children at an early age. Why not wait, and buy your embryos later, after your work career is over? Thus childlessness is likely to spread among young and middle-aged couples; sexagenarians who raise infants may be far more common. The post-retirement family could become a recognized social institution.

BIO-PARENTS AND PRO-PARENTS

If a smaller number of families raise children, however, why do the children have to be their own? Why not a system under which "professional parents" take on the childrearing function for others?

Raising children, after all, requires skills that are by no means universal. We don't let "just anyone" perform brain surgery or, for that matter, sell stocks and bonds. Even the lowest ranking civil servant is required to pass tests proving competence. Yet we allow virtually anyone, almost without regard for mental or moral qualification, to try his or her hand at raising young human beings, so long as these humans are biological offspring. Despite the increasing complexity of the task, parenthood remains the greatest single preserve of the amateur.

■ ■ ■

Parental professionals would not be therapists, but actual family units assigned to, and well paid for, rearing children. Such families might be multi-generational by design, offering children in them an opportunity to observe and learn from a variety of adult models, as was the case in the old farm homestead. With the adults paid to be professional parents, they would be freed of the occupational necessity to relocate repeatedly. Such families would take in new children as old ones "graduate" so that age-segregation would be minimized.

COMMUNES AND HOMOSEXUAL DADDIES

Quite a different alternative lies in the communal family. As transience increases the loneliness and alienation in society, we can anticipate increasing experimentation with various forms of group marriage. The banding together of several adults and children into a single "family" provides a kind of insurance against isolation. Even if one or two members of the household leave, the remaining members have one another. Communes are springing up modeled after those described by psychologist B. F. Skinner in *Walden Two* and by novelist Robert Rimmer in *The Harrad Experiment* and *Proposition 31*. In the latter work, Rimmer seriously proposes the legalization of a "corporate family" in which from three to six adults adopt a single name, live and raise children in common, and legally incorporate to obtain certain economic and tax advantages.

■ ■ ■

Still another type of family unit likely to win adherents in the future might be called the "geriatric commune"—a group marriage of elderly people drawn together in a common search for companionship and assistance. Disengaged from the productive economy that makes mobility necessary, they will settle in a single place, band together, pool funds, collectively hire domestic or nursing help, and proceed—within limits—to have the "time of their lives."

Communalism runs counter to the pressure for ever greater geographical and social mobility generated by the thrust toward super-industrialism. It presupposes groups of people who "stay put." For this reason, communal experiments will first proliferate among those in the society who are free from the industrial discipline— the retired population, the young, the dropouts, the students, as well as among self-employed professional and technical people. Later, when advanced technology and information systems make it possible for much of the work of society to be done at home via computer-telecommunication hookups, communalism will become feasible for larger numbers.

We shall, however, also see many more "family" units consisting of a single unmarried adult and one or more children. Nor will all of these adults be women. It is already possible in some places for unmarried men to adopt children. In 1965 in Oregon, for example, a thirty-eight-year-old musician named Tony Piazza became the first unmarried man in that state, and perhaps in the United States, to be granted the right to adopt a baby. Courts are more readily granting custody to divorced fathers, too. In London, photographer Michael Cooper, married at twenty and divorced soon after, won the right to raise his infant son, and expressed an interest in adopting other children. Observing that he did not

particularly wish to remarry, but that he liked children, Cooper mused aloud: "I
wish you could just ask beautiful women to have babies for you. Or any woman
you liked, or who had something you admired. Ideally, I'd like a big house full of
children—all different colors, shapes and sizes." Romantic? Unmanly? Perhaps.
Yet attitudes like these will be widely held by men in the future.

■ ■ ■

As homosexuality becomes more socially acceptable, we may even begin to
find families based on homosexual "marriages" with the partners adopting children. Whether these children would be of the same or opposite sex remains to be
seen. But the rapidity with which homosexuality is winning respectability in the
techno-societies distinctly points in this direction. In Holland not long ago a
Catholic priest "married" two homosexuals, explaining to critics that "they are
among the faithful to be helped." England has rewritten its relevant legislation;
homosexual relations between consenting adults are no longer considered a
crime. And in the United States a meeting of Episcopal clergymen concluded
publicly that homosexuality might, under certain circumstances, be adjudged
"good." The day may also come when a court decides that a couple of stable, well
educated homosexuals might make decent "parents."

We might also see the gradual relaxation of bars against polygamy. Polyga-
mous families exist even now, more widely than generally believed, in the
midst of "normal" society. Writer Ben Merson, after visiting several such families
in Utah where polygamy is still regarded as essential by certain Mormon fundamentalists, estimated that there are some 30,000 people living in underground
family units of this type in the United States. As sexual attitudes loosen up, as
property rights become less important because of rising affluence, the social
repression of polygamy may come to be regarded as irrational. This shift may be
facilitated by the very mobility that compels men to spend considerable time away
from their present homes. The old male fantasy of the Captain's Paradise may
become a reality for some, although it is likely that, under such circumstances, the
wives left behind will demand extramarital sexual rights. Yesterday's "captain"
would hardly consider this possibility. Tomorrow's may feel quite differently
about it.

Still another family form is even now springing up in our midst, a novel
childrearing unit that I call the "aggregate family"—a family based on relationships between divorced and remarried couples, in which all the children become
part of "one big family." Though sociologists have paid little attention as yet to
this phenomenon, it is already so prevalent that it formed the basis for a hilarious
scene in a recent American movie entitled *Divorce American Style*. We may
expect aggregate families to take on increasing importance in the decades ahead.

Childless marriage, professional parenthood, post-retirement childrearing,
corporate families, communes, geriatric group marriages, homosexual family
units, polygamy—these, then, are a few of the family forms and practices with
which innovative minorities will experiment in the decades ahead. Not all of us,
however, will be willing to participate in such experimentation. What of the
majority?

Minorities experiment; majorities cling to the forms of the past. It is safe to say that large numbers of people will refuse to jettison the conventional idea of marriage or the familiar family forms. They will, no doubt, continue searching for happiness within the orthodox format. Yet, even they will be forced to innovate in the end, for the odds against success may prove overwhelming.

The orthodox format presupposes that two young people will "find" one another and marry. It presupposes that the two will fulfill certain psychological needs in one another, and that the two personalities will develop over the years, more or less in tandem, so that they continue to fulfill each other's needs. It further presupposes that this process will last "until death do us part."

These expectations are built deeply into our culture. It is no longer respectable, as it once was, to marry for anything but love. Love has changed from a peripheral concern of the family into its primary justification. Indeed, the pursuit of love through family life has become, for many, the very purpose of life itself.

Love, however, is defined in terms of this notion of shared growth. It is seen as a beautiful mesh of complementary needs, flowing into and out of one another, fulfilling the loved ones, and producing feelings of warmth, tenderness and devotion. Unhappy husbands often complain that they have "left their wives behind" in terms of social, educational or intellectual growth. Partners in successful marriages are said to "grow together."

This "parallel development" theory of love carries endorsement from marriage counsellors, psychologists and sociologists. Thus, says sociologist Nelson Foote, a specialist on the family, the quality of the relationship between husband and wife is dependent upon "the degree of matching in their phases of distinct but comparable development."

If love is a product of shared growth, however, and we are to measure success in marriage by the degree to which matched development actually occurs, it becomes possible to make a strong and ominous prediction about the future.

It is possible to demonstrate that, even in a relatively stagnant society, the mathematical odds are heavily stacked against any couple achieving this ideal of parallel growth. The odds for success positively plummet, however, when the rate of change in society accelerates, as it now is doing. In a fast-moving society, in which many things change, not once, but repeatedly, in which the husband moves up and down a variety of economic and social scales, in which the family is again and again torn loose from home and community, in which individuals move further from their parents, further from the religion of origin, and further from traditional values, it is almost miraculous if two people develop at anything like comparable rates.

If, at the same time, average life expectancy rises from, say, fifty to seventy years, thereby lengthening the term during which this acrobatic feat of matched development is supposed to be maintained, the odds against success become absolutely astronomical. Thus, Nelson Foote writes with wry understatement: "To expect a marriage to last indefinitely under modern conditions is to expect a lot." To ask love to last indefinitely is to expect even more. Transience and novelty are both in league against it.

It is this change in the statistical odds against love that accounts for the high divorce and separation rates in most of the techno-societies. The faster the rate of change and the longer the life span, the worse these odds grow. Something has to crack.

In point of fact, of course, something has already cracked—and it is the old insistence on permanence. Millions of men and women now adopt what appears to them to be a sensible and conservative strategy. Rather than opting for some offbeat variety of the family, they marry conventionally, they attempt to make it "work," and then, when the paths of the partners diverge beyond an acceptable point, they divorce or depart. Most of them go on to search for a new partner whose developmental stage, at that moment, matches their own.

As human relationships grow more transient and modular, the pursuit of love becomes, if anything, more frenzied. But the temporal expectations change. As conventional marriage proves itself less and less capable of delivering on its promise of lifelong love, therefore, we can anticipate open public acceptance of temporary marriages. Instead of wedding "until death us do part," couples will enter into matrimony knowing from the first that the relationship is likely to be short-lived.

They will know, too, that when the paths of husband and wife diverge, when there is too great a discrepancy in developmental stages, they may call it quits—without shock or embarrassment, perhaps even without some of the pain that goes with divorce today. And when the opportunity presents itself, they will marry again . . . and again . . . and again.

Serial marriage—a pattern of successive temporary marriages—is cut to order for the Age of Transience in which all man's relationships, all his ties with the environment, shrink in duration. It is the natural, the inevitable outgrowth of a social order in which automobiles are rented, dolls traded in, and dresses discarded after one-time use. It is the mainstream marriage pattern of tomorrow.

■ ■ ■

MARRIAGE TRAJECTORIES

As serial marriages become more common, we shall begin to characterize people not in terms of their present marital status, but in terms of their marriage career or "trajectory." This trajectory will be formed by the decisions they make at certain vital turning points in their lives.

For most people, the first such juncture will arrive in youth, when they enter into "trial marriage." Even now the young people of the United States and Europe are engaged in a mass experiment with probationary marriage, with or without benefit of ceremony. The staidest of United States universities are beginning to wink at the practice of co-ed housekeeping among their students. Acceptance of trail marriage is even growing among certain religious philosophers. Thus we hear the German theologian Siegfried Keil of Marburg University urge what he terms "recognized premarriage." In Canada, Father Jacques Lazure has publicly proposed "probationary marriages" of three to eighteen months.

In the past, social pressures and lack of money restricted experimentation with trial marriage to a relative handful. In the future, both these limiting forces will evaporate. Trial marriage will be the first step in the serial marriage "careers" that millions will pursue.

A second critical life juncture for the people of the future will occur when the trial marriage ends. At this point, couples may choose to formalize their relationship and stay together into the next stage. Or they may terminate it and seek out new partners. In either case, they will then face several options. They may prefer to go childless. They may choose to have, adopt or "buy" one or more children. They may decide to raise these children themselves or to farm them out to professional parents. Such decisions will be made, by and large, in the early twenties—by which time many young adults will already be well into their second marriages.

A third significant turning point in the marital career will come, as it does today, when the children finally leave home. The end of parenthood proves excruciating for many, particularly women who, once the children are gone, find themselves without a *raison d'être*. Even today divorces result from the failure of the couple to adapt to this traumatic break in continuity.

Among the more conventional couples of tomorrow who choose to raise their own children in the time-honored fashion, this will continue to be a particularly painful time. It will, however, strike earlier. Young people today already leave home sooner than their counterparts a generation ago. They will probably depart even earlier tomorrow. Masses of youngsters will move off, whether into trial marriage or not, in their mid-teens. Thus we may anticipate that the middle and late thirties will be another important breakpoint in the marital careers of millions. Many at that juncture will enter into their third marriage.

This third marriage will bring together two people for what could well turn out to be the longest uninterrupted stretch of matrimony in their lives—from, say, the late thirties until one of the partners dies. This may, in fact, turn out to be the only "real" marriage, the basis of the only truly durable marital relationship. During this time two mature people, presumably with well-matched interests and complementary psychological needs, and with a sense of being at comparable stages of personality development, will be able to look forward to a relationship with a decent statistical probability of enduring.

Not all these marriages will survive until death, however, for the family will still face a fourth crisis point. This will come, as it does now for so many, when one or both of the partners retire from work. The abrupt change in daily routine brought about by this development places great strain on the couple. Some couples will go the path of the post-retirement family, choosing this moment to begin the task of raising children. This may overcome for them the vacuum that so many couples now face after reaching the end of their occupational lives. (Today many women go to work when they finish raising children; tomorrow many will reverse that pattern, working first and childrearing next.) Other couples will overcome the crisis of retirement in other ways, fashioning both together a new set of habits, interests and activities. Still others will find the transition too

Traditionally, the nuclear family has been the most valued institution in American culture, in theory if not always in reality. Does the family have a future as well as a history? What are the forces in contemporary life that are breaking down its central place in our culture?

difficult, and will simply sever their ties and enter the pool of "in-betweens"—the floating reserve of temporarily unmarried persons.

■ ■ ■

Children in this super-industrial society will grow up with an ever enlarging circle of what might be called "semi-siblings"—a whole clan of boys and girls brought into the world by their successive sets of parents. What becomes of such "aggregate" families will be fascinating to observe. Semi-sibs may turn out to be like cousins, today. They may help one another professionally or in time of need. But they will also present the society with novel problems. Should semi-sibs marry, for example?

Surely, the whole relationship of the child to the family will be dramatically altered. Except perhaps in communal groupings, the family will lose what little remains of its power to transmit values to the younger generation. This will further accelerate the pace of change and intensify the problems that go with it.

BIBLIOGRAPHIC NOTE

The daily newspaper and the journals of opinion may be the best place to find analyses of society in the 1970s, but the following accounts approach our bewildering age from a variety of ideological perspectives: Christopher Lasch, *The Culture of Narcissism: American Life in the Age of Diminishing Expectations* (1979); Peter F. Drucker, *The Age of Discontinuity: Guidelines to Our Changing Society* (1979); Theodore Roszak, *Person-Planet: The Creative Disintegration of Industrial Society* (1978); Lester C. Thurow, *The Zero-Sum Society: Distribution and the Possibilities for Economic Change* (1980); George Gilder, *Wealth and Poverty* (1981). Mary Jo Bane, *Here to Stay: American Families in the Twentieth Century* (1976), argues that despite changes in life style, the family will survive.

Appendix

MATERIALS FOR RESEARCH AND WRITING

The materials in this section should be used only as they are useful to you. The assignments in the text suggest some of the ways that you can use them to your best advantage. You can familiarize yourself with the techniques of researching and writing your family's history by reading the first essay in this section. The questions, charts, and questionnaires that end this section can be used as aids in interviewing family members and writing up results. Do not think that you must fill in every space, answer every question, retrieve every bit of requested information. Instead, select what seems most pertinent to your investigations. As you uncover documents and conduct your oral interviews, return to this section to refresh your memory. Questions, possible areas, and information that you rejected or overlooked the first time through may seem, on second glance, necessary to your work.

RESEARCHING AND WRITING
YOUR FAMILY HISTORY

Below are some suggestions about how to proceed to search for your family history. Not all the suggestions will be useful to you; some suggestions may take longer to apply than the time you have in your class to do your project. But searching for your ancestors and studying your family history can become a lifetime hobby. You, or a member of your family, may want to continue your search after the school year is over.

The task of the historian is to collect as much information as possible about a person, an event, or a movement; to sift the relevant from the irrelevant, to organize the surviving data; and then to interpret the evidence by writing a story that attempts to make sense out of the past. Of course, the past can never be recaptured or reconstructed exactly. The information available is always incomplete and often contradictory, since witnesses remember the same event differently. In addition, each historian approaches the evidence with a particular point of view and purpose. All history is necessarily subjective, therefore, but that is why it is interesting and important.

There is a special thrill in coming across an old letter written when your grandmother was a young girl, in discovering the name of an ancestor in a census record, or in talking about what life was like sixty years ago with a great-aunt. It is a thrill of recognition, a realization that you have made a personal connection with the past. But going beyond that flash of recognition—learning how to interpret and understand this past—is a more difficult task.

A WORD ABOUT TAKING NOTES AND KEEPING RECORDS

As you acquire information about your family, you will need to devise a systematic way to organize your notes. Otherwise, you will end up with many bits and pieces of paper with incomplete information, and you may have a difficult time locating the notes you need. There are several charts and forms in this Appendix, but you will need to supplement them with blank sheets of the same size. If you take all your notes on the same size paper and label each sheet carefully, they will be easier to organize. *Write on only one side of the paper.* This may seem like a waste, but when you spread your notes on a table or even on the floor, writing on the back may easily be lost. *Take notes carefully and be complete.* When you are copying a document or recording data from a gravestone or from a court record, take notes as if you were never going to see the document again—in many cases you probably will not. Make sure you record complete references to the sources you use so that you, or someone else, can retrace your steps. If it is a book, you need the author, place, and date of publication, publisher, the complete title, and the specific pages. If you are using a court document, you usually need a volume number and a number for the document in addition to the date. If it is a gravestone, you might give directions for finding the cemetery. (Locating a single stone in a large cemetery can be an all-day job.) Most libraries and courthouses now have photocopy machines, and for a small charge you can get an exact copy of a document or a page from a book. This saves time and eliminates the possibility of error, but be sure to write the source on each photocopy. Make a list of those sources consulted that contained no information useful to your project. This will prevent a second trip to the same source at a later date. *Above all be careful, be organized, and be clear.*

If you start with yourself, you will discover that you already know something about your family's history (probably more than you realize). When and where were you born? When and where were your brothers and sisters, parents and grandparents born? How many times have you moved? Can you reconstruct in your mind the appearance of the house in which you lived at ten? Where did everyone sleep? Where did the family sit at the table? Taking notes of things you cannot remember may be useful, since you can later ask a relative.

INTERVIEWING RELATIVES

After you have written down all the information about your family that you can remember, it is time to approach other family members—your parents, grandparents, uncles and aunts, or anyone who survives and is able to talk to you. It is

Mid-nineteenth-century daguerreotypes of a newly married couple.

A stereograph view from the 1880s. Often a family posed proudly in front of their house for the photographer. Can you find a similar photo in your collection?

Julia Maloney Sullivan Hughes (1859–1959) was born in County Cork, Ireland, and emigrated to the United States at the age of thirteen, never to return to Ireland. She spent over fifty years "in service" in middle-class homes in and around New York City. Twice widowed, she lived until the age of 100, spending her last thirty years in Oswego, New York, in the home of her daughter Mary and son-in-law James F. Watts. In this picture, taken in the mid-1930s, she holds her grandson, Jim, coeditor of this book.

amazing how much about your family you can learn and how far back in time you can go. If you have a grandmother who is eighty years old and she remembers things her grandmother told her about her childhood, you may be able to recover an oral tradition that goes back to the early part of the nineteenth century. A word of caution is in order before you begin your interviewing.

Interviewing is a delicate art at best. Although it has special benefits, interviewing one's parents and grandparents may also cause special problems. The family should be informed of the purpose of this project so that fears of embarrassment or invasion of privacy can be allayed. Assurance must be given that no use beyond the classroom is contemplated and, if you think it necessary, a commitment can be made for prior clearance before the paper is submitted.

349

Talking to relatives about your family's history can be a rewarding experience, but you should use your judgment and common sense about the most effective way to approach them. The best interviewers are those who have an interest in their subject and have done a careful job of preparation before they begin to interview. You should begin by doing as much research as possible before you conduct your interviews, utilizing what you have learned from the earlier chapters of this book. The next step is to gather as much useful information as you can by asking specific questions of your parents and grandparents: place of birth, date of marriage, grandmother's maiden name, and so on. It is probably better to fill out the questionnaires at the end of this Appendix yourself rather than to ask your relatives to do it, because forms have a tendency to stifle talk. See "Questions to Ask Your Grandmother" on pages 386–387 for some possible subjects to cover in your interviews.

As you move to the more substantive questions, it is usually best to structure your interview loosely. Reading a list of prepared questions will be stilted and formal, so use the suggested questions and topics as guides only. (Of course, being fairly unstructured in your interview does not mean being unprepared.) Try to ask open-ended questions that stimulate, rather than questions that can only be answered by yes or no or questions so broad that they inhibit a response. Thus, instead of asking, "Was the depression economically difficult for you?" try inquiring, "Where did you work and how much were you paid?" Or, instead of the nonspecific question, "Where were you during World War II?" try asking, "What was the single most significant thing that happened to you during the war?" Moreover, a simple question like "What do you remember eating for Sunday dinner when you were a child?" may yield surprising information on family structure, standard of living, the role of religion, and so on. Be ready to ask follow-up questions, and be flexible enough to alter your plan and pursue a topic that you had not considered.

Do not overlook mundane topics, since you may later be able to use the information in your analysis. Seemingly inconsequential details may be of significance—holiday traditions, for instance, or the role of music in the home. If your ancestors were born in hospitals, who paid the bill? If not, who delivered the child, and what reciprocal gestures were expected as a result? In other words, concentrate on the areas of life your relatives know best, not their opinion of world leaders, unless, of course, they actually knew those famous people.

Your major role as interviewer is to listen carefully—not an easy job—and to act as a guide and director of the conversation. Try not to let your own preconceived ideas influence your questions or your responses to answers, and do not assume that your parents and grandparents share your value system. Guard against overly sophisticated questions; try to keep them simple and direct.

If you have a tape recorder readily available, it may prove useful, but tape may not be the best way to record your interviews. The machine, reproducing every detail of what is said, may frighten or inhibit some people. Transcribing the tapes at a later time can also be very difficult. Some interviewers prefer to take brief notes during the interview, and then to write up a summary and impressions immediately afterward. Whatever method you choose for recording your interview, try to make the situation as natural and relaxed as possible. The length of time you can talk at one session will vary, depending on the age and personality of the person to whom you are talking, as well as on your attitude and mood. Most interviewers find that two hours is the absolute maximum for one interview session. Several short sessions may be more effective than one long session, because that gives you time in between to go over what has been accomplished, to fill in gaps, to formulate new questions. If a relative lives a long distance from you, or if all of your sources of information are far away, questions may be sent through the mail. Letters are a poor substitute for face-to-face conversations, however, and consequently the facts-by-mail approach should be supplemented by interviews the next time you return home.

Human memory is often unpredictable and unreliable, especially as people grow older. The documents, pictures, and clippings you have collected should help trigger memories and establish a time sequence. Remember that you are interested in general trends, thoughts, feelings, and overall meaning more than in establishing and confirming each fact. Being a historian is in some ways like playing detective, but beware of overplaying the role. Most families have stories or legends about the family's past that have been passed from one generation to another. It is important to try to separate fact from myth, but legends and stories can also be important. As you proceed in a flexible and open manner, you will learn a great deal. You will also acquire a new understanding and appreciation for your own heritage.

Some useful books on interviewing and oral history are:

1. Brady, John. *The Craft of Interviewing.* Cincinnati, Ohio: Writers Digest, 1976.
2. Gordon, Raymond L. *Interviewing: Strategy, Techniques and Tactics.* Homewood, Ill.: Dorsey Press, 1969.
3. Ives, Edward D. *The Tape-Recorded Interviews: A Manual for Field Workers* in *Folklore and Oral History,* Knoxville: University of Tennessee Press, 1980.
4. Sherwood, Hugh C. *The Journalistic Interview.* New York: Harper & Row, 1972. Designed for the journalist but useful for anyone doing interviewing.
5. Wigginton, Eliot. *Foxfire.* 6 vols. New York: Anchor Press/Doubleday, 1972, 1980. Contains interviews of long-time residents of rural Georgia conducted by high-school students.

SOURCES FOR FAMILY HISTORY IN THE HOME

Most history books are based on research in written records. Diaries, letters, newspapers, and reports are the stuff out of which written history is created. You may never have thought about it, but every family has its own archives where primary sources for family history can be found. You may find papers and memorabilia from the past in an old box, a trunk, a desk drawer, or a file cabinet in your parents' and grandparents' homes. How much has been saved and how useful it is will vary a great deal from one family to another, but in addition to an oral tradition almost all families preserve some of the following written records and physical artifacts.

Birth Records

Not only do birth certificates provide the official record of an individual's date and place of birth, but they often give the age, occupation, and birthplaces of both parents as well as the mother's maiden name. A birth certificate for your father may reveal that the first name he always used was really his middle name, or that your grandfather was born in Ireland and was a carpenter and your mother was born in Massachusetts. There may be an official record of birth in the town or city where you or your ancestor was born. Sometimes, for recent births, you may have to supply proof of relationship to obtain the official document. In some cases, when an official record was not made or the original record has been destroyed, church records, school records, family Bible records, or the testimony of relatives may be taken in place of the official record. Of course, people born in other countries and immigrating at an early age may not know exactly when they were born. If you find a birth certificate that contradicts the information on a cemetery stone or in an obituary, the official birth certificate is usually the more accurate.

Death Certificates

These are also official documents and contain information on parents, including the maiden name of the mother of the deceased, cause of death, and usually place and date of death.

Marriage Certificates

These will give you correct names of both partners, where they were born, and the place and date of marriage. Both death and marriage certificates are recorded and can usually be obtained for a small fee, but first you have to know when and where the event took place.

Naturalization Papers

In addition to the date and place of birth, such papers record the nationality as well as the age, date of arrival in the United States, date of naturalization, and, in some cases, the parents' names. If you cannot find these papers and know that an ancestor was naturalized, it is possible to locate the records, but it is often a difficult task. The records for those naturalized before 1840 are available at the National Archives and at Federal Records Centers. Some other records, especially for the New England states, 1789–1906, are in the National Archives. Records of state and local courts are available in the state archives or occasionally in county court houses. After 1906 there was a regular and complicated procedure established that included a formal petition and examination and a certificate of naturalization. These records are usually difficult to obtain if less than fifty years old. Remember that many immigrants were not naturalized, but that children born in American were automatically citizens.

Discharge Papers from the Armed Forces

These often give date and place of birth or of induction as well as the highest rank achieved, number of years served, military unit, and discharge date and place.

Letters, Diaries, Account Books, etc.

We know a great deal about some American families because they left a large amount of material behind. The Adams family of Massachusetts, for example,

Naturalization papers, a Declaration of Intention to become a citizen, Revolutionary War pension files, even the manifests of slave ships can help us trace our ancestors. Even more, they can help us to imagine what it was like to be alive in another time and place.

which produced two Presidents and several scholars, diplomats, and business-men, left an enormous volume of letters, diaries, and other writings that have enabled historians to reconstruct the family's history in great detail over several generations. The letters of a less famous Georgia family have been published in Robert Manson Myers, ed., *Children of Pride* (New Haven, Conn.: Yale University Press, 1972). Most families have not saved the letters written among family members, but perhaps you will be lucky and come across the love letters written between your grandfather and grandmother before they were married, or the account book kept by an ancestor who was a storekeeper or blacksmith, or the diary of someone who fought in the Civil War. If you should discover some interesting family letters or a diary, you should contact your local or state historical society. Most archives and historical societies are becoming increas-ingly interested in preserving the papers of anonymous people. They might be interested in copying the papers and would usually return the originals to you.

Even if you cannot find a trunk full of old letters, you may be able to find a few items that have been tucked away in a drawer or perhaps in an old book. There might even be some letters written by you when you were a child, or a postcard mailed home by your father.

Family Bibles

Many nineteenth-century families owned a family Bible. Sometimes these were large and elaborate, but at other times they were smaller in size. Often these Bibles contained a place to record births, deaths, and marriages. Usually the family records section was placed between the Old and New Testaments, but it could be in the front or in the back or the entries could be written wherever there was a blank space. You need to be something of a detective to analyze these records. If the dates go back before the date the Bible was printed and all the handwriting is the same, you know they were added later. Someone wrote the information at a later date, probably from memory, and therefore there may be possibilities of inaccuracies. If you find a family Bible in the possession of a relative, ask for a photocopy of the family information for your records. Family Bibles were often used as a hiding place for valuable letters and papers, so look carefully. Family information was often written or pasted into dictionaries and other such books, and these may be profitably investigated as well.

Newspaper Clippings, Deeds, Diplomas, etc.

Many families clip news items that relate to the family—the story of a wedding, an obituary, or perhaps a fiftieth wedding anniversary. Look for these in desk drawers, in scrapbooks, or wherever valuable things are kept in the house. You may also find high-school or Sunday-school certificates or deeds of purchase for a house. There may be old school yearbooks, dance programs, or accounts of sporting events. All of these things had significance for a relative, and if he or she is still alive they may trigger a memory that can lead to an interesting story. Again, do not overlook the books in the house, some of which may have inscrip-tions, notes, or other writings. Cookbooks should not be overlooked. Sometimes cookbooks or recipes may have been passed down from mother to daughter and may give you some idea of the meals served in your grandmother's house.

Family Bibles and, less frequently, samplers are great research prizes, since traditionally they contained basic family records. You should inquire, perhaps of the oldest surviving member of your family, about the record-keeping habits of the past. Is there an old Bible hidden away somewhere? Which of your ancestors did needlework? Have you ever seen a sampler?

Other Objects in the Home

As you browse through the attic or the basement of your own home or that of a grandparent, think of yourself as an archaeologist uncovering the remnants of another civilization. Perhaps you will find an old radio or phonograph, a flatiron that was heated on top of a stove, or a chamber pot and pitcher that recall a day before indoor plumbing. In the basement you may find old canning jars or bottles, possibly a coal hod, or even a horse harness. Maybe your family has preserved quilts or tablecloths from an earlier time, or a sampler that has the record of a family cross-stitched into the cloth. Perhaps there is a silver spoon with initials on it, or a table that was a wedding gift to great-grandparents. Are there pieces of furniture or dishes that have been cherished by several generations? Can you find out the stories that go with them?

The following books may be useful in identifying objects and aiding your thoughts about the way people lived with those objects:

1. Cotter, John. *Aboveground Archeology*. Washington, D.C.: U.S. Government Printing Office, 1975. This is available for 60 cents by writing to the Government Printing Office, Washington, D.C. 20402.
2. Winchester, Alice. *How to Know American Antiques*. New York: Signet, 1951. This work identifies the age and style of furniture and other objects.
3. Munsey, Cecil. *Illustrated Guide to Collecting Bottles*. New York: Hawthorn, 1970.
4. The Sears, Roebuck and Montgomery Ward catalogues. Two have been republished: *1897 Sears Catalogue*. New York: Chelsea House, 1968; and *1927 Sears Catalogue*. New York: Crown, 1970. These may prove useful in identifying objects you find, and they may also help to stimulate the memory of those you are interviewing.
5. Andrew, Wayne. *Architecture, Ambition and Americans*. New York: Harper & Row, 1955. Changing architectural styles are discussed in a lively style.
6. *Life. America's Arts and Skills*. New York: Time-Life Books, 1968. This well-illustrated book includes discussion of architecture, tools, and furniture.

Photographs

Almost every family can document at least a portion of its history with photographs. Some families may even have home movies that date from the 1940s and 1950s. There may be old daguerreotypes or tintypes from the middle of the nineteenth century tucked away in grandfather's bureau drawers. Or there may be some old stereograph photos—two identical images that were viewed through a stereoscope to give the illusion of three dimensions.

Perhaps you can find a family album from the late nineteenth century; such an album, covered with rich red cloth, was usually placed next to the family Bible in

Four generations of women in one family. This photo was taken about 1898 in Chicago. The great-grandmother was born about 1835. How many generations are alive in your family?

Sometimes family documents and photographs get torn and damaged during the crises and turmoil that we all live through. Yet even a torn photograph can bring back memories and become a priceless momento of the past. This is a photo of the Wilkes family of Chester, South Carolina, taken in 1937, before they moved north. It was taken to be sent to Wilkes' daughter who lived with her aunt and had not seen her father or her stepmother in seven years.

the middle-class Victorian home and contained pictures of stern-looking ancestors. The family album was a prized possession in many homes, especially when the family was separated by great distances. Sons and daughters, aunts and uncles moved to the city or to the West, but they could be recalled by studying their pictures. Unfortunately, many families did not take the time to give names to the portraits (since at the time everyone knew who they were), so that today many people are anonymous. There are often many clues for your family history in these albums and perhaps there is a grandmother or great-aunt who will still remember some of the faces. But even if you cannot tell exactly who they are, you can still learn something of their personalities and the time in which they lived by studying the clothes they wore and the poses they affected.

Not every family has preserved nineteenth-century photos, but almost every family has snapshots of twentieth-century events—family picnics, school pictures, weddings. Most families seem to take pictures on vacations or during holidays. Perhaps you can take a lesson from the unlabeled pictures from the past and help your parents or grandparents label their pictures. Even pictures taken over a ten- or twenty-year period will allow you to study changing styles in dress, hair, automobiles, and home furnishings.

Some useful books to consult in interpreting such photos are:

1. Akeret, Robert. *Photoanalysis: How to Interpret the Hidden Psychological Meaning of Personal and Public Photographs.* New York: Pocket Books, 1973.
2. Davies, Thomas L. *Shoots: A Guide to Your Family's Photographic Heritage.* Danbury, N.H.: Addison House, 1977.
3. Green, Jonathan, ed. *The Snapshot.* Millerton, N.Y.: Aperture, 1974.
4. Noren, Catherine Hanf. *The Camera & My Family.* New York: Knopf, 1976.
5. Taft, Robert. *Photography and the American Scene.* 1938. Reprint. New York: Dover, 1964.
6. Welling, William. *Collector's Guide to Nineteenth Century Photographs.* New York: Collier, 1976.

WRITING TO RELATIVES

As you look through your family archives, you may need to write to relatives living in distant places. Be polite, explain why you are interested in information on the family, and what use you are going to make of it. Keep your requests simple, at least in the first letter. Since elderly people often have difficulty with their eyesight, you should probably type or print your letter. Enclose a self-addressed stamped envelope to make the reply as easy as possible.

You may discover in writing to relatives that someone in your family has prepared a genealogy. It may be a few pages of handwritten notes recording births and deaths, or it may be an elaborate, published book tracing many branches of the family to the original immigrant ancestor. But you should not accept the facts as accurate just because they are written or even published. Use whatever information you can find, but check the facts whenever you can and remember that family history is more than genealogy.

SOURCES IN THE COMMUNITY

The best place to start your study of your own family is with yourself and those relatives who are still alive. The next place to go is to the sources preserved by the family. (These two stages can often go on simultaneously.) Eventually you will exhaust the resources of your family archives and you will need to look to more public sources.

Families separated by distance often exchanged snapshots as a means of staying in touch. These were sent by a woman in Nova Scotia, Alice Burns (pictured at left), to her niece Elizabeth in Boston. Her two sons are among the group at right. Perhaps some of your relatives have collected similar shots over the years.

Cemeteries

Gravestones are fascinating to study even if you have no knowledge of the people buried beneath them. The triumphs and tragedies, the human stories of another era, are all preserved in stone. There is a special thrill if you can locate the gravestone of a great-grandparent. In addition, gravestones can sometimes provide valuable genealogical information not available elsewhere. If you know where your ancestors lived (the most important clue for unlocking the secrets of the past generations), you may well be able to find where they are buried, although not everyone was buried near where he or she lived. The smaller the town, city, borough, or parish, or the closer you can pinpoint a residence in a rural county, the easier it will be to find an ancestor's grave. A detailed topographical map will help you in your search, but you still may look through several cemeteries before finding the stones you are looking for. Some you will never find, but the search itself is part of the fun. Gravestones may vary from the simple slate markers of the eighteenth and early nineteenth centuries to the more elaborate and ornamental granite and marble stones of a later period. The inscriptions and carvings can sometimes give you a clue as to the occupation of the deceased and even how he or she died. They can also tell you something about people's religious beliefs and their attitudes toward death in a particular time. Many early stones

Where are your ancestors buried? Are they interred in different places, perhaps indicating the family's migratory history? What information is recorded on the tombstones you have seen? Can simple birth and death dates lead you to such additional information as obituaries, birth certificates, and names and addresses of ancestors?

contained hand-carved death's heads, cherubs, urns, and willows. One early and fairly common rhyme was:

As you are now,
So once was I;
As I am now,
So you must be.
So prepare for death
And follow me.

A popular hobby is gravestone rubbing. You can try this with some very simple equipment, but remember the best results come from the old slate stones (usually those before 1810), though the technique can be used on later stones. You will need a roll of masking tape, a large pad or roll of paper, and a box of black lumber-marking wax crayons. Clean the stone, tape the paper over the stone, and, then, using the side of the crayon, rub until the image comes through.

COPY OF CERTIFICATE OF DEATH
STATE OF VERMONT

DH-VS-5x-25M-53

Certificate No.

1. FULL NAME OF DECEASED (First) (Middle) (Last)	2. DATE OF DEATH (Month) (Day) (Year)
Nellie Sarah Anderson	November 22 - 1954

3. PLACE OF DEATH	4. USUAL RESIDENCE (If institution residence before admission)
a. COUNTY Caledonia	a. STATE Vt. — b. COUNTY Cal
b. CITY OR TOWN (If rural, please state) Lyndonville — c. LENGTH OF STAY (In this place) 4 weeks	c. CITY OR TOWN (If rural, please state) Lyndonville
d. NAME OF HOSPITAL OR INSTITUTION (If not in hospital, give street address) Carlton Basner	d. STREET ADDRESS (If rural, give R. F. D. number)

5. SEX	6. COLOR OR RACE	7. MARITAL STATUS (Check one)	8. DATE OF BIRTH	9. AGE (In years last birthday)	If under 1 year Months Days	If under 24 h Hours Min
Female	White	S☐ M☐ W☒ D☐	May 20-1868	86		

10a. USUAL OCCUPATION (Kind of work done most of working life) Housewife	10b. BUSINESS OR INDUSTRY own home	11. BIRTHPLACE Craftsbury, Vt.	12. CITIZEN OF WHAT COUNTRY U.S.A.

13. FATHER'S NAME Job Allen	15. MOTHER'S MAIDEN NAME June Chase
14. FATHER'S BIRTHPLACE (Town) (State or Country) Burke, Vt.	16. MOTHER'S BIRTHPLACE (Town) (State or Country) Craftsbury	17. NAME OF HUSBAND OR WIF

18. WAS DECEASED EVER IN U.S. ARMED FORCES? (Yes, no, unknown) (Give war & dates of service)	19. SOCIAL SECURITY NO.	20. INFORMANT'S NAME (Person giving this informati Mrs. Lola Latham

Medical Certification

21.			DURATION
I. DISEASE OR CONDITION DIRECTLY LEADING TO DEATH. This does not mean the mode of dying, such as heart failure, asthenia, etc. It means the disease, injury or complications which caused death.	(a) Arterio Sclerosis		
ANTECEDENT CAUSES. Morbid conditions, if any, giving rise to the above cause (a) stating the underlying cause last.	(b) DUE TO		
	(c)		
II. OTHER SIGNIFICANT CONDITIONS (Contributing to the death but not related to disease or condition causing it)			

22. DATE OF OPERATION	22a. MAJOR FINDINGS OF OPERATION	23. AUTOPSY Yes☐ No
24a. ACCIDENT, SUICIDE, HOMICIDE (Specify)	24b. PLACE OF INJURY (In home, farm, factory, street, etc.) — 24c. CITY OR TOWN COUNTY	STATE
24d. TIME OF INJURY (Month, day, year) (hour) m	24e. INJURY OCCURRED While at work ☐ Not at work ☐ — 24f. HOW DID INJURY OCCUR?	

25. I hereby certify that I attended the deceased from July 19 54 to Nov. 22, 19 54 that I last saw deceased a on Nov. 22, 19 54 and that death occurred at 3:20 a m, from the cause and on the date stated above.

26a. SIGNATURE (Degree or Title) A. L. LEONARD M.D.	26b. ADDRESS Lyndonville Vt.	26c. DATE SIGNI 11-22-54
27a. BURIAL, CREMATION, REMOVAL (Specify) Burial	27b. DATE Nov. 24, 1954	27c. NAME OF CEMETERY OR CREMATORY Andersonville	27d. LOCATION (Town or County) (S Glover Vt.
28. DATE REC'D BY TOWN OR CITY CLERK November 22,1954	29. CLERK'S SIGNATURE S. R. LANG (Clerk's signature)	30. FUNERAL DIRECTOR'S SIGNATURE HENRY F. CLAPP, Craftsbury Common, Vt. ADDRESS

Attest: *S. R. Lang* Date: December 22, 1954

A typical death certificate. Notice that you can learn the father's and mother's names and birthplaces from such certificates.

Usually you will have to go over the stone several times. If you prefer to photograph the stones, go over the inscription with white chalk to make it more legible in the picture. A slow, black and white film, such as Kodak Panatomic X, will give you the best results.

Sometimes the data on the gravestone are inaccurate because the stones were erected years after the deaths. You may also discover that the dates are not always exact: "Died in the sixty-eighth year of his age," or "Died at age sixty-seven years, seven months, and two days" are both common inscriptions, Sometimes the cemetery records in the custodian's or the town clerk's office may be more accurate and complete than is the cemetery stone itself. The inscriptions from many cemeteries have been copied and placed in historical societies or in genealogical libraries.

Some useful books in reconnoitering cemeteries are:

1. Newman, John J. *Cemetery Transcribing: Preparations and Procedures*. Technical Leaflet 9. American Association of State and Local History, 1315 Eighth Avenue, South Nashville, Tenn. 37203. 50 cents.
2. Gillon, Edmund Vincent, Jr. *Early New England Gravestone Rubbings*. New York: Dover, 1966.

Vital Records

The official records of birth, marriage, divorce, and death usually are recorded by the town, city, borough, or occasionally the county. Sometimes the older records are compiled and are also available at the library or archives of a state. If you know the town where an ancestor died or was born, you may write for assistance to the town clerk or the city archivist, giving as much information as you have (the more exact the information, the more likely you will be successful). You should always enclose a stamped self-addressed envelope and offer to pay a reasonable fee for the search. If you are not exactly sure where to write, you may write to the Superintendent of Documents, U.S. Government Printing Office, Washington, D.C. 20402 for three pamphlets: *Where to Write for Birth and Death Records*, DHEW Pub. No. HRA 75–1142; *Where to Write for Marriage Records*, DHEW Pub. No. HSM 72–1144; and *Where to Write for Divorce Records*, DHEW Pub. No. HRA 75–1145 (Public Health Service Publications 630A, 630B, 630C). For old records, consult the state-by-state list in an article by Harold Clarke Durrell, *New England Historical and Genealogical Register 90* (January 1936), 9–31. There is also a good list in *How to Trace Your Family Tree* (Garden City: Dolphin, 1975), compiled by the staff of the American Genealogical Research Institute.

Obituaries

Your ancestors may not have been important enough to have an obituary in the *New York Times*, though it may be worth your while to check the *New York Times Index*. Some libraries also have indexes to obituaries in other newspapers, including the *Boston Transcript, 1875–1930*. A more likely source is the local newspaper in the community where your ancestor lived. Ordinary people often are given extensive obituaries in the local press.

Church Records

In many communities, the churches kept records of births, deaths, and marriages, as well as records of who joined the church. Unlike vital records, these are often hard to locate. If you have located a town where an ancestor lived and can find no vital records, try to locate the pastor of the church to which he or she may have belonged. Some church records have been collected. There is a good chapter in Gilbert Doane, *Searching for Your Ancestors* (New York: Bantam, 1974), which lists references and depositories.

The record of the purchase and the sale of land is another valuable source for those tracing the history of their family. Some of the early records also include the former residence of the buyer, and this can be a valuable clue. These records are usually kept at the town or city level, but in some states they may be at the county court house, and the older records may have been collected in the state archives. You may want to write to local or state historical and genealogical societies for additional information. As in the case of vital records and church records, you may discover that many records have been destroyed by fires and other disasters.

Maps

A good map may be an invaluable source for finding where your ancestors lived and for locating cemeteries and villages. The detailed geodetic survey maps available for most parts of the country can be useful. But even more valuable are the old maps kept in historical societies, which can give you information about a town or city as it existed a century ago. Sometimes these maps include the owner of a farm or store and, in a city, the numbers for each block.

Wills and Probate Records

Various documents in probate courts (usually at the county courthouse in the county where your ancestors lived) can be useful in tracing your family and finding interesting information about them. Wills and papers relating to the settling of an estate usually give the names of the heirs, but along with the probate records there often are inventories of the estate of the deceased. These documents list both the objects and the property owned by the ancestor, allowing you to reconstruct the interior of his or her house and to imagine life in another era. If you cannot get to the county seat, clerks of probate courts will usually supply any documents relating to the settling of a particular individual's estate if you have the date of death. There usually is a small fee. Wills and probate records may also be filed with land records.

City Directories

Most cities of even moderate size publish directories and have done so since the early part of the nineteenth century. These list the place of residence and the business of most people living in the city. The directories can help you tell when someone moved into and left a particular place. Local historical societies, public libraries, and city archives usually have files of these directories. There currently is a microfilm project that will copy all directories before 1840. Some states also published directories listing the town officers and the businesses in the various towns and cities.

County and City Histories

There was a great flurry of interest in local history after the centennial, and many cities, towns, and counties prepared histories that are often useful if you know where your ancestors lived in 1880 or 1890. Often these local histories give information on the various families then residing there, and one did not always need to be prominent to get into one of these histories. Sometimes they are accompanied by biographical volumes that again might prove useful in your search, but remember many of these books were financed by those who had their biographies included. Local histories can usually be found in town and county libraries as well as in state historical society libraries and in such major libraries as the Newberry Library in Chicago, the New York Public Library, and the Library of Congress.

Pension Records

If you had an ancestor who served in a war the chances are good that there is some record of his service or of a pension granted to him or his widow in the National Archives. Often in order to substantiate a claim, a considerable amount of family information was given. For veterans of the Revolution, Indian Wars, the War of 1812, and the Mexican, Civil, and Spanish American wars, you can write for information, but first you need the proper forms. It may be helpful to read *Military Service Records in the National Archives of the United States* (General Information Leaflet No. #7), or send directly for forms to Military Service Records, National Archives, Washington, D.C. 20408. World War I and World War II records should be requested at the United States Veterans' office in your state, but these records rarely have family information.

Census Records

The national census, taken every ten years beginning in 1790, can be helpful in tracing your ancestors, but there are limitations to its usefulness. Some states such as New York have also taken censuses, and these can also be valuable. The 1900 national census is the most recent one that is available for research, but the 1910 census was scheduled for release in 1982. Those after that date are open selectively for genealogical research on your own family. If the person listed in the census is still alive, that person has to apply for the records. If the person is dead, then a next of kin may apply. Information and forms can be secured by writing to Application of Search of Census Records, BC600 Personal Census Service Branch, Bureau of the Census, Pittsburg, Kans. 66732. The 1890 census was almost completely destroyed by fire. The censuses from 1790 through 1840 list only the name of the head of the household and certain other facts about those other people living in the house. For example, the 1790 census lists the name of the head of the family, the number of free white males over sixteen, the number of free white males under sixteen, the number of free white females, the number of free black persons, and the number of slaves. The 1790 census has been published for ten of the thirteen original colonies plus Maine and Vermont, and copies can be located in the state historical societies and most major research libraries. The 1820 census lists the head of the family, the number of free white males and females under ten, the number of free white males ten to sixteen, the number of white males and females sixteen to eighteen, the number of free white males and females eighteen to twenty-six, twenty-six to forty-five, and over forty-five. It also includes statistics on the number of naturalized aliens, the number of persons

SCHEDULE I.—Free Inhabitants in *Craftsbury* in the County of *Orleans* State of *Vermont* enumerated by me, on the 24 day of *Augt* 1850 *Saml Chamberlin* Ass't Marshal. 30

Dwelling-houses numbered in the order of visitation.	Families numbered in the order of visitation.	The Name of every Person whose usual place of abode on the first day of June, 1850, was in this family.	Age.	Sex.	Color.	Profession, Occupation, or Trade of each Male Person over 15 years of age.	Value of Real Estate owned.	Place of Birth. Naming the State, Territory, or Country.	Married within the year.	Attended School within the year.	Persons over 20 y'rs of age who cannot read and write.	Whether deaf and dumb, blind, insane, idiotic, pauper, or convict.	
1	2	3	4	5	6	7	8	9	10	11	12	13	
		Sarah Farrington	80	f		none		N.H.				Pauper	1
		Do Gilford	31	m		Farmer		Mass					2
		Mary Ann	35	f				V.t.					3
		Lorinzo	1	m				"					4
		Geore	6	m				"		1			5
392	392	Robert Mordy	60	m		Farmer	3800	Scotland					6
		Augusta	40	f				V.t.					7
		Thomas	16	m		"		"		1			8
		Matilda	14	f				"		1			9
		Janett	11	f				"		1			10
		Robert	7	m				"		1			11
		David	2	m				"					12
393	393	Wm Graham	40	m		Laborer		Scotland					13
		John Sharp	22	m		"		N.Y.					14
		James Rine	22	m		"		Canada					15
		Mary Haggan	21	f				Ireland					16
394	394	Harold Whitney	54	m		Farmer	1800	Ct					17
		Albert H.	20	m				N.Y.					18
		James	18	m		"		"		1			19
		Clarissa	53	f				N.H.					20
		Susan Batchelder	19	f				N.Y.		1			21
395	395	Helen F Hall	24	f		Carpenter	1200	"					22
		Sarah B	22	f				"					23
		Lafaette	1	m				Mass					24
		Wm N Beech	27	m		Farmer		N.Y.					25
		Melinda	24	f				"					26
		Wm Eugene	7/12	m				"					27
		James M Coxter	31	m		Laborer		"					28
396	396	Josiah Allen	59	m		Farmer	1500	"					29
		Mary	49	f				"					30
		Job W	20	m		Farmer		"					31
		James	18	m				"		1			32
		Willard	12	m				"		1			33
397	397	Lewis Hart	48	m		Farmer	2000	"					34
		Lucy "	80	f				"					35
		Betsey	52	f				"					36
		Martin	43	m				"					37
398	398	John Davis	30	m		C	2010	"					38
		Jame Gurd	42	m		"		"					39
		Annis	47	f				Tenn.					40
		Annett	8	f				V.t.		1			41
		Curlos Skinner	15	m				"		1			42

This is a page from the 1850 census.

engaged in agriculture, commerce, and manufacturing, the number of free blacks and slaves, and the number of persons except Indians not taxed.

The most useful censuses are those from 1850 to 1910, all of which list the name and age of everyone in the household. They also list the value of property and professions of those over fifteen. The 1880 census gives name, age, sex, color of each person, the relationship of each person to the head of the household, and the place of birth of the mother and father of the person listed. This last item alone can provide the clue that can lead you back at least one more generation. The 1900 census can also be valuable because it lists the birthplaces of parents, and if immigrants, the year of immigration and naturalization.

The census is on microfilm in the National Archives in Washington, and there are copies at many other locations such as Federal Records Centers and libraries.

366   In order to find your ancestors in the census, you need to know where they were living in the year of the census. If they lived in a large city, you need to know the ward, otherwise it will be a long search. City maps can help if you have the street address. The census, like any document, is not always accurate; people were missed in 1850 just as they were in 1980. The census taker often misspelled names or got the age of a child wrong. Even when you have all the necessary information, you may search through the microfilm reels for hours before coming across your ancestor, but as Alex Haley recalls, there is a special thrill in actually finding your own people in the official census records.

Records of the Church of Jesus Christ of Latter Day Saints

Many church records are possible sources of information on family history, but the Church of Jesus Christ of Latter Day Saints in Salt Lake City, Utah, has special resources. The Mormons believe that the family will survive in the future paradise, so every Mormon is obligated to trace his or her ancestry as far back as possible. For this reason the church has copied vital records, land records, probate records, family Bibles, and other material of all kinds from all over the world, but especially from the United States and Europe. There are more than 1 million reels of microfilm in the vaults in Salt Lake City. You can consult many of these records if you go there. You also can consult many records at branch libraries, and some material can be researched for you. For information, write to The Genealogical Department, Church of Jesus Christ of Latter Day Saints, 50 East North Temple Street, Salt Lake City, Utah 84150.

Books for More Information

There are thousands of books and articles written about the science of genealogy. If you become seriously interested in tracing your family's history, you will want to consult some of them. The following titles suggest places where you might start:

1. *Genealogy Beginners Manual.* This pamphlet was prepared by the staff of the Newberry Library, 60 West Walton Street, Chicago, Ill. 60610.
2. *How to Trace Your Family Tree.* American Genealogical Research Staff. Garden City, N.Y.: Dolphin, 1975.
3. Blockson, Charles L., with Ron Fry. *Black Genealogy.* Englewood Cliffs, N.J.: Prentice-Hall, 1977.
4. Doane, Gilbert H. *Searching for Your Ancestors.* New York: Bantam, 1974.
5. Everton, George B., et al. *The Handybook for Genealogists.* Logan, Utah: Everton, 1971.
6. Williams, Ethel W. *Know Your Ancestors.* Rutland, Vt.: Charles E. Tuttle, 1960.
7. *Tracing Your Ancestors in Canada.* Available from Information, Ottawa, Ontario, Canada.
8. Rottenberg, Dan. *Finding Our Fathers: A Guidebook to Jewish Genealogy.* New York: Random House, 1977.
9. Walker, James Dent. *Black Genealogy: How to Begin.* Available from Georgia Center for Continuing Education, Athens, Ga. 30602.
10. Greenwood, Val D. *Researcher's Guide to American Genealogy.* Baltimore, Md.: Genealogical Publishing Co., 1974.
11. Lichtman, Allan J. *Your Family History: How to Use Oral History, Personal Family Archives, and Public Documents to Discover Your Heritage.* New York: Vintage, 1978.

If you cannot find naturalization papers or other records relating to your immigrant ancestors, perhaps you can find your ancestor's name on a passenger list. The more information you have about date of arrival, port of entry, and the name of the vessel, the more likely you are to be successful. The passenger list records are not complete. Many have been destroyed; for example, there were two fires in San Francisco making it difficult to trace people who landed in that city, but see Louis J. Rasmussen, *San Francisco Passenger Lists*, 4 vols. (Ship 'N Rail Series, San Francisco Historic Records, 1976). The records in the National Archives go back as far as 1798, but most relate to the period from 1825 to 1945. A useful guide is Harold Lancour, *A Bibliography of Ships' Passenger Lists, 1538–1825: Being a Guide to Published Lists of Early Immigrants to North America* (New York: New York Public Library, 1963). For later records, see the very useful book *Guide to Genealogical Records in the National Archives* (Washington, D.C.: U.S. Government Printing Office, 1964). The best records seem to be for New York, Boston, Philadelphia, and Baltimore. Not to be overlooked are the records of travelers' aid societies, which often helped recent arrivals. The Philadelphia Jewish Archives Center (625 Walnut Street), for example, has records kept by a travelers' aid society for Jewish immigrants arriving in Philadelphia (with many going on to other cities) from 1885 to 1920. Slaves coming into the United States or to the American colonies were not listed by name, as Alex Haley discovered, but listed only by the number on each ship.

TRACING YOUR ANCESTORS WHILE OVERSEAS

If some day you want to search for your ancestors in Ireland, Italy, Sweden, or England, you should make sure you have done all the work possible in the United States before you go. Perhaps you still have relatives in the village your ancestors came from; that makes the task easier and more pleasant. Just as in tracing your ancestors on this side of the Atlantic, your task is made easier if you know the village or place that your ancestors came from. You might want to consult Leslie G. Pine, *The Genealogist's Encyclopedia* (New York: Weybright and Talley, 1969), which lists archives and record depositories in many countries; also *Genealogical Research: Methods and Sources*, 2 vols. (Washington, D.C.: American Society of Genealogists, 1960, 1971); and Dan Rottenberg, *Finding Our Fathers*. If you go to Europe or Africa, you should not expect to find too much. Remember, it took Alex Haley a great deal of time, money, and luck to find his African roots.

A WORD OR TWO OF WARNING

Beware of the letter that offers to provide your family with a coat of arms or to trace your family tree for a fee. What you are likely to receive is a pamphlet containing the origins of your name and perhaps a few famous people who share the name with you, with no effort to prove your connections to those people; or you may get an expensive coat of arms that in all probability has no connection to your family. If you must hire someone to trace your family history, write to the

Board of Certification of Genealogists, 1307 New Hampshire Avenue N.W., Washington, D.C. 20036.

TRACING YOUR FAMILY HISTORY IF ADOPTED

If you are adopted or an orphan your problems are obviously complicated. Some states, however, are beginning to open up adoption records in response to the growing concern on the part of many adopted children about their real parents. There are many successful stories of adopted children who have found their roots, so that, even though difficult, the search is not impossible. Two books that describe the search of adopted or illegitimate children for their families are: Betty Jean Lifton, *Twice Born: Memoirs of an Adopted Daughter* (New York: Penguin, 1976); and Rod McKuen, *Finding My Father: One Man's Search for Identity* (New York: Coward, 1976).

ETHNIC GROUPS

Many people will discover that the trail of their ancestors disappears after a generation or two, and many others will find it impossible to recover the name of that first immigrant who came to America. But we all can discover the ethnic mix in our backgrounds, and with a little research and a lot of imagination, we can reconstruct what it must have been like for our ancestors.

The references listed below may be of some help. The list is by no means complete, but many of the books contain extensive bibliographies.

General Accounts

Carlson, Lewis H. and George A. Colburn, eds. *In Their Place: White America Defines Her Minorities, 1850–1950.* New York: Wiley, 1972. Essays on Indians, Afro-Americans, Chicanos, Chinese, Japanese, Jews, and immigration policy.

Coleman, Terry. *Going to America.* Garden City, N.Y.: Anchor, 1973.

Davis, Allen F. and Mark H. Haller, eds. *The Peoples of Philadelphia: A History of Ethnic Groups and Lower Class Life, 1790–1940.* Philadelphia: Temple University Press, 1973. Essays on blacks, Jews, Poles, Irish, and Italians.

Dinnerstein, Leonard and Frederic C. Jaher. *The Aliens: A History of Ethnic Minorities in America.* New York: Appleton-Century-Crofts, 1970. Essays on many ethnic groups.

———and David M. Reimers. *Ethnic Americans: A History of Immigration and Assimilation.* New York: Dodd, Mead, 1975.

Handlin, Oscar, ed. *Children of the Uprooted.* New York: Grosset & Dunlap, 1966. An anthology.

Hansen, Marcus Lee. *Atlantic Migration, 1607–1860.* 1940. Reprint. Gloucester, Mass.: Peter Smith, n.d. Deals mostly with the European background.

Herberg, Will. *Protestant, Catholic, Jew.* rev. ed. Garden City, N.Y.: Doubleday/Anchor, 1955. An essay on the major American religious groups.

Morison, Samuel Eliot. *The European Discovery of America: The Northern Voyages.*

New York: Oxford University Press, 1971. Deals with the expansion of Europe and the voyages of discovery.

Novotny, Ann. *Strangers at the Door: Ellis Island, Castle Garden, and the Great Migration to America*. Riverside, Conn.: Chatham, 1971. Illustrated account of immigration.

Palmer, Robert R. and Joel Colton. *The History of the Modern World*. 5th ed. New York: Knopf, 1977.

Thernstrom, Stephan, ed. *Harvard Encyclopedia of American Ethnic Groups*. Cambridge, Mass.: Harvard University Press, 1980. Perhaps the single most important source and a good place to begin your search.

Racial and Ethnic Groups

Afro-Americans

Curtin, Philip D. *The Atlantic Slave Trade: A Census*. Madison: University of Wisconsin Press, 1969.

Fishel, Leslie H., Jr., and Benjamin Quarles. *The Negro American: A Brief Documentary History*. rev ed. Glenview, Ill.: Scott Foresman, 1970.

Franklin, John Hope. *From Slavery to Freedom*. 4th ed. New York: Random House, 1974.

Gutman, Herbert G. *The Black Family in Slavery & Freedom, 1750–1925*. New York: Pantheon, 1976.

Haley, Alex. *Roots: The Saga of an American Family*. Garden City, N.Y.: Doubleday, 1976. Fiction but still a fascinating story.

Lerner, Gerda. *Black Women in White America: A Documentary History*. New York: Pantheon, 1972.

Meier, August and Elliott M. Rudwick, eds. *The Making of Black America*. Studies in American Negro Life Series. New York: Atheneum, 1969.

American Indians

Brandon, William. *The American Heritage Book of the Indians*. New York: Dell, 1964.

Driver, Harold E. *Indians of North America*. 2d ed. Chicago: University of Chicago Press, 1969.

Josephy, Alvin M., Jr. *The Indian Heritage of America*. New York: Knopf, 1968.

Levine, Stuart and Nancy O. Lurie. *The American Indian Today*. Deland, Fla.: Everett-Edwards, 1968.

Washburn, Wilcomb E. *The Indian in America*. New York: Harper and Row, 1975.

Armenians

Vartan, Malcolm H. *Armenians in America*. New York: Pilgrim Press, 1919.

British (English, Scotch, Scotch-Irish, Welsh)

Berthoff, Rowland T. *British Immigrants in Industrial America, 1789–1950*. 1953. Reprint. New York: Russell & Russell, 1970.

Graham, Ian C. *Colonists from Scotland: Emigration to the United States, 1707–1783*. Ithaca, N.Y.: Cornell University Press, 1956.

Leyburn, James G. *The Scotch-Irish: A Social History*. 1944. Reprint. Chapel Hill: University of North Carolina Press, 1962.

Cooledge, Mary R. *Chinese Immigration*. New York: Holt, 1909.

Sandmeyer, E. C. *The Anti-Chinese Movement in California*. Urbana: University of Illinois Press, 1939.

Czechs

Capek, Thomas. *The Czechs in America*. 1920. Reprint. American Immigration Collection Series, no. 1. New York: Arno Press, 1969.

Dutch

Lucas, Henry S. *Netherlanders in America: Dutch Immigration to the United States and Canada, 1789–1950*. Ann Arbor: University of Michigan Press, 1955.

French-Canadians

Ducharme, Jacques. *Shadows of the Trees: The Story of French-Canadians in New England*. New York: Harper & Row, 1943.

Wade, Mason. *The French Canadians, 1760–1945*. New York: Macmillan, 1955.

Germans

O'Connor, Richard. *The German-Americans*. Boston: Little, Brown, 1968.

Rothan, Emmet H. *The German Catholic Immigrant in the United States, 1830–1860*. Washington, D.C.: Catholic University of America Press, 1946.

Schrader, Frederick F. *The Germans in the Making of America*. 1924. Reprint. Americana Series, no. 47. New York: Haskell House, 1972.

Greeks

Saloutos, Theodore. *The Greeks in the United States*. Cambridge, Mass.: Harvard University Press, 1964.

Hungarians

Lengyel, Emil. *Americans from Hungary*. 1948. Reprint. Westport, Conn.: Greenwood Press, n.d.

Irish

Clark, Dennis. *The Irish in Philadelphia: Ten Generations of Urban Experience*. Philadelphia: Temple University Press, 1974.

Handlin, Oscar. *Boston's Immigrants: A Study in Acculturation*. rev. ed. Cambridge, Mass.: Harvard University Press, 1959.

Schrier, Arnold. *Ireland and the American Emigration, 1850–1900*. 1958. Reprint. New York: Russell & Russell, 1970.

Wittke, Carl. *The Irish in America*. 1956. Reprint. New York: Russell & Russell, 1970.

Italians

Barzini, Luigi. *The Italians*. New York: Atheneum, 1964.

Covello, Leonard. *The Social Background of the Italo-American School Child*. New York:
Humanities Press, 1967.

Gambino, Richard. *Blood of My Blood*. New York: Doubleday, 1974.

Gans, Herbert J. *The Urban Villagers: Group and Class in the Life of Italo-Americans*. New York: Free Press, 1962.

Nelli, Humbert S. *The Italians in Chicago, 1880–1930: A Study in Ethnic Mobility*. New York: Oxford University Press, 1973.

Japanese

Ichihashi, Yamato. *Japanese in the United States*. 1932. Reprint. American Immigration Collection Series, no. 1. New York: Arno Press, 1969.

Kitano, Harry H. *Japanese Americans: The Evolution of a Subculture*. Englewood Cliffs, N.J.: Prentice-Hall, 1969.

Jews

Handlin, Oscar. *Adventure in Freedom*. 1954. Reprint. American History and Culture in the Twentieth Century Series. Port Washington, N.Y.: Kennikat Press, 1971.

Howe, Irving. *World of Our Fathers: The Journey of the East European Jews to America and the Life They Found and Made*. New York: Harcourt Brace Jovanovich, 1976.

Rischin, Moses. *The Promised City: New York's Jews, 1870–1914*. Cambridge, Mass.: Harvard University Press, 1962.

Schoener, Allon. *Portal to America: The Lower East Side, 1870–1925*. New York: Holt, Rinehart and Winston, 1967.

Sklare, Marshall, ed. *The Jews: Social Patterns of an American Group*. New York: Free Press, 1958.

Mexicans

Gamio, Manuel. *Mexican Immigration to the United States*. 1930. Reprint. American Immigration Collection Series, no. 1. New York: Arno Press, 1969.

McWilliams, Carey. *North from Mexico: The Spanish-Speaking People of the United States*. 1949. Reprint. Westport, Conn.: Greenwood Press, 1961.

Samora, Julian, ed. *La Raza: Forgotten Americans*. Notre Dame, Ind.: University of Notre Dame Press, 1966.

Norwegians

Blegen, Theodore C. *Norwegian Migration to America, 1825–1860*. 1931. Reprint. American Immigration Collection Series, no. 1. New York: Arno Press, 1969.

Poles

Fox, Paul. *The Poles in America*. 1922. Reprint. American Immigration Collection Series, no. 2. New York: Arno Press, 1970.

Thomas, William I. and Znaniecki, Florian. *The Polish Peasant in Europe and America*. 5 vols., 1918–1920. Reprint in 2 vols. New York: Octagon, 1971.

Puerto Ricans

Lewis, Oscar. *La Vida: A Puerto Rican Family in the Culture of Poverty, San Juan and New York*. New York: Random House, 1966.

372 Padilla, Elena. *Up from Puerto Rico*. New York: Columbia University Press, 1958.

Russians

Davis, Jerome. *The Russian Immigrant*. 1922. Reprint. American Immigration Collection Series, no. 2. New York: Arno Press, 1970.

Slavs

Balch, Emily G. *Our Slavic Fellow Citizens*. 1910. Reprint. American Immigration Collection Series, no. 1. New York: Arno Press, 1969.

Swedes

Janson, Florence, E. *The Background of Swedish Immigration, 1840−1930*. 1931. Reprint. American Immigration Collection Series, no. 2. New York: Arno Press, 1970.

Syrians

Hitti, Philip. *The Syrians in America*. New York: Holt, Rinehart and Winston, 1924.

Ukrainians

Halich, Wasyl. *Ukrainians in the United States*. 1937. Reprint. American Immigration Series, no. 2. New York: Arno Press, 1970.

THE WHYS AND HOWS OF WRITING YOUR PAPER

Any individual's past is the essence of the millions.

—Alex Haley

This book has tried to help you relate your personal past to a larger history. The main question it has posed is: What is there in your own history that has brought you to your present position? We believe it is important to ask that question because an investigation of the longer-range historical forces that have influenced you may explain a great deal more about yourself than immediate, short-range factors.

A key event in the past that may well tell you much about your present position is your ancestors' uprooting and resettlement in America. We hope that you have already learned something about this often heroic chapter of your family's history. Do you have a theory now about why they came across the ocean? Surely, except for the Africans and others who came in chains, hope for a better life was a motivation. Perhaps they came to escape anti-Semitic outrages or famine, like the eastern European Jews and the Irish; or perhaps to flee from war and conscription, like the Germans. There were, of course, many other reasons: religious persecution drove out many, including the Puritans, the earliest European-Americans. And, class oppression uprooted southern European and Asian peasants, from Greece to China. In general, then, they left because the societies in which they were born were inflexible, with children following parents in the same class positions, living the same lives, held by the same traditional bonds of culture. The changes that migration brought (or failed to bring) should be illuminating to you, especially through the comparisons with the present that this information should invite. Why, for instance, do most Americans now stay in school so much longer than past generations did? How has home life changed in the last three generations of your family's history? What has happened to your family's standard of living over the past fifty years? How do you account for the changes?

This series of questions attempts to uncover the structure of contemporary American society by asking you to retrace the path by which you arrived at your present position. Your investigation is a *historical* one because it leads you to understand the attitudes and values taught you throughout childhood as the outcome of your ancestors' experiences in a particular historical epoch. Ultimately, the question you should try to answer is whether history has been rewarding or alienating for you and your family. To find out requires some careful thinking and planning during the course of your research.

First, you should decide on the scope of your paper, that is, how much you want to do in relation to what is expected of you in your course. Is it enough, for example, for you to write a paper focusing on a particular aspect of family living to

374 gain some insight into the influence of history? Or should your paper be a fuller, more traditional effort?

Although you need not follow either model, let us assume for now that you are interested in writing a detailed description and analysis. The first suggestion is that you thoroughly familiarize yourself with the information that you have accumulated. Review all your material a few times. Two or three hours spent in mastering the data will permit you to go on to the next step.

A series of questions must be asked of the material, since the isolated facts you have collected are virtually useless until some framework of meaning is given to them. Some of the facts must be emphasized and others discarded, and those emphasized must be put into a sequence that produces some conclusion. The essence of planning lies in deciding which questions are to be asked of the historical record and which problems are to be solved. Familiarity with your research materials should reveal some major areas of inquiry. Perhaps you have discovered one especially interesting and influential person in your family who might provide a focal point for your essay. Or, possibly, there was a crucial incident—a move, a crisis, an accomplishment, a disaster—that you can use as a key. If you can pinpoint neither a person nor an event, try thinking in terms of the social factors discussed in this book. For example, place of residence may seem to be important, so that you can concentrate on the interactions between your ancestors and their locality: their coming, settlement, development through time, and assumption of position in the local social structure. Racism, war, economic class, or any other large historical force that may turn up throughout your research into the past two or three generations of your family can form the basis for structuring the family's history.

This structure, to reiterate, will be developed by the questions you pose. Your assumptions about what was most important in your family's history will be closely related to your hypothesis, that is, the historical argument you are making. You may initially develop a hypothesis that, when applied to your facts, loses its appeal. There may be too little evidence to support your theory (or too much counterevidence), thus forcing you to modify the hypothesis. This process is not unusual, and, in any case, the resulting argument is very much strengthened by it. As you look at your research notes, the important evidence is whatever helps you to explain the questions that you are interested in having answered. But, exercise care in determining the validity of the data before you.

The product of your efforts should be an essay that is organized around a central hypothesis, accounts for change over time, clearly identifies the causes of the change, and seeks to analyze the larger historical meanings associated with the family's story. As you measure your family's progress—in economic advancement, social mobility, educational change, political involvement— remember that your task is not to glorify or to condemn the past, but to understand it. Understanding your historical legacy, in turn, allows you some insight into those economic and social forces most significant to your existence. Or, as Sören Kierkegaard, the existentialist philosopher, expressed it, "One has to live life in the present but can only understand life from its history."

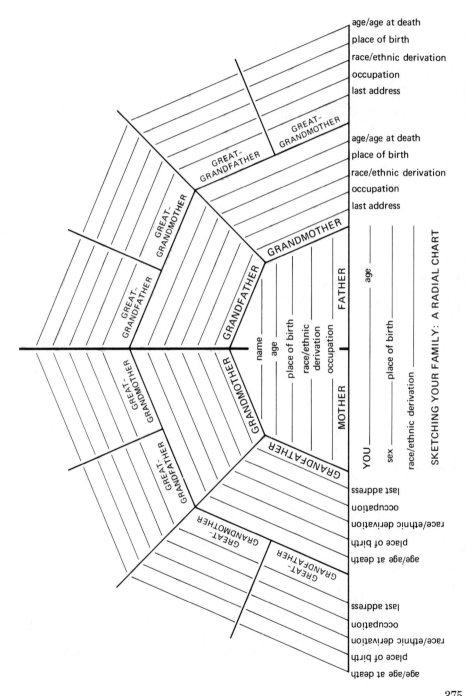

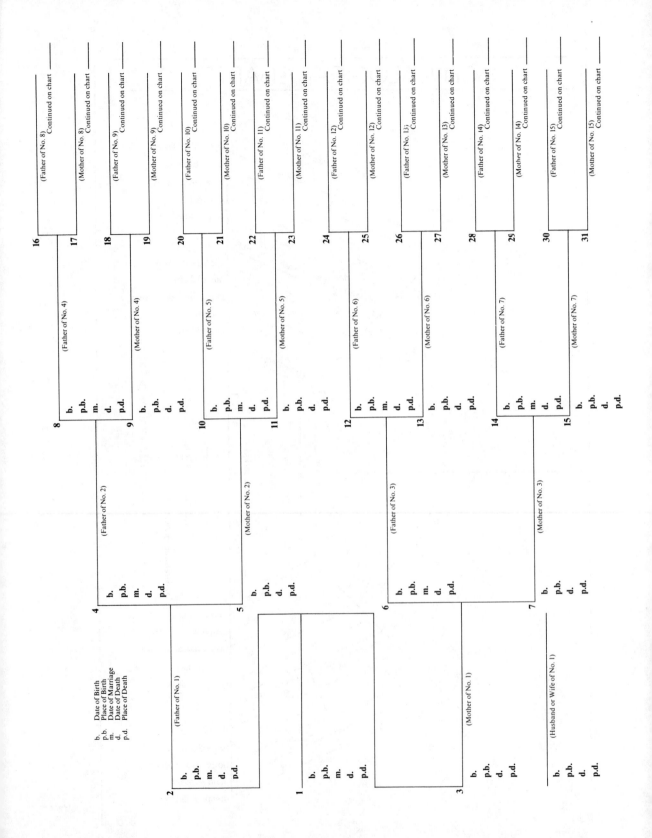

Yourself

name _____ age/date of birth _____

home address _____ city/state _____

place of birth _____ citizenship _____

number of siblings _____ their ages _____

places of residence since birth

_____ years there _____ left in 19_____

_____ years there _____ left in 19_____

_____ years there _____ left in 19_____

_____ years there _____ left in 19_____

religion _____ same as parents _____

leisure-time activities _____

_____

_____

number of hours of television watching averaged each week _____

military service _____

_____

racial/ethnic identification (if any) _____

languages spoken in the home _____

your social and economic class _____

_____

_____

_____

advantages/disadvantages of your education to this point _____

_____

_____

_____

_____

job/career choice after graduation _____

_____

_____

Your Father

name _____ age _____

place of birth _____ date of birth _____

schooling (years) _____ vocational training (in) _____

occupations

1. _____ where _____ when _____

2. _____ where _____ when _____

3. _____ where _____ when _____

approximate income level _____

all residence movements

from _____ to _____ when _____ why _____ how _____

from _____ to _____ when _____ why _____ how _____

from _____ to _____ when _____ why _____ how _____

religion _____

political/social affiliations _____

leisure-time activities _____

military service (length, rank, experiences, recollections) _____

_____

date and place of marriage to your mother _____

   age of bride _____ age of groom _____

   previous or subsequent marriages _____

   number of children of this marriage _____ of other marriages _____

number of people living in the home now

   adults _____ children under 18 _____

   frequency of contact with relatives _____

associations with ethnic derivation _____

_____

general attitudes toward American life as fulfilling expectations _____

_____

recollections of childhood _____

_____

specific information regarding his own parents _____

_____

Your Mother

name (inc. maiden name) _____ age _____

place of birth _____ date of birth _____

schooling (years) _____ vocational training (in) _____

occupations

1. _____ where _____ when _____

2. _____ where _____ when _____

3. _____ where _____ when _____

approximate income level _____

all residence movements up to marriage

from _____ to _____ when _____ why _____ how _____

from _____ to _____ when _____ why _____ how _____

from _____ to _____ when _____ why _____ how _____

religion _____

political/social affiliations _____

leisure-time activities _____

_____

date and place of marriage to your father _____

   age of bride _____age of groom _____

   previous or subsequent marriages _____

   number of children of this marriage _____ of other marriages _____

associations with ethnic derivation _____

_____

_____

general attitudes toward contemporary women's movement _____

_____

_____

general attitudes toward American life as fulfilling expectations _____

_____

_____

recollections of childhood _____

_____

specific information regarding her own parents _____

_____

Your Father's Father

name _____ age/age at death _____

place of birth _____ date of birth _____

schooling (years) _____ vocational training (in) _____

occupations

1. _____ where _____ when _____

2. _____ where _____ when _____

3. _____ where _____ when _____

all migrations (movement of the family residence)

from _____ to _____ when _____ why _____ how _____

from _____ to _____ when _____ why _____ how _____

from _____ to _____ when _____ why _____ how _____

religion _____

political/social affiliations _____

leisure-time activities _____

_____

date and place of marriage to your father's mother _____

   age of groom _____ age of bride _____

   previous or subsequent marriages _____

image of homeland after leaving (if immigrant to United States); or image of area

of identification (e.g., Africa) _____

_____

_____

_____

_____

   length of contact with old country after leaving _____

general attitudes toward American life as fulfilling expectations ____

_____

_____

recollections of childhood _____

_____

_____

_____

specific information regarding his own parents _____

_____

Your Father's Mother

name _____ age/age at death _____

place of birth _____ date of birth _____

schooling (years) _____ vocational training (in) _____

occupations

1. _____ where _____ when _____

2. _____ where _____ when _____

3. _____ where _____ when _____

all migrations (movement of the family residence)

from _____ to _____ when _____ why _____ how _____

from _____ to _____ when _____ why _____ how _____

from _____ to _____ when _____ why _____ how _____

religion _____

political/social affiliations _____

leisure-time activities _____

_____

date and place of marriage to your father's father _____

   age of bride _____age of groom _____

   previous or subsequent marriages _____

image of homeland after leaving (if immigrant to United States); or image of area

of identification (e.g., Africa) _____

_____

_____

_____

   length of contact with old country after leaving _____

general attitudes toward American life as fulfilling expectations _____

_____

_____

_____

recollections of childhood _____

_____

_____

specific information regarding her own parents _____

_____

Your Mother's Father

name _____ age/age at death _____

place of birth _____ date of birth _____

schooling (years) _____ vocational training (in) _____

occupations

1. _____ where _____ when _____

2. _____ where _____ when _____

3. _____ where _____ when _____

all migrations (movement of the family residence)

from _____ to _____ when _____ why _____ how _____

from _____ to _____ when _____ why _____ how _____

from _____ to _____ when _____ why _____ how _____

religion _____

political/social affiliations _____

leisure-time activities _____

_____

date and place of marriage to your mother's mother _____

  age of groom _____ age of bride _____

  previous or subsequent marriages _____

image of homeland after leaving (if immigrant to United States); or image of area of identification (e.g., Africa) _____

_____

_____

_____

  length of contact with old country after leaving _____

general attitudes toward American life as fulfilling expectations _____

_____

_____

_____

recollections of childhood _____

_____

_____

specific information regarding his own parents _____

_____

_____

Your Mother's Mother

name _____ age/age at death _____

place of birth _____ date of birth _____

schooling (years) _____ vocational training (in) _____

occupations

1. _____ where _____ when _____

2. _____ where _____ when _____

3. _____ where _____ when _____

all migrations (movement of the family residence)

from _____ to _____ when _____ why _____ how _____

from _____ to _____ when _____ why _____ how _____

from _____ to _____ when _____ why _____ how _____

religion _____

political/social affiliations _____

leisure-time activities _____

_____

date and place of marriage to your mother's father _____

   age of bride _____ age of groom _____

   previous or subsequent marriages _____

image of homeland after leaving (if immigrant to United States); or image of area

of identification (e.g., Africa) _____

_____

_____

   length of contact with old country after leaving _____

general attitudes toward American life as fulfilling expectations _____

_____

_____

recollections of childhood _____

_____

_____

specific information regarding her own parents _____

_____

_____

_____

A Step-Parent

name _____ age _____

place of birth _____ date of birth _____

schooling (years) _____ vocational training (in) _____

occupations

1. _____ where _____ when _____

2. _____ where _____ when _____

3. _____ where _____ when _____

all residence movements

from _____ to _____ when _____ why _____ how _____

from _____ to _____ when _____ why _____ how _____

from _____ to _____ when _____ why _____ how _____

religion _____

political/social affiliations _____

leisure-time activities _____

_____

married to your _____

   date and place of marriage _____

   age of groom _____age of bride _____

   previous or subsequent marriages _____

associations with ethnic derivation _____

_____

_____

_____

general attitudes toward American life as fulfilling expectations _____

_____

_____

recollections of childhood _____

_____

_____

specific information regarding his or her own parents _____

_____

_____

Siblings of Your Father and Your Mother

father's siblings

name _____ age/age at death _____ present hometown _____

name _____ age/age at death _____ present hometown _____

name _____ age/age at death _____ present hometown _____

name _____ age/age at death _____ present hometown _____

occupations _____

_____

_____

_____

_____

frequency of contact with your own family _____

_____

_____

_____

mother's siblings

name _____ age/age at death _____ present hometown _____

name _____ age/age at death _____ present hometown _____

name _____ age/age at death _____ present hometown _____

name _____ age/age at death _____ present hometown _____

occupations _____

_____

_____

_____

_____

frequency of contact with your own family _____

_____

_____

_____

QUESTIONS TO ASK
YOUR GRANDMOTHER

Many of these questions, of course, you could ask your grandfather, but, with women in our society living an average of seven to eight years longer than do men, more grandmothers survive. Even if none of the older generation in your family has survived, it is worth talking to any seventy- or eighty-year old. You may not want to ask all these questions, and you certainly would not want to ask them all in one session. You may want to change the order to fit the nature of your conversation. But do talk to the older members of your family. The preservation of generational memory is important for you and for your grandmother.

Where were you born? in a hospital? in your home?

Who attended your birth? a physician? a midwife?

How many brothers and sisters did you have?

What are your first memories?

What kind of toys did you play with?

Did you have grandparents, aunts, uncles, or other relatives living with you? or nearby?

Did anyone else live in the house?

What kind of clothes did you wear? Did your parents purchase them or make them?

Were you treated differently from your brothers?

What racial or ethnic group did you come from? When did the first member of your family come to the United States? What religious group did you come from? How important was religion in your family?

Can you remember a family meal when you were a child? What kind of food was served? Who served the food? Who sat around the table? Were there prayers before eating? Were there special family customs? Who was in command of the table? your mother, father, or grandparents?

What special holidays or events did your family celebrate? Did relatives come to these special occasions? Can you recall how people acted and how they dressed?

How did your family obtain food? How much did they grow? Where did they buy the rest? Can you recall any favorite recipes? What kind of stove did they have? Can you describe the preparation of a meal? Have any special recipes been preserved in your family?

Did you have a piano or other musical instruments in the house?

How was the house lighted? How was it heated? Did you have an icebox?

Can you recall the way the rooms were arranged? Who slept where? Can you picture the furniture?

Can you describe "washday"? Did you have a washing machine? Did you make your own soap?

Where did you go to school? Can you recall your teachers? or any other incidents?

What did you do for fun when you were in school? Did you also have to work?

Did your family move when you were young? Can you recall your feelings about these moves?

How did you travel? by horse and wagon? by streetcar or train?

How frequently and how far did you travel when you were a child?

Do you remember the first automobile in your neighborhood? the first radio?

How did you meet men when you were a young woman? Were young women treated differently from young men? How did you meet your husband?

When you were a young woman, what kinds of clothes did you wear? Did you buy them or make them?

What did you do in the summer?

Did you work when you were a young woman? in the home or outside the home? Did most of your friends work?

What do you know about your family surname? Were the names ever changed?

Are there traditional first names, or middle names, in your family? What is their significance?

What stories, traditions, legends have come down to you about your parents, grandparents, or other ancestors?

Were there any famous or infamous members of your family?

Are there any stories of fortunes made and lost, or almost made, in your family?

Is there a family cemetery or burial plot? Where are members of your family buried?

Does your family have any heirlooms or objects that have survived? What are the stories connected with them?

Does your family have photo albums, scrapbooks, slides, home movies? Are there letters, diaries, genealogies, or other family records?

About the Authors

J. F. Watts is Professor of History at The City College of the City University of New York, where he has taught since 1965. He teaches courses in social and diplomatic history, has produced programs for radio and television, and made historical films. Recently he has written on such subjects as Senator Joseph McCarthy and Irish-American ethnicity.

Allen F. Davis is Professor of History at Temple University. He has also taught at Wayne State University and the University of Missouri. His Ph.D. is from the University of Wisconsin. He was formerly Executive Director of the American Studies Association and has lectured widely in the United States and Europe. He is the author of *Spearheads for Reform* and *American Heroine: The Life and Legend of Jane Addams.* He is the editor of *For Better or Worse* and is the co-editor of *Conflict and Consensus in American History, The Peoples of Philadelphia,* and other books.

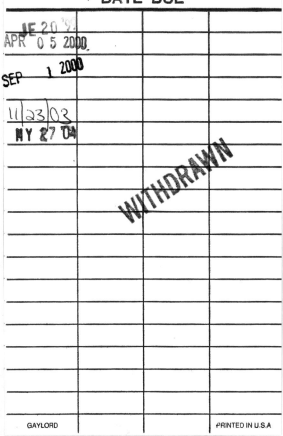